NEW HISTORICISM AND CULTURAL MATERIALISM

NEW HISTORICISM AND CULTURAL MATERIALISM

A READER

Edited by
Kiernan Ryan
Fellow and Director of Studies in English at New Hall,
University of Cambridge

A member of the Hodder Headline Group
LONDON • NEW YORK • SYDNEY • AUCKLAND

First published in Great Britain 1996 by
Arnold, a member of the Hodder Headline Group,
338 Euston Road, London NW1 3BH

Co-published in the United States of America by
Oxford University Press Inc.,
198 Madison Avenue, New York, NY 10016.

British Library Cataloguing in Publication Data
A catalogue record for this book is available from the British Library

Library of Congress Cataloging-in-Publication Data
New historicism and cultural materialism : a reader / Kiernan Ryan
[editor].
    p.   cm.
    Includes bibliographical references and index.
    ISBN 0-340-66307-3 (hb.) — ISBN 0-340-61458-7 (pbk.)
    1. Criticism.   2. Historicism.   3. Marxist criticism.
4. Materialism in literature.   I. Ryan. Kiernan, 1950–
PN81.N4317   1996
801'.95 — dc20   96-5594
                                                       CIP

ISBN 0 340 61458 7 (Pb)
ISBN 0 340 66307 3 (Hb)

2 3 4 5 6 7 8 9 10

Composition by Phoenix Photosetting, Chatham, Kent
Printed and bound in Great Britain by JW Arrowsmith Ltd, Bristol

Contents

Acknowledgements   vii

Introduction   ix

Section One: Sources
Introduction   1
  1   Clifford Geertz, 'The Impact of the Concept of Culture on the
       Concept of Man'   5
  2   Michel Foucault, 'Panopticism'   11
  3   Louis Althusser, 'Ideology and Ideological State Apparatuses'   17
  4   Raymond Williams, 'Base and Superstructure in Marxist Cultural
       Theory'   22
  5   Jacques Derrida, 'Différance'   28
  6   Walter Benjamin, 'Theses on the Philosophy of History'   32

Section Two: Standpoints
Introduction   41
  7   Catherine Gallagher, 'Marxism and the New Historicism'   45
  8   Stephen Greenblatt, 'Resonance and Wonder'   55
  9   Alan Sinfield, 'Cultural Materialism, *Othello*, and the Politics of
       Plausibility'   61
 10   Catherine Belsey, 'Towards Cultural History – in Theory and
       Practice'   82
 11   Lee Patterson, 'Historical Criticism and the Claims of Humanism'   92
 12   Marjorie Levinson, 'The New Historicism: Back to the Future'   102

Section Three: Soundings
Introduction   113
 13   Jonathan Goldberg, '*Measure for Measure* as Social Text'   117
 14   Francis Barker and Peter Hulme, '"Nymphs and Reapers Heavily
       Vanish": The Discursive Con-texts of *The Tempest*'   125
 15   John Bender, '*Robinson Crusoe* and the Rise of the Penitentiary'   138
 16   Heather Glen, 'Blake's "London": The Language of Experience'   146

17 Nancy Armstrong, 'The Politics of Domestic Fiction: Dickens, Thackeray and the Brontës'   157
18 Jerome McGann, 'The Third World of Criticism: From Aeschylus to Ezra Pound'   166

Bibliography   183

Index   207

Acknowledgements

The editor and publishers would like to thank the following for permission to use copyright material in this book.

The author and Blackwell for the extract from Stephen Greenblatt, 'Resonance and Wonder', in *Literary Theory Today*, ed. Peter Collier and Helga Geyer-Ryan (1990); the author and Blackwell for Jerome McGann, 'The Third World of Criticism', in Marjorie Levinson, Marilyn Butler, Jerome McGann and Paul Hamilton, *Rethinking Historicism: Critical Readings in Romantic History* (1989); the author and Blackwell for extracts from Marjorie Levinson, 'The New Historicism: Back to the Future', in Marjorie Levinson, Marilyn Butler, Jerome McGann and Paul Hamilton, *Rethinking Historicism: Critical Readings in Romantic History* (1989); the author and Cambridge University Press for the extract from Heather Glen, *Vision and Disenchantment: Blake's 'Songs' and Wordsworth's 'Lyrical Ballads'* (1983); Éditions La Découverte and Verso/New Left Books for the extract from Louis Althusser, *Lenin and Philosophy and Other Essays* (1971), © Maspéro/La Découverte, Paris, 1969; Catherine Gallagher for 'Marxism and the New Historicism', in *The New Historicism*, ed. H. Aram Veeser (1989); Harcourt Brace & Company, Harvard University Press and Suhrkamp Verlag for 'Theses on the Philosophy of History', from *Illuminations* by Walter Benjamin, translated by Harry Zohn, copyright © 1955 by Suhrkamp Verlag, Frankfurt a. M., English translation copyright © 1968 by Harcourt Brace & Company, reprinted by permission of Harcourt Brace & Company. 'Theses on the Philosophy of History' will be included in the forthcoming collected works of Walter Benjamin, to be published by Harvard University Press; Johns Hopkins University Press for the extract from Jonathan Goldberg, *James I and the Politics of Literature: Jonson, Shakespeare, Donne and their Contemporaries* (1983), © 1983 by The Johns Hopkins University Press; Oxford University Press for the extract from *Desire and Domestic Fiction: A Political History of the Novel* by Nancy Armstrong, copyright © 1987 by Oxford University Press, Inc., reprinted by permission; Oxford University Press and the University of California Press for 'Cultural Materialism, *Othello*, and the Politics of Plausibility', © Alan Sinfield 1992, reprinted from *Faultlines* by Alan Sinfield (1992) by permission of Oxford University Press, copyright © 1992 The Regents of the University of California; Penguin Books Ltd and Georges Borchardt, Inc., for the extract from Michel Foucault, *Discipline and Punish: The Birth of the Prison*, trans. Alan Sheridan (Harmondsworth,1979),

Introduction

Any commentator rash enough to pass sentence on a powerful new critical movement before its star has plainly waned is tempting fate. But few pundits of recent times have proved quite so ill-advised as those who wrote off cultural materialism and new historicism as transient fads of the 1980s before the 1980s themselves had turned into the past. The fact that the validity of these critical practices is no longer being debated with the same ferocity and frequency as it was during the decade that cradled them might seem to be a sign that their charm has already faded and their credibility is in decline. On closer inspection, however, the abatement of urgent theoretical contention confirms that nothing could be further from the truth. The flood of articles and essays striving to define, compare, refute or defend new historicism and cultural materialism has begun to ebb not because criticism has clearly moved beyond these modes of study, leaving their assumptions and procedures bobbing in its wake, but because these assumptions and procedures have been so completely absorbed into mainstream critical practice as to have become virtually invisible. Nothing testifies so eloquently to the triumph of a new academic dispensation as the reluctance of its adherents to acknowledge its sway, and their instinctive disavowal of their debt to those who laid its foundations. Departments of literature on both sides of the Atlantic are now densely populated with critics, scholars and students who would never dream of identifying themselves as a new historicist or a cultural materialist, preferring to reserve the label for the handful of high-profile individuals whose principles and strategies they blatantly share.

For once, the indecent haste with which the discipline tends to shrink-wrap the latest kind of criticism and stack it alongside the rival brands has worked in favour of the new commodity. While new historicism and cultural materialism appeared to have been cordoned off by classification as mere extensions of consumer choice, as plausible alternatives to formalist, psychoanalytic, feminist, Marxist and poststructuralist perspectives, they were busy recruiting these perspectives to their cause and expanding their regime to the point where it has become the effective horizon of advanced literary study in every period. If that seems an outlandish claim, a glance at the Bibliography riding shotgun at the rear of this Reader should help to quell disbelief. Critics who think that new historicism and cultural materialism are chiefly rooted in the Renaissance studies that nurtured them, with occasional offshoots sprouting up in studies of subsequent eras, are badly out of date. The same goes for those in thrall to the delusion that the new historicists are a relatively compact faction of American critics led by Stephen Greenblatt and Catherine Gallagher, while their cultural materialist cousins across the Atlantic could hold their annual meeting, chaired by Alan Sinfield and Jonathan Dollimore, in a reasonably commodious telephone booth. For the initial conquest of Renaissance studies has now expanded into a global colonization of English and American literary history, producing a wealth of exciting, innovative work by a multitude of scholars on everything from the *Canterbury Tales* to the *Cantos*.

The landscape and boundaries of literary studies have already changed dramatically as a result, and the need for a map of the transfigured terrain is made all the more urgent by the fact that the scale and consequences of the transformation remain largely unacknowledged. If a new consensus is indeed emerging about what counts as criticism, and about what kind of criticism matters most, it becomes especially important to keep the terms of that consensus in focus and open to debate. This volume aims to do just that. By tracing the intellectual genealogy of new historicism and cultural materialism, by identifying and discussing the theoretical principles at stake in their critical practice, and by illustrating the application of that practice to a pantheon of canonical authors ranging from Aeschylus to Ezra Pound, it seeks to do justice to the achievement of this critical enterprise and at the same time keep it controversial.

This is a far from simple task. But the first step towards accomplishing it must be to resist the temptation to which previous compendia have succumbed, and refuse to let cultural materialism be displaced, annexed or engulfed by new historicism. Neither the large tracts of common ground they share, nor their mutual resistance to clear-cut definition should dispose one to repress or veil the vital distinctions and productive tensions between them. To divorce or conflate the two approaches is to surrender the opportunity for a dialogue likely to shed fresh light on the changing politics of interpretation. But such a dialogue is unlikely to develop without a sharper sense of what new historicism and cultural materialism stand for, and both kinds of criticism have proved notoriously difficult to pin down. The reluctance of prominent practitioners to be unequivocally identified with either camp (an attitude one can readily understand, since few of us like being labelled) only compounds the difficulty. It is impossible to discern beneath the diversity of new historicist or cultural materialist practice a single, unifying theory or consistent critical method. Whereas Marxist, psychoanalytic or deconstructive readings all too often secrete a doctrine which governs their transactions, the sort of criticism explored in these pages defies reduction to a school or creed, and might more profitably be regarded as a flexible repertoire of strategies and techniques. In fact, it may be that this elusive, protean quality of new historicism and cultural materialism, their capacity to incorporate, adapt and improvise instead of hardening into dogma, is their greatest strength and the secret of their rampant appeal.

What is needed in place of canned formulas is a way of thinking about this critical movement which registers the affinities and the disparities between cultural materialism and new historicism without simply polarizing them or subordinating one to the other. My own belief is that these approaches are best viewed as occupying a range of distinct positions or options on the same critical continuum. New historicism and cultural materialism are united by their compulsion to relate literature to history, to treat texts as indivisible from contexts, and to do so from a politically charged perspective forged in the present. But they are divided by the different routes they take to reach this goal, and by the different conclusions they draw once they have reached it.

Nor should either new historicism or cultural materialism be regarded as a cohesive, uniform endeavour in itself. (For this reason I think it wiser to keep both terms uncapitalized, although I have naturally respected the capitalized usage preferred by some of the contributors to this volume.) On the contrary: both afford their congregations an attractively broad church, in which diverse theoretical influences and critical emphases are embraced. It strikes me as much more helpful, therefore, to speak of a single wide spectrum of radical historicist criticism, and to use 'cultural materialism' and 'new historicism' as shorthand for the two dominant tendencies displayed in various inflections across that spectrum. For this permits us to recognize the conflicts and the continuities between and within both kinds of criticism, and discourages us from perceiving them as starkly opposed British and American persuasions, to whose firm tenets particular critics have deliberately subscribed. It obliges us to redefine the situation more subtly and plausibly as one in which dissident American scholars can find themselves more at home with cultural materialist assumptions; in which radical British readings can thrive when transplanted into transatlantic hotbeds of new historicism; and in which individual critics may adopt different positions on the spectrum at different times, depending on their aims and the nature of the text being tackled, so that trying to lock them into a single posture becomes a sterile aspiration.

Not the least virtue of viewing matters in more graduated, less adversarial terms is that it furnishes this book with a more constructive framework for the student of this critical formation. Because too many anthologies of this kind turn out to be jumbles of disconnected essays on incongruous themes, I have tried to design a frankly polemical Reader with a cogent rationale and a coherent plot. The book is divided into three interlocking sections, each prefaced by a brief introduction which brings its six extracts into focus and signposts their connections with the extracts that precede or succeed them. The extracts in each section have been chosen to exemplify the full gamut of perspectives shaping the debate about how and why literature should be restored to the past in order to make it count in the present. Thus each section blazes its own trail across the same critical territory, setting out from the kingdom whose authors may speak only of what was, and arriving in the realm whose secular scripture is revered for its gift of prophecy, for its power to foretell what we might become. En route it encounters a wealth of contrasting beliefs and practices: the view that literary texts should not be worshipped above other texts and the unshaken conviction that they deserve their exalted status; the indictment of imaginative works as confederates of oppression and their enlistment as cohorts in the ranks of resistance; the contention that radical critics can make a difference in the world in which books are read, and detached contemplation of the origins of our impotence, our entanglement in a world-wide web of signs which has placed the reality of history beyond reach.

The first section ('Sources') tracks these ideas back to an international constellation of thinkers who exerted a decisive influence on the development of cultural materialism and new historicism: the American cultural anthropologist Clifford Geertz, the French social scientist and intellectual historian Michel Foucault, the British critic and cultural theorist Raymond Williams, the French Marxist philosopher Louis Althusser, the German cultural and literary critic Walter Benjamin, and the French philosopher and founder of deconstruction Jacques Derrida. The middle section of the reader ('Standpoints') reflects the impact of these initiatives on the vigorous theoretical controversies provoked by new historicism and cultural materialism. It provides a forum in which leading exponents and critics of both approaches can be heard making a case for what they take to be the vital issues and objectives. The lineup features both British and American critics, who have been chosen not only for their intrinsic importance and the diversity of their views, but also for the collective breadth of their expertise, which covers nineteenth-century fiction (Catherine Gallagher), medieval literature (Lee Patterson) and Romantic poetry (Marjorie Levinson) in addition to Renaissance studies (Catherine Belsey, Alan Sinfield and Stephen Greenblatt). An even wider range of critical competence is displayed in the final section of the book ('Soundings'), which carries the debate forward through a series of exemplary readings of specific works. These readings disclose the direct influence on critical practice of figures such as Foucault, Williams and Benjamin, but they also demonstrate vividly how new historicism and cultural materialism can transform our perception of the masterpieces most of us study and teach.

Those who are familiar with the field surveyed by this volume may well be aghast at what has been excluded in the interests of cohesion. Some of my omissions, it must be confessed, excite few regrets: the jaundiced pose and grim pontifications of Jonathan Dollimore, for example, would sort ill with a selection convinced of the value of canonical literature. But the absence of Antonio Gramsci and Mikhail Bakhtin from the 'Sources' section is another matter, as is the neglect of important essays on gender, race and imperialism in the second section, and the lamentable lack of 'Soundings' of medieval criticism (especially the work of David Aers or Paul Strohm) and studies of American literature (by Walter Benn Michaels, Michael Rogin and Jane Tompkins in particular). What the Reader has lost in catholicity, however, it has gained, I trust, in clarity of shape and purpose. Those who wish to chart the full extent of its suppressions will find them amply mapped in the comprehensive Bibliography, which should compensate in some measure for all the indispensable material that wound up on the cutting-room floor.

The Bibliography is meant to serve both as a means of expanding the theoretical horizons of the book and as a practical resource for students keen to explore the application of radical historicist criticism to a particular era, culture or body of writing. It opens with a selection of key works by the principal progenitors of this mode of criticism, including those showcased in Section One and those ruled out by the dictates of space. This is followed by two lists of books and essays devoted to the wider debates about the study of history and culture in which new historicism and cultural materialism are inevitably involved. The fourth part of the Bibliography confirms just how intense and sustained the theoretical controversy surrounding both approaches has been, filling in the gaps between the 'Standpoints' framed in Section Two. Parts V to XI comprise a unique catalogue of the most valuable criticism produced in this vein to date in medieval studies, Renaissance studies, eighteenth-century studies, Romantic studies, Victorian studies, twentieth-century studies and American studies. Any lingering doubts about the rise and rise and steady spread of radical historicist criticism should be dispatched by the last two segments of the Bibliography, which list the publishers' series and the academic journals expressly spawned to feed the huge appetite for this sort of work.

What are the basic aims of this critical movement? There are strong clues concealed in the terms 'new historicism' and 'cultural materialism' themselves, whose implications it is worth pausing to unpack. The former phrase is foreshadowed as early as 1969 in Roy Harvey Pearce's book, *Historicism Once More*; it crops up explicitly a few years later in the title of Wesley Morris's *Toward a New Historicism* (1972); and Michael McCanles seems to have been the first to bring it to bear on early modern studies in his essay, 'The Authentic Discourse of the Renaissance' (*Diacritics* 10:1 [1980], pp. 77–87). But it is Stephen Greenblatt who gets the credit for slipping the term into circulation in its current sense in his introduction to 'The Forms of Power and the Power of Forms in the Renaissance', a special issue of *Genre* (15:1–2 [1982]) devoted to what was already billed as a fresh departure in critical practice. To advertise a *new* historicism is to promise a displacement of previous modes of critical historicism, which are thereby consigned to obsolescence. New historicists cold-shoulder approaches that claim to ground their accounts of literature in a factual historical reality that can be recovered and related to the poems, plays and novels that reflect it. Nor will they have any truck with criticism which reduces works to expressions of some grand providential design, whether Marxist, Christian or humanist. Both positivist and metaphysical versions of historicism are ditched in favour of a history perceived as accessible through its textual traces alone and irreducible to a single master narrative; and the idea of the work as a suffix of the social or biographical realm, as a mere mirror of its age or its author's mind, yields to a belief in the text's active role in constructing what qualifies as reality.

None the less, it might be argued that the term 'new historicism' is oxymoronic, because the word 'new' betrays an adherence to the concept of modernity, and thus to a linear vision of history as progress, which rebukes the sceptical implications of the word 'historicism', stilling the postmodern irony shimmering in its final syllable. Nor does the complexity of the term's connotations end there. The phrase 'new historicism' adverts also to the 'new criticism' in which so many of its American luminaries were first schooled, but whose principles and procedures it seeks to demolish. Whereas the new critic believed that the best interests of the work were served by treating it as autotelic, by isolating its analysis from extraneous considerations of time, place and function, and focusing on its intrinsic properties as a verbal icon, the new historicist insists on situating the text, on stitching it back into the intertextual quilt of its initial context. The aim is to dethrone and demystify the privileged literary work: to destroy its immunity to infection by circumstance and other kinds of text, and to rob it of political innocence by exposing its discreet commitments, its subtle collusions in the cultural struggle for power. Yet insofar as new historicism turns history itself into a text and treats all texts as literary texts susceptible to the same interpretive techniques, its divorce from the new criticism may not be as absolute as it seems. For despite the violent differences between them, both approaches contrive to make material history vanish: the one by severing the work from the world, the other by reducing the real to the written. The poststructuralist price of the return to history is the evaporation of the world that produced all these words; and the debt new historicism owes to deconstruction allows it to seem, in this respect at least, the culmination rather than the termination of the new critical enterprise.

That impression is strengthened by reflecting on the alias under which new historicism commonly travels. In *Renaissance Self-Fashioning* (1980), a couple of years before he launched the latter term, Greenblatt had described what he was developing as a 'cultural poetics', and he returned to this definition of his critical practice – a definition he prefers to its more popular rival – in the introductory chapter of *Shakespearean Negotiations* (1988). As a watchword, 'cultural poetics' exchanges a stress on the historicity of texts for a concern with the textuality of culture. In this sense it marks the posthumous expansion of new criticism to embrace not merely the detached canonical work but the entire cultural formation, to which the resources of close textual analysis can now be applied. The term 'poetics' recalls too the structuralist endeavour to grasp its object synchronically and spatially as a system of relations, suppressing its diachronic involvement in the process of historical change. Such an emphasis sits quite comfortably, of course, with a criticism which has collapsed the old historicist distinctions between base and superstructure, culture and society, literary and non-literary texts. For those distinctions reveal a devotion not only to causal explanations, but to moral and aesthetic judgements whose reliance on a teleological account of history soon surfaces. Cultural poetics, by contrast, perceives literature as only one element of the whole cultural configuration whose distinctive rhetoric it undertakes to read. Instead of elevating one cultural practice above the rest, and either sealing off its texts for special scrutiny or explaining them as products of some fundamental process, the new historicist mounts an interdisciplinary campaign to track the culture's chief tropes as they move back and forth between its various discursive domains.

The attractions of such an approach are plain. Seeing the literature of a period as part of a larger symbolic economy, as one of the many sites of exchange through which the defining signs of a culture circulate, levels dubious hierarchical distinctions and wires works back up to all the other social spheres from which they have been disconnected. At the same time, it accords poems, plays and novels a creative, reciprocal role in the shaping of their time, which it refuses to construe as a chapter in an unfolding historical narrative. The danger, however, as the anthropological overtones of the term 'cultural' suggest, is that the vital sense of history as continuous transformation may be stunned in the process, and replaced by a vision of the past as a sequence of discrete constellations devoid of consequence for the present.

It is a danger to which cultural materialism is not immune, given that it shares the new historicist predilection for splicing texts back into their cultural formation and the new historicist distrust of *grands récits*. But the summons to pursue a *materialist* critique of culture, as opposed to establishing a cultural *poetics*, speaks volumes about the differences between these two styles of radical criticism. The term 'cultural materialism' was coined by Raymond Williams to describe the theory and practice he first mapped out in *Marxism and Literature* (1977). It was picked up in the 1980s by Dollimore and Sinfield, who hijacked it for the subtitle of their groundbreaking anthology *Political Shakespeare: New Essays in Cultural Materialism* (1985), and it swiftly acquired authority as the banner round which an eclectic array of initiatives could rally. Those who felt pulled towards this pole of radical historicism saw culture less as a self-determined system of representations to be appraised in subsequent detachment, and more as an arena in which the battle for the meaning of those representations continued to be fought. Cultural materialists are concerned as much with the culture of the present as with the culture of the past, which matters insofar as it can be brought to bear constructively on our current political predicament. No one could accuse new historicism of being blind to the way its modern standpoint colours its reconstructions of the past, or of generating readings of the canon bereft of political relevance to our time. But cultural materialism seeks actively and explicitly to use the literature of yesterday to change the world today. It is a brazenly engaged critical stance, committed to activating the dissident potential of past texts in order to challenge the present conservative consensus inside the educational institutions where it is forged.

The more reserved gaze of the new historicist is drawn back towards the past, its awareness of its own modernity a reminder of the past's alterity and the risk of finding in the other the reflection of oneself; while the embattled gaze of the cultural materialist is fixed from the start on the present, whose demands dictate the questions to be addressed to the cultures and the texts of former times. New historicists are prone to regard cultures as regimes of constraint, designed to absorb resistance or ultimately turn it to their own account. In this scenario, not surprisingly, works of literature tend to be cast as conspirators in the plots hatched by power to secure our subjection. Even when works are allowed to have been politically ambivalent or progressive in their day, the overriding implication is that they *no longer* have anything subversive to say to us, since they belong to a superseded world. Most cultural materialists, to be sure, would agree that most literature once served as an agent of acquiescence, in cahoots with the dominant interests of its culture. But they would also argue that there is no reason why it should still fulfil that function now. For their concept of culture sees hegemony as a vulnerable, unstable condition, continually undermined by the interests it excludes or violates, and constantly compelled to shore itself up in order to survive. The most responsive imaginative writing, however conservative its original intent or effect, cannot help betraying, directly or obliquely, the impact of this perpetual struggle for power. So a key task for the cultural materialist is to read the canon against the grain: to amplify the voices of the disenfranchised, to expose the guilty political unconscious of the text, to deepen and widen the faultlines in its legitimation of the status quo.

The phrase 'cultural materialism' is haunted, after all, by the name of its notorious ancestor, historical materialism, whose Marxist legacy it both salutes and transmutes. The echo carries with it a potent sense of belonging to an unbroken tradition of resistance and dissent, while the pointed revision identifies the realm of culture as a site of contestation no less crucial than the economic realm itself. If culture is the place where consent is won or undone, then occupying that domain in order to appropriate or demolish its most treasured monuments may be one of the most effective ways of sapping the credibility of the present dispensation. At the same time, the *materialist* slant of the enterprise keeps its textual business earthed in the stubborn realities to which writing and reading are bound: realities which can never be divorced from discourse, but which must not be reduced to it either. Cultural materialists underwrite the new historicist acceptance of the textuality of history, but they are less apt to leave the world immured for life in the prisonhouse of language. They are equally wary of succumbing to the charm of evolutionary versions of history, and with historical materialism as a progenitor they certainly need to be. Nevertheless, although they lack the confidence of earlier generations of Marxist intellectuals, their disillusionment is not so complete as to deny them a sense of the past's answerability for what we are now and what lies ahead of us.

Indeed, the most promising developments in recent radical historicist criticism have been concerned with opening up the horizon of futurity, which cultural poetics and cultural materialism as a rule have repressed to their cost. If you want to recover the sheer strangeness of a bygone age, you could scarcely do better than watch a new historicist at work, patiently embedding a familiar Elizabethan drama or Victorian novel in unfamiliar contexts, evoked in all their density by means of pungent anecdotes and arcane documents culled from the archives. If you wish, on the other hand, to rescue *Persuasion* or *The Duchess of Malfi* from their thraldom to the class-bound, patriarchal culture that sired them, you could do worse than try the cultural materialist tack of wrenching modern relevance from their reactionary clutches. (There is even a brand of cultural materialism, epitomized by the work of Terence Hawkes and Gary Taylor on Shakespeare, which frees you to make of any text whatever present needs demand, on the grounds that there are no constraints built into the text to stop you.) You may feel that the new historicist reliance on concepts drawn from market capitalism, poststructuralist discourse and Foucault's carceral obsessions fosters readings that owe more to the imperatives of modernity than to the priorities of the past. And you may note that cultural materialism cannot ride roughshod over the original import it ascribes to the work without conceding its historical validity – unless it resorts to the expedient of draining it of import altogether. But whichever manoeuvre you find more congenial, notwithstanding such reservations, neither is open to the possibility that literature may be shaped as much by the impulse of anticipation as by the limits of its first location.

For the beginnings of a radical historicist criticism which *is* open to that possibility, we need to turn to critics who have taken their cue from Benjamin rather than Foucault, and to back up the appeal to Benjamin by enlisting the aid of Theodor Adorno, Herbert Marcuse and above all Ernst Bloch, all of whom have made powerful contributions to the evolution of a utopian aesthetics and the liberation of literature from a petrified historicism. The influence of Benjamin can be traced in several essays in this volume, but it is most apparent in the pieces by Marjorie Levinson and Jerome McGann, who point to a way of addressing texts that might dissolve the bind in which we are placed by most shades of radical historicist criticism. New historicism and cultural materialism have enriched the field of literary studies by letting all the other disciplines in on the act, plugging texts back into historical contexts, probing literature's implication in social, racial and sexual oppression, and giving criticism a political edge and pertinence it had generally lacked. Yet they have also closed things down insofar as they have locked critics into either a past-bound or a modernizing posture. For readings that are purely retrospective, however conscious of their anchorage in the present they may be, and analyses that turn such retrospective readings inside out to make them fit the current political agenda, paralyse literature and history alike.

They do so because, despite their proclaimed aversion to totalities and teleologies, their rear-view perspective casts literature as the genetically doomed creation of a preconceived time and culture. This is nowhere more apparent than in the new historicists' use of arresting anecdotes to root their interpretations in the quirky stuff of history. Apart from exuding an antiquarian whiff of authenticity, the anecdote signals the critic's commitment to local rather than global knowledge, to *petits* as opposed to *grands récits*. As a strategy of estrangement the anecdote works admirably at first, forcing readers to drop their stale assumptions about books and backgrounds, and confront the work and its world afresh in all their idiosyncrasy. But in the end the eccentric anecdote repeatedly turns out to be a synecdoche, an exemplary illustration of a pervasive cultural logic, which even the wildest imaginations of the age are powerless to escape. A similar problem arises when cultural materialists foreground figures, groups and experiences sidelined or repressed by the conventional ambitions of the text. Switching the focus to the colonized, the criminal, the insane, the enslaved and the exploited has proved an invaluable move, and has changed the way our classic texts are read for good; but it leaves the original balance of power within those texts intact, since the notion that they might unhinge hierarchy itself has been ruled out in advance as unthinkable. The trouble, in other words, is that too many exponents of cultural poetics and cultural materialism are curbed by their remorselessly diagnostic attitude to literature, hamstrung by their invulnerability to the work's enigmas and mutations.

Hence the importance, if this radical historicist movement is to remain vital, of developing more dialogic forms of criticism, which respect the power of texts from the remote and recent past to call our deepest preconceptions into question, disclosing insights into its world and our own that hindsight deemed impossible. If that means acknowledging something incalculable, something indecipherable in the most appealing works that defies appropriation, so much the better. For it might at least be a sign that the poem or play is being seen with real historical imagination as the unpredictable result of an author wrestling with words under equally unpredictable conditions. Any serious attempt to accommodate the strangeness of the cultural past should surely begin with amazement that works as unexpected – as *gratuitous* – as

Wuthering Heights, Lyrical Ballads, Gulliver's Travels or *Dr Faustus* got written at all. Overfamiliarity with the canon can breed a contempt which takes such texts for granted or even writes them off as obsolete, and which is blind to their capacity to revise their meaning under the shifting circumstances of their subsequent reception.

There is also, of course, more than a touch of disingenuousness in critiques of the canon which are parasitic upon its appeal, and which only enhance the authority of the books they depose, even as they feed off the iconoclastic frisson they provoke. Perhaps there is more to the canon after all than meets most critics' eyes, which have been prone for too long to take the interpretations for the text. If there is, then one thing is for sure: radical historicism is unlikely to discover it, unless it is prepared to bring really close reading in from the cold and graft it into the heart of its practice. One can see why it was so important to send the discredited axioms of new critical analysis, practical criticism and unbridled deconstruction to Siberia, and the last thing that is needed is their complete rehabilitation. But it is astonishing to observe how much new historicist and cultural materialist criticism hardly engages with the verbal detail of texts at all. Even where textual quotations and allusions abound, their purpose is normally to act as broad illustrations or enactments of a conviction that precedes them, rather than as chances to unravel the mysteries of a unique weave of words. Radical historicist criticism is undoubtedly the poorer for its reluctance to meet the complex demands of a text's diction and formal refinements; for in the end only a precise local knowledge of the literary work, acquired through a 'thick description' of decisive verbal effects, will allow the critic to determine how far the work's complicity with power truly extends, and how far beyond our own horizon it may already have reached.

Liberating as it has clearly been to tear down the wall between literary and other sorts of discourse, the widespread belief that more than arbitrary convention divides *Hamlet* from contemporary homilies may have been abandoned prematurely nonetheless. The recent publication of books such as Paul Fry's *A Defense of Poetry: Reflections on the Occasion of Writing* (1995) and Mark Edmundson's *Literature Against Philosophy, Plato to Derrida: A Defence of Poetry* (1995) show that, for some theorists at least, the question of whether literature is a privileged form of expression is far from settled. If new historicism and cultural materialism fail to reopen this question by expanding their expectations of literary texts and rising to the challenge of close reading, their capacity to convince may well decline. But if they do manage to transmute themselves into a criticism as eager to unfold the future as it is keen to invade the past, I have a hunch that they will prove the classic texts of British and American culture to be more invaluable than anyone has yet suspected.

SECTION ONE

Sources

This section provides a concise anthology of some of the main theoretical influences on new historicist and cultural materialist criticism. It opens with an extract from Clifford Geertz's classic collection of essays on anthropology, *The Interpretation of Cultures*. From 'The Impact of the Concept of Culture on the Concept of Man' it is not difficult to infer the reasons for the impact of Geertz on the work of Stephen Greenblatt in particular and thus on the evolution of cultural poetics in general. Geertz demolishes the myth that culture is an attribute recently acquired by man, the latest stratum to be stacked on top of our biological, social and psychological dispositions. Far from being a belated, supplementary dimension of our development, the cultural capacity to signify was constitutive of the human animal from the start: 'there is no such thing', Geertz asserts, 'as a human nature independent of culture'. To understand human beings, therefore, we need to grasp them as 'cultural artifacts', whose significance is to be found inscribed in the specificity of local circumstance and concrete detail. Or as Greenblatt puts it in his own contribution to this volume in Section Two, 'interest lies not in the abstract universal but in particular, contingent cases, the selves fashioned and acting according to the generative rules and conflicts of a given culture'. As his closing quote from Robert Lowell's poem about Hawthorne suggests, Geertz's anthropology has a natural attraction for critics anxious to link literature to a wider semiotic system, and ideally equipped to read the whole of human culture as a literary text. His insistence on the primacy and inclusiveness of culture dovetails with the poststructuralist conversion of the real into the written and the dissident critic's redesignation of culture as a central site of political struggle.

It consorts readily too, in the mind of the new historicist, with the vision of Michel Foucault, inasmuch as Geertz and Foucault both authorize a preoccupation with 'selves fashioned and acting according to the generative rules and conflicts of a given culture'. Cultural materialism owes much to Foucault too; but, as Alan Sinfield's essay in the next section confirms, its stress tends to fall on the conflicts rather than the rules, on Foucault's warrant to detect fractures in the edifice of power rather than his stronger case for regarding power as ubiquitous and irresistible. Nowhere is that case more forcefully made than in the chapter on 'Panopticism' from *Discipline and Punish*, the book which, along with volume 1 of *The History of Sexuality* (1978), has had the most pervasive influence of all Foucault's works on radical historicist criticism. In the extract included here, Foucault chronicles two crucial stages in the formation of the modern society of the spectacle. The disciplinary regime of the plague-stricken town and the coercive transparency of Bentham's penitentiary dramatize the sinister logic of a carceral culture we still inhabit. They also incriminate writing and spectating as vital instruments of surveillance and control, and critics have been quick to seize this cue to indict the novel and the theatre as intrinsically complicit with oppression. The flipside of Foucault's magnification of power may well be a reciprocal compassion for its victims – the lunatics, lepers, vagabonds and criminals whose marginalization cultural materialists in particular are eager to reverse. But the contributions by Jonathan Goldberg, John Bender and Nancy Armstrong to Section Three suggest that it is in the exposure of fiction and drama as secret agents of hegemony that his chief critical legacy resides.

Despite the blatant differences between them, Foucault himself is plainly an heir of the Marxist philosopher Louis Althusser, whose theory of ideology and art constitutes, as chapters 7, 9 and 12 testify, an important tributary of new historicism and cultural materialism in its own right. Foucault explains how, through panopticism,

> A real subjection is born mechanically from a fictitious relation. So it is not necessary to use force to constrain the convict to good behaviour, the madman to calm, the worker to work, the schoolboy to application, the patient to the observation of the regulations. . . . He who is subjected to a field of visibility, and who knows it, assumes responsibility for the constraints of power; he makes them play spontaneously upon himself; he inscribes in himself the power relation in which he simultaneously plays both roles; he becomes the principle of his own subjection.

This is Foucault's revamping of Althusser's celebrated thesis that 'Ideology represents the imaginary relationship of individuals to their real conditions of existence'. In his seminal essay 'Ideology and Ideological State Apparatuses' Althusser explodes the common misconception of ideology as a cynical mystification of reality foisted upon the exploited by the exploiters to sustain the status quo. Far from being an externally imposed illusion, ideology involves a structural distortion of perception, a subconscious warping of the imagination, fostered in the individual by the institutions through which she or he is socialized. If the delusion that all is as it should be could be dispelled by rational argument alone, those who own and rule would have been toppled long ago; but from infancy onwards people learn to live their own subjection as the condition they desire, which is what makes change so difficult to achieve. It is less difficult to understand the appeal of this thesis to the politically disappointed generation of 1968, to whose ranks the first wave of radical historicists largely belonged. Some of these critics conscripted Althusser to back up their disenchanted view of literature as an intractably ideological practice; others adopted Althusser's own view of literature as a privileged means of exposing ideology to critique; and both groups were grateful for his insistence that the production of ideology is a material practice in actual social institutions, because it made education an ideal stage at which to sabotage the production process.

From the perspective of Raymond Williams, the founding father of cultural materialism, both Foucault's notion of power and Althusser's version of ideology appear intolerably monolothic. Keen though the latter and their acolytes are to defend themselves against such charges, their rebuttals are inevitably dwarfed by their grim image of humanity in thrall to forces beyond its control. In search of a more complex model of culture, which can account for the fact of change and cope with the movement of history, Williams turns to the concept of hegemony devised by the Italian Marxist Antonio Gramsci. The virtue of Gramsci's idea of hegemony is that it acknowledges the depth to which ruling beliefs and values can saturate society, while refusing (unlike Foucault) to dispense with the reality of class conflict and the brute fact of domination. Above all, it allows Williams to trade in the crude Marxist theory of economic base and cultural superstructure for an incomparably subtler analysis of culture as a whole way of life in motion. The fresh distinctions he draws in 'Base and Superstructure in Marxist Cultural Theory' between the dominant, the residual and the emergent dimensions of a given culture, and between alternative positions that can be incorporated by the reigning formation and oppositional perspectives that cannot, have proved extraordinarily fruitful for literary criticism. Williams does stress that 'we cannot separate literature and art from other kinds of social practice, in such a way as to make them subject to quite special and distinct laws'; and he is prepared to concede that 'most writing, in any period, including our own, is a form of contribution to the effective dominant culture'. But he also maintains (in a much-cited sentence) that 'no mode of production, and therefore no dominant society or order of society, and therefore no dominant culture, in reality exhausts the full range of human practice, human energy, human intention'. So his cultural theory also recognizes the capacity of literature not only to escape absorption, but to envisage standpoints as yet unvoiced.

Despite his dissolution of base and superstructure into a subsuming, horizontal concept of culture, Williams is never in danger of collapsing reality into writing, of taking the world for a book, in the way that the doyen of deconstruction, Jacques Derrida, is frequently apt to do. Williams's work is suffused with a firm sense of where reading ends and living begins, and of history as not only a discursive construct, but what gets made and remade by men and women, for better and for worse, beyond the library and the lecture hall. Derrida's persuasive dissemination of the view that we can have no access to reality that is not mediated by language, no glimpse of history that is not refracted through representation, has bred a proper scepticism in new historicists and cultural materialists about the authority of the documents they deal with and the objectivity of their own accounts of them. But one does not need to read far into the groundbreaking definition of *différance* reprinted here to appreciate how easily Derrida could also promote, among new historicists in particular, the contraction of history to story, on the grounds that narratives are all that we know, and the disappearance of the world behind the global web of textuality woven round it. Derrida picks up Saussure's proposition that 'language has neither ideas nor sounds that existed before the linguistic system, but only conceptual and phonic differences that have issued from the system', and drives it to the point where the differential play of meaning is not only the precondition of thought itself, but the causeless cause of our capacity to think historically in the first place, to divide past from present and present from future. The differential effects of language have obviously been produced, Derrida admits, 'but they are effects which do not find their cause in a subject or a substance', because 'there is no presence before and outside semiological difference'. Being cast adrift forever on the shoreless seas of textuality does have its advantages, however. The empirical materiality of history may have vanished, but at least all the old metaphysical ideas of history have vanished along with it, including the notion of history as 'background' or as the bedrock reality that literature subsequently mirrors or misrepresents. Indeed, as Catherine Belsey contends in chapter 10, *différance* may ultimately pave the way for a non-metaphysical return to history, and for a kind of historical criticism intent on undoing the ambitions of ideology through a militant textual practice.

Section One concludes with perhaps the best-known text penned by the messianic Marxist philosopher, Walter Benjamin. Completed in spring 1940 by a Jew fated to take his own life a few months later while fleeing from the Nazis, 'Theses on the Philosophy of History' is understandably less disposed than Derrida to let political realities evaporate under the pressure of intellectual concern. Every one of the theses is electrically charged by the state of crisis, the climate of commitment, in which its author composed it. At the same time, Benjamin is as anxious as Derrida to avoid placing glib theological constructions on history. The entire piece is a sardonic assault on historicism by a man wedded to a theory of historical materialism from which fantasies of retrospective empathy and inevitable progress have been purged. Progress for Benjamin is Klee's angel hurled backwards into the future from Paradise, as the wreckage – the dreadful human cost of history – piles up before his appalled gaze. So 'The historical materialist leaves it to others to be drained by the whore called "Once upon a time" in historicism's bordello', preferring to take 'a tiger's leap into the past' in order to 'blast open the continuum of history'. The only escape from the impasse of providence or nostalgia is to identify the point at which the needs of the present intersect with the unrealized potential of an earlier era; to release a different destiny for the present by releasing the prefigurative energies of the unredeemed past: 'As flowers turn toward the sun, by dint of a secret heliotropism the past strives to turn toward that sun which is rising in the sky of history.' Critics raring to put Benjamin's philosophy of history into practice are advised, however, to approach their literary quarry with the utmost caution, for 'There is no document of civilization which is not at the same time a document of barbarism'. As a consequence, neither the past nor the literature of the past can be redeemed by the present for the future unless historians and critics are prepared to brush history and read texts 'against the grain' of their original inclination. A fine example of reading against the grain is provided by Francis Barker and Peter Hulme's essay on *The Tempest* in the final section of the Reader; while the richer opportunities in store for a criticism tuned to the frequency of the future are explored in the contributions by Marjorie Levinson (chapter 12) and Jerome McGann (chapter 18).

Clifford Geertz

From *The Impact of the Concept of Culture on the Concept of Man*

The Interpretation of Cultures: Selected Essays, Basic Books: New York, 1973, pp. 46–54.

The traditional view of the relations between the biological and the cultural advance of man was that the former, the biological, was for all intents and purposes completed before the latter, the cultural, began. That is to say, it was again stratigraphic: Man's physical being evolved, through the usual mechanisms of genetic variation and natural selection, up to the point where his anatomical structure had arrived at more or less the status at which we find it today; then cultural development got under way. At some particular stage in his phylogenetic history, a marginal genetic change of some sort rendered him capable of producing and carrying culture, and thenceforth his form of adaptive response to environmental pressures was almost exclusively cultural rather than genetic. As he spread over the globe, he wore furs in cold climates and loin cloths (or nothing at all) in warm ones; he didn't alter his innate mode of response to environmental temperature. He made weapons to extend his inherited predatory powers and cooked foods to render a wider range of them digestible. Man became man, the story continues, when, having crossed some mental Rubicon, he became able to transmit 'knowledge, belief, law, morals, custom' (to quote the items of Sir Edward Tylor's classical definition of culture) to his descendants and his neighbours through teaching and to acquire them from his ancestors and his neighbours through learning. After that magical moment, the advance of the hominids depended almost entirely on cultural accumulation, on the slow growth of conventional practices, rather than, as it had for ages past, on physical organic change.

The only trouble is that such a moment does not seem to have existed. By the most recent estimates the transition to the cultural mode of life took the genus *Homo* several million years to accomplish; and stretched out in such a manner, it involved not one or a handful of marginal genetic changes but a long, complex, and closely ordered sequence of them.

In the current view, the evolution of *Homo sapiens* – modern man – out of his immediate pre*sapiens* background got definitely under way nearly four million years ago with the appearance of the now famous Australopithecines – the so-called ape men of southern and eastern Africa – and culminated with the emergence of *sapiens* himself only some one to two or three hundred thousand years ago. Thus, as at least elemental forms of cultural, or if you wish protocultural, activity (simple toolmaking, hunting, and so on) seem to have been present among some of the Australopithecines, there was an overlap of, as I say, well over a million years between the beginning of culture and the appearance of man as we know him today. The precise dates – which are tentative and which further research may later alter in one direction or another – are not critical; what is critical is that there was an overlap and that it was a very extended one. The final phases (final to date, at any rate) of the phylogenetic history of man took place in the same grand geological era – the so-called Ice Age – as the initial phases of his cultural history. Men have birthdays, but man does not.

What this means is that culture, rather than being added on, so to speak, to a finished or virtually finished animal, was ingredient, and centrally ingredient, in the production of that animal itself. The slow, steady, almost glacial growth of culture through the Ice Age altered the balance of selection pressures for the evolving *Homo* in such a way as to play a major directive role in his evolution. The perfection of tools, the adoption of organized hunting and gathering practices, the beginnings of true family organization, the discovery of fire, and, most critically, though it is as yet extremely difficult to trace it out in any detail, the increasing reliance upon systems of significant symbols (language, art, myth, ritual) for orientation, communication, and self-control all created for man a new environment to which he was then obliged to adapt. As culture, step by infinitesimal step, accumulated and developed, a selective advantage was given to those individuals in the population most able to take advantage of it – the effective hunter, the persistent gatherer, the adept toolmaker, the resourceful leader – until what had been a small-brained, protohuman *Australopithecus* became the large-brained fully human *Homo sapiens*. Between the cultural pattern, the body, and the brain, a positive feedback system was created in which each shaped the progress of the other, a system in which the interaction among increasing tool use, the changing anatomy of the hand, and the expanding representation of the thumb on the cortex is only one of the more graphic examples. By submitting himself to governance by symbolically mediated programmes for producing artifacts, organizing social life, or expressing emotions, man determined, if unwittingly, the culminating stages of his own biological destiny. Quite literally, though quite inadvertently, he created himself.

Though, as I mentioned, there were a number of important changes in the gross anatomy of genus *Homo* during this period of his crystallization – in skull shape, dentition, thumb size, and so on – by far the most important and dramatic were those that evidently took place in the central nervous system; for this was the period when the human brain, and most particularly the forebrain, ballooned into its present top-heavy proportions. The technical problems are complicated and controversial here; but the main point is that though the Australopithecines had a torso and arm configuration not drastically different from our own, and a pelvis and leg formation at least well-launched toward our own, they had cranial capacities hardly larger than those of the living apes – that is to say, about a third to a half of our own. What sets true men off most distinctly from protomen is apparently not overall bodily form but complexity of nervous organization. The overlap period of cultural and biological change seems to have consisted in an intense concentration on neural development and perhaps associated refinements of various behaviours – of the hands, bipedal locomotion, and so on – for which the basic anatomical foundations – mobile shoulders and wrists, a broadened ilium, and so on – had already been securely laid. In itself, this is perhaps not altogether startling; but, combined with what I have already said, it suggests some conclusions about what sort of animal man is that are, I think, rather far not only from those of the eighteenth century but from those of the anthropology of only ten or fifteen years ago.

Most bluntly, it suggests that there is no such thing as a human nature independent of culture. Men without culture would not be the clever savages of Golding's *Lord of the Flies* thrown back upon the cruel wisdom of their animal instincts; nor would they be the nature's noblemen of Enlightenment primitivism or even, as classical anthropological theory would imply, intrinsically talented apes who had somehow failed to find themselves. They would be unworkable monstrosities with very few useful instincts, fewer recognizable sentiments, and no intellect: mental basket cases. As our central nervous system – and most particularly its crowning curse and glory, the neocortex – grew up in great part in interaction with culture, it is incapable of directing our behaviour or organizing our experience without the guidance provided by systems of significant symbols. What happened to us in the Ice Age is that we were obliged to abandon the regularity and precision of detailed genetic control over our conduct for the flexibility and adaptability of a more generalized, though of course no less real, genetic control over it. To supply the additional information necessary to be able to act, we were forced, in turn, to rely more and more heavily on cultural sources – the accumulated fund of significant symbols. Such symbols are thus not mere expressions, instrumentalities, or correlates of our biological, psychological, and social existence; they are prerequisites of it. Without men, no culture, certainly; but equally, and more significantly, without culture, no men.

We are, in sum, incomplete or unfinished animals who complete or finish ourselves through culture – and not through culture in general but through highly particular forms of it: Dobuan and Javanese, Hopi and Italian, upper-class and lower-class, academic and commercial. Man's great capacity for learning, his plasticity, has often been remarked, but what is even more critical is his extreme dependence upon a certain sort of learning: the attainment of concepts, the apprehension and application of specific systems of symbolic meaning. Beavers build dams, birds build nests, bees locate food, baboons organize social groups, and mice mate on the basis of forms of learning that rest predominantly on the instructions encoded in their genes and evoked by appropriate patterns of external stimuli: physical keys inserted into organic locks. But men build dams or shelters, locate food, organize their social groups, or find sexual partners under the guidance of instructions encoded in flow charts and blueprints, hunting lore, moral systems and aesthetic judgments: conceptual structures moulding formless talents.

We live, as one writer has neatly put it, in an 'information gap'. Between what our body tells us and what we have to know in order to function, there is a vacuum we must fill ourselves, and we fill it with information (or misinformation) provided by our culture. The boundary between what is innately controlled and what is culturally controlled in human behaviour is an ill-defined and wavering one. Some things are, for all intents and purposes, entirely controlled intrinsically: we need no more cultural guidance to learn how to breathe than a fish needs to learn how to swim. Others are almost certainly largely cultural; we do not attempt to explain on a genetic basis why some men put their trust in centralized planning and others in the free market, though it might be an amusing exercise. Almost all complex human behaviour is, of course, the interactive, nonadditive outcome of the two. Our capacity to speak is surely innate; our capacity to speak English is surely cultural. Smiling at pleasing stimuli and frowning at unpleasing ones are surely in some degree genetically determined (even apes screw up their faces at noxious odours); but sardonic smiling and burlesque frowning are equally surely predominantly cultural, as is perhaps demonstrated by the Balinese definition of a madman as someone who, like an American, smiles when there is nothing to laugh at. Between the basic ground plans for our life that our genes lay down – the capacity to speak or to smile – and the precise behaviour we in fact execute – speaking English in a certain tone of voice, smiling enigmatically in a delicate social situation – lies a complex set of significant symbols under whose direction we transform the first into the second, the ground plans into the activity.

Our ideas, our values, our acts, even our emotions, are, like our nervous system itself, cultural products – products manufactured, indeed, out of tendencies, capacities, and dispositions with which we were born, but manufactured nonetheless. Chartres is made of stone and glass. But it is not just stone and glass; it is a cathedral, and not only a cathedral, but a particular cathedral built at a particular time by certain members of a particular society. To understand what it means, to perceive it for what it is, you need to know rather more than the generic properties of stone and glass and rather more than what is common to all cathedrals. You need to understand also – and, in my opinion, most critically – the specific concepts of the relations among God, man, and architecture that, since they have governed its creation, it consequently embodies. It is no different with men: they, too, every last one of them, are cultural artifacts.

Whatever differences they may show, the approaches to the definition of human nature adopted by the Enlightenment and by classical anthropology have one thing in common: they are both basically typological. They endeavour to construct an image of man as a model, an archetype, a Platonic idea or an Aristotelian form, with respect to which actual men – you, me, Churchill, Hitler, and the Bornean headhunter – are but reflections, distortions, approximations. In the Enlightenment case, the elements of this essential type were to be uncovered by stripping the trappings of culture away from actual men and seeing what then was left – natural man. In classical anthropology, it was to be uncovered by factoring out the commonalities in culture and seeing what then appeared – consensual man. In either case, the result is the same as that which tends to emerge in all typological approaches to scientific problems generally: the differences among individuals and among groups of individuals are rendered secondary. Individuality comes to be seen as eccentricity, distinctiveness as accidental deviation from the only legitimate object of study for the true scientist: the underlying, unchanging, normative type. In such an approach, however elaborately formulated and resourcefully defended, living detail is drowned in dead stereotype: we are in quest of a metaphysical entity, Man with a capital 'M', in the interests of which we sacrifice the empirical entity we in fact encounter, man with a small 'm'.

The sacrifice is, however, as unnecessary as it is unavailing. There is no opposition between general theoretical understanding and circumstantial understanding, between synoptic vision and a fine eye for detail. It is, in fact, by its power to draw general propositions out of particular phenomena that a scientific theory – indeed, science itself – is to be judged. If we want to discover what man amounts to, we can only find it in what men are: and what men are, above all other things, is various. It is in understanding that variousness – its range, its nature, its basis, and its implications – that we shall come to construct a concept of human nature that, more than a statistical shadow and less than a primitivist dream, has both substance and truth.

It is here, to come round finally to my title, that the concept of culture has its impact on the concept of man. When seen as a set of symbolic devices for controlling behaviour, extrasomatic sources of information, culture provides the link between what men are intrinsically capable of becoming and what they actually, one by one, in fact become. Becoming human is becoming individual, and we become individual under the guidance of cultural patterns, historically created systems of meaning in terms of which we give form, order, point, and direction to our lives. And the cultural patterns involved are not general but specific – not just 'marriage' but a particular set of notions about what men and women are like, how spouses should treat one another, or who should properly marry whom; not just 'religion' but belief in the wheel of karma, the observance of a month of fasting, or the practice of cattle sacrifice. Man is to be defined neither by his innate capacities alone, as the Enlightenment sought to do, nor by his actual behaviours alone, as much of contemporary social science seeks to do, but rather by the link between them, by the way in which the first is transformed into the second, his generic potentialities focused into his specific performances. It is in man's *career*, in its characteristic course, that we can discern, however dimly, his nature, and though culture is but one element in determining that course, it is hardly the least important. As culture shaped us as a single species – and is no doubt still shaping us – so too it shapes us as separate individuals. This, neither an unchanging subcultural self nor an established cross-cultural consensus, is what we really have in common.

Oddly enough – though on second thought, perhaps not so oddly – many of our subjects seem to realize this more clearly than we anthropologists ourselves. In Java, for example, where I have done much of my work, the people quite flatly say, 'To be human is to be Javanese.' Small children, boors, simpletons, the insane, the flagrantly immoral, are said to be *ndurung djawa*, 'not yet Javanese'. A 'normal' adult capable of acting in terms of the highly elaborate system of etiquette, possessed of the delicate aesthetic perceptions associated with music, dance, drama, and textile design, responsive to the subtle promptings of the divine residing in the stillnesses of each individual's inward-turning consciousness, is *sampun djawa*, 'already Javanese', that is, already human. To be human is not just to breathe; it is to control one's breathing, by yogalike techniques, so as to hear in inhalation and exhalation the literal voice of God pronouncing His own name – 'hu Allah'. It is not just to talk, it is to utter the appropriate words and phrases in the appropriate social situations in the appropriate tone of voice and with the appropriate evasive indirection. It is not just to eat; it is to prefer certain foods cooked in certain ways and to follow a rigid table etiquette in consuming them. It is not even just to feel but to feel certain quite distinctively Javanese (and essentially untranslatable) emotions – 'patience', 'detachment', 'resignation', 'respect'.

To be human here is thus not to be Everyman; it is to be a particular kind of man, and of course men differ: 'Other fields,' the Javanese say, 'other grasshoppers.' Within the society, differences are recognized, too – the way a rice peasant becomes human and Javanese differs from the way a civil servant does. This is not a matter of tolerance and ethical relativism, for not all ways of being human are regarded as equally admirable by far; the way the local Chinese go about it is, for example, intensely dispraised. The point is that there are different ways; and to shift to the anthropologist's perspective now, it is in a systematic review and analysis of these – of the Plains Indian's bravura, the Hindu's obsessiveness, the Frenchman's rationalism, the Berber's anarchism, the American's optimism (to list a series of tags I should not like to have to defend as such) – that we shall find out what it is, or can be, to be a man.

We must, in short, descend into detail, past the misleading tags, past the metaphysical types, past the empty similarities to grasp firmly the essential character of not only the various cultures but the various sorts of individuals within each culture, if we wish to encounter humanity face to face. In this area, the road to the general, to the revelatory simplicities of science, lies through a concern with the particular, the circumstantial, the concrete, but a concern organized and directed in terms of the sort of theoretical analyses that I have touched upon – analyses of physical evolution, of the functioning of the nervous system, of social organization, of psychological process, of cultural patterning, and so on – and, most especially, in terms of the interplay among them. That is to say, the road lies, like any genuine Quest, through a terrifying complexity.

'Leave him alone for a moment or two,' Robert Lowell writes, not as one might suspect of the anthropologist but of that other eccentric inquirer into the nature of man, Nathaniel Hawthorne.

> Leave him alone for a moment or two,
> and you'll see him with his head
> bent down, brooding, brooding,
> eyes fixed on some chip,
> some stone, some common plant,
> the commonest thing,
> as if it were the clue.
> The disturbed eyes rise,
> furtive, foiled, dissatisfied
> from meditation on the true
> and insignificant.[1]

Bent over his own chips, stones, and common plants, the anthropologist broods, too, upon the true and insignificant, glimpsing in it, or so he thinks, fleetingly and insecurely, the disturbing, changeful image of himself.

---

[1] From 'Hawthorne', in *For the Union Dead* (New York: Farrar, Straus & Giroux, 1964), p. 39.

2   Michel Foucault

From *Panopticism*

Discipline and Punish: The Birth of the Prison, trans. Alan Sheridan,
Penguin Books: Harmondsworth, 1979, pp. 195–203.

The following, according to an order published at the end of the seventeenth
century, were the measures to be taken when the plague appeared in a town.[1]
   First, a strict spatial partitioning: the closing of the town and its outlying
districts, a prohibition to leave the town on pain of death, the killing of all stray
animals; the division of the town into distinct quarters, each governed by an
intendant. Each street is placed under the authority of a syndic, who keeps it
under surveillance; if he leaves the street, he will be condemned to death. On
the appointed day, everyone is ordered to stay indoors: it is forbidden to leave
on pain of death. The syndic himself comes to lock the door of each house
from the outside; he takes the key with him and hands it over to the intendant
of the quarter; the intendant keeps it until the end of the quarantine. Each
family will have made its own provisions; but, for bread and wine, small
wooden canals are set up between the street and the interior of the houses, thus
allowing each person to receive his ration without communicating with the
suppliers and other residents; meat, fish and herbs will be hoisted up into the
houses with pulleys and baskets. If it is absolutely necessary to leave the
house, it will be done in turn, avoiding any meeting. Only the intendants,
syndics and guards will move about the streets and also, between the infected
houses, from one corpse to another, the 'crows', who can be left to die: these
are 'people of little substance who carry the sick, bury the dead, clean and do
many vile and abject offices'. It is a segmented, immobile, frozen space. Each
individual is fixed in his place. And, if he moves, he does so at the risk of his
life, contagion or punishment.
   Inspection functions ceaselessly. The gaze is alert everywhere: 'A
considerable body of militia, commanded by good officers and men of
substance', guards at the gates, at the town hall and in every quarter to ensure
the prompt obedience of the people and the most absolute authority of the
magistrates, 'as also to observe all disorder, theft and extortion'. At each of the
town gates there will be an observation post; at the end of each street sentinels.
Every day, the intendant visits the quarter in his charge, inquires whether the
syndics have carried out their tasks, whether the inhabitants have anything to
complain of; they 'observe their actions'. Every day, too, the syndic goes into
the street for which he is responsible; stops before each house: gets all the
inhabitants to appear at the windows (those who live overlooking the
courtyard will be allocated a window looking onto the street at which no one

---

[1] Archives militaires de Vincennes, A 1,516 91 sc. Pièce. This regulation is broadly similar to
a whole series of others that date from the same period and earlier.

but they may show themselves); he calls each of them by name; informs himself as to the state of each and every one of them – 'in which respect the inhabitants will be compelled to speak the truth under pain of death'; if someone does not appear at the window, the syndic must ask why: 'In this way he will find out easily enough whether dead or sick are being concealed.' Everyone locked up in his cage, everyone at his window, answering to his name and showing himself when asked – it is the great review of the living and the dead.

This surveillance is based on a system of permanent registration: reports from the syndics to the intendants, from the intendants to the magistrates or mayor. At the beginning of the 'lock up', the role of each of the inhabitants present in the town is laid down, one by one; this document bears 'the name, age, sex of everyone, notwithstanding his condition': a copy is sent to the intendant of the quarter, another to the office of the town hall, another to enable the syndic to make his daily roll call. Everything that may be observed during the course of the visits – deaths, illnesses, complaints, irregularities – is noted down and transmitted to the intendants and magistrates. The magistrates have complete control over medical treatment; they have appointed a physician in charge; no other practitioner may treat, no apothecary prepare medicine, no confessor visit a sick person without having received from him a written note 'to prevent anyone from concealing and dealing with those sick of the contagion, unknown to the magistrates'. The registration of the pathological must be constantly centralized. The relation of each individual to his disease and to his death passes through the representatives of power, the registration they make of it, the decisions they take on it.

Five or six days after the beginning of the quarantine, the process of purifying the houses one by one is begun. All the inhabitants are made to leave; in each room 'the furniture and goods' are raised from the ground or suspended from the air; perfume is poured around the room; after carefully sealing the windows, doors and even the keyholes with wax, the perfume is set alight. Finally, the entire house is closed while the perfume is consumed; those who have carried out the work are searched, as they were on entry, 'in the presence of the residents of the house, to see that they did not have something on their persons as they left that they did not have on entering'. Four hours later, the residents are allowed to re-enter their homes.

This enclosed, segmented space, observed at every point, in which the individuals are inserted in a fixed place, in which the slightest movements are supervised, in which all events are recorded, in which an uninterrupted work of writing links the centre and periphery, in which power is exercised without division, according to a continuous hierarchical figure, in which each individual is constantly located, examined and distributed among the living beings, the sick and the dead – all this constitutes a compact model of the disciplinary mechanism. The plague is met by order; its function is to sort out every possible confusion: that of the disease, which is transmitted when bodies are mixed together; that of the evil, which is increased when fear and death overcome prohibitions. It lays down for each individual his place, his body, his disease and his death, his well-being, by means of an omnipresent and omniscient power that subdivides itself in a regular, uninterrupted way even to the ultimate determination of the individual, of what characterizes him, of what belongs to him, of what happens to him. Against the plague, which is a mixture, discipline brings into play its power, which is one of analysis. A whole literary fiction of the festival grew up around the plague: suspended laws, lifted prohibitions, the frenzy of passing time, bodies mingling together without respect, individuals unmasked, abandoning their statutory identity and the figure under which they had been recognized, allowing a quite different truth to appear. But there was also a political dream of the plague, which was exactly its reverse: not the collective festival, but strict divisions; not laws transgressed, but the penetration of regulation into even the smallest details of everyday life through the mediation of the complete hierarchy that assured the capillary functioning of power; not masks that were put on and taken off, but the assignment to each individual of his 'true' name, his 'true' place, his 'true' body, his 'true' disease. The plague as a form, at once real and imaginary, of disorder had as its medical and political correlative discipline. Behind the disciplinary mechanisms can be read the haunting memory of 'contagions', of the plague, of rebellions, crimes, vagabondage, desertions, people who appear and disappear, live and die in disorder.

If it is true that the leper gave rise to rituals of exclusion, which to a certain extent provided the model for and general form of the great Confinement, then the plague gave rise to disciplinary projects. Rather than the massive, binary division between one set of people and another, it called for multiple separations, individualizing distributions, an organization in depth of surveillance and control, an intensification and a ramification of power. The leper was caught up in a practice of rejection, of exile-enclosure; he was left to his doom in a mass among which it was useless to differentiate; those sick of the plague were caught up in a meticulous tactical partitioning in which individual differentiations were the constricting effects of a power that multiplied, articulated and subdivided itself; the great confinement on the one hand; the correct training on the other. The leper and his separation; the plague and its segmentations. The first is marked; the second analysed and distributed. The exile of the leper and the arrest of the plague do not bring with them the same political dream. The first is that of a pure community, the second that of a disciplined society. Two ways of exercising power over men, of controlling their relations, of separating out their dangerous mixtures. The plague-stricken town, traversed throughout with hierarchy, surveillance, observation, writing; the town immobilized by the functioning of an extensive power that bears in a distinct way over all individual bodies – this is the utopia of the perfectly governed city. The plague (envisaged as a possibility at least) is the trial in the course of which one may define ideally the exercise of disciplinary power. In order to make rights and laws function according to pure theory, the jurists place themselves in imagination in the state of nature; in order to see perfect disciplines functioning, rulers dreamt of the state of plague. Underlying disciplinary projects the image of the plague stands for all forms of confusion and disorder; just as the image of the leper, cut off from all human contact, underlies projects of exclusion.

They are different projects, then, but not incompatible ones. We see them coming slowly together, and it is the peculiarity of the nineteenth century that it applied to the space of exclusion of which the leper was the symbolic inhabitant (beggars, vagabonds, madmen and the disorderly formed the real population) the technique of power proper to disciplinary partitioning. Treat 'lepers' as 'plague victims', project the subtle segmentations of discipline onto the confused space of internment, combine it with the methods of analytical distribution proper to power, individualize the excluded, but use procedures of individualization to mark exclusion – this is what was operated regularly by disciplinary power from the beginning of the nineteenth century in the psychiatric asylum, the penitentiary, the reformatory, the approved school and, to some extent, the hospital. Generally speaking, all the authorities exercising individual control function according to a double mode; that of binary division and branding (mad/sane; dangerous/harmless; normal/abnormal); and that of coercive assignment, of differential distribution (who he is; where he must be; how he is to be characterized; how he is to be recognized; how a constant surveillance is to be exercised over him in an individual way, etc.). On the one hand, the lepers are treated as plague victims; the tactics of individualizing disciplines are imposed on the excluded; and, on the other hand, the universality of disciplinary controls makes it possible to brand the 'leper' and to bring into play against him the dualistic mechanisms of exclusion. The constant division between the normal and the abnormal, to which every individual is subjected, brings us back to our own time, by applying the binary branding and exile of the leper to quite different objects; the existence of a whole set of techniques and institutions for measuring, supervising and correcting the abnormal brings into play the disciplinary mechanisms to which the fear of the plague gave rise. All the mechanisms of power which, even today, are disposed around the abnormal individual, to brand him and to alter him, are composed of those two forms from which they distantly derive.

Bentham's *Panopticon* is the architectural figure of this composition. We know the principle on which it was based: at the periphery, an annular building; at the centre, a tower; this tower is pierced with wide windows that open onto the inner side of the ring; the peripheric building is divided into cells, each of which extends the whole width of the building; they have two windows, one on the inside, corresponding to the windows of the tower; the other, on the outside, allows the light to cross the cell from one end to the other. All that is needed, then, is to place a supervisor in a central tower and to shut up in each cell a madman, a patient, a condemned man, a worker or a schoolboy. By the effect of backlighting, one can observe from the tower, standing out precisely against the light, the small captive shadows in the cells of the periphery. They are like so many cages, so many small theatres, in which each actor is alone, perfectly individualized and constantly visible. The panoptic mechanism arranges spatial unities that make it possible to see constantly and to recognize immediately. In short, it reverses the principle of the dungeon; or rather of its three functions – to enclose, to deprive of light and to hide – it preserves only the first and eliminates the other two. Full lighting and the eye of a supervisor capture better than darkness, which ultimately protected. Visibility is a trap.

To begin with, this made it possible – as a negative effect – to avoid those compact, swarming, howling masses that were to be found in places of confinement, those painted by Goya or described by Howard. Each individual, in his place, is securely confined to a cell from which he is seen from the front by the supervisor; but the side walls prevent him from coming into contact with his companions. He is seen, but he does not see; he is the object of information, never a subject in communication. The arrangement of his room, opposite the central tower, imposes on him an axial visibility; but the divisions of the ring, those separated cells, imply a lateral invisibility. And this invisibility is a guarantee of order. If the inmates are convicts, there is no danger of a plot, an attempt at collective escape, the planning of new crimes for the future, bad reciprocal influences; if they are patients, there is no danger of contagion; if they are madmen there is no risk of their committing violence upon one another; if they are schoolchildren, there is no copying, no noise, no chatter, no waste of time; if they are workers there are no disorders, no theft, no coalitions, none of those distractions that slow down the rate of work, make it less perfect or cause accidents. The crowd, a compact mass, a locus of multiple exchanges, individualities merging together, a collective effect, is abolished and replaced by a collection of separated individualities. From the point of view of the guardian, it is replaced by a multiplicity that can be numbered and supervised; from the point of view of the inmates, by a sequestered and observed solitude.[2]

Hence the major effect of the Panopticon: to induce in the inmate a state of conscious and permanent visibility that assures the automatic functioning of power. So to arrange things that the surveillance is permanent in its effects, even if it is discontinuous in its action; that the perfection of power should tend to render its actual exercise unnecessary; that this architectural apparatus should be a machine for creating and sustaining a power relation independent of the person who exercises it; in short, that the inmates should be caught up in a power situation of which they are themselves the bearers. To achieve this, it is at once too much and too little that the prisoner should be constantly observed by an inspector: too little, for what matters is that he knows himself to be observed; too much, because he has no need in fact of being so. In view of this, Bentham laid down the principle that power should be visible and unverifiable. Visible: the inmate will constantly have before his eyes the tall outline of the central tower from which he is spied upon. Unverifiable: the inmate must never know whether he is being looked at at any one moment; but he must be sure that he may always be so. In order to make the presence or absence of the inspector unverifiable, so that the prisoners, in their cells, cannot even see a shadow, Bentham envisaged not only venetian blinds on the windows of the central observation hall, but, on the inside, partitions that intersected the hall at right angles and, in order to pass from one quarter to the other, not doors but zig-zag openings; for the slightest noise, a gleam of light, a brightness in a half-opened door would betray the presence of the guardian.[3] The Panopticon is a machine for dissociating the see/being seen dyad: in the

[2] Jeremy Bentham, *Works*, ed. John Bowring (Edinburgh: W. Tait, 1843), IV, pp. 60–4.
[3] In the *Postscript to the Panopticon*, 1791, Bentham adds dark inspection galleries painted in black around the inspector's lodge, each making it possible to observe two storeys of cells.

peripheric ring, one is totally seen, without ever seeing; in the central tower, one sees everything without ever being seen.[4]

It is an important mechanism, for it automatizes and disindividualizes power. Power has its principle not so much in a person as in a certain concerted distribution of bodies, surfaces, lights, gazes; in an arrangement whose internal mechanisms produce the relation in which individuals are caught up. The ceremonies, the rituals, the marks by which the sovereign's surplus power was manifested are useless. There is a machinery that assures dissymmetry, disequilibrium, difference. Consequently, it does not matter who exercises power. Any individual, taken almost at random, can operate the machine: in the absence of the director, his family, his friends, his visitors, even his servants.[5] Similarly, it does not matter what motive animates him: the curiosity of the indiscreet, the malice of a child, the thirst for knowledge of a philosopher who wishes to visit this museum of human nature, or the perversity of those who take pleasure in spying and punishing. The more numerous those anonymous and temporary observers are, the greater the risk for the inmate of being surprised and the greater his anxious awareness of being observed. The Panopticon is a marvellous machine which, whatever use one may wish to put it to, produces homogeneous effects of power.

A real subjection is born mechanically from a fictitious relation. So it is not necessary to use force to constrain the convict to good behaviour, the madman to calm, the worker to work, the schoolboy to application, the patient to the observation of the regulations. Bentham was surprised that panoptic institutions could be so light: there were no more bars, no more chains, no more heavy locks; all that was needed was that the separations should be clear and the openings well arranged. The heaviness of the old 'houses of security', with their fortress-like architecture, could be replaced by the simple, economic geometry of a 'house of certainty'. The efficiency of power, its constraining force have, in a sense, passed over to the other side – to the side of its surface of application. He who is subjected to a field of visibility, and who knows it, assumes responsibility for the constraints of power; he makes them play spontaneously upon himself; he inscribes in himself the power relation in which he simultaneously plays both roles; he becomes the principle of his own subjection. By this very fact, the external power may throw off its physical weight; it tends to the non-corporal; and, the more it approaches this limit, the more constant, profound and permanent are its effects: it is a perpetual victory that avoids any physical confrontation and which is always decided in advance.

---

[4] In his first version of the *Panopticon*, Bentham had also imagined an acoustic surveillance, operated by means of pipes leading from the cells to the central tower. In the *Postscript* he abandoned the idea, perhaps because he could not introduce into it the principle of dissymmetry and prevent the prisoners from hearing the inspector as well as the inspector hearing them. Julius tried to develop a system of dissymmetrical listening (N.H. Julius, *Leçons sur les prisons*, I, 1831).

[5] Bentham, *Works*, IV, p. 45.

3 Louis Althusser

From *Ideology and Ideological State Apparatuses*

Lenin and Philosophy and other Essays, trans. Ben Brewster, New Left
Books: London, 1971, pp. 152–9.

Ideology is a 'Representation' of the Imaginary Relationship of Individuals to their Real Conditions of Existence

In order to approach my central thesis on the structure and functioning of ideology, I shall first present two theses, one negative, the other positive. The first
concerns the object which is 'represented' in the imaginary form of ideology,
the second concerns the materiality of ideology.

THESIS I: Ideology represents the imaginary relationship of individuals to
their real conditions of existence.

We commonly call religious ideology, ethical ideology, legal ideology,
political ideology, etc., so many 'world outlooks'. Of course, assuming that we
do not live one of these ideologies as the truth (e.g. 'believe' in God, Duty,
Justice, etc. . . .), we admit that the ideology we are discussing from a critical
point of view, examining it as the ethnologist examines the myths of a 'primitive society', that these 'world outlooks' are largely imaginary, i.e. do not 'correspond to reality'.

However, while admitting that they do not correspond to reality, i.e. that
they constitute an illusion, we admit that they do make allusion to reality, and
that they need only be 'interpreted' to discover the reality of the world behind
their imaginary representation of that world (ideology = *illusion/allusion*).

There are different types of interpretation, the most famous of which are the
mechanistic type, current in the eighteenth century (God is the imaginary representation of the real King), and the '*hermeneutic*' interpretation, inaugurated
by the earliest Church fathers, and revived by Feuerbach and the theologico-
philosophical school which descends from him, e.g. the theologian Barth (to
Feuerbach, for example, God is the essence of real Man). The essential point
is that on condition that we interpret the imaginary transposition (and inversion) of ideology we arrive at the conclusion that in ideology 'men represent
their real conditions of existence to themselves in an imaginary form'.

Unfortunately, this interpretation leaves one small problem unsettled: why
do men 'need' this imaginary transposition of their real conditions of existence
in order to 'represent to themselves' their real conditions of existence?

The first answer (that of the eighteenth century) proposes a simple solution: Priests or Despots are responsible. They 'forged' the Beautiful Lies so
that, in the belief that they were obeying God, men would in fact obey the
Priests and Despots, who are usually in alliance in their imposture, the
Priests acting in the interests of the Despots or *vice versa*, according to the
political positions of the 'theoreticians' concerned. There is therefore a
cause for the imaginary transposition of the real conditions of existence: that

cause is the existence of a small number of cynical men who base their domination and exploitation of the 'people' on a falsified representation of the world which they have imagined in order to enslave other minds by dominating their imaginations.

The second answer (that of Feuerbach, taken over word for word by Marx in his Early Works) is more 'profound', i.e. just as false. It, too, seeks and finds a cause for the imaginary transposition and distortion of men's real conditions of existence, in short, for the alienation in the imaginary of the representation of men's conditions of existence. This cause is no longer Priests or Despots, nor their active imagination and the passive imagination of their victims. This cause is the material alienation which reigns in the conditions of existence of men themselves. This is how, in *The Jewish Question* and elsewhere, Marx defends the Feuerbachian idea that men make themselves an alienated (= imaginary) representation of their conditions of existence because these conditions of existence are themselves alienating (in the *1844 Manuscripts*: because these conditions are dominated by the essence of alienated society – '*alienated labour*').

All these interpretations thus take literally the thesis which they presuppose, and on which they depend, i.e. that what is reflected in the imaginary representation of the world found in an ideology is the conditions of existence of men, i.e. their real world.

Now I can return to a thesis which I have already advanced: it is not their real conditions of existence, their real world, that 'men' 'represent to themselves' in ideology, but above all it is their relation to those conditions of existence which is represented to them there. It is this relation which is at the centre of every ideological, i.e. imaginary, representation of the real world. It is this relation that contains the 'cause' which has to explain the imaginary distortion of the ideological representation of the real world. Or rather, to leave aside the language of causality it is necessary to advance the thesis that it is the *imaginary nature of this relation* which underlies all the imaginary distortion that we can observe (if we do not live in its truth) in all ideology.

To speak in a Marxist language, if it is true that the representation of the real conditions of existence of the individuals occupying the posts of agents of production, exploitation, repression, ideologization and scientific practice, does in the last analysis arise from the relations of production, and from relations deriving from the relations of production, we can say the following: all ideology represents in its necessarily imaginary distortion not the existing relations of production (and the other relations that derive from them), but above all the (imaginary) relationship of individuals to the relations of production and the relations that derive from them. What is represented in ideology is therefore not the system of the real relations which govern the existence of individuals, but the imaginary relation of those individuals to the real relations in which they live.

If this is the case, the question of the 'cause' of the imaginary distortion of the real relations in ideology disappears and must be replaced by a different question: why is the representation given to individuals of their (individual) relation to the social relations which govern their conditions of existence and their collective and individual life necessarily an imaginary relation? And what is the nature of this imaginariness? Posed in this way, the question explodes the solution by a 'clique',[1] by a group of individuals (Priests or Despots) who are the authors of the great ideological mystification, just as it explodes the solution by the alienated character of the real world. We shall see why later in my exposition. For the moment I shall go no further.

THESIS II: Ideology has a material existence.

I have already touched on this thesis by saying that the 'ideas' or 'representations', etc., which seem to make up ideology do not have an ideal (*idéale* or *idéelle*) or spiritual existence, but a material existence. I even suggested that the ideal (*idéale, idéelle*) and spiritual existence of 'ideas' arises exclusively in an ideology of the 'idea' and of ideology, and let me add, in an ideology of what seems to have 'founded' this conception since the emergence of the sciences, i.e. what the practicians of the sciences represent to themselves in their spontaneous ideology as 'ideas', true or false. Of course, presented in affirmative form, this thesis is unproven. I simply ask that the reader be favourably disposed towards it, say, in the name of materialism. A long series of arguments would be necessary to prove it.

This hypothetical thesis of the not spiritual but material existence of 'ideas' or other 'representations' is indeed necessary if we are to advance in our analysis of the nature of ideology. Or rather, it is merely useful to us in order the better to reveal what every at all serious analysis of any ideology will immediately and empirically show to every observer, however critical.

While discussing the ideological State apparatuses and their practices, I said that each of them was the realization of an ideology (the unity of these different regional ideologies – religious, ethical, legal, political, aesthetic, etc. – being assured by their subjection to the ruling ideology). I now return to this thesis: an ideology always exists in an apparatus, and its practice, or practices. This existence is material.

Of course, the material existence of the ideology in an apparatus and its practices does not have the same modality as the material existence of a paving-stone or a rifle. But, at the risk of being taken for a Neo-Aristotelian (NB Marx had a very high regard for Aristotle), I shall say that 'matter is discussed in many senses', or rather that it exists in different modalities, all rooted in the last instance in 'physical' matter.

Having said this, let me move straight on and see what happens to the 'individuals' who live in ideology, i.e. in a determinate (religious, ethical, etc.) representation of the world whose imaginary distortion depends on their imaginary relation to their conditions of existence, in other words, in the last instance, to the relations of production and to class relations (ideology = an imaginary relation to real relations). I shall say that this imaginary relation is itself endowed with a material existence.

Now I observe the following.

An individual believes in God, or Duty, or Justice, etc. This belief derives (for everyone, i.e. for all those who live in an ideological representation of ideology, which reduces ideology to ideas endowed by definition with a spiritual

---

[1] I use this very modern term deliberately. For even in Communist circles, unfortunately, it is a commonplace to 'explain' some political deviation (left or right opportunism) by the action of a 'clique'.

existence) from the ideas of the individual concerned, i.e. from him as a subject with a consciousness which contains the ideas of his belief. In this way, i.e. by means of the absolutely ideological 'conceptual' device (*dispositif*) thus set up (a subject endowed with a consciousness in which he freely forms or freely recognizes ideas in which he believes), the (material) attitude of the subject concerned naturally follows.

The individual in question behaves in such and such a way, adopts such and such a practical attitude, and, what is more, participates in certain regular practices which are those of the ideological apparatus on which 'depend' the ideas which he has in all consciousness freely chosen as a subject. If he believes in God, he goes to Church to attend mass, kneels, prays, confesses, does penance (once it was material in the ordinary sense of the term) and naturally repents and so on. If he believes in Duty, he will have the corresponding attitudes, inscribed in ritual practices 'according to the correct principles'. If he believes in Justice, he will submit unconditionally to the rules of the Law, and may even protest when they are violated, sign petitions, take part in a demonstration, etc.

Throughout this schema we observe that the ideological representation of ideology is itself forced to recognize that every 'subject' endowed with a 'consciousness' and believing in the 'ideas' that his 'consciousness' inspires in him and freely accepts, must '*act* according to his ideas', must therefore inscribe his own ideas as a free subject in the actions of his material practice. If he does not do so, 'that is wicked'.

Indeed, if he does not do what he ought to do as a function of what he believes, it is because he does something else, which, still as a function of the same idealist scheme, implies that he has other ideas in his head as well as those he proclaims, and that he acts according to these other ideas, as a man who is either 'inconsistent' ('no one is willingly evil') or cynical, or perverse.

In every case, the ideology of ideology thus recognizes, despite its imaginary distortion, that the 'ideas' of a human subject exist in his actions, or ought to exist in his actions, and if that is not the case, it lends him other ideas corresponding to the actions (however perverse) that he does perform. This ideology talks of actions: I shall talk of actions inserted into *practices*. *And* I shall point out that these practices are governed by the *rituals* in which these practices are inscribed, within the *material existence of an ideological apparatus*, be it only a small part of that apparatus: a small mass in a small church, a funeral, a minor match at a sports club, a school day, a political party meeting, etc.

Besides, we are indebted to Pascal's defensive 'dialectic' for the wonderful formula which will enable us to invert the order of the notional schema of ideology. Pascal says more or less: 'Kneel down, move your lips in prayer, and you will believe.' He thus scandalously inverts the order of things, bringing, like Christ, not peace but strife, and in addition something hardly Christian (for woe to him who brings scandal into the world!) – scandal itself. A fortunate scandal which makes him stick with Jansenist defiance to a language that directly names the reality.

I will be allowed to leave Pascal to the arguments of his ideological struggle with the religious ideological State apparatus of his day. And I shall be expected to use a more directly Marxist vocabulary, if that is possible, for we are advancing in still poorly explored domains.

I shall therefore say that, where only a single subject (such and such an individual) is concerned, the existence of the ideas of his belief is material in that *his ideas are his material actions inserted into material practices governed by material rituals which are themselves defined by the material ideological apparatus from which derive the ideas of that subject.* Naturally, the four inscriptions of the adjective 'material' in my proposition must be affected by different modalities: the materialities of a displacement for going to mass, of kneeling down, of the gesture of the sign of the cross, or of the *mea culpa*, of a sentence, of a prayer, of an act of contrition, of a penitence, of a gaze, of a hand-shake, of an external verbal discourse or an 'internal' verbal discourse (consciousness), are not one and the same materiality. I shall leave on one side the problem of a theory of the differences between the modalities of materiality.

It remains that in this inverted presentation of things, we are not dealing with an 'inversion' at all, since it is clear that certain notions have purely and simply disappeared from our presentation, whereas others on the contrary survive, and new terms appear.

Disappeared: the term *ideas.*

Survive: the terms *subject, consciousness, belief, actions.*

Appear: the terms *practices, rituals, ideological apparatus.*

It is therefore not an inversion or overturning (except in the sense in which one might say a government or a glass is overturned), but a reshuffle (of a non-ministerial type), a rather strange reshuffle, since we obtain the following result.

Ideas have disappeared as such (insofar as they are endowed with an ideal or spiritual existence), to the precise extent that it has emerged that their existence is inscribed in the actions of practices governed by rituals defined in the last instance by an ideological apparatus. It therefore appears that the subject acts insofar as he is acted by the following system (set out in the order of its real determination): ideology existing in a material ideological apparatus, prescribing material practices governed by a material ritual, which practices exist in the material actions of a subject acting in all consciousness according to his belief.

But this very presentation reveals that we have retained the following notions: subject, consciousness, belief, actions. From this series I shall immediately extract the decisive central term on which everything else depends: the notion of the *subject.*

And I shall immediately set down two conjoint theses:

1 there is no practice except by and in an ideology;
2 there is no ideology except by the subject and for subjects.

From *Base and Superstructure in Marxist Cultural Theory*

Problems in Materialism and Culture, Verso: London, 1980, pp. 37–45.

The Complexity of Hegemony

It is Gramsci's great contribution to have emphasized hegemony, and also to have understood it at a depth which is, I think, rare. For hegemony supposes the existence of something which is truly total, which is not merely secondary or superstructural, like the weak sense of ideology, but which is lived at such a depth, which saturates the society to such an extent, and which, as Gramsci put it, even constitutes the substance and limit of common sense for most people under its sway, that it corresponds to the reality of social experience very much more clearly than any notions derived from the formula of base and superstructure. For if ideology were merely some abstract, imposed set of notions, if our social and political and cultural ideas and assumptions and habits were merely the result of specific manipulation, of a kind of overt training which might be simply ended or withdrawn, then the society would be very much easier to move and to change than in practice it has ever been or is. This notion of hegemony as deeply saturating the consciousness of a society seems to me to be fundamental. And hegemony has the advantage over general notions of totality, that it at the same time emphasizes the facts of domination.

Yet there are times when I hear discussions of hegemony and feel that it too, as a concept, is being dragged back to the relatively simple, uniform and static notion which 'superstructure' in ordinary use had become. Indeed I think that we have to give a very complex account of hegemony if we are talking about any real social formation. Above all we have to give an account which allows for its elements of real and constant change. We have to emphasize that hegemony is not singular; indeed that its own internal structures are highly complex, and have continually to be renewed, recreated and defended; and by the same token, that they can be continually challenged and in certain respects modified. That is why instead of speaking simply of 'the hegemony', 'a hegemony', I would propose a model which allows for this kind of variation and contradiction, its sets of alternatives and its processes of change.

For one thing that is evident in some of the best Marxist cultural analysis is that it is very much more at home in what one might call *epochal* questions than in what one has to call *historical* questions. That is to say, it is usually very much better at distinguishing the large features of different epochs of society, as commonly between feudal and bourgeois, than at distinguishing between different phases of bourgeois society, and different moments within these phases: that true historical process which demands a much greater precision and delicacy of analysis than the always striking epochal analysis which is concerned with main lineaments and features.

The theoretical model which I have been trying to work with is this. I would say first that in any society, in any particular period, there is a central system of practices, meanings and values, which we can properly call dominant and effective. This implies no presumption about its value. All I am saying is that it is central. Indeed I would call it a corporate system, but this might be confusing, since Gramsci uses 'corporate' to mean the subordinate as opposed to the general and dominant elements of hegemony. In any case what I have in mind is the central, effective and dominant system of meanings and values, which are not merely abstract but which are organized and lived. That is why hegemony is not to be understood at the level of mere opinion or mere manipulation. It is a whole body of practices and expectations; our assignments of energy, our ordinary understanding of the nature of man and of his world. It is a set of meanings and values which as they are experienced as practices appear as reciprocally confirming. It thus constitutes a sense of reality for most people in the society, a sense of absolute because experienced reality beyond which it is very difficult for most members of the society to move, in most areas of their lives. But this is not, except in the operation of a moment of abstract analysis, in any sense a static system. On the contrary we can only understand an effective and dominant culture if we understand the real social process on which it depends: I mean the process of incorporation. The modes of incorporation are of great social significance. The educational institutions are usually the main agencies of the transmission of an effective dominant culture, and this is now a major economic as well as a cultural activity; indeed it is both in the same moment. Moreover, at a philosophical level, at the true level of theory and at the level of the history of various practices, there is a process which I call the *selective tradition*: that which, within the terms of an effective dominant culture, is always passed off as *'the* tradition', *'the* significant past'. But always the selectivity is the point; the way in which from a whole possible area of past and present, certain meanings and practices are chosen for emphasis, certain other meanings and practices are neglected and excluded. Even more crucially, some of these meanings and practices are reinterpreted, diluted, or put into forms which support or at least do not contradict other elements within the effective dominant culture. The processes of education; the processes of a much wider social training within institutions like the family; the practical definitions and organization of work; the selective tradition at an intellectual and theoretical level: all these forces are involved in a continual making and remaking of an effective dominant culture, and on them, as experienced, as built into our living, its reality depends. If what we learn there were merely an imposed ideology, or if it were only the isolable meanings and practices of the ruling class, or of a section of the ruling class, which gets imposed on others, occupying merely the top of our minds, it would be – and one would be glad – a very much easier thing to overthrow.

It is not only the depths to which this process reaches, selecting and organizing and interpreting our experience. It is also that it is continually active and adjusting; it isn't just the past, the dry husks of ideology which we can more easily discard. And this can only be so, in a complex society, if it is something more substantial and more flexible than any abstract imposed ideology. Thus we have to recognize the alternative meanings and values, the alternative opinions and attitudes, even some alternative senses of the world, which can be accommodated and tolerated within a particular effective and dominant culture. This has been much under-emphasized in our notions of a superstructure, and even in some notions of hegemony. And the under-emphasis opens the way for retreat to an indifferent complexity. In the practice of politics, for example, there are certain truly incorporated modes of what are nevertheless, within those terms, real oppositions, that are felt and fought out. Their existence within the incorporation is recognizable by the fact that, whatever the degree of internal conflict or internal variation, they do not in practice go beyond the limits of the central effective and dominant definitions. This is true, for example, of the practice of parliamentary politics, though its internal oppositions are real. It is true about a whole range of practices and arguments, in any real society, which can by no means be reduced to an ideological cover, but which can nevertheless be properly analysed as in my sense corporate, if we find that, whatever the degree of internal controversy and variation, they do not in the end exceed the limits of the central corporate definitions.

But if we are to say this, we have to think again about the sources of that which is not corporate; of those practices, experiences, meanings, values which are not part of the effective dominant culture. We can express this in two ways. There is clearly something that we can call alternative to the effective dominant culture, and there is something else that we can call oppositional, in a true sense. The degree of existence of these alternative and oppositional forms is itself a matter of constant historical variation in real circumstances. In certain societies it is possible to find areas of social life in which quite real alternatives are at least left alone. (If they are made available, of course, they are part of the corporate organization.) The existence of the possibility of opposition, and of its articulation, its degree of openness, and so on, again depends on very precise social and political forces. The facts of alternative and oppositional forms of social life and culture, in relation to the effective and dominant culture, have then to be recognized as subject to historical variation, and as having sources which are very significant as a fact about the dominant culture itself.

Residual and Emergent Cultures

I have next to introduce a further distinction, between *residual* and *emergent* forms, both of alternative and of oppositional culture. By 'residual' I mean that some experiences, meanings and values, which cannot be verified or cannot be expressed in terms of the dominant culture, are nevertheless lived and practised on the basis of the residue – cultural as well as social – of some previous social formation. There is a real case of this in certain religious values, by contrast with the very evident incorporation of most religious meanings and values into the dominant system. The same is true, in a culture like Britain, of certain notions derived from a rural past, which have a very significant popularity. A residual culture is usually at some distance from the effective dominant culture, but one has to recognize that, in real cultural activities, it may get incorporated into it. This is because some part of it, some version of it – and especially if the residue is from some major area of the past – will in many cases have had to be incorporated if the effective dominant culture is to make sense in those areas. It is also because at certain points a dominant culture cannot allow too much of this kind of practice and experience outside itself, at least without risk. Thus the pressures are real, but certain genuinely residual meanings and practices in some important cases survive.

By 'emergent' I mean, first, that new meanings and values, new practices, new significances and experiences, are continually being created. But there is then a much earlier attempt to incorporate them, just because they are part – and yet not a defined part – of effective contemporary practice. Indeed it is significant in our own period how very early this attempt is, how alert the dominant culture now is to anything that can be seen as emergent. We have then to see, first, as it were a temporal relation between a dominant culture and on the one hand a residual and on the other hand an emergent culture. But we can only understand this if we can make distinctions, that usually require very precise analysis, between residual-incorporated and residual not incorporated, and between emergent-incorporated and emergent not incorporated. It is an important fact about any particular society, how far it reaches into the whole range of human practices and experiences in an attempt at incorporation. It may be true of some earlier phases of bourgeois society, for example, that there were some areas of experience which it was willing to dispense with, which it was prepared to assign as the sphere of private or artistic life, and as being no particular business of society or the state. This went along with certain kinds of political tolerance, even if the reality of that tolerance was malign neglect. But I am sure it is true of the society that has come into existence since the last war, that progressively, because of developments in the social character of labour, in the social character of communications, and in the social character of decision, it extends much further than ever before in capitalist society into certain hitherto resigned areas of experience and practice and meaning. Thus the effective decision, as to whether a practice is alternative or oppositional, is often now made within a very much narrower scope. There is a simple theoretical distinction between alternative and oppositional, that is to say between someone who simply finds a different way to live and wishes to be left alone with it, and someone who finds a different way to live and wants to change the society in its light. This is usually the difference between individual and small-group solutions to social crisis and those solutions which properly belong to political and ultimately revolutionary practice. But it is often a very narrow line, in reality, between alternative and oppositional. A meaning or a practice may be tolerated as a deviation, and yet still be seen only as another particular way to live. But as the necessary area of effective dominance extends, the same meanings and practices can be seen by the dominant culture, not merely as disregarding or despising it, but as challenging it.

Now it is crucial to any Marxist theory of culture that it can give an adequate explanation of the sources of these practices and meanings. We can understand, from an ordinary historical approach, at least some of the sources of residual meanings and practices. These are the results of earlier social formations, in which certain real meanings and values were generated. In the subsequent default of a particular phase of a dominant culture, there is then a reaching back to those meanings and values which were created in real societies in the past, and which still seem to have some significance because they represent areas of human experience, aspiration and achievement, which the dominant culture undervalues or opposes, or even cannot recognize. But our hardest task, theoretically, is to find a non-metaphysical and non-subjectivist explanation of emergent cultural practice. Moreover, part of our answer to this question bears on the process of persistence of residual practices.

Class and Human Practice

We have indeed one source to hand from the central body of Marxist theory. We have the formation of a new class, the coming to consciousness of a new class. This remains, without doubt, quite centrally important. Of course, in itself, this process of formation complicates any simple model of base and superstructure. It also complicates some of the ordinary versions of hegemony, although it was Gramsci's whole purpose to see and to create by organization that hegemony of a proletarian kind which would be capable of challenging the bourgeois hegemony. We have then one central source of new practice, in the emergence of a new class. But we have also to recognize certain other kinds of source, and in cultural practice some of these are very important. I would say that we can recognize them on the basis of this proposition: that no mode of production, and therefore no dominant society or order of society, and therefore no dominant culture, in reality exhausts the full range of human practice, human energy, human intention (this range is not the inventory of some original 'human nature' but, on the contrary, is that extraordinary range of variations, both practised and imagined, of which human beings are and have shown themselves to be capable). Indeed it seems to me that this emphasis is not merely a negative proposition, allowing us to account for certain things which happen outside the dominant mode. On the contrary, it is a fact about the modes of domination that they select from and consequently exclude the full range of actual and possible human practice. The difficulties of human practice outside or against the dominant mode are, of course, real. It depends very much whether it is in an area in which the dominant class and the dominant culture have an interest and a stake. If the interest and the stake are explicit, many new practices will be reached for, and if possible incorporated, or else extirpated with extraordinary vigour. But in certain areas, there will be in certain periods practices and meanings which are not reached for. There will be areas of practice and meaning which, almost by definition from its own limited character, or in its profound deformation, the dominant culture is unable in any real terms to recognize. This gives us a bearing on the observable difference between, for example, the practices of a capitalist state and a state like the contemporary Soviet Union in relation to writers. Since from the whole Marxist tradition literature was seen as an important activity, indeed a crucial activity, the Soviet state is very much sharper in investigating areas where different versions of practice, different meanings and values, are being attempted and expressed. In capitalist practice, if the thing is not making a profit, or if it is not being widely circulated, then it can for some time be overlooked, at least while it remains alternative. When it becomes oppositional in an explicit way, it does, of course, get approached or attacked.

I am saying then that in relation to the full range of human practice at any one time, the dominant mode is a conscious selection and organization. At least in its fully formed state it is conscious. But there are always sources of actual human practice which it neglects or excludes. And these can be different in quality from the developing and articulate interests of a rising class. They can include, for example, alternative perceptions of others, in immediate personal relationships, or new perceptions of material and media, in art and science, and within certain limits these new perceptions can be practised. The relations between the two kinds of source – the emerging class and either the dominatively excluded or the more generally new practices – are by no means necessarily contradictory. At times they can be very close, and on the relations between them much in political practice depends. But culturally and as a matter of theory the areas can be seen as distinct.

Now if we go back to the cultural question in its most usual form – what are the relations between art and society, or literature and society? – in the light of the preceding discussion, we have to say first that there are no relations between literature and society in that abstracted way. The literature is there from the beginning as a practice in the society. Indeed until it and all other practices are present, the society cannot be seen as fully formed. A society is not fully available for analysis until each of its practices is included. But if we make that emphasis we must make a corresponding emphasis: that we cannot separate literature and art from other kinds of social practice, in such a way as to make them subject to quite special and distinct laws. They may have quite specific features as practices, but they cannot be separated from the general social process. Indeed one way of emphasizing this is to say, to insist, that literature is not restricted to operating in any one of the sectors I have been seeking to describe in this model. It would be easy to say, it is a familiar rhetoric, that literature operates in the emergent cultural sector, that it represents the new feelings, the new meanings, the new values. We might persuade ourselves of this theoretically, by abstract argument, but when we read much literature, over the whole range, without the sleight-of-hand of calling Literature only that which we have already selected as embodying certain meanings and values at a certain scale of intensity, we are bound to recognize that the act of writing, the practices of discourse in writing and speech, the making of novels and poems and plays and theories, all this activity takes place in all areas of the culture.

Literature appears by no means only in the emergent sector, which is always, in fact, quite rare. A great deal of writing is of a residual kind, and this has been deeply true of much English literature in the last half century. Some of its fundamental meanings and values have belonged to the cultural achievements of long-past stages of society. So widespread is this fact, and the habits of mind it supports, that in many minds 'literature' and 'the past' acquire a certain identity, and it is then said that there is now no literature: all that glory is over. Yet most writing, in any period, including our own, is a form of contribution to the effective dominant culture. Indeed many of the specific qualities of literature – its capacity to embody and enact and perform certain meanings and values, or to create in single particular ways what would be otherwise merely general truths – enable it to fulfil this effective function with great power. To literature, of course, we must add the visual arts and music, and in our own society the powerful arts of film and of broadcasting. But the general theoretical point should be clear. If we are looking for the relations between literature and society, we cannot either separate out this one practice from a formed body of other practices, nor when we have identified a particular practice can we give it a uniform, static and ahistorical relation to some abstract social formation. The arts of writing and the arts of creation and performance, over their whole range, are parts of the cultural process in all the different ways, the different sectors, that I have been seeking to describe. They contribute to the effective dominant culture and are a central articulation of it. They embody residual meanings and values, not all of which are incorporated, though many are. They express also and significantly some emergent practices and meanings, yet some of these may eventually be incorporated, as they reach people and begin to move them. Thus it was very evident in the sixties, in some of the emergent arts of performance, that the dominant culture reached out to transform, or seek to transform, them. In this process, of course, the dominant culture itself changes, not in its central formation, but in many of its articulated features. But then in a modern society it must always change in this way, if it is to remain dominant, if it is still to be felt as in real ways central in all our many activities and interests.

---

5   Jacques Derrida

From *Différance*

Margins of Philosophy, trans. Alan Bass, University of Chicago Press: Chicago, 1982, pp. 9–13.

Let us start, since we are already there, from the problematic of the sign and of writing. The sign is usually said to be put in the place of the thing itself, the present thing, 'thing' here standing equally for meaning or referent. The sign represents the present in its absence. It takes the place of the present. When we cannot grasp or show the thing, state the present, the being-present, when the present cannot be presented, we signify, we go through the detour of the sign. We take or give signs. We signal. The sign, in this sense, is deferred presence. Whether we are concerned with the verbal or the written sign, with the monetary sign, or with electoral delegation and political representation, the circulation of signs defers the moment in which we can encounter the thing itself, make it ours, consume or expend it, touch it, see it, intuit its presence. What I am describing here in order to define it is the classically determined structure of the sign in all the banality of its characteristics – signification as the *différance* of temporization. And this structure presupposes that the sign, which defers presence, is conceivable only on the *basis* of the presence that it defers and *moving toward* the deferred presence that it aims to reappropriate. According to this classical semiology, the substitution of the sign for the thing itself is both *secondary* and *provisional*: secondary due to an original and lost presence from which the sign thus derives; provisional as concerns this final and missing presence toward which the sign in this sense is a movement of mediation.

In attempting to put into question these traits of the provisional secondariness of the substitute, one would come to see something like an originary *différance*; but one could no longer call it originary or final in the extent to which the values of origin, archi-, *telos*, *eskhaton*, etc. have always denoted presence – *ousia*, *parousia*.[1] To put into question the secondary and provisional characteristics of the sign, to oppose to them an 'originary' *différance*, therefore would have two consequences.

1   One could no longer include *différance* in the concept of the sign, which always has meant the representation of a presence, and has been constituted in a system (thought or language) governed by and moving toward presence.
2   And thereby one puts into question the authority of presence, or of its simple symmetrical opposite, absence or lack. Thus one questions the limit which has always constrained us, which still constrains us – as inhabitants of a language and a system of thought – to formulate the meaning of Being in general as presence or absence, in the categories of being or beingness (*ousia*). Already it appears that the type of question to which we are redirected is, let us say, of the Heideggerian type, and that *différance seems* to lead back to the ontico-ontological difference. I will be permitted to hold off on this reference. I will note only that between difference as temporization–temporalization, which can no longer be conceived within the horizon of the present, and what Heidegger says in *Being and Time* about temporalization as the transcendental horizon of the question of Being, which must be liberated from its traditional, metaphysical domination by the present and the now, there is a strict communication, even though not an exhaustive and irreducibly necessary one.

But first let us remain within the semiological problematic in order to see *différance* as temporization and *différance* as spacing conjoined. Most of the semiological or linguistic researches that dominate the field of thought today, whether due to their own results or to the regulatory model that they find themselves acknowledging everywhere, refer genealogically to Saussure (correctly or incorrectly) as their common inaugurator. Now Saussure first of all is the thinker who put the *arbitrary character of the sign* and the *differential character* of the sign at the very foundation of general semiology, particularly linguistics. And, as we know, these two motifs – arbitrary and differential – are inseparable in his view. There can be arbitrariness only because the system of signs is constituted solely by the differences in terms, and not by their plenitude. The elements of signification function due not to the compact force of their nuclei but rather to the network of oppositions that distinguishes them, and then relates them one to another. 'Arbitrary and differential', says Saussure, 'are two correlative characteristics.'
Now this principle of difference, as the condition for signification, affects the *totality* of the sign, that is the sign as both signified and signifier. The signified is the concept, the ideal meaning; and the signifier is what Saussure calls

[1]   *Ousia* and *parousia* imply presence as both origin and end, the founding principle (*arkhe-*) as that toward which one moves (*telos*, *eskhaton*). [Translator's note.]

the 'image', the 'psychical imprint' of a material, physical – for example, acoustical – phenomenon. We do not have to go into all the problems posed by these definitions here. Let us cite Saussure only at the point which interests us: 'The conceptual side of value is made up solely of relations and differences with respect to the other terms of language, and the same can be said of its material side. . . . Everything that has been said up to this point boils down to this: in language there are only differences. Even more important: a difference generally implies positive terms between which the difference is set up; but in language there are only differences *without positive terms*. Whether we take the signified or the signifier, language has neither ideas nor sounds that existed before the linguistic system, but only conceptual and phonic differences that have issued from the system. The idea or phonic substance that a sign contains is of less importance than the other signs that surround it.'[2]

The first consequence to be drawn from this is that the signified concept is never present in and of itself, in a sufficient presence that would refer only to itself. Essentially and lawfully, every concept is inscribed in a chain or in a system within which it refers to the other, to other concepts, by means of the systematic play of differences. Such a play, *différance*, is thus no longer simply a concept, but rather the possibility of conceptuality, of a conceptual process and system in general. For the same reason, *différance*, which is not a concept, is not simply a word, that is, what is generally represented as the calm, present, and self-referential unity of concept and phonic material. Later we will look into the word in general.

The difference of which Saussure speaks is itself, therefore, neither a concept nor a word among others. The same can be said, *a fortiori*, of *différance*. And we are thereby led to explicate the relation of one to the other.

In a language, in the *system* of language, there are only differences. Therefore a taxonomical operation can undertake the systematic, statistical, and classificatory inventory of a language. But, on the one hand, these differences *play*: in language, in speech too, and in the exchange between language and speech. On the other hand, these differences are themselves *effects*. They have not fallen from the sky fully formed, and are no more inscribed in a *topos noetos*, than they are prescribed in the grey matter of the brain. If the word 'history' did not in and of itself convey the motif of a final repression of difference, one could say that only differences can be 'historical' from the outset and in each of their aspects.

What is written as *différance*, then, will be the playing movement that 'produces' – by means of something that is not simply an activity – these differences, these effects of difference. This does not mean that the *différance* that produces differences is somehow before them, in a simple and unmodified – in-different – present. *Différance* is the non-full, non-simple, structured and differentiating origin of differences. Thus, the name 'origin' no longer suits it.

Since language, which Saussure says is a classification, has not fallen from the sky, its differences have been produced, are produced effects, but they are

² Ferdinand de Saussure, *Course in General Linguistics*, trans. Wade Baskin (New York: Philosophical Library, 1959), pp. 117-18, 120. [Translator's note.]

effects which do not find their cause in a subject or a substance, in a thing in general, a being that is somewhere present, thereby eluding the play of *différance*. If such a presence were implied in the concept of cause in general, in the most classical fashion, we then would have to speak of an effect without a cause, which very quickly would lead to speaking of no effect at all. I have attempted to indicate a way out of the closure of this framework via the 'trace', which is no more an effect than it has a cause, but which in and of itself, outside its text, is not sufficient to operate the necessary transgression.

Since there is no presence before and outside semiological difference, what Saussure has written about language can be extended to the sign in general: 'Language is necessary in order for speech to be intelligible and to produce all of its effects; but the latter is necessary in order for language to be established; historically, the fact of speech always comes first.'[3]

Retaining at least the framework, if not the content, of this requirement formulated by Saussure, we will designate as *différance* the movement according to which language, or any code, any system of referral in general, is constituted 'historically' as a weave of differences. 'Is constituted', 'is produced', 'is created', 'movement', 'historically', etc., necessarily being understood beyond the metaphysical language in which they are retained, along with all their implications. We ought to demonstrate why concepts like *production*, constitution, and history remain in complicity with what is at issue here. But this would take me too far today – toward the theory of the representation of the 'circle' in which we appear to be enclosed – and I utilize such concepts, like many others, only for their strategic convenience and in order to undertake their deconstruction at the currently most decisive point. In any event, it will be understood, by means of the circle in which we appear to be engaged, that as it is written here, *différance* is no more static than it is genetic, no more structural than historical. Or is no less so; and to object to this on the basis of the oldest of metaphysical oppositions (for example, by setting some generative point of view against a structural-taxonomical point of view, or vice versa) would be, above all, not to read what here is missing from orthographical ethics. Such oppositions have not the least pertinence to *différance*, which makes the thinking of it uneasy and uncomfortable.

Now if we consider the chain in which *différance* lends itself to a certain number of non-synonymous substitutions, according to the necessity of the context, why have recourse to the 'reserve', to 'archi-writing', to the 'archi-trace', to 'spacing', that is, to the 'supplement', or to the *pharmakon,* and soon to the hymen, to the margin-mark-march, etc.[4]

---

[3] Saussure, *Course in General Linguistics*, p. 18. [Translator's note.]

[4] All these terms refer to writing and inscribe *différance* within themselves, as Derrida says, according to the context. The supplement (*supplément*) is Rousseau's word to describe writing (analyzed in *Of Grammatology*, trans. Gayatri Spivak [Baltimore, Md: Johns Hopkins University Press, 1976]). It means *both* the missing piece and the extra piece. The *pharmakon* is Plato's word for writing (analyzed in 'Plato's Pharmacy' in *Dissemination*, trans. Barbara Johnson [Chicago: University of Chicago Press, 1981]), meaning *both* remedy and poison; the hymen (*l'hymen*) comes from Derrida's analysis of Mallarmé's writing and Mallarmé's reflections on writing ('The Double Session' in *Dissemination*) and refers *both* to virginity and to consummation; *marge-marque-marche* is the series *en différance* that Derrida applies to Sollers's *Nombres* ('Dissemination' in *Dissemination*). [Translator's note.]

Let us go on. It is because of *différance* that the movement of signification is possible only if each so-called 'present' element, each element
appearing on the scene of presence, is related to something other than itself,
thereby keeping within itself the mark of the past element, and already letting itself be vitiated by the mark of its relation to the future element, this
trace being related no less to what is called the future than to what is called
the past, and constituting what is called the present by means of this very
relation to what it is not: what it absolutely is not, not even a past or a
future as a modified present. An interval must separate the present from
what it is not in order for the present to be itself, but this interval that constitutes it as present must, by the same token, divide the present in and of
itself, thereby also dividing, along with the present, everything that is
thought on the basis of the present, that is, in our metaphysical language,
every being, and singularly substance or the subject. In constituting itself,
in dividing itself dynamically, this interval is what might be called *spacing*,
the becoming-space of time or the becoming-time of space (*temporization*).
And it is this constitution of the present, as an 'originary' and irreducibly
non-simple (and therefore, *stricto sensu* non-originary) synthesis of marks,
or traces of retentions and protentions (to reproduce analogically and provisionally a phenomenological and transcendental language that soon will
reveal itself to be inadequate), that I propose to call archi-writing, archi-
trace, or *différance*. Which (is) (simultaneously) spacing (and) temporization.

6   Walter Benjamin

Theses on the Philosophy of History

Illuminations, ed. Hannah Arendt, trans. Harry Zohn, Fontana: London,
1973, pp. 255–66.

I

The story is told of an automaton constructed in such a way that it could play
a winning game of chess, answering each move of an opponent with a coun-
termove. A puppet in Turkish attire and with a hookah in its mouth sat before
a chessboard placed on a large table. A system of mirrors created the illusion
that this table was transparent from all sides. Actually, a little hunchback who
was an expert chess player sat inside and guided the puppet's hand by means
of strings. One can imagine a philosophical counterpart to this device. The
puppet called 'historical materialism' is to win all the time. It can easily be a
match for anyone if it enlists the services of theology, which today, as we
know, is wizened and has to keep out of sight.

II

'One of the most remarkable characteristics of human nature', writes Lotze, 'is, alongside so much selfishness in specific instances, the freedom from envy which the present displays toward the future.' Reflection shows us that our image of happiness is thoroughly coloured by the time to which the course of our own existence has assigned us. The kind of happiness that could arouse envy in us exists only in the air we have breathed, among people we could have talked to, women who could have given themselves to us. In other words, our image of happiness is indissolubly bound up with the image of redemption. The same applies to our view of the past, which is the concern of history. The past carries with it a temporal index by which it is referred to redemption. There is a secret agreement between past generations and the present one. Our coming was expected on earth. Like every generation that preceded us, we have been endowed with a *weak* Messianic power, a power to which the past has a claim. That claim cannot be settled cheaply. Historical materialists are aware of that.

III

A chronicler who recites events without distinguishing between major and minor ones acts in accordance with the following truth: nothing that has ever happened should be regarded as lost for history. To be sure, only a redeemed mankind receives the fullness of its past – which is to say, only for a redeemed mankind has its past become citable in all its moments. Each moment it has lived becomes a *citation à l'ordre du jour* – and that day is Judgment Day.

IV

Seek for food and clothing first, then
the Kingdom of God shall be added unto you.

Hegel, 1807

The class struggle, which is always present to a historian influenced by Marx, is a fight for the crude and material things without which no refined and spiritual things could exist. Nevertheless, it is not in the form of the spoils which fall to the victor that the latter make their presence felt in the class struggle. They manifest themselves in this struggle as courage, humour, cunning, and fortitude. They have retroactive force and will constantly call in question every victory, past and present, of the rulers. As flowers turn toward the sun, by dint of a secret heliotropism the past strives to turn toward that sun which is rising in the sky of history. A historical materialist must be aware of this most inconspicuous of all transformations.

V

The true picture of the past flits by. The past can be seized only as an image which flashes up at the instant when it can be recognized and is never seen again. 'The truth will not run away from us': in the historical outlook of historicism these words of Gottfried Keller mark the exact point where historical materialism cuts through historicism. For every image of the past that is not recognized by the present as one of its own concerns threatens to disappear irretrievably. (The good tidings which the historian of the past brings with throbbing heart may be lost in a void the very moment he opens his mouth.)

VI

To articulate the past historically does not mean to recognize it 'the way it really was' (Ranke). It means to seize hold of a memory as it flashes up at a moment of danger. Historical materialism wishes to retain that image of the past which unexpectedly appears to man singled out by history at a moment of danger. The danger affects both the content of the tradition and its receivers. The same threat hangs over both: that of becoming a tool of the ruling classes. In every era the attempt must be made anew to wrest tradition away from a conformism that is about to overpower it. The Messiah comes not only as the redeemer, he comes as the subduer of Antichrist. Only that historian will have the gift of fanning the spark of hope in the past who is firmly convinced that *even the dead* will not be safe from the enemy if he wins. And this enemy has not ceased to be victorious.

VII

Consider the darkness and the great cold
In this vale which resounds with misery.

Brecht, *The Threepenny Opera*

To historians who wish to relive an era, Fustel de Coulanges recommends that they blot out everything they know about the later course of history. There is no better way of characterizing the method with which historical materialism has broken. It is a process of empathy whose origin is the indolence of the heart, *acedia*, which despairs of grasping and holding the genuine historical image as it flares up briefly. Among medieval theologians it was regarded as the root cause of sadness. Flaubert, who was familiar with it, wrote: '*Peu de gens devineront combien il a fallu être triste pour ressusciter Carthage.*'[1] The nature of this sadness stands out more clearly if one asks with whom the adherents of historicism actually empathize. The answer is inevitable: with the victor. And all rulers are the heirs of those who conquered before them. Hence, empathy with the victor invariably benefits the rulers. Historical materialists know what that means. Whoever has emerged victorious participates to this day in the triumphal procession in which the present rulers step over those who are lying prostrate. According to traditional practice, the spoils are carried along in the procession. They are called cultural treasures, and a historical

---

[1] 'Few will be able to guess how sad one had to be in order to resuscitate Carthage.' [Translator's note.]

materialist views them with cautious detachment. For without exception the cultural treasures he surveys have an origin which he cannot contemplate without horror. They owe their existence not only to the efforts of the great minds and talents who have created them, but also to the anonymous toil of their contemporaries. There is no document of civilization which is not at the same time a document of barbarism. And just as such a document is not free of barbarism, barbarism taints also the manner in which it was transmitted from one owner to another. A historical materialist therefore dissociates himself from it as far as possible. He regards it as his task to brush history against the grain.

VIII

The tradition of the oppressed teaches us that the 'state of emergency' in which we live is not the exception but the rule. We must attain to a conception of history that is in keeping with this insight. Then we shall clearly realize that it is our task to bring about a real state of emergency, and this will improve our position in the struggle against Fascism. One reason why Fascism has a chance is that in the name of progress its opponents treat it as a historical norm. The current amazement that the things we are experiencing are 'still' possible in the twentieth century is *not* philosophical. This amazement is not the beginning of knowledge – unless it is the knowledge that the view of history which gives rise to it is untenable.

IX

Mein Flügel ist zum Schwung bereit,
ich kehrte gern zurück,
denn blieb ich auch lebendige Zeit,
ich hätte wenig Glück.

Gerhard Scholem, 'Gruss vom Angelus'[2]

A Klee painting named 'Angelus Novus' shows an angel looking as though he is about to move away from something he is fixedly contemplating. His eyes are staring, his mouth is open, his wings are spread. This is how one pictures the angel of history. His face is turned toward the past. Where we perceive a chain of events, he sees one single catastrophe which keeps piling wreckage upon wreckage and hurls it in front of his feet. The angel would like to stay, awaken the dead, and make whole what has been smashed. But a storm is blowing from Paradise; it has got caught in his wings with such violence that the angel can no longer close them. This storm irresistibly propels him into the future to which his back is turned, while the pile of debris before him grows skyward. This storm is what we call progress.

---

[2] *My wing is ready for flight, / I would like to turn back. / If I stayed timeless time, / I would have little luck.* [Translator's note.]

X

The themes which monastic discipline assigned to friars for meditation were designed to turn them away from the world and its affairs. The thoughts which we are developing here originate from similar considerations. At a moment when the politicians in whom the opponents of Fascism had placed their hopes are prostrate and confirm their defeat by betraying their own cause, these observations are intended to disentangle the political worldlings from the snares in which the traitors have entrapped them. Our consideration proceeds from the insight that the politicians' stubborn faith in progress, their confidence in their 'mass basis', and, finally, their servile integration in an uncontrollable apparatus have been three aspects of the same thing. It seeks to convey an idea of the high price our accustomed thinking will have to pay for a conception of history that avoids any complicity with the thinking to which these politicians continue to adhere.

XI

The conformism which has been part and parcel of Social Democracy from the beginning attaches not only to its political tactics but to its economic views as well. It is one reason for its later breakdown. Nothing has corrupted the German working class so much as the notion that it was moving with the current. It regarded technological developments as the fall of the stream with which it thought it was moving. From there it was but a step to the illusion that the factory work which was supposed to tend toward technological progress constituted a political achievement. The old Protestant ethics of work was resurrected among German workers in secularized form. The Gotha Programme[3] already bears traces of this confusion, defining labour as 'the source of all wealth and all culture'. Smelling a rat, Marx countered that ' . . . the man who possesses no other property than his labour power' must of necessity become 'the slave of other men who have made themselves the owners. . . '. However, the confusion spread, and soon thereafter Josef Dietzgen proclaimed: 'The saviour of modern times is called work. The . . . improvement . . . of labour constitutes the wealth which is now able to accomplish what no redeemer has ever been able to do.' This vulgar-Marxist conception of the nature of labour bypasses the question of how its products might benefit the workers while still not being at their disposal. It recognizes only the progress in the mastery of nature, not the retrogression of society; it already displays the technocratic features later encountered in Fascism. Among these is a conception of nature which differs ominously from the one in the Socialist utopias before the 1848 revolution. The new conception of labour amounts to the exploitation of nature, which with naive complacency is contrasted with the exploitation of

---

[3] The Gotha Congress of 1875 united the two German Socialist parties, one led by Ferdinand Lassalle, the other by Karl Marx and Wilhelm Liebknecht. The programme, drafted by Liebknecht and Lassalle, was severely attacked by Marx in London. See his 'Critique of the Gotha Programme'. [Translator's note.]

the proletariat. Compared with this positivistic conception, Fourier's fantasies, which have so often been ridiculed, prove to be surprisingly sound. According to Fourier, as a result of efficient co-operative labour, four moons would illuminate the earthly night, the ice would recede from the poles, sea water would no longer taste salty, and beasts of prey would do man's bidding. All this illustrates a kind of labour which, far from exploiting nature, is capable of delivering her of the creations which lie dormant in her womb as potentials. Nature, which, as Dietzgen puts it, 'exists gratis', is a complement to the corrupted conception of labour.

XII

We need history, but not the way a spoiled loafer
in the garden of knowledge needs it.
Nietzsche, *Of the Use and Abuse of History*

Not man or men but the struggling, oppressed class itself is the depository of historical knowledge. In Marx it appears as the last enslaved class, as the avenger that completes the task of liberation in the name of generations of the downtrodden. This conviction, which had a brief resurgence in the Spartacist group,[4] has always been objectionable to Social Democrats. Within three decades they managed virtually to erase the name of Blanqui, though it had been the rallying sound that had reverberated through the preceding century. Social Democracy thought fit to assign to the working class the role of the redeemer of future generations, in this way cutting the sinews of its greatest strength. This training made the working class forget both its hatred and its spirit of sacrifice, for both are nourished by the image of enslaved ancestors rather than that of liberated grandchildren.

XIII

Every day our cause becomes clearer and people get smarter.
Wilhelm Dietzgen, *Die Religion der Sozialdemokratie*

Social Democratic theory, and even more its practice, have been formed by a conception of progress which did not adhere to reality but made dogmatic claims. Progress as pictured in the minds of Social Democrats was, first of all, the progress of mankind itself (and not just advances in men's ability and knowledge). Secondly, it was something boundless, in keeping with the infinite perfectibility of mankind. Thirdly, progress was regarded as irresistible, something that automatically pursued a straight or spiral course. Each of these predicates is controversial and open to criticism. However, when the chips are down, criticism must penetrate beyond these predicates and focus on some-

---

[4] Leftist group, founded by Karl Liebknecht and Rosa Luxemburg at the beginning of World War I in opposition to the pro-war policies of the German Socialist party, later absorbed by the Communist party. [Translator's note.]

thing that they have in common. The concept of the historical progress of mankind cannot be sundered from the concept of its progression through a homogeneous, empty time. A critique of the concept of such a progression must be the basis of any criticism of the concept of progress itself.

XIV

Origin is the goal.

Karl Kraus, *Worte in Versen*, Vol. I

History is the subject of a structure whose site is not homogeneous, empty time, but time filled by the presence of the now [*Jetztzeit*].[5] Thus, to Robespierre ancient Rome was a past charged with the time of the now which he blasted out of the continuum of history. The French Revolution viewed itself as Rome reincarnate. It evoked ancient Rome the way fashion evokes costumes of the past. Fashion has a flair for the topical, no matter where it stirs in the thickets of long ago; it is a tiger's leap into the past. This jump, however, takes place in an arena where the ruling class gives the commands. The same leap in the open air of history is the dialectical one, which is how Marx understood the revolution.

XV

The awareness that they are about to make the continuum of history explode is characteristic of the revolutionary classes at the moment of their action. The great revolution introduced a new calendar. The initial day of a calendar serves as a historical time-lapse camera. And, basically, it is the same day that keeps recurring in the guise of holidays, which are days of remembrance. Thus the calendars do not measure time as clocks do; they are monuments of a historical consciousness of which not the slightest trace has been apparent in Europe in the past hundred years. In the July revolution an incident occurred which showed this consciousness still alive. On the first evening of fighting it turned out that the clocks in towers were being fired on simultaneously and independently from several places in Paris. An eye-witness, who may have owed his insight to the rhyme, wrote as follows:

> Qui le croirait! on dit, qu'irrités contre l'heure
> De nouveaux Josués au pied de chaque tour,
> Tiraient sur les cadrans pour arrêter le jour.[6]

---

[5] Benjamin says *'Jetztzeit'* and indicates by the quotation marks that he does not simply mean an equivalent to *Gegenwart*, that is, present. He clearly is thinking of the mystical *nunc stans*. [Translator's note.]

[6] Who would have believed it! We are told that new Joshuas at the foot of every tower, as though irritated with time itself, fired at the dials in order to stop the day. [Translator's note.]

XVI

A historical materialist cannot do without the notion of a present which is not a transition, but in which time stands still and has come to a stop. For this notion defines the present in which he himself is writing history. Historicism gives the 'eternal' image of the past; historical materialism supplies a unique experience with the past. The historical materialist leaves it to others to be drained by the whore called 'Once upon a time' in historicism's bordello. He remains in control of his powers, man enough to blast open the continuum of history.

XVII

Historicism rightly culminates in universal history. Materialistic historiography differs from it as to method more clearly than from any other kind. Universal history has no theoretical armature. Its method is additive; it musters a mass of data to fill the homogeneous, empty time. Materialistic historiography, on the other hand, is based on a constructive principle. Thinking involves not only the flow of thoughts, but their arrest as well. Where thinking suddenly stops in a configuration pregnant with tensions, it gives that configuration a shock, by which it crystallizes into a monad. A historical materialist approaches a historical subject only where he encounters it as a monad. In this structure he recognizes the sign of a Messianic cessation of happening, or, put differently, a revolutionary chance in the fight for the oppressed past. He takes cognizance of it in order to blast a specific era out of the homogeneous course of history – blasting a specific life out of the era or a specific work out of the lifework. As a result of this method the lifework is preserved in this work and at the same time cancelled;[7] in the lifework, the era; and in the era, the entire course of history. The nourishing fruit of the historically understood contains time as a precious but tasteless seed.

XVIII

'In relation to the history of organic life on earth,' writes a modern biologist, 'the paltry fifty millennia of *homo sapiens* constitute something like two seconds at the close of a twenty-four-hour day. On this scale, the history of civilized mankind would fill one-fifth of the last second of the last hour.' The present, which, as a model of Messianic time, comprises the entire history of mankind in an enormous abridgment, coincides exactly with the stature which the history of mankind has in the universe.

---

[7] The Hegelian term *aufheben* in its threefold meaning: to preserve, to elevate, to cancel. [Translator's note.]

A

Historicism contents itself with establishing a causal connection between various moments in history. But no fact that is a cause is for that very reason historical. It became historical posthumously, as it were, through events that may be separated from it by thousands of years. A historian who takes this as his point of departure stops telling the sequence of events like the beads of a rosary. Instead, he grasps the constellation which his own era has formed with a definite earlier one. Thus he establishes a conception of the present as the 'time of the now' which is shot through with chips of Messianic time.

B

The soothsayers who found out from time what it had in store certainly did not experience time as either homogeneous or empty. Anyone who keeps this in mind will perhaps get an idea of how past times were experienced in remembrance – namely, in just the same way. We know that the Jews were prohibited from investigating the future. The Torah and the prayers instruct them in remembrance, however. This stripped the future of its magic, to which all those succumb who turn to the soothsayers for enlightenment. This does not imply, however, that for the Jews the future turned into homogeneous, empty time. For every second of time was the strait gate through which the Messiah might enter.

SECTION TWO
Standpoints

This section spans the full range of radical historicist positions, staging a debate between six of the most cogent advocates and antagonists of new historicism and cultural materialism. The debate begins with two essays which set out to defend new historicism against the misconceptions and distortions inflicted upon it by hostile critics, and to clarify in the process their authors' understanding of what this kind of criticism actually entails. In the first essay Catherine Gallagher vigorously rebuts the charge of political disillusionment and defeatism frequently levelled at new historicists by Marxists and other oppositional critical schools. Through a fascinating history of her own intellectual and political development, to which Althusser, Derrida and Foucault (see Section One) contributed, she argues 'that American radicalism of the sixties and early seventies bred just those preoccupations that have tended to separate new historicist from Marxist critics in the eighties and that the former preserve and continue, rather than react against, many of the characteristic tendencies of New Left thought'. Chief among these tendencies is the rejection as naive of 'the left formalist's belief in a privileged realm of representation and her optimism about the efficacy of exposing ideological contradictions' through the analysis of literature. The new historicist usually seeks instead 'to show that under certain historical circumstances, the display of ideological contradictions is completely consonant with the maintenance of oppressive social relations'. This may be bad news for radical critics keen to recruit literature to the cause as an inherently progressive force, but it is meant to be politically bracing rather than demoralizing, a sobering reminder of how completely the most transgressive texts and the dissident critic can be coopted. In this sense, Gallagher concludes, far from being a quietistic, conservative critical practice, 'New historicism confronts Marxism now partly as an amplified record of Marxism's own edgiest, uneasiest voices.'

Stephen Greenblatt's essay 'Resonance and Wonder' targets three fundamental regards in which new historicism has been, in his judgement, seriously misunderstood or misrepresented. The first misapprehension is that new historicism denies human beings the agency to resist or transform their circumstances, portraying characters, authors and other protagonists of the past as the helpless dupes of historical determinism. Greenblatt insists against this that cultural poetics 'does not posit historical processes as unalterable and inexorable, but it does tend to discover limits or constraints upon individual intervention: actions that appear to be single are disclosed as multiple; the apparently isolated power of the individual genius turns out to be bound up with collective, social energy; a gesture of dissent may be an element in a larger legitimation process, while an attempt to stabilize the order of things may turn out to subvert it.' Greenblatt is equally impatient with those who claim that his absorption in the Renaissance involves a disengagement from the imperatives of the present, and who demand that he spell out boldly his political position and goals. His theoretical assumptions and value judgements, as he points out, patently inform every sentence he writes; while the culture of the Renaissance bewitched him precisely because 'it seemed to be powerfully linked to the present both analogically and causally. This two-fold link at once called forth and qualified my value judgements: called them forth because my response to the past was inextricably bound up with my response to the present; qualified them because the analysis of the past revealed the complex, unsettling historical genealogy of the very judgements I was making.' Finally, Greenblatt addresses the accusation that new historicism has swapped a concern with the literary work for a fixation on texts, events and practices remarkable only for their obscurity and eccentricity. To regard medical treatises, witchcraft trials or fashion as irrelevant to the study of a period's plays and poetry is to betray, in Greenblatt's eyes, a woeful blindness to the ways in which a culture's diverse discourses constantly transgress the boundaries between them. Nor does the charting of these transgressions prevent his retaining, he believes, a capacity to be dazzled by the unique radiance of a literary masterpiece.

Gallagher and Greenblatt are at pains to refute or complicate simplistic views of cultural poetics, which ignore their assurances that no work of art is inherently and forever doomed to function in a conservative manner, since the work's effect is liable to change as the context of its reception changes. Having taken that point on board, however, it still seems broadly true that new historicists find evidence of art conspiring with coercion more persuasive, that they are temperamentally drawn to what Alan Sinfield calls in his essay 'the "entrapment model" of ideology and power, whereby even, or especially, manoeuvres that seem designed to challenge the system help to maintain it'. Sinfield has no quarrel with the assumption that most literature originally toiled to shore up the validity of the dominant ideology, to 'negotiate the faultlines that distress the prevailing conditions of plausibility'. But as a cultural materialist he prefers to activate the dissident modern potential of past masterpieces by exposing these cracks in the coherence of the stories they tell us. Sinfield enlists Althusser, Foucault and especially Raymond Williams to buttress his contention that 'dissident potential derives . . . from conflict and contradiction that the social order inevitably produces within itself, even as it attempts to sustain itself. Despite their power, dominant ideological formations are always, in practice, under pressure, striving to substantiate their claim to superior plausibility in the face of diverse disturbances.' And, as Sinfield's own highly plausible accounts of *Othello*, *Henry V* and *Macbeth* attest, there are few places where the disruptive consequences of that pressure can be more vividly apprehended than in the classic texts of the literary canon. For these powerful narratives 'contribute to the perpetual contest of stories that constitutes culture: its representations, and our critical accounts of them, reinforce or challenge prevailing notions of what the world is like, of how it might be.'

The kind of cultural history proposed by Catherine Belsey in the essay that succeeds Sinfield's shares, as its author acknowledges, a good deal of common ground with cultural materialism. 'Wherever there is a history of subjection to norms and truths', writes Belsey, 'there is also a history of resistances.' The trouble with new historicist work, she argues, is that all too often, under the obvious influence of Foucault, 'power is represented as seamless and all-pervasive, while resistance, where it exists at all, is seen as ultimately self-deceived'. The cultural history Belsey has in mind, by contrast, 'is a story of conflicting interests, of heroic refusals, of textual uncertainties. It tells of power, but of power which always entails the possibility of resistance.' This story also owes a fair bit to Foucault, though to a much less prominent strain in his thought, as well as to Althusser's theses on ideology and Raymond Williams's dynamic, agonistic concept of culture. But its most significant debt is to Derrida, whose reputation for being 'contemptuous of history' Belsey regards as unwarranted by his work. Derrida's notion of textuality as intrinsically unstable puts a distinctive spin on Belsey's enterprise, marking it off in important respects from the cultural materialist projects it otherwise resembles. Thus Jonathan Dollimore's characteristically coarse brand of cultural materialism is upbraided for relegating culture to a subordinate, vicarious political role, and failing to identify it 'as itself the place where norms are specified and contested, knowledges affirmed and challenged, and subjectivity produced and disrupted'. Moreover, the radical critic's task, if Derrida is deployed, can scarcely be confined to redeeming reactionary works by reading them against the grain of their supposed intention. For in the semantic volatility of every cultural text, in its constitutive refusal to freeze into final meaning, Belsey perceives the promise of a critical practice through which texts might unravel and exceed even the most enlightened constructions forced upon them.

The extract from Lee Patterson's *Negotiating the Past: The Historical Understanding of Medieval Literature* kicks off with a trenchant critique of new historicism's 'totalizing vision of an entrapping world organized not primarily but exclusively by structures of domination and submission'. Belsey and Sinfield would doubtless applaud Patterson's overture, but one suspects that they would be as scandalized as any new historicist by what it paves the way for. The defences mounted by Gallagher and Greenblatt at the start of this section are unlikely to cut any ice with Patterson. He castigates new historicism for 'suppressing the individual in favour of the general and the disparate in favour of the homogenous'; for recycling rather than refuting the old historicism; for permitting the written to obliterate the real; for kissing historical explanation and thus political commitment goodbye; and for finding itself caught, in short, 'in a conservative political posture', which 'is best understood as an unintended embarrassment'. For Patterson, any radical historicism worth its salt should not only respect the independent, primary materiality of the histories texts refract; it should also confront the inescapable need for a non-teleological grand narrative, without which such criticism can have little point or purchase. What Patterson recommends above all is a reconsideration, though in no sense a simple revival, of humanist categories which most new historicists and cultural materialists would be appalled to see back on the agenda. We surrender at our peril, he warns, an attention to the author's intention, despite its vulnerability to reversal, because 'simply to set aside these intentions and purposes as unworthy of discussion is effectively to silence dissent'. We cannot go back to the transhistorical bourgeois subject, but we cannot afford to ditch the concept of the individual either; for 'To deprive the human agent of any purchase upon the social whole is to signal the end of a politics we desperately need.' By the same token, Patterson believes, it is fatal to abolish the idea of literature as a distinctive form of discourse, which can give us access to otherwise hidden reaches of historical experience. That ability to unlock secrets of the past hinges in turn, however, on converting modern critical monologues, in which the past is colonized by hindsight, into dialogues in which the past is an equal partner with unpredictable things to say.

A provocative sketch of what such dialogues would involve and could accomplish is furnished by the final essay in this section, 'The New Historicism: Back to the Future' by Marjorie Levinson. (It strikes me as unlikely to be a coincidence, incidentally, that this fresh departure within radical historicism should be sponsored by a medievalist and a Romanticist, both of whom are estranged from the world of early modern studies in which new historicism and cultural materialism were reared.) Levinson's chief, overt debt is to Walter Benjamin's essay 'The Task of the Translator', but anyone who has read Benjamin's 'Theses on the Philosophy of History' in Section One will recognize their constant, covert presence too. Most committed criticism to date has found itself trapped in an intolerable bind when it addresses a work from an earlier era: 'namely, a privileging of the text's original or its most belated position. If we choose not to rehearse the politics produced for the work by the way it got written and, initially, read, then we must crisply depose the authority of first things, which is to say, we transfer that authority to last or latest things.' Neither of these courses can begin to do justice to the scope of the problem. What we need instead, in Levinson's view, is an approach which is able

> to articulate the literatures of the past in such a way as to accommodate the contingency of the present – the wilfulness of our textual politics – and at the same time, to configurate that freedom with the particular past that is retextualized. We want a framework that will explain the objective value of a belated criticism, one which reads into the work anticipations that were *not* present in the text's contemporary life, only in its posthumous existence, an existence that turns around and *plants itself* in the past.

Not the least virtues of such an approach would be its readiness to grant texts the proleptic power to dictate their subsequent import, and its confession of its own myopia as the child of a moment fated to be some future's past.

7 Catherine Gallagher

Marxism and the New Historicism

The New Historicism, ed. H. Aram Veeser, Routledge: London, 1989 pp. 37–48.

Critics of the 'new historicism' have given wildly different accounts of its political implications, but they generally agree that its politics are obnoxious. Charged on the one hand with being a crude version of Marxism and on the other with being a formalist equivalent of colonialism,[1] the new historicism attracts an unusual amount of specifically political criticism for a criticism whose politics are so difficult to specify. One could, of course, simply stand back, amused, and let the countervailing charges collide and explode each other, but one might also be curious about why a phenomenon of such apparent political indeterminacy should seem such a general political irritant.

There is no mystery about why the new historicism's politics should attract speculation. Although there has been a certain amount of controversy over just what the new historicism is, what constitutes its essence and what its accidents, most of its adherents and opponents would probably agree that it entails reading literary and nonliterary texts as constituents of historical discourses that are both inside and outside of texts and that its practitioners generally posit no fixed hierarchy of cause and effect as they trace the connections among texts, discourses, power, and the constitution of subjectivity. Since these are the issues new historicists study, it's hardly surprising that they have kindled speculation about their own discursive contexts, commitments to and negotiations of power, or the constitution of their historical subjectivity. Such speculation is obviously very much in the spirit of their own inquiries and can hardly be called impertinent or irrelevant.

However, the insistence on finding a *single*, unequivocal political meaning for this critical practice, indeed in some cases on reducing it to a politics or a relation to power, is puzzling and certainly runs counter to what seem to me to be new historicism's most valuable insights: that no cultural or critical practice is simply a politics in disguise, that such practices are seldom *intrinsically* either liberatory or oppressive, that they seldom contain their politics as an essence but rather occupy particular historical situations from which they enter

---

[1] For the former charge, see Edward Pechter, 'The New Historicism and Its Discontents: Politicizing Renaissance Drama', *PMLA* 102 (1987), pp. 292–303; for the latter see Carolyn Porter, 'Are We Being Historical Yet?', *South Atlantic Quarterly* 87 (1988), pp. 743–86. An argument similar to but less substantial and sophisticated than Porter's is made by Marguerite Waller in 'Academic Tootsie: The Denial of Difference and the Difference It Makes', *Diacritics* 17:1 (1987), pp. 2–20. It must be noted that all of the above and most of the critics yet to be cited here focus their attacks on the work of Stephen Greenblatt. I've attempted in this article to discuss only those charges that seem to me applicable to other critics, outside the field of Renaissance literature, who are routinely called new historicists.

into various exchanges, or negotiations, with practices designated 'political'. The search for the new historicism's political essence can be seen as a rejection of these insights. Critics on both the right and left seem offended by this refusal to grant that literature and, by extension, criticism either ideally transcend politics or simply are politics when properly decoded.

To ask what is the intrinsic political meaning or content of the new historicism, then, is to pose the question in terms that wipe out the assumptions on which many critics who are routinely called new historicists might base a reply. Consequently, the following remarks proceed from a different question: what are the historical situations of the new historicism and how have these defined the nature of its exchanges with explicitly political discourses?

Having formulated this more congenial question, I must at once admit my inability to answer it adequately. I have neither the space nor the knowledge to identify the situations and sources of such a vast and various phenomenon; I can only write from what may seem a highly unusual perspective, that of critics who have arrived at new historicist positions via continental Marxist theory and 1960s radical politics. Marxist critics[2] have themselves called attention to this filiation by accusing new historicists of 'left disillusionment'. Whereas I acknowledge the 'left' inspiration in the work of many new historicists, I disagree that 'disillusionment' intervened between our current work and our more 'optimistic' youth. I'll be arguing, on the contrary, that American radicalism of the sixties and early seventies bred just those preoccupations that have tended to separate new historicist from Marxist critics in the eighties and that the former preserve and continue, rather than react against, many of the characteristic tendencies of New Left thought. I'll be concentrating especially on new historicism's residual formalism, its problematization of representation, and its dual critique and historicization of the subject.

We should bear in mind that American left-wing literary critics had developed a strong, optimistic and politically problematic brand of formalism a generation before the New Left. In its most independent and intelligent sectors, the American left offered its children in the post-war years a politics that had already begun to transfer its hopes from the traditional agent of revolutionary change, the proletariat, to a variety of 'subversive' cultural practices, the most prominent of which was aesthetic modernism. The transferral had started in the earlier belief that modernism was a support for revolutionary social change of an anti-Stalinist kind; writers such as Philip Rahv, William Phillips, Dwight Macdonald, Harold Rosenberg, and Mary McCarthy, were reacting in the 1930s against the popular front for its Stalinism, its uncritical embrace of Democratic Party politics and its sentimental, traditional cultural nationalism. The very difficulty of modernist forms, they believed, cut against the grain of American conservatism. Hence we find Harold Rosenberg, for example, trying even in the 1940s to yoke the modern working class, modernist culture, traditionless America, and his own immigrant experience into one complex of radical forces. But the joining soon

---

[2] Carolyn Porter uses this term, quoting Walter Cohen's 'Political Criticism of Shakespeare', in Jean E. Howard and Marion F. O'Connor, eds, *Shakespeare Reproduced: The Text in History and Ideology* (New York and London: Methuen, 1987).

became a substitution of elements whereby cultural modernism and the rootless intellectual were increasingly valued as the privileged representations of latent and repressed social contradictions.

The generation of cultural critics that came of age in the 1960s, therefore, might have inherited a belief in the political efficacy of certain aesthetic forms, for left formalism had reached a high level of sophistication before the war. If these aspiring critics had then merely read the available continental Marxist aesthetic theory in the sixties and early seventies, they might have stayed very much within this legacy. The Marxist criticism that circulated most widely in those years tended to be the work of Western Marxists, especially Lukács and members of the Frankfurt School. From these sources one might have picked up a number of different critical orientations toward the dominant culture. For example, one would probably have learned that culture as a realm differentiated itself from the social whole during the period of bourgeois ascendancy for the purpose of creating false resolutions for social contradictions. Its function, according to this account, was to create a consciousness capable of at once acknowledging these contradictions and justifying them by ascribing them to any number of supra-social causes. The Marxist literary critic committed to this model of bourgeois culture saw her job as the undoing of the false resolution, the detection in the text of the original contradiction and the formal signs of its irresolvability. She believed that identifying such signs exposed the false ideological solution, that turning the text back on its moments of instability confronted the culture with things it could not stand to acknowledge.

Alternatively, to take another influential Western Marxist commonplace from that period, she might have viewed the bourgeois work of art's imperfect attempts at harmonious resolution as expressions of utopian hopes and hence as potential incitements to subversive realizations. To be sure, the job of the critic was still the exposure of the gap between conflict and resolution, for the reader must be made to understand that only action in the social world could resolve the conflict. Nevertheless, the imperfect formal reconciliation itself became in this view more than a functional component of bourgeois ideology; it became a disfunctional moment as well, a vision of fulfilment not yet achieved and hence a disturbance of the status quo.

A third strand of continental Marxist aesthetics, that of the Brecht revival of the late sixties, probably also had an effect on this generation of critics. Brechtian aesthetics emphasized, like the other available Marxisms, the role of culture and cultural analysis in exposing ideological contradictions. Among Brechtians, moreover, a critic with close ties to American Left formalism might have felt very much at home, since, despite serious political differences, both tendencies believed in the almost magical subversive power of modernist forms. But whether pro- or anti-modernist, whether cognitive or affective in its orientation, whether concentrating on critical or creative practice, the continental Marxist aesthetics that was being circulated in this country in the late sixties and early seventies tended to confirm the left formalist's belief in a privileged realm of representation and her optimism about the efficacy of exposing ideological contradictions.

Such confirmation, however, might easily have collided with the implied cultural and aesthetic assumptions of the life one was actually living in the late sixties. For this generation of critics was not just reading Marxist aesthetic theory produced decades earlier; many of its members were also living, reading, writing and acting the political culture of the New Left. And it is to that culture, inchoate as it was, that we should look for several important departures from what had been the influential Marxist models.

First, for a variety of reasons, the New Left dispensed with what we might call a politics of substitution that relied on a hierarchy of causation to determine just what the crucial contradictions were. Most obviously, the intellectual activist herself did not claim to stand or speak for some other oppressed group. New Left activists notoriously invoked the principle of individual and group liberation in justifying rebellion instead of invoking their connection to the objective interests of a universal class. In the 1940s, Harold Rosenberg had taken pains to show that the ideological crisis informing his own immigrant experience could be traced back, not just to other conflicts, but to the one conflict that counted: class conflict. In contrast, New Left intellectuals generally avoided the implicit causal hierarchy of such analyses and their logic of substitution.

For example, in New Left rhetoric particular struggles were often joined to the general interest through a logic of decentred distribution, in which each group, in speaking for itself, spoke against a 'system' that was oppressing all. This was the case at the outset of the 'movement', when middle-class, white, civil rights activists learned that they could not think of themselves as representing or even as altruistically aiding black people, for altruism implied condescension. Indeed, the roots of the movement in black civil rights struggles was no doubt a strong factor obviating the rhetoric of representation for white radicals,[3] who claimed instead to be freeing themselves from racism. And the avoidance of substitutional politics only increased as group after group claimed the legitimacy of action on its own behalf.

This is not to deny the importance of such slogans as 'serve the people' or the vehemence of New Left anti-middle-class sentiments. But the slogan, after all, only proves my general point: 'the people' was a category designed to include oneself and anyone else content to join a decentred coalition of disaffected groups. Certainly, solidarity was as important to the radicals of the sixties as it had been to those of the thirties, but the grounds of solidarity had shifted from an identification with a designated specific class to a recognition of shared oppressions that cut across class divisions. Moreover, 'serving the people' was often imagined to be a means of self-transformation, even the realization and liberation of self stifled by middle-class conventionality.

Thus, because of its sociological base in groups outside the organized traditional proletariat – its reliance on upwardly mobile sectors of racial minorities, women of all races, and college students in general – important segments of the New Left devised a profoundly anti-representational form of political activism. One no longer needed to justify her own cause by claiming that it ultimately substituted for the crucial cause, the cause of the universal class. Instead, one could believe that a number of local contests, a number of micro-contradictions, would condense into a systemic crisis, a revolutionary conjunction.

---

[3] I am grateful to Houston Baker for this suggestion.

All of this has been said before, but its consequences for the budding cultural critic have generally not been remarked. First, it led to an emphasis, still very influential in 'oppositional' American criticism, on indeterminant negativity. It was no longer necessary, indeed it was impossible, to specify the inverse positive valence on every group's oppositional stance toward the 'system'. Indeed, in certain quarters, indeterminant negativity came to be seen as superior to positive programmes because less liable to cooptation. Negativity and marginality became values in themselves.

Second, but perhaps more important for the future of literary studies in general, was simply the collapse of the logic of representation itself. There was no longer a privileged realm of representation any more than there was a privileged referent. Cultural activity itself in this context began discarding its claim to separate status; lived and symbolic experience were consciously merged in guerrilla theatre, in happenings, in attempts to live a radical culture. Everything was equally symbolic and immanent, readable and opaque, and something (unspecified) in excess of itself.

This, rather than continental Marxist theory, was the intellectual and political experience that prepared the way for the American reception of French poststructuralist thought in left-wing circles, where it was often filtered through an increasingly attenuated Althusserianism. For some, Althusserianism became a step toward re-Marxification, for others it was a step toward the deconstructive critique of representation. In either case it reformulated the problem of the constitution of the subject, giving it a new, linguistic emphasis. When this was then supplemented by Jacques Derrida's work, a method of analysis resulted that accorded with some aspects of New Left political thought and contravened others. Specifically, although Derridean critiques also decentred a 'system', collapsed the distinction between things and signs, and concentrated on the fungibility of a series of diacritical moments, they often defined the system as nothing but its diacritical moments and implied that those moments displace one another in an endless chain of signification instead of condensing in a revolutionary conjunction. What came to be called 'deconstruction', then, could be used both to confirm important New Left tenets and, at the very time when the movement was losing momentum, to provide an explanation for that loss.

Many of us, however, found that we could neither renew our faith in Marxism nor convert to deconstruction, for neither seemed sufficient to explain the permutations of our own historical subjectivities and our relationship to a system of power, which we still imagined as decentred, but which we no longer viewed as easily vulnerable to its own contradictions. At this juncture, the process that had begun when the hierarchy of contradictions was abandoned, the process of rethinking the relationship between power and apparently oppositional subjectivity, became exigent. This was not so much a process of disillusionment as it was an extension of our belief in the efficacy of combining personal and political self-reflection. Was it possible, we asked, that certain forms of subjectivity that felt oppositional were really a means by which power relations were maintained? Was a politics organized by the discourse of liberation inevitably caught inside modern America's terms of power? Was it theoretically possible even to differentiate the individual subject from a system of power relationships?

This sort of self-questioning had extensive left-wing credentials, not only in the works of Louis Althusser, but also in Herbert Marcuse's highly influential repressive desublimation thesis. Such self-questioning became all the more urgent as feminist self-consciousness spread among activists. Indeed, the women's liberation movement taught us several things that are apposite here. First, it forced us to see that the more 'personal' and 'mundane' the issues, the more resistance to change we encountered. We could achieve what at the time seemed virtual generational consensus for abolishing the draft, winning a strike, reorganizing a university, ending the war, and passing affirmative action laws. But there was no such consensus about sharing the housework, reorganizing childcare, exposing family violence, or ending exploitative sexual relations. In the early years of the women's liberation movement, we were repeatedly told that we were siphoning off energy from significant political activities and wasting it in trivial, personal confrontations. Of course, we took such resistance, including the very rhetoric of triviality, as a token of the radical significance of our movement. Finally, we thought, we had penetrated the deepest, least questioned and most inaccessible region of social formation: the formation of ourselves as gendered subjects.

Thus we went beyond dismantling the old hierarchy of significance and began erecting a new one in which those aspects of life whose continuity was assured by their classification under the category of the trivial came to seem the most important. But this lesson had a second implication as well; by focusing attention on our gendered individuation as the deepest moment of social oppression, some of us called into question the political reliability of our own subjectivity. We effectively collapsed the self/society division and began regarding our 'normal' consciousness and 'natural' inclinations as profoundly untrustworthy. We, along with our erstwhile political optimism, became for ourselves the objects of a hermeneutics of suspicion. We wondered at our pre-feminist radical consciousness, which had imagined social arrangements to be relatively fragile. Could the illusion of fragility maintained by a belief that the system could not bear an exposure of its contradictions be a functioning part of its endurance? This was not the end of politics for many of us, but it was the end of a naive faith in the transparency of our own political consciousness.

The women's liberation movement had a third relevant consequence. We became fascinated with the history of gender, of how things have changed and how they don't change. The work of the Annales school and other anthropologically inspired historians gave some methodological direction in the mid-seventies, and in those years Michel Foucault's work appeared, addressing exactly the issues that preoccupied us.

These were the seed years for the new historicist work that has been appearing in the eighties. In many ways this work has maintained New Left assumptions about the sources, nature, and sites of social conflict and about the issue of representation. Instead of resubscribing, as some Marxist critics have, to a historical meta-narrative of class conflict, we have tended to insist that power cannot be equated with economic or state power, that its sites of activity, and hence of resistance, are also in the micro-politics of daily life. The traditionally important economic and political agents and events have been displaced or supplemented by people and phenomena that once seemed wholly insignificant, indeed outside of history: women, criminals, the insane, sexual practices and discourses, fairs, festivals, plays of all kinds. Just as in the sixties, the effort in the eighties has been to question and destabilize the distinctions between sign systems and things, the representation and the represented, history and text.

In all of these ways, much new historicist work can be said to possess a remarkable continuity with certain cultural assumptions of the New Left. But the work has also exposed and taken off from a number of contested moments within those assumptions, especially those regarding form and ideological contradiction. Despite the critique of substitutionalist politics and the supposed de-privileging of a realm of representation during the sixties and seventies, left formalism managed to thrive. In its Althusserian form, it tended, ironically, to reestablish many former Hegelian notions about the special status of art as a displayer of ideological contradictions. The art form, according to Althusser and Pierre Macherey, created internal distantiations which allow us to 'see' the gaps and fissures, the points of stress and incoherence, inside the dominant ideology. 'Seeing' was not to be confused with 'knowing'; nevertheless, Althusserian literary criticism in practice made very little of this distinction and proceeded as if form were in itself revelatory.[4] This did not entail the privileging of any particular form, but of all forms. It was against such claims for the automatic subversiveness of art, as well as parallel deconstructive claims for literature's self-referential and therefore anti-ideological rhetoricity, that many new historicists directed their critiques. Their effort was, and still is, to show that under certain historical circumstances, the display of ideological contradictions is completely consonant with the maintenance of oppressive social relations. New historicists were often bent on proving that the relationship between form and ideology was neither one of simple affirmation, in which form papers over ideological gaps, nor one of subversive negation, in which form exposes ideology and thereby helps render it powerless. The contribution of the new historicism has been to identify a third alternative in which the very antagonism between literature and ideology becomes, in specific historical environments, a powerful and socially functional mode of constructing subjectivity.

This could be seen as the final de-privileging of the realm of representation, the final blow to left formalism, and hence a further extension of a New Left tendency. But it is precisely this mode of construing the relationship between literature and ideology that other left-wing critics have found not only quietistic in its implications but also formalist[5] in its assumptions. I will treat the second of these charges first, since it seems to me undeniable. The actual procedures of many new historicist analyses are often not very different from those of left formalists. We too often take the text as a constant, the very instability of which is stable across time, so that its historical impact can be determined from an analysis of its structures and the logic of their disintegration when set against other discourses. Historical reception studies

---

[4] Michael Sprinker has recently explicated this distinction in *Imaginary Relations: Aesthetics and Ideology in the Theory of Historical Materialism* (New York: Verso, 1987). See especially pp. 101–4 and 267–95.

[5] On the issue of formalism, see Cohen, 'Political Criticism of Shakespeare'.

are sometimes suggested as an antidote to such formalism,[6] and, despite the fact that these often import their own epistemological *naïveté*, they certainly deserve much more of our attention than they currently receive. However, there is no simple solution to the problem of formalism – one variant of the problem of textuality – in historical studies; we can only hope to maintain a productive tension between the textualist and historicist dimensions of our work.

The charge of quietism in response to attacks on left formalism returns us to the issue with which we began, the issue of the relationship between politics and criticism. To argue that it is inherently quietistic to deny literature an inherent politics is, first of all, to reason tautologically. Such reasoning begins with the assumption that everything has *a* politics; a denial of this assumption must also have *a* politics, no doubt reactionary. Such reasoning is impervious to evidence; the accusers need not do the difficult work of examining how critical orientations interact with specific political initiatives, even in the most immediate arena of academic politics. They need not ask, for example, what impact the new historicism has had on curricula in literature departments, whether or not it has had a role in introducing non-canonical texts into the classroom, or in making students of literature more aware of the history and significance of such phenomena as imperialism, slavery, and gender differentiation in western culture. It is my guess, although the evidence is yet to be gathered, that new historicists have been, along with Marxists and feminists, fairly active in achieving these goals, which are generally considered to be on the 'left' of the academic political spectrum.

All this is oddly irrelevant to critics of the new historicism on the left, while it forms the basis of political complaints coming from the right.[7] Left-wing critics would concede that new historicists often read the right texts and ask the right questions, but they complain that such readings yield the wrong answers. Specifically, they tend to complain that new historicists fail to emphasize that the text is a site of subversive potential and that the critic's job is to activate it.[8] They imply that the new historicist, in describing how texts may create modern subjectivity by playing the literary against the ideological, somehow becomes

---

[6]   Both Porter and Cohen have made this suggestion.

[7]   According to David Brooks of *The Wall Street Journal* the new historicism is a left-wing plot to destroy the canon and substitute a political agenda for a loving exploration of 'literary excellence': 'Annabel Patterson of Duke is typical. She uses Shakespeare, she says, as a vehicle to illuminate the way 17th-century society mistreated women, the working class and minorities. This emphasis is called the New Historicism.' ('From Western Lit to Westerns as Lit', *The Wall Street Journal*, 2 February 1988, p. 24, cols 3–5.) And according to *Newsweek,* new historicism is one among many schools prescribing 'the study of books not because of their moral or esthetic value but because they permit the professor to advance a political, often Marxist agenda'. (David Lehman, 'Deconstructing de Man's Life: An Academic Idol Falls Into Disgrace', *Newsweek*, 15 February 1988, p. 62.) Frederick Crews, to whom these sentiments are attributed in the article, has energetically repudiated them in a letter to the editor, insisting that they are Lehman's own construction. There may be a certain amount of confusion evident in these mass-media attacks, but they are, in their own way, arguably accurate about the new historicism's usual affiliations in the overall politics of the discipline.

[8]   See both Cohen, 'Political Criticism of Shakespeare', and Waller, 'Academic Tootsie'.

complicit in the process described.[9] There are many versions of this argument, some more persuasive than others, but they share a dismay at the new historicist's tendency to identify precisely the things in texts that had been named subversive, destabilizing, and self-distantiating, as inscriptions of the formative moments, not the disruptions, of the liberal subject. The negativity of literary culture is not denied but is rather re-presented as a potential basis of its positivity. Such a representation seems in itself quietistic to some critics because it apparently presents culture as achieving, through its very fracturing, an inescapable totalizing control. It could thus, the argument runs, convince people of the uselessness of opposition. And it certainly discredits the left-formalist assumptions that have underwritten much of this generation's emotional investment in the study of literature.

There is no doubt, then, that those new historicists who emphasize that modern subjectivity is subtended by what we might call a sub-tension pose a challenge to the usual methods of left-wing criticism. But it does not follow that this is a reactionary or quietistic challenge to the left. Indeed, one can find no more generally agreed-upon proposition in all sectors of literary criticism than the proposition that literature shakes us up and disturbs our moral equilibrium (liberal humanism), destabilizes the subject (deconstruction), and self-distantiates ideological formations (Marxism). New historicists find the terms of this consensus fascinating, and far from imagining that it has a politics, simply point to the ways in which it can take the place of many politics. As D.A. Miller has succinctly expressed it, 'even if it were true that literature exercises a destabilizing function in our culture, the current consensus that it does so does not.'[10] By posing challenges to the left-wing version of this consensus, indeed by simply pointing out that there is such a consensus, new historicists on the left ask more traditional leftists to see how the 'subversion hypothesis', to use Miller's words again, 'tends to function within the overbearing cultural "mythologies" that will already have appropriated it'. This is not an attempt to demoralize the left, but it can be seen as an attempt to de-moralize our relationship to literature, to interrupt the moral narrative of literature's benign disruptions with which we soothe ourselves.

What is the political import of this interruption? It doesn't have *one*. Even if its political origins were wholly comprised in the history I have sketched – of course, they are not – its tendencies and potential affiliations are never fully determined. We can reasonably predict, however, that new historicism's most active interlocutors will continue to be Marxists and other 'oppositional' critics, and that the effects of their debate might be to alter long-standing critical procedures. For new historicism and Marxism are nudging one another

---

[9] For the argument that new historicists themselves repeat the marginalization and/or containment of disruptive elements accomplished by the discursive practices they analyse, see Porter, 'Are We Being Historical Yet?', and Lynda Boose, 'The Family in Shakespeare Studies; or – Studies in the Family of Shakespeareans; or – The Politics of Politics', *Renaissance Quarterly* 40 (1987), pp. 707–42.

[10] D.A. Miller, *The Novel and the Police* (Berkeley, Calif.: University of California Press, 1987), p. xi.

toward previously undeveloped evidentiary bases for their conclusions and away from a belief in the self-consistency or constant 'difference' of the text over time that warrants deriving historical effect from formal features or 'rigorous' readings.

But we probably cannot predict a happy collaboration in the future, because some new historicists will continue to resist the goal of synthesizing their historical, literary-critical, and political consciousnesses into one coherent entity. The new historicist, unlike the Marxist, is under no nominal compulsion to achieve consistency. She may even insist that historical curiosity can develop independently of political concerns; there may be no political impulse whatsoever behind her desire to historicize literature. This is not to claim that the desire for historical knowledge is itself historically unplaced or 'objective'; it is, rather, to insist that the impulses, norms, and standards of a discipline called history, which has achieved a high level of autonomy in the late twentieth century, are a profound part of the subjectivity of some scholars and do not in all cases require political ignition.

Moreover, even for those of us whose political and historical concerns quite clearly overlap, a perfect confluence between the two might arouse more suspicion than satisfaction, for what would such a confluence be based on but the myth of a self-consistent subject impervious to divisions of disciplinary boundaries and outside the constraints of disciplinary standards? The demands that one so often hears on the left for self-placement, for exposing the political bases of one's intellectual endeavours, for coming clean about one's political agenda, for reading and interpreting everything as a feminist or a Marxist or an anti-imperialist, for getting to and shoring up a solid political foundation for all of one's endeavours, demands often made in the name of historical self-consciousness, resound only in a historical vacuum, so deeply do they mistake the constitution of modern subjectivity.

One could retort, using the analyses of some new historicists, that this modern subject, whose supposed non-identity often facilitates the circulation of disciplinary power, is precisely what needs to be overcome. Such a retort would temporarily reverse the positions of the interlocutors, for the people who call for a single political-historical-critical enterprise often celebrate the subversive potential of the non-identical subject, while the new historicist finds herself insisting on the very non-identity she has so often shown to be part of disciplinary processes. In doing so, however, new historicists have not claimed that the historical experience of nonidentity is merely chimerical and can be overcome by simply dismissing it as a literary effect underneath which some essential consistency can be unearthed. In fact, it does not follow from new historicist arguments either that the subject can or should be reconstituted on an identitarian model. Rather, the effort of this criticism has been to trace the creation of modern subjectivity in the necessary failures of the effort to produce a stable subject. It is difficult to see how attempts at producing stable critical subjects on a political model will escape repeating this circuit, will not result once again in an experience of decentred helplessness.

Of course, many of the points I'm making here come from inside the Marxist tradition; Lukács, Adorno, Althusser, indeed, Marx himself all warned against subordinating theory, critique, or historical scholarship to practical political goals. New historicism confronts Marxism now partly as an amplified record of Marxism's own edgiest, uneasiest voices. Those Marxists who listen carefully may hear many of their own unanswered doubts and questions. To dismiss such challenges as the mere echoes of a reactionary defeatism would be a serious mistake.

8 Stephen Greenblatt

From *Resonance and Wonder*

Literary Theory Today, ed. Peter Collier and Helga Geyer-Ryan, Polity Press: Cambridge, 1990, pp. 74–9.

The new historicism, like the Holy Roman Empire, constantly belies its own name. The *American Heritage Dictionary* gives three meanings for the term 'historicism':

1. The belief that processes are at work in history that man can do little to alter. 2. The theory that the historian must avoid all value judgments in his study of past periods or former cultures. 3. Veneration of the past or of tradition.

Most of the writing labelled 'new historicist', and certainly my own work, has set itself resolutely against each of these positions.

(1) 'The belief that processes are at work in history that man can do little to alter.' This formulation rests upon a simultaneous abstraction and evacuation of human agency. The men and women who find themselves making concrete choices in given circumstances at particular times are transformed into something called 'man'. And this colourless, nameless collective being cannot significantly intervene in the 'processes . . . at work in history', processes that are thus mysteriously alienated from all of those who enact them.

New historicism, by contrast, eschews the use of the term 'man'; interest lies not in the abstract universal but in particular, contingent cases, the selves fashioned and acting according to the generative rules and conflicts of a given culture. And these selves, conditioned by the expectations of their class, gender, religion, race and national identity, are constantly effecting changes in the course of history. Indeed if there is any inevitability in the new historicism's vision of history it is this insistence on agency, for even inaction or extreme marginality is understood to possess meaning and therefore to imply intention. Every form of behaviour, in this view, is a strategy: taking up arms or taking flight are significant social actions, but so is staying put, minding one's business, turning one's face to the wall. Agency is virtually inescapable.

Inescapable but not simple: new historicism, as I understand it, does not posit historical processes as unalterable and inexorable, but it does tend to discover limits or constraints upon individual intervention: actions that appear to be single are disclosed as multiple; the apparently isolated power of the individual genius turns out to be bound up with collective, social energy; a gesture of dissent may be an element in a larger legitimation process, while an attempt to stabilize the order of things may turn out to subvert it. And political valencies may change, sometimes abruptly: there are no guarantees, no absolute, formal assurances that what seems progressive in one set of contingent circumstances will not come to seem reactionary in another.

The new historicism's insistence on the pervasiveness of agency has apparently led some of its critics to find in it a Nietzschean celebration of the ruthless will to power, while its ironic and sceptical reappraisal of the cult of heroic individualism has led others to find in it a pessimistic doctrine of human helplessness. Hence, for example, from a Marxist perspective Walter Cohen criticizes the new historicism as a 'liberal disillusionment' that finds that 'any apparent site of resistance ultimately serves the interests of power', while from a liberal humanist perspective, Edward Pechter proclaims that 'anyone who, like me, is reluctant to accept the will to power as the defining human essence will probably have trouble with the critical procedures of the new historicists and with their interpretative conclusions.'[1] But the very idea of a 'defining human essence' is precisely what critics like me find vacuous and untenable, as I do Pechter's counter-claim that love rather than power makes the world go round. Cohen's critique is more plausible, but it rests upon his assertion that new historicism argues that '*any* apparent site of resistance' is ultimately co-opted. Some are, some aren't.

I argued in *Shakespearean Negotiations* that the sites of resistance in Shakespeare's second tetralogy are co-opted in the plays' ironic, complex but finally celebratory affirmation of charismatic kingship. That is, the formal structure and rhetorical strategy of the plays make it difficult for audiences to withhold their consent from the triumph of Prince Hal. That triumph is shown to rest upon a claustrophobic narrowing of pleasure, a hypocritical manipulation of appearances, and a systematic betrayal of friendship, and yet these manifestations of bad faith only contrive to increase the spectators' knowing pleasure and the ratification of applause. The subversive perceptions do not disappear but, in so far as they remain within the structure of the play, they are contained and indeed serve to heighten a power they would appear to question.

I did not propose that all manifestations of resistance in all literature (or even in all plays by Shakespeare) were co-opted – one can readily think of plays where the forces of ideological containment break down. And yet characterizations of this essay in particular, and new historicism in general, repeatedly refer to a supposed argument that any resistance is

[1] Walter Cohen, 'Political Criticism of Shakespeare', in Jean E. Howard and Marion F. O'Connor, eds, *Shakespeare Reproduced: The Text in History and Ideology* (New York and London: Methuen, 1987), p. 33; Edward Pechter, 'The New Historicism and its Discontents: Politicizing Renaissance Drama', *PMLA* 102:3 (1987), p. 301.

impossible.[2] A particularizing argument about the subject position projected by a set of plays is at once simplified and turned into a universal
principle from which contingency and hence history itself is erased.

Moreover, even the argument about Shakespeare's second tetralogy is
misunderstood if it is thought to foreclose the possibility of dissent or change
or the radical alteration of the processes of history. The point is that certain
aesthetic and political structures work to contain the subversive perceptions
they generate, not that those perceptions simply wither away. On the contrary,
they may be pried loose from the order with which they were bound up and
may serve to fashion a new and radically different set of structures. How else
could change ever come about? No one is forced – except perhaps in school –
to take aesthetic or political wholes as sacrosanct. The order of things is never
simply a given: it takes labour to produce, sustain, reproduce, and transmit the
way things are, and this labour may be withheld or transformed. Structures
may be broken in pieces, the pieces altered, inverted, rearranged. Everything
can be different than it is; everything could have been different than it was. But
it will not do to imagine that this alteration is easy, automatic, without cost or
obligation. My objection was to the notion that the rich ironies in the history
plays were themselves inherently liberating, that to savour the tetralogy's
sceptical cunning was to participate in an act of political resistance. In general
I find dubious the assertion that certain rhetorical features in much-loved
literary works constitute authentic acts of political subversion; the fact that this
assertion is now heard from the left – when in my college days it was more
often heard from the right – does not make it in most instances any less fatuous
and presumptuous. I wished to show, at least in the case of Shakespeare's
histories and in several analogous discourses, how a set of representational and
political practices in the late sixteenth century could produce and even batten
upon what appeared to be their own subversion.

To show this is the case is not to give up on the possibility of altering
historical processes – if this is historicism I want no part of it – but rather to
eschew an aestheticized and idealized politics of the liberal imagination.

(2) 'The theory that the historian must avoid all value judgments in his study
of past periods or former cultures.' Once again, if this is an essential tenet of
historicism, then the new historicism belies its name. My own critical practice
was decisively shaped by the America of the 1960s and early 1970s, and
especially by the opposition to the Viet Nam War. Writing that was not
engaged, that withheld judgements, that failed to connect the present with the
past seemed worthless. Such connection could be made either by analogy or
causality; that is, a particular set of historical circumstances could be

---

[2] 'The new historicists and cultural materialists', one typical summary puts it, 'represent,
and by representing, reproduce in their new history of ideas, a world which is hierarchical,
authoritarian, hegemonic, unsubvertable. . . . In this world picture, Stephen Greenblatt has
poignantly asserted, there can be no subversion – and certainly not for us!' (C.T. Neely,
'Constructing the Subject: Feminist Practice and the New Renaissance Discourses', *English
Literary Renaissance* 18 [1988], p. 10). Poignantly or otherwise, I asserted no such thing; I
argued that the spectator of the history plays was continually tantalized by a resistance
simultaneously powerful and deferred.

represented in such a way as to bring out homologies with aspects of the present or, alternatively, those circumstances could be analysed as the generative forces that led to the modern condition. In either mode, value judgments were implicated, because a neutral or indifferent relation to the present seemed impossible. Or rather it seemed overwhelmingly clear that neutrality was itself a political position, a decision to support the official policies in both the state and the academy.

To study the culture of sixteenth-century England did not present itself as an escape from the turmoil of the present; it seemed rather an intervention, a mode of relation. The fascination for me of the Renaissance was that it seemed to be powerfully linked to the present both analogically and causally. This two-fold link at once called forth and qualified my value judgements: called them forth because my response to the past was inextricably bound up with my response to the present; qualified them because the analysis of the past revealed the complex, unsettling historical genealogy of the very judgements I was making. To study Renaissance culture, then, was simultaneously to feel more rooted and more estranged in my own values.[3]

Other critics associated with the new historicism – Louis Montrose, Don Wayne and Catherine Gallagher, among others – have written directly and forcefully about their own subject position and have made more explicit than I the nature of this engagement.[4] If I have not done so to the same extent, it is not because I believe that my values are somehow suspended in my study of the past but because I believe they are pervasive: in the textual and visual traces I choose to analyse, in the stories I choose to tell, in the cultural conjunctions I attempt to make, in my syntax, adjectives, pronouns. 'The new historicism', Jean Howard has written in a lively critique, 'needs at every point to be more overtly self-conscious of its methods and its theoretical assumptions, since what one discovers about the historical place and function of literary texts is in large measure a function of the angle from which one looks and the assumptions that enable the investigation.'[5] I am certainly not opposed to methodological self-consciousness, but I am less inclined to see overtness – an explicit articulation of one's values and methods – as inherently necessary or virtuous. Nor, though I believe that one's values are everywhere engaged in one's work, do I think that there need be a perfect integration of those values and the objects one is studying. On the contrary, some of the most interesting and powerful ideas in cultural criticism occur precisely at moments of

---

[3] See my *Renaissance Self-Fashioning: From More to Shakespeare* (Chicago: University of Chicago Press, 1980), pp. 174–5: 'We are situated at the close of the cultural movement initiated in the Renaissance; the places in which our social and psychological world seems to be cracking apart are those structural joints visible when it was first constructed.'

[4] Louis Adrian Montrose, 'Renaissance Literary Studies and the Subject of History', *English Literary Renaissance* 16 (1986), pp. 5–12; Don Wayne, 'Power, Politics, and the Shakespearean Text: Recent Criticism in England and the United States', in Howard and O'Connor, eds, *Shakespeare Reproduced*, pp. 47–67; Catherine Gallagher, 'Marxism and the New Historicism', in H. Aram Veeser, ed., *The New Historicism* (New York and London: Routledge, 1989), pp. 37–48.

[5] Jean E. Howard, 'The New Historicism in Renaissance Studies', in Arthur F. Kinney and Dan S. Collins, eds, *Renaissance Historicism: Selections from 'English Literary Renaissance'* (Amherst, Mass.: University of Massachusetts Press, 1987), pp. 32–3.

disjunction, disintegration, unevenness. A criticism that never encounters obstacles, that celebrates predictable heroines and rounds up the usual suspects, that finds confirmation of its values everywhere it turns, is quite simply boring.

If there is then no suspension of value judgments in the new historicism, there is at the same time a complication of those judgments, what I have called a sense of estrangement. This estrangement is bound up with the abandonment of a belief in historical inevitability, for, with this abandonment, the values of the present could no longer seem the necessary outcome of an irreversible teleological progression, whether of enlightenment or decline. An older historicism that proclaimed self-consciously that it had avoided all value judgments in its account of the past – that it had given us historical reality *wie es eigentlich gewesen* – did not thereby avoid all value judgements; it simply provided a misleading account of what it had actually done. In this sense the new historicism, for all its acknowledgement of engagement and partiality, is slightly less likely than the older historicism to impose its values belligerently on the past, for those values seem historically contingent.

(3) 'Veneration of the past or of tradition.' The third definition of historicism obviously sits in a strange relation to the second, but they are not simply alternatives. The apparent eschewing of value judgments was often accompanied by a still more apparent admiration, however cloaked as objective description, of the past. One of the most oppressive qualities of my own literary training was its relentlessly celebratory character: literary criticism was and largely remains a kind of secular theodicy. Every decision made by a great artist could be shown to be a brilliant one; works that had seemed flawed and uneven to an earlier generation of critics bent on displaying discriminations in taste were now revealed to be organic masterpieces. A standard critical assignment in my student years was to show how a text that seemed to break in parts was really a complex whole: thousands of pages were dutifully churned out to prove that the zany subplot of *The Changeling* was cunningly integrated into the tragic main plot, or that every tedious bit of clowning in *Doctor Faustus* was richly significant. Behind these exercises was the assumption that great works of art were triumphs of resolution, that they were, in Bakhtin's term, monological – the mature expression of a single artistic intention. When this formalism was combined, as it often was, with both ego-psychology and historicism, it posited aesthetic integration as the reflection of the artist's psychic integration and posited that psychic integration as the triumphant expression of a healthy, integrated community. Accounts of Shakespeare's relation to Elizabethan culture were particularly prone to this air of veneration, since the Romantic cult of poetic genius could be conjoined with the still older political cult that had been created around the figure of the Virgin Queen.

Here again new historicist critics have swerved in a different direction. They have been more interested in unresolved conflict and contradiction than in integration; they are as concerned with the margins as with the centre; and they have turned from a celebration of achieved aesthetic order to an exploration of the ideological and material bases for the production of this order. Traditional formalism and historicism, twin legacies of early nineteenth-century

Germany, shared a vision of high culture as a harmonizing domain of reconciliation based upon an aesthetic labour that transcends specific economic or political determinants. What is missing is psychic, social, and material resistance, a stubborn, unassimilable otherness, a sense of distance and difference. New historicism has attempted to restore this distance; hence its characteristic concerns have seemed to some critics off-centre or strange. 'New historicists', writes Walter Cohen, 'are likely to seize upon something out of the way, obscure, even bizarre: dreams, popular or aristocratic festivals, denunciations of witchcraft, sexual treatises, diaries and autobiographies, descriptions of clothing, reports on disease, birth and death records, accounts of insanity.'[6] What is fascinating to me is that concerns like these should have come to seem bizarre, especially to a subtle and intelligent Marxist critic who is committed to the historical understanding of culture. That they have done so indicates how narrow the boundaries of historical understanding had become, how much these boundaries needed to be broken.

For none of the cultural practices on Cohen's list (and one could extend it considerably) is or should be 'out of the way' in a study of Renaissance literature or art; on the contrary, each is directly in the way of coming to terms with the period's methods of regulating the body, its conscious and unconscious psychic strategies, its ways of defining and dealing with marginals and deviants, its mechanisms for the display of power and the expression of discontent, its treatment of women. If such concerns have been rendered 'obscure', it is because of a disabling idea of causality that confines the legitimate field of historical agency within absurdly restrictive boundaries. The world is parcelled out between a predictable group of stereotypical causes and a large, dimly lit mass of raw materials that the artist chooses to fashion.

The new historicist critics are interested in such cultural expressions as witchcraft accusations, medical manuals, or clothing not as raw materials but as 'cooked' – complex symbolic and material articulations of the imaginative and ideological structures of the society that produced them. Consequently, there is a tendency in at least some new historicist writings (certainly in my own) for the focus to be partially displaced from the work of art that is their formal occasion onto the related practices that had been adduced ostensibly in order to illuminate that work. It is difficult to keep those practices in the background if the very concept of historical background has been called into question.

I have tried to deal with the problem of focus by developing a notion of cultural negotiation and exchange, that is, by examining the points at which one cultural practice intersects with another, borrowing its forms and intensities or attempting to ward off unwelcome appropriations. But it would be misleading to imagine that there is a complete homogenization of interest; my own concern remains centrally with imaginative literature, and not only because other cultural structures resonate powerfully within it. If I do not approach works of art in a spirit of veneration, I do approach them in a spirit that is best described as wonder. Wonder has not been alien to literary criticism, but it has been associated (if only implicitly) with formalism rather than historicism. I wish to extend this wonder beyond the formal boundaries of works of art, just as I wish to intensify resonance within those boundaries.

---

[6] Cohen, 'Political Criticism of Shakespeare', pp. 33–4.

9   Alan Sinfield

Cultural Materialism, Othello, *and the Politics of Plausibility*

Faultlines: Cultural Materialism and the Politics of Dissident Reading,
Clarendon Press, Oxford, 1992, pp. 29–51.

' 'Tis apt and of great credit'

Cassio, in Shakespeare's *Othello*, is discovered in a drunken brawl. He
laments: 'Reputation, reputation, I ha' lost my reputation!' (2.3.254).[1] Iago
replies, 'You have lost no reputation at all, unless you repute yourself such a
loser' (2.3.261–3), but this assertion is absurd (though attractive), since
reputation is by definition a social construct, concerned entirely with one's
standing in the eyes of others. In fact, language and reality are always
interactive, dependent upon social recognition; reputation is only a specially
explicit instance. Meaning, communication, language work only because they
are shared. If you invent your own language, no one else will understand you;
if you persist, you will be thought mad. Iago is telling Cassio to disregard the
social basis of language, to make up his own meanings for words; it is the more
perverse because Iago is the great manipulator of the prevailing stories of his
society.

Stephen Greenblatt has remarked how Othello's identity depends upon a
constant performance of his 'story';[2] when in difficulty, his immediate move is
to rehearse his nobility and service to the state. Actually, all the characters in
Othello are telling stories, and to convince others even more than themselves.
At the start, Iago and Roderigo are concocting a story – a sexist and racist story
about how Desdemona is in 'the gross clasps of a lascivious Moor' (1.1.126).
Brabantio believes this story and repeats it to the Senate, but Othello contests
it with his 'tale':

> I will a round unvarnish'd tale deliver,
> Of my whole course of love.
>
> (1.3.90–1)

[1] *Othello* is quoted from the New Arden edition, ed. M.R. Ridley (London: Methuen, 1962).
An earlier version of parts of this paper, entitled 'Othello and the Politics of Character', was
published in Manuel Barbeito, ed., *In Mortal Shakespeare: Radical Readings* (Santiago:
Universidad de Santiago de Compostela, 1989).

[2] Stephen Greenblatt, *Renaissance Self-Fashioning: From More to Shakespeare* (Chicago:
University of Chicago Press, 1980), p. 245 and also pp. 234–9, and Greenblatt, 'Psychoanalysis
and Renaissance Culture', in Patricia Parker and David Quint, eds, *Literary Theory/Renaissance
Texts* (Baltimore, Md: Johns Hopkins University Press, 1986), p. 218. On stories in *Othello*, see
further Jonathan Goldberg, 'Shakespearean Inscriptions: The Voicing of Power', in Patricia
Parker and Geoffrey Hartman, eds, *Shakespeare and the Question of Theory* (New York:
Methuen, 1985), pp. 131–2.

The tale is – that Othello told a story. Brabantio 'Still question'd me the story of my life' (1.3.129), and this story attracted Desdemona. She asked to hear it through, observing,

> if I had a friend that lov'd her,
> I should but teach him how to tell my story,
> And that would woo her.

(1.3.163–5)

So the action advances through a contest of stories, and *the conditions of plausibility* are therefore crucial – they determine which stories will be believed. Brabantio's case is that Othello must have enchanted Desdemona – anything else is implausible:

> She is abus'd, stol'n from me and corrupted,
> By spells and medicines, bought of mountebanks,
> For nature so preposterously to err,
> (Being not deficient, blind, or lame of sense,)
> Sans witchcraft could not.

(1.3.60–4)

To Brabantio, for Desdemona to love Othello would be preposterous, an error of nature. To make this case, he depends on the plausibility, to the Senate, of the notion that Blacks are inferior outsiders. This, evidently, is a good move. Even characters who want to support Othello's story accept that he is superficially inappropriate as a husband for Desdemona. She says as much herself when she declares, 'I saw Othello's visage in his mind' (1.3.252): this means, he may look like a black man but really he is very nice. And the Duke finally tells Brabantio: 'Your son-in-law is far more fair than black' (1.3.290) – meaning, Othello doesn't have many of those unpleasant characteristics that we all know belong to Blacks, he is really quite like a white man.

With the conditions of plausibility so stacked against him, two main strategies are available to Othello, and he uses both. One is to appear very calm and responsible – as the Venetians imagine themselves to be. But also, and shrewdly, he uses the racist idea of himself as exotic: he says he has experienced 'hair-breadth scapes', redemption from slavery, hills 'whose heads touch heaven', cannibals, anthropophagi, 'and men whose heads / Do grow beneath their shoulders' (1.3.129–45). These adventures are of course implausible – but not when attributed to an exotic. Othello has little credit by normal upper-class Venetian criteria, but when he plays on his strangeness, the Venetians tolerate him, for he is granting, in more benign form, part of Brabantio's case.

Partly, perhaps, because the senators need Othello to fight the Turks for them, they allow his story to prevail. However, this is not, of course, the end of the story. Iago repeats his racist and sexist tale to Othello, and persuades him of its credibility:

> I know our country disposition well . . .
> She did deceive her father, marrying you . . .
> Not to affect many proposed matches,
> Of her own clime, complexion, and degree,
> Whereto we see in all things nature tends . . .

(3.3.205, 210, 233–5)

Othello is persuaded of his inferiority and of Desdemona's inconstancy, and he proceeds to act as if they were true. 'Haply, for I am black', he muses (3.3.267), and begins to take the role of the 'erring barbarian' (1.3.356–7) that he is alleged to be. As Ania Loomba puts it, 'Othello moves from being a colonised subject existing on the terms of white Venetian society and trying to internalise its ideology, towards being marginalised, outcast and alienated from it in every way, until he occupies his "true" position as its other.'[3] It is very difficult not to be influenced by a story, even about yourself, when everyone else is insisting upon it. So in the last lines of the play, when he wants to reassert himself, Othello 'recognizes' himself as what Venetian culture has really believed him to be: an ignorant, barbaric outsider – like, he says, the 'base Indian' who threw away a pearl. Virtually, this is what Althusser means by 'interpellation': Venice hails Othello as a barbarian, and he acknowledges that it is he they mean.[4]

Iago remarks that the notion that Desdemona loves Cassio is 'apt and of great credit' (2.1.282); and that his advice to Cassio to press Desdemona for his reinstatement is 'Probal to thinking' (2.3.329). Iago's stories work because they are plausible to Roderigo, Brabantio, the Senate, even to Othello himself. As Peter Stallybrass has observed, Iago is convincing not because he is 'superhumanly ingenious but, to the contrary, because his is the voice of "common sense", the ceaseless repetition of the always-already "known", the culturally "given".'[5] The racism and sexism in the play should not be traced just to Iago's character, therefore, or to his arbitrary devilishness, but to the Venetian culture that sets the conditions of plausibility.

The Production of Ideology

I have spoken of stories because I want an inclusive term that will key in my theory to the continuous and familiar discourses of everyday life. But in effect I have been addressing the production of ideology. Societies need to produce materially to continue – they need food, shelter, warmth; goods to exchange with other societies; a transport and information infrastructure to carry those processes. Also, they have to produce ideologically (Althusser makes this argument at the start of his essay on ideological state apparatuses).[6] They need

[3] Ania Loomba, *Gender, Race, Renaissance Drama* (Manchester: Manchester University Press, 1989), p. 48. See also Doris Adler, 'The Rhetoric of *Black* and *White* in *Othello*', *Shakespeare Quarterly* 25 (1974), pp. 248–57.

[4] Louis Althusser, 'Ideological State Apparatuses', in Althusser, *Lenin and Philosophy and Other Essays*, trans. Ben Brewster (London: New Left Books, 1971), pp. 160–5.

[5] Peter Stallybrass, 'Patriarchal Territories: The Body Enclosed', in Margaret W. Ferguson, Maureen Quilligan and Nancy J. Vickers, eds, *Rewriting the Renaissance* (Chicago: University of Chicago Press, 1986), p. 139. Greenblatt makes a comparable point about Jews in Marlowe's *Jew of Malta*, though in *Othello* he stresses Iago's 'ceaseless narrative invention': see *Renaissance Self-Fashioning*, pp. 208, 235. On Blacks in Shakespearean England, see Loomba, *Gender, Race, Renaissance Drama*, pp. 42–52; Ruth Cowhig, 'Blacks in English Renaissance Drama and the Role of Shakespeare's *Othello*', in David Dabydeen, ed., *The Black Presence in English Literature* (Manchester: Manchester University Press, 1985).

[6] Althusser, *Lenin and Philosophy*, pp. 123–8. For further elaboration of the theory presented here, see Alan Sinfield, *Literature, Politics and Culture in Postwar Britain* (Oxford: Basil Blackwell; Berkeley, Calif.: University of California Press, 1989), Ch. 3.

knowledges to keep material production going – diverse technical skills and wisdoms in agriculture, industry, science, medicine, economics, law, geography, languages, politics, and so on. And they need understandings, intuitive and explicit, of a system of social relationships within which the whole process can take place more or less evenly. Ideology produces, makes plausible, concepts and systems to explain who we are, who the others are, how the world works.

The strength of ideology derives from the way it gets to be common sense; it 'goes without saying'. For its production is not an external process, stories are not outside ourselves, something we just hear or read about. Ideology makes sense for us – of us – because it is already proceeding when we arrive in the world, and we come to consciousness in its terms. As the world shapes itself around and through us, certain interpretations of experience strike us as plausible: they fit with what we have experienced already, and are confirmed by others around us. So we complete what Colin Sumner calls a 'circle of social reality': 'understanding produces its own social reality at the same time as social reality produces its own understanding.'[7] This is apparent when we observe how people in other cultures than our own make good sense of the world in ways that seem strange to us: their outlook is supported by their social context. For them, those frameworks of perception, maps of meaning, work.

The conditions of plausibility are therefore crucial. They govern our understandings of the world and how to live in it, thereby seeming to define the scope of feasible political change. Most societies retain their current shape, not because dissidents are penalized or incorporated, though they are, but because many people believe that things have to take more or less their present form – that improvement is not feasible, at least through the methods to hand. That is why one recognizes a dominant ideology: were there not such a powerful (plausible) discourse, people would not acquiesce in the injustice and humiliation that they experience. To insist on ideological construction is not to deny individual agency (though it makes individual agency less interesting). Rather, the same structure informs individuals and the society. Anthony Giddens compares the utterance of a grammatical sentence, which is governed by the lexicon and syntactical rules that constitute the language, but is individual and, through its utterance, may both confirm and slightly modify the language.[8]

Ideology is produced everywhere and all the time in the social order, but some institutions – by definition, those that usually corroborate the prevailing power arrangements – are vastly more powerful than others. The stories they endorse are more difficult to challenge, even to disbelieve. Such institutions, and the people in them, are also constituted in ideology; they are figures in its stories. At the same time, I would not want to lose a traditional sense of the power elite in the state exercising authority, through the ideological framework it both inhabits and maintains, over subordinate groups. This process may be observed in Shakespearean plays, where the most effective

[7]   Colin Sumner, *Reading Ideologies* (London and New York: Academic Press, 1979), p. 288.
[8]   Anthony Giddens, *Central Problems in Social Theory* (London: Macmillan, 1979), pp. 69–71, 77–8. Giddens's development of *langue* and *parole* is anticipated in Michel Foucault, *The Order of Things,* trans. Alan Sheridan (London: Tavistock, 1970), p. 380.

stories are given specific scope and direction by powerful men. They authorize scripts, we may say, that the other characters resist only with difficulty. Very often this does not require any remarkable intervention, or seems to involve only a 'restoration of order', for the preferences of the ruling elite are already attuned to the system as it is already running. Conversely, scripting from below by lower-order characters immediately appears subversive; consider Shylock, Malvolio, Don John, Iago, Edmund, Macbeth, Caliban. Women may disturb the system (I return to this shortly), and in early comedies they are allowed to script, sometimes even in violation of parental wishes, but their scripts lead to the surrender of their power in the larger story of marriage. Elsewhere, women who script men are bad – Goneril and Regan, Lady Macbeth, the Queen in *Cymbeline*. Generally, the scripting of women by men is presented as good for them. Miranda's marriage in *The Tempest* seems to be all that Prospero has designed it to be. In *Measure for Measure*, Isabella is given by the Duke the script she ought to want – all the men in the play have conspired to draw her away from an independent life in the convent. To be sure, these are not the scripts of men only. As Stephen Orgel remarks, the plays must have appealed to the women in the audience as well: these were the fantasies of a whole culture.[9] But insofar as they show the powerful dominating the modes in which ideology is realized, these plays record an insight into ideology and power.

The state is the most powerful scriptor; it is best placed to enforce its story. In *Othello,* the Duke offers Brabantio, for use against Desdemona's alleged enchanter, 'the bloody book of law' (1.3.67–70): the ruling elite have written this, and they decree who shall apply it. At the end of the play, Othello tries to control the story that will survive him – 'When you shall these unlucky deeds relate, / Speak of them as they are . . .' (5.2.342–3). However, the very last lines are spoken by Lodovico, the Venetian nobleman and representative of the Senate: 'Myself will straight aboard, and to the state / This heavy act with heavy heart relate.' The state and the ruling elite will tell Othello's story in the way they choose. They will try to control Iago's story as well, torturing him until he speaks what they want to hear: the state falls back on direct coercion when its domination of the conditions of plausibility falters. Through violence against Iago, the state means to make manifest his violence while legitimating its own.

The relation between violence and the ideological power of the state may be glimpsed in the way Othello justifies himself, in his last speech, as a good Venetian: he boasts of killing someone. Not Desdemona – that, he now agrees, was bad – but 'a malignant and a turban'd Turk', who 'Beat a Venetian, and traduc'd the state'. Othello says he 'took by the throat the circumcised dog, / And smote him thus' (5.2.352–7). And so, upon this recollection, Othello stabs himself, recognizing himself, for the last time, as an outsider, a discredit to the social order he has been persuaded to respect. Innumerable critics discuss

⁹ Stephen Orgel, 'Nobody's Perfect: Or Why Did the English Stage Take Boys for Women?', *South Atlantic Quarterly* 88 (1989), pp. 8–10. Jonathan Goldberg writes of the Duke's scripting in *Measure For Measure* in his *James I and the Politics of Literature* (Baltimore, Md: Johns Hopkins University Press, 1983), pp. 230–9. See also Steven Mullaney, *The Place of the Stage* (Chicago: University of Chicago Press, 1988), pp. 107–10.

Othello's suicide, but I haven't noticed them worrying about the murdered Turk. Being malignant, circumcised, and wearing a turban into the bargain, he seems not to require the sensitive attention of literary critics in Britain and North America. The character critic might take this reported murder as a last-minute revelation of Othello's long-standing propensity to desperate violence when people say things he doesn't like. But the violence here is not Othello's alone, any more than Venetian racism and sexism are particular to individuals. Othello's murder of the Turk is the kind of thing the Venetian state likes – or so we must assume, since Othello is in good standing in Venice as a state servant, and presents the story to enhance his credit. 'He was great of heart', Cassio enthuses (5.2.362), pleased that he has found something to retrieve his respect for Othello. In respect of murdering state enemies, at least, he was a good citizen.

It is a definition of the state, almost, that it claims a monopoly of legitimate violence, and the exercise of that violence is justified through stories about the barbarity of those who are constituted as its demonized others. For the Venetians, as for the Elizabethans, the Turks were among the barbarians.[10] In actuality, in most states that we know of, the civilized and the barbaric are not very different from each other; that is why maintaining the distinction is such a constant ideological task. It is not altogether Othello's personal achievement, or his personal failure, therefore, when he kills himself declaring, with respect to the Turk, that he 'smote him thus'. Othello becomes a good subject once more by accepting within himself the state's distinction between civilized and barbaric. This 'explains' how he has come to murder Desdemona: it was the barbarian beneath, or rather in, the skin. And when he kills himself it is even better, because he eradicates the intolerable confusion of finding both the citizen and the alien in the same body. Othello's particular circumstances bring into visibility, for those who want to see, the violence upon which the state and its civilization rest.

Structure and Individuals

My argument has reached the point where I have to address the scope for dissidence within ideological construction. 'The class which is the ruling material force is, at the same time, its ruling intellectual force. The class which has the means of material production at its disposal, has control at the same time over the means of mental production', Marx and Engels declare in *The German Ideology*.[11] The point is surely only sensible: groups with material power will dominate the institutions that deal with ideas. That is why people

[10] On attitudes to Turks, see Simon Shepherd, *Marlowe and the Politics of Elizabethan Theatre* (New York: St Martin's Press, 1986), pp. 142–9. The later part of Othello's career, in fact, has been devoted entirely to state violence – as Martin Orkin has suggested, he is sent to Cyprus to secure it for the colonial power: see Orkin, *Shakespeare against Apartheid* (Craighall, South Africa: Ad. Donker, 1987), pp. 88–96.

[11] Karl Marx and Friedrich Engels, *The German Ideology* (London: Lawrence and Wishart, 1965), p. 61. See further Althusser, *Lenin and Philosophy*, pp. 139–42; Pierre Bourdieu, 'Cultural Reproduction and Social Reproduction', in Richard Brown, ed., *Knowledge, Education and Cultural Change* (London: Tavistock, 1973).

can be persuaded to believe things that are neither just, humane, nor to their advantage. The issue is pressed harder in modern cultural theory. In work deriving from Althusser and Foucault, distinct as those two sources are, ideological constructedness, not just of our ideas but of our subjectivities, seems to control the scope for dissident thought and expression. This is a key question: if we come to consciousness within a language that is continuous with the power structures that sustain the social order, how can we conceive, let alone organize, resistance?

The issue has been raised sharply by feminist critics, in particular Lynda E. Boose and Carol Thomas Neely. They accuse both new historicism and cultural materialism of theorizing power as an unbreakable system of containment, a system that positions subordinate groups as effects of the dominant, so that female identity, for instance, appears to be something fathered upon women by patriarchy.[12] How, it is asked, can women produce a dissident perspective from such a complicit ideological base? And so with other subordinated groups: if the conditions of plausibility persuade black or gay people to assume subjectivities that suit the maintenance of the social order, how is a radical black or gay consciousness to arise?

Kathleen McLuskie's argument that *Measure for Measure* and *King Lear* are organized from a male point of view has received particular attention. There is no way, McLuskie says, to find feminist heroines in Regan and Goneril, the wicked women, or in the good woman, Cordelia. Feminist criticism 'is restricted to exposing its own exclusion from the text'.[13] The alternative feminist position, which we may term a humanist or essentialist feminism, is stated by Carolyn Ruth Swift Lenz, Gayle Greene, and Carol Thomas Neely in their ground-breaking collection of essays, *The Woman's Part*. They believe feminist critics should, typically, be finding that Shakespeare's women characters are *not* male constructions – not 'the saints, monsters, or whores their critics have often perceived them to be'. Rather, 'like the male characters the women are complex and flawed, like them capable of passion and pain, growth and decay.'[14] This perspective is evidently at odds with the approach I am presenting. In my view, when traditional critics perceive Shakespearean women characters in terms of stereotypes, they are often more or less right. Such critics recognize in the plays the ideological structures that our cultures have been producing. My dispute with them begins when they admire the patterns they find and collaborate in rendering them

---

[12] See Lynda E. Boose, 'The Family in Shakespearean Studies; or – Studies in the Family of Shakespeareans; or – the Politics of Politics', *Renaissance Quarterly* 40 (1987), pp. 707–42; Carol Thomas Neely, 'Constructing the Subject: Feminist Practice and the New Renaissance Discourses', *English Literary Renaissance* 18 (1988), pp. 5–18.

[13] Kathleen McLuskie, 'The Patriarchal Bard: Feminist Criticism and Shakespeare', in Jonathan Dollimore and Alan Sinfield, eds, *Political Shakespeare* (Manchester: Manchester University Press; Ithaca, NY: Cornell University Press, 1985), p. 97. For a reply to her critics by Kathleen McLuskie, see her *Renaissance Dramatists* (Hemel Hempstead: Harvester Wheatsheaf, 1989), pp. 224–9; and for further comment, Jonathan Dollimore, 'Shakespeare, Cultural Materialism, Feminism and Marxist Humanism', *New Literary History* 21 (1990), pp. 471–93.

[14] Carolyn Ruth Swift Lenz, Gayle Greene and Carol Thomas Neely, eds, *The Woman's Part* (Urbana, Ill.: University of Illinois Press, 1980), p. 5.

plausible, instead of offering a critique of them. As McLuskie says, we should attend to 'the narrative, poetic and theatrical strategies which construct the plays' meanings and position the audience to understand their events from a particular point of view'.[15]

There are in fact two issues here. One is whether there is (for women or men) any such fullness of personhood as Lenz, Greene, and Neely propose, or whether subjectivity is, as I have been arguing, an effect of cultural production. The other is the authority of Shakespeare: can we reasonably assume that he anticipated a progressive modern sexual politics? As McLuskie points out, he was working within 'an entertainment industry which, as far as we know, had no women shareholders, actors, writers, or stage hands' (p. 92). Ultimately these issues converge: the idea that Shakespearean texts tune into an essential humanity, transcending cultural production, is aligned with the idea that individual characters do that. As Lynda Boose says, the question is whether the human being is conceived as inscribing 'at least something universal that transcends history, or as an entity completely produced by its historical culture'. Boose credits McLuskie with 'unblinkered honesty', but complains that one has 'to renounce completely one's pleasure in Shakespeare and embrace instead the rigorous comforts of ideological correctness'.[16] Maybe one does (try listening again to the words of most Christmas carols); but pleasure in Shakespeare is a complex phenomenon, and it may not be altogether incompatible with a critical attitude to ideology in the plays.

The essentialist-humanist approach to literature and sexual politics depends upon the belief that the individual is the probable, indeed necessary, source of truth and meaning. Literary significance and personal significance seem to derive from and speak to individual consciousnesses. But thinking of ourselves as essentially individual tends to efface processes of cultural production and, in the same movement, leads us to imagine ourselves to be autonomous, self-determining. It is not individuals but power structures that produce the system within which we live and think, and focusing upon the individual makes it hard to discern those structures; and if we discern them, hard to do much about them, since that would require collective action. To adopt the instance offered by Richard Ohmann in his book *English in America*, each of us buys an automobile because we need it to get around, and none of us, individually, does much damage to the environment or other people. But from that position it is hard to get to address, much less do anything about, whether we should be living in an automobile culture at all.[17]

I believe feminist anxiety about derogation of the individual in cultural materialism is misplaced, since personal subjectivity and agency are, anyway, unlikely sources of dissident identity and action. Political awareness does not

[15] McLuskie, 'The Patriarchal Bard', p. 92.

[16] Boose, 'The Family in Shakespearean Studies', pp. 734, 726, 724. See also Ann Thompson, '"The warrant of womanhood": Shakespeare and Feminist Criticism', in Graham Holderness, ed., *The Shakespeare Myth* (Manchester: Manchester University Press, 1988); Judith Newton, 'History as Usual?: Feminism and the New Historicism', *Cultural Critique* 9 (1988), pp. 87–121.

[17] Richard Ohmann, *English in America* (New York: Oxford University Press, 1976), p. 313. See V.N. Voloshinov, *Marxism and the Philosophy of Language*, trans. Ladislav Matejka and I.R. Titunik (New York and London: Seminar Press, 1973), pp. 17–24, 83–98.

arise out of an essential, individual self-consciousness of class, race, nation, gender, or sexual orientation; but from involvement in *a milieu, a subculture.* 'In acquiring one's conception of the world one belongs to a particular grouping which is that of all the social elements which share the same mode of thinking and acting', Gramsci observes.[18] It is through such sharing that one may learn to inhabit plausible oppositional preoccupations and forms – ways of relating to others – and hence develop a plausible oppositional selfhood. That is how successful movements have worked.

These issues have been most thoroughly considered by recent theorists of lesbian identity. Judith Butler argues against a universalist concept, 'woman', not only on the ground that it effaces diversities of time and place, but also because it is oppressive: it necessarily involves 'the exclusion of those who fail to conform to unspoken normative requirements of the subject'.[19] Butler asks if 'unity' is indeed necessary for effective political action, pointing out that 'the articulation of an identity within available cultural terms instates a definition that forecloses in advance the emergence of new identity concepts in and through politically engaged actions' (p. 15). For agency to operate, Butler points out, a 'doer' does not have to be in place first; rather, she or he is constructed through the deed. Identity develops, precisely, in the process of signification: 'identity is always already signified, and yet continues to signify as it circulates within various interlocking discourses' (pp. 142–3). So 'construction is not opposed to agency; it is the necessary scene of agency, the very terms in which agency is articulated and becomes culturally intelligible' (p. 147). Identity is not that which produces culture, nor even that which is produced as a static entity by culture: rather, the two are the same process.

If these arguments are correct, then it is not necessary to envisage, as Neely does, 'some area of "femaleness" that is part biological, part psychical, part experiential, part cultural and that is not utterly inscribed by and in thrall to patriarchal ideology and that makes possible female discourse'.[20] 'Female discourse' will be the discourse that women work out together at a historical conjuncture, and it will be rendered plausible by social interaction, especially among women. Desdemona gets closest to seeing what is going on when she talks with Emilia (what she needs is a refuge for battered wives); Othello gets it wrong because he has no reliable friends with whom to check out his perceptions. Subcultures constitute consciousness, in principle, in the same way that dominant ideologies do – but in partly dissident forms. In that bit of the world where the subculture runs, you can feel confident, as we used to say, that Black is beautiful, gay is good: there, those stories work, they build their own kinds of interactive plausibility. Validating the individual may seem attractive because it appears to empower him or her, but actually it undervalues potential resources of collective understanding and resistance.

---

[18] Antonio Gramsci, *Selections from the Prison Notebooks,* ed. and trans. Quintin Hoare and Geoffrey Nowell-Smith (London: Lawrence and Wishart, 1971), p. 324.

[19] Judith Butler, *Gender Trouble* (London: Routledge, 1990), p. 6. See Celia Kitzinger, *The Social Construction of Lesbianism* (London: Sage, 1987). Diana Fuss asks: 'Is politics based on identity, or is identity based on politics?' (*Essentially Speaking* [London: Routledge, 1989], p. 100, and see Ch. 6).

[20] Neely, 'Constructing the Subject', p. 7.

Entrapment and Faultlines

While the ideology of individualism is associated mainly with traditional modes of literary criticism, the poststructuralist vein in recent cultural work, including new historicism, has also helped to obscure the importance of collectivities and social location. A principal theoretical task in such work has been to reassess the earlier Marxist base/superstructure model, whereby culture was seen as a one-way effect of economic organization. (In apparent ignorance of this work, much of which has been conducted in Europe, J. Hillis Miller supposes that people of 'the so-called left' hold 'an unexamined ideology of the material base'.[21]) It was necessary to abandon that model, but in the process, as Peter Nicholls has pointed out, the tendency in new historicism has been 'to replace a model of mechanical causality with one of structural homology'. And this works to 'displace the concepts of production and class which would initiate a thematics of historical change'. Homology discovers synchronic structural connectedness without determination, sometimes without pressure or tension. Hence 'the problem of ideology becomes a purely superstructural one.'[22] The agency that has sunk from view, following Nicholls's argument, is that, not of individuals, but of classes, class fractions, and groups. Yet Marx was surely right to envisage such collectivities as the feasible agents of historical change.

New historicism has been drawn to what I call the 'entrapment model' of ideology and power, whereby even, or especially, manoeuvres that seem designed to challenge the system help to maintain it. Don E. Wayne says new historicism has often shown 'how different kinds of discourse intersect, contradict, destabilize, cancel, or modify each other . . . seek[ing] to demonstrate how a dominant ideology will give a certain rein to alternative discourses, ultimately appropriating their vitality and containing their oppositional force'.[23] The issue informs the ambiguous title of *Renaissance Self-Fashioning*: Stephen Greenblatt's central figures aspired to fashion themselves, but he finds that their selves were fashioned for them. So Wyatt

[21] J. Hillis Miller, 'Presidential Address, 1986: The Triumph of Theory, the Resistance to Reading, and the Question of the Material Base', *PMLA* 102 (1987), pp. 290–1. Cf. Raymond Williams, 'Base and Superstructure in Marxist Cultural Theory', *New Left Review* 82 (1973), pp. 3–16; reprinted in Williams, *Problems in Materialism and Culture* (London: Verso, 1980; New York: Schocken Books, 1981). James Holstun, 'Ranting at the New Historicism', *English Literary Renaissance* 19 (1989), pp. 189–225, makes more effort than most to address European/Marxist work.

[22] Peter Nicholls, 'State of the Art: Old Problems and the New Historicism', *Journal of American Studies* 23 (1989), pp. 428, 429.

[23] Don E. Wayne, 'New Historicism', in Martin Coyle, Peter Garside, Malcolm Kelsall and John Peck, eds, *Encyclopedia of Literature and Criticism* (London: Routledge, 1990), p. 795. I am grateful to Professor Wayne for showing this essay to me in typescript. Further on this topic, see Jean E. Howard and Marion F. O'Connor, 'Introduction', Don E. Wayne, 'Power, Politics and the Shakespearean Text: Recent Criticism in England and the United States' and Walter Cohen, 'Political Criticism of Shakespeare', all in Jean E. Howard and Marion F. O'Connor, eds, *Shakespeare Reproduced* (London: Methuen, 1987); Louis Montrose, 'Professing the Renaissance: The Poetics and Politics of Culture', in H. Aram Veeser, ed., *The New Historicism* (New York: Routledge, 1989), pp. 20–4; Alan Liu, 'The Power of Formalism: The New Historicism', *English Literary History* 56 (1989), pp. 721–77.

'cannot fashion himself in opposition to power and the conventions power deploys; on the contrary, those conventions are precisely what constitute Wyatt's self-fashioning.'[24] Hence Carolyn Porter's complaint that the subordinate seems a mere discursive effect of the dominant in new historicism.[25]

Of course, not all work generally dubbed 'new historicist' takes such a line (not that of Louis Adrian Montrose). Nor is entrapment only here at issue – it arises generally in functionalism, structuralism, and Althusserian Marxism. Greenblatt has recently denied proposing that resistance is always coopted, and he is in my view right to say that his 'Invisible Bullets' essay has often been misinterpreted.[26] I associate the entrapment model with new historicism nevertheless, because its treatment there has been distinctively subtle, powerful, and pressured, and because it is, of course, not by chance that this aspect of new historicism has been emphasized. The notion that dissidence is characteristically contained has caught the imagination of the profession. Therefore, even while acknowledging the diversity and specificity of actual writing (which I draw upon frequently in the pages that follow), it is the aspect of new historicist thought that has to be addressed.

An instance that confronts the entrapment model at its heart is the risk that the legally constituted ruler might not be able to control the military apparatus. Valuable new historicist analyses, considering the interaction of the monarch and the court, have tended to discover 'power' moving in an apparently unbreakable circle – proceeding from and returning to the monarch. But although absolutist ideology represents the ruler as the necessary and sufficient source of national unity, the early modern state depended in the last analysis, like other states, upon military force. The obvious instance is the Earl of Essex's rebellion in 1601. With the queen ageing and military success in Cadiz to his credit, it was easy for the charismatic earl to suppose that he should not remain subordinate. Ideological and military power threaten to split apart; it is a faultline in the political structure. Indeed, army coups against legitimate but militarily dependent political leaders still occur all the time. In the United States, during the Korean War, General Douglas MacArthur believed he could override the authority of President Harry S. Truman.

In *Macbeth*, Duncan has the legitimacy but Macbeth is the best fighter. Duncan cannot but delegate power to subordinates, who may turn it back upon him – the initial rebellion is that of the Thane of Cawdor, in whom Duncan says he 'built / An absolute trust'.[27] If the thought of revolt can enter the mind of Cawdor, then it will occur to Macbeth, and others; its source is not just personal (Macbeth's ambition). Of course, it is crucial to the ideology of absolutism to deny that the state suffers such a structural flaw. Hence the projection of the whole issue onto a supernatural backdrop of good and evil,

[24] Greenblatt, *Renaissance Self-Fashioning,* pp. 120, 209–14.
[25] Carolyn Porter, 'Are We Being Historical Yet?', *South Atlantic Quarterly* 87 (1988), pp. 743–86; see also Porter, 'History and Literature: "After the New Historicism"', *New Literary History* 21 (1990), pp. 253–72.
[26] Stephen J. Greenblatt, *Learning to Curse: Essays in Early Modern Culture* (London: Routledge, 1990), pp. 164–6.
[27] Shakespeare, *Macbeth,* ed. Kenneth Muir, 9th edn (London: Methuen, 1962), 1.4.12–13.

and the implication that disruption must derive, or be crucially reinforced, from outside (by the Weird Sisters and the distinctively demonic Lady Macbeth). Macbeth's mistake, arguably, is that he falls for Duncan's ideology and loses his nerve. However, this does not mean that absolutist ideology was inevitably successful – when Charles I tried to insist upon it there was a revolution.

Henry V offers a magical resolution of this faultline by presenting the legitimate king as the triumphant war leader. The pressure of aspiration and anxiety around the matter may be gauged from the reference to Essex by the Chorus of Act 5. In the most specific contemporary allusion in any Shakespeare play, Henry V's return from France is compared first to Caesar's return as conqueror to Rome and then to Essex's anticipated return from Ireland:

> As, by a lower but by loving likelihood,
> Were now the general of our gracious empress,
> As in good time he may, from Ireland coming,
> Bringing rebellion broached on his sword,
> How many would the peaceful city quit
> To welcome him! much more, and much more cause,
> Did they this Harry.[28]

Notice the prudent qualification that this is 'a lower . . . likelihood' insofar as Essex is but 'the general of our gracious empress'; Harry would be welcomed 'much more, and much more cause'. The text strives to envisage a leader whose power, unlike that of the queen, would be uncontestable, but yet at the same time that of the queen. Promoting Elizabeth to empress (of Ireland) seems to give her a further edge over her commander. Even so the comparisons refuse to stabilize, for Henry V himself has just been likened to a caesar, and Julius Caesar threatened the government after his triumphal entry into Rome. And Elizabeth becomes empress only through Essex's military success, and that very success would enhance his potential for revolt. With the city specified as 'peaceful', it seems only thoughtful to wonder whether it would remain so. However, faultlines are by definition resistant to the fantasies that would erase them. The epilogue to *Henry V* has to record that the absolutist pyramid collapsed with the accession of Henry VI, who, precisely, was not the strongest military leader. And Essex failed to mobilize sufficient support to bring Elizabeth within his power.

My argument is that dissident potential derives ultimately not from essential qualities in individuals (though they have qualities) but from conflict and contradiction that the social order inevitably produces within itself, even as it attempts to sustain itself. Despite their power, dominant ideological formations are always, in practice, under pressure, striving to substantiate their claim to superior plausibility in the face of diverse disturbances. Hence Raymond Williams's observation that ideology has always to be *produced*: 'Social orders and cultural orders must be seen as being actively made: actively and continuously, or they may quite quickly break down.'[29] Conflict

---

[28] William Shakespeare, *King Henry V*, ed. J.H. Walter (London: Methuen, 1954), 5. Chorus. 29–35.

[29] Raymond Williams, *Culture* (Glasgow: Fontana, 1981), p. 201.

and contradiction stem from the very strategies through which ideologies strive to contain the expectations that they need to generate. This is where failure – inability or refusal – to identify one's interests with the dominant may occur, and hence where dissidence may arise. In this argument the dominant and subordinate are structurally linked, but not in the way criticized by Carolyn Porter when she says that although 'masterless men' (her instance) may ultimately have been controlled, 'their subversive resistance cannot [therefore] be understood simply as the product of the dominant culture's power.'[30] It was the Elizabethan social structure that produced unemployed labourers, and military leaders, but it could not then prevent such figures conceiving and enacting dissident practices, especially if they were able to constitute milieux within which dissidence might be rendered plausible.

Desdemona's Defiance

Another key point at which to confront the entrapment model concerns the scope of women. *Othello*, like many contemporary texts, betrays an obsessive concern with disorder; the ideology and power of the ruling elite are reasserted at the end of the play, but equilibrium is not, by any means, easily regained. The specific disruption stems from Desdemona's marital choice.[31] At her first entrance, her father asks her: 'Do you perceive in all this noble company, / Where most you owe obedience?' She replies that she sees 'a divided duty' – to her father and her husband:

I am hitherto your daughter: but here's my husband:
And so much duty as my mother show'd
To you, preferring you before her father,
So much I challenge, that I may profess,
Due to the Moor my Lord.

(1.3.179–89)

And to justify the latter allegiance, she declares: 'I did love the Moor, to live with him' (1.2.248).

This is a paradigm instance. For, in her use of the idea of a divided duty to justify elopement with an inappropriate man, Desdemona has not discovered a distinctive, radical insight (any more than Cordelia does when she uses it). She is offering a straightforward elaboration of official doctrine, which said that a woman should obey the male head of her family, who should be first her father

---

[30] Porter, 'Are We Being Historical Yet?', p. 774. For important recent discussions of the scope for movement in the early modern state, see Richard Cust and Ann Hughes, eds, *Conflict in Early Stuart England* (London: Longman, 1989), esp. Johann Sommerville, 'Ideology, Property and the Constitution'.

[31] I am not happy that race and sexuality tend to feature in distinct parts of this chapter; in this respect, my wish to clarify certain theoretical arguments has produced some simplification. Of course, race and sexuality are intertwined, in *Othello* as elsewhere. See Loomba, *Gender, Race, Renaissance Drama*, pp. 48–62; Karen Newman, '"And wash the Ethiop white": Femininity and the Monstrous in *Othello*', in Howard and O'Connor, eds, *Shakespeare Reproduced*; Jonathan Dollimore, *Sexual Dissidence* (Oxford: Oxford University Press, 1991), Part 4.

(or failing that a brother or uncle), then her husband. Before marriage, the former; afterwards, the latter. Ideally, from the point of view of the social order, it would all be straightforward. The woman's transition from daughter to wife – from one set of duties to another – would be accomplished smoothly, with the agreement of all parties. But things could go wrong here; it was an insecure moment in patriarchy. The danger derived from a fundamental complication in the ideology of gender relations. Marriage was the institution through which property arrangements were made and inheritance secured, but it was supposed also to be a fulfilling personal relationship. It was held that the people being married should act in obedience to their parents, but also that they should love each other.[32] The 'divided duty' was not especially Desdemona's problem, therefore; it is how the world was set up for her.

The Reformation intensified the issue by shifting both the status and the nature of marriage. The Catholic church held that the three reasons for matrimony were, first, to beget children; second, to avoid carnal sin; and third, for mutual help and comfort. Protestants stressed the third objective, often promoting it to first place; the homily 'Of the State of Matrimony' says: 'it is instituted of God, to the intent that man and woman should live lawfully in a perpetual friendly fellowship, to bring forth fruit, and to avoid fornication.'[33] Thus protestants defined marriage more positively, as a mutual, fulfilling, reciprocal relationship. However, they were not prepared to abandon patriarchal authority; it was too important to the system. In *Arcadia*, Philip Sidney presents an ideal marriage of reciprocity and mutual love, that of Argalus and Parthenia: 'A happy couple: he joying in her, she joying in herself, but in herself, because she enjoyed him: both increasing their riches by giving to each other; each making one life double, because they made a double life one.' However, the passage concludes: 'he ruling, because she would obey, or rather because she would obey, she therein ruling.'[34] Does this mean that Parthenia was fulfilled in her subordinate role; or that by appearing submissive she managed to insinuate her own way? Neither seems ideal. In *The Anatomy of Melancholy*, Robert Burton displays a protestant enthusiasm: 'You know marriage is honourable, a blessed calling, appointed by God himself in paradise; it breeds true peace, tranquillity, content and happiness.' But the elaboration is tricky: 'The husband rules her as head, but she again commands his heart, he is her servant, she his only joy and content.'[35] The alternation of head and heart

---

[32] I set out this argument in Alan Sinfield, *Literature in Protestant England, 1560–1660* (London: Croom Helm, 1983), Ch. 4. See also Juliet Dusinberre, *Shakespeare and the Nature of Women* (London: Macmillan, 1976); Simon Shepherd, *Amazons and Warrior Women* (Brighton: Harvester, 1981), pp. 53–6, 107–18; Catherine Belsey, *The Subject of Tragedy* (London: Methuen, 1985), Ch. 7; Dympna Callaghan, *Woman and Gender in Renaissance Tragedy* (Atlantic Highlands, NJ: Humanities Press, 1989), Ch. 2 *et passim*; McLuskie, *Renaissance Dramatists*, pp. 31–9, 50–5 *et passim*.

[33] *Certain Sermons or Homilies* (London: Society for Promoting Religious Knowledge, 1899), p. 534.

[34] Sir Philip Sidney, *Arcadia*, ed. Maurice Evans (Harmondsworth: Penguin Books, 1977), p. 501.

[35] Robert Burton, *The Anatomy of Melancholy*, ed. Holbrook Jackson (London: Dent, 1932), 3: 52–3.

sounds reciprocal but is not, for we know that the head should rule the heart. Then the strong phrasing of 'servant' reverses altogether the initial priority, introducing language more appropriate to romantic love; and finally 'only joy and content' seems to privilege the wife but also places upon her an obligation to please. Coercion and liberty jostle together unresolved, and this is characteristic of protestant attitudes.

In fact, protestantism actually strengthened patriarchal authority. The removal of the mediatory priest threw upon the head of household responsibility for the spiritual life and devout conduct of the family. Also, there was a decline in the significance of great magnates who might stand between subject and monarch. From these developments, protestants devised a comprehensive doctrine of social control, with a double chain of authority running from God to the husband to the individual, and from God to the monarch to the subject. The homily 'Against Disobedience and Wilful Rebellion' derives earthly rule from God and parallels the responsibilities of the monarch and the head of household.[36] Indeed, the latter could be said to have the more important role. 'A master in his family hath all the offices of Christ, for he must rule, and teach, and pray; rule like a king, and teach like a prophet, and pray like a priest', Henry Smith declared in 'A Preparative to Marriage' (1591). This leaves little space for independence for offspring, or anyone else in the household. Smith says parents must control marital choice because, after all, they have the property: 'If children may not make other contracts without [parents'] good will, shall they contract marriage, which have nothing to maintain it after, unless they return to beg of them whom they scorned before?'[37] As with other business deals, it is wrong to enter into marriage unless you can sustain the costs. This was one extreme; at the other, only radicals like the Digger Gerrard Winstanley proposed that 'every man and woman shall have the free liberty to marry whom they love.'[38] In between, most commentators fudged the question, suggesting that children might exercise a right of refusal, or that even if they didn't like their spouses at first, they would learn to get on. 'A couple is that whereby two persons standing in mutual relation to each other are combined together, as it were, into one. And of these two the one is always higher and beareth rule: the other is lower and yieldeth subjection', William Perkins declared.[39] The boundaries are plainly unclear, and conflict is therefore likely. Hence the awkward bullying and wheedling in the disagreements between Portia and Bassanio, Caesar and Portia, Othello and Desdemona, Macbeth and Lady Macbeth, Leontes and Hermione. Lawrence Stone says dutiful children experienced 'an impossible conflict of role models. They had to try to reconcile the often incompatible demands for obedience to parental wishes on the one hand and expectations of

[36] *Certain Sermons*, p. 589.

[37] Henry Smith, *Works*, with a Memoir by Thomas Fuller (Edinburgh, 1886), 1: 32, 19.

[38] Gerrard Winstanley, *Works*, ed. G.H. Sabine (Ithaca, NY: Cornell University Press, 1941), p. 599.

[39] William Perkins, *Christian Economy* (1609), in *The Work of William Perkins*, ed. Ian Breward (Abingdon: Sutton Courtenay Press, 1970), pp. 418–19.

affection in marriage on the other.'[40] At this point, the dominant ideology had not quite got its act together.

Parental influence over marriage in early modern England is nowadays often regarded simply as an instance of the oppressiveness of patriarchy, but that is not quite all. The ambiguity of official doctrine afforded one distinct point at which a woman such as Desdemona could produce a crisis in the patriarchal story. 'Despite the economic and social mechanisms that reinforced parental authority, it was in marriage that parents were most often defied', Dympna Callaghan observes.[41] All too often, such defiance provoked physical and mental violence; at the least it must have felt very unpleasant. That is how it is when you disturb the system – the tendency of ideology is, precisely, to produce good subjects who feel uncomfortable when they transgress. But contradictions in the ideology of marriage produced, nevertheless, an opportunity for dissidence, and even before the appearance of Othello, we are told, Desdemona was exploiting it – refusing 'The wealthy curled darlings of our nation' (1.2.68). Her more extreme action – marrying without parental permission, outside the ruling oligarchy, and outside the race – is so disruptive that the chief (male) council of the state delays its business. 'For if such actions may have passage free,' Brabantio says, 'Bond-slaves, and pagans, shall our statesmen be' (1.2.98). Desdemona throws the system into disarray – and just when the men are busy with one of their wars – killing people because of their honour and their property – proving their masculinity to each other.

To be sure, Desdemona was claiming only what Louis Montrose calls 'the limited privilege of giving herself',[42] and her moment of power ends once the men have accepted her marriage. But then dissident opportunities always are limited – otherwise we would not be living as we do. Revolutionary change is rare and usually dependent upon a prior buildup of small breaks; often there are great personal costs. The point of principle is that scope for dissident understanding and action occurs not because women characters, Shakespeare, and feminist readers have a privileged vantage point outside the dominant, but because the social order *cannot but produce* faultlines through which its own criteria of plausibility fall into contest and disarray. This has been theorized by Stuart Hall and his colleagues at the Centre for Contemporary Cultural Studies at the University of Birmingham:

[40] Lawrence Stone, *The Family, Sex and Marriage in England, 1500–1800* (London: Weidenfeld and Nicolson, 1977), p. 137. See also *op. cit.*, pp. 151–9, 178–91, 195–302; Charles and Katherine George, *The Protestant Mind of the English Reformation* (Princeton, NJ: Princeton University Press, 1961), pp. 257–94; Christopher Hill, *Society and Puritanism in Pre-Revolutionary England* (London: Panther, 1969), pp. 429–67; Louis Adrian Montrose, '"Shaping Fantasies": Figurations of Gender and Power in Elizabethan Culture', in Stephen Greenblatt, ed., *Representing the English Renaissance* (Berkeley, Calif.: University of California Press, 1988), pp. 37–40; Lisa Jardine, *Still Harping on Daughters* (Brighton: Harvester Press, 1983), Ch. 3; Leonard Tennenhouse, *Power on Display* (London: Methuen, 1986), pp. 17–30, 147–54; Patrick Collinson, *The Birthpangs of Protestant England* (London: Macmillan, 1988), Ch. 3.

[41] Callaghan, *Woman and Gender*, p. 21; also pp. 19–22, 101–5. On women's scope for negotiation, see also Ann Rosalind Jones, *The Currency of Eros: Women's Love Lyric in Europe, 1540–1620* (Bloomington, Ind.: Indiana University Press, 1990), pp. 1–10.

[42] Montrose, '"Shaping Fantasies"', p. 37. For the thought that the men in *Othello* are preoccupied with their masculinity but ineffectual, see Carol Thomas Neely, *Broken Nuptials in Shakespeare's Plays* (New Haven, Conn.: Yale University Press, 1985), pp. 119–22.

the dominant culture of a complex society is never a homogeneous structure. It is layered, reflecting different interests within the dominant class (e.g. an aristocratic versus a bourgeois outlook), containing different traces from the past (e.g. religious ideas within a largely secular culture), as well as emergent elements in the present. Subordinate cultures will not always be in open conflict with it. They may, for long periods, coexist with it, negotiate the spaces and gaps in it, make inroads into it, 'warrenning [*sic*] it from within'.[43]

Observe that this account does not offer to decide whether or not dissidence will be contained; it may not even be actualized, but may lie dormant, becoming disruptive only at certain conjunctures. But if ideology is so intricately 'layered', with so many potential modes of relation to it, it cannot but allow awareness of its own operations. In *Othello*, Emilia takes notable steps towards a dissident perception:

> But I do think it is their husbands' faults
> If wives do fall: say, that they slack their duties,
> And pour our treasures into foreign laps;
> Or else break out in peevish jealousies,
> Throwing restraint upon us; or say they strike us . . .
>
> (4.3.86–90)

Emilia has heard the doctrine of mutual fulfilment in marriage, and from the gap between it and her experience, she is well able to mount a critique of the double standard. At faultlines, such as I am proposing here, a dissident perspective may be discovered and articulated.

The crisis over marital choice illustrates how stories work in culture. It appears again and again – in *A Midsummer Night's Dream*, *The Merchant of Venice*, *The Taming of the Shrew*, *Romeo and Juliet*, *Measure for Measure*, *King Lear*, *The Winter's Tale*, *The Tempest*. Roughly speaking, in comedies parents are eventually reconciled to children's wishes; in tragedies (as in *Othello*), precipitate actions without parental authority lead to disaster. And in writing, on through the ensuing centuries until the late nineteenth century, the arranged- versus the love-match is a recurring theme in literature. This is how culture elaborates itself. In these texts, through diverse genres and institutions, people were talking to each other about an aspect of their life that they found hard to handle. When a part of our worldview threatens disruption by manifestly failing to cohere with the rest, then we reorganize and retell its story, trying to get it into shape – back into the old shape if we are conservative-minded, or into a new shape if we are more adventurous. The question of the arranged- versus the love-match died out in fiction in the late nineteenth century because then, for most people in Britain, it was resolved in favour of children's preferences, and therefore became uninteresting (but not, however, for British families deriving recently from Asia). The other great point at which the woman could disturb the system was by loving a man not her husband, and that is why adultery is such a prominent theme in literature.

---

[43] John Clarke, Stuart Hall, Tony Jefferson, and Brian Roberts, 'Subcultures, Cultures and Class', in Stuart Hall and Tony Jefferson, eds, *Resistance through Rituals* (London: Hutchinson; Birmingham: Centre for Contemporary Cultural Studies, 1976), p. 12. The final phrase is quoted from E.P. Thompson's essay 'The Peculiarities of the English'.

It upsets the husband's honour, his masculinity, and (through the bearing of illegitimate children) his property. Even the rumour of Desdemona's adultery is enough to send powerful men in the state into another anxiety.

This is why it is not unpromising to seek in literature our preoccupations with class, race, gender, and sexual orientation: it is likely that literary texts will address just such controversial aspects of our ideological formation. Those faultline stories are the ones that require most assiduous and continuous reworking; they address the awkward, unresolved issues, the ones in which the conditions of plausibility are in dispute. For authors and readers, after all, want writing to be interesting. The task for a political criticism, then, is to observe how stories negotiate the faultlines that distress the prevailing conditions of plausibility.

Reading Dissidence

The reason why textual analysis can so readily demonstrate dissidence being incorporated is that dissidence operates, necessarily, with reference to dominant structures. It has to invoke those structures to oppose them, and therefore can always, ipso facto, be discovered reinscribing that which it proposes to critique. 'Power relations are always two-way; that is to say, however subordinate an actor may be in a social relationship, the very fact of involvement in that relationship gives him or her a certain amount of power over the other', Anthony Giddens observes.[44] The inter-involvement of resistance and control is systemic: it derives from the way language and culture get articulated. Any utterance is bounded by the other utterances that the language makes possible. Its shape is the correlative of theirs: as with the duck/rabbit drawing, when you see the duck the rabbit lurks round its edges, constituting an alternative that may spring into visibility. Any position supposes its intrinsic *op*-position. All stories comprise within themselves the ghosts of the alternative stories they are trying to exclude.

It does not follow, therefore, that the outcome of the inter-involvement of resistance and control must be the incorporation of the subordinate. Indeed, Foucault says the same, though he is often taken as the theorist of entrapment. In *The History of Sexuality: An Introduction*, he says there is no 'great Refusal', but envisages 'a plurality of resistances . . . spread over time and space at varying densities, at times mobilising groups or individuals in a definitive way'. He *denies* that these must be 'only a reaction or rebound, forming with respect to the basic domination an underside that is in the end always passive, doomed to perpetual defeat'.[45] In fact, a dissident text may

[44] Giddens, *Central Problems*, p. 6. See further Raymond Williams, *Marxism and Literature* (Oxford: Oxford University Press, 1977), pp. 108–27; Fredric Jameson, 'Reification and Utopia in Mass Culture', *Social Text* 1 (1979), pp. 144–8; Colin Gordon, 'Afterword', in Michel Foucault, *Power/Knowledge*, ed. and trans. Colin Gordon (Brighton: Harvester Press, 1980).

[45] Michel Foucault, *The History of Sexuality: Volume 1: An Introduction*, trans. Robert Hurley (New York: Vintage Books, 1980), pp. 95–6. Also, as Jonathan Culler has remarked, Foucault's exposure of the ubiquity of regulatory practices may itself be experienced as liberatory: Culler, *Framing the Sign* (Oxford: Blackwell, 1988), pp. 66–7.

derive its leverage, its purchase, precisely from its partial implication with the dominant. It may embarrass the dominant by appropriating its concepts and imagery. For instance, it seems clear that nineteenth-century legal, medical, and sexological discourses on homosexuality made possible new forms of control; but, at the same time, they also made possible what Foucault terms 'a "reverse" discourse', whereby 'homosexuality began to speak in its own behalf, to demand that its legitimacy or "naturality" be acknowledged, often in the same vocabulary, using the same categories by which it was medically disqualified.'[46] Deviancy returns from abjection by deploying just those terms that relegated it there in the first place. A dominant discourse cannot prevent 'abuse' of its resources. Even a text that aspires to contain a subordinate perspective must first bring it into visibility; even to misrepresent, one must present. And once that has happened, there can be no guarantee that the subordinate will stay safely in its prescribed place. Readers do not have to respect closures – we do not, for instance, have to accept that the independent women characters in Shakespearean comedies find their proper destinies in the marriage deals at the ends of those plays. We can insist on our sense that the middle of such a text arouses expectations that exceed the closure.

Conversely, a text that aspires to dissidence cannot control meaning either. It is bound to slide into disabling nuances that it fails to anticipate, and it cannot prevent the drawing of reactionary inferences by readers who want to do that. (Among other things, this might serve as a case against ultra-leftism, by which I mean the complacency of finding everyone else to be ideologically suspect.) There can be no security in textuality: no scriptor can control the reading of his or her text. And when, in any instance, either incorporation or resistance turns out to be the more successful, that is not in the nature of things. It is because of *their relative strengths in that situation.* So it is not quite as Jonathan Goldberg has recently put it, turning the entrapment model inside out, that 'dominant discourses allow their own subversion precisely because hegemonic control is an impossible dream, a self-deluding fantasy.'[47] Either outcome depends on the specific balance of historical forces. Essex's rebellion failed because he could not muster adequate support on the day. It is the same with competence. Williams remarks that the development of writing reinforced cultural divisions, but also that 'there was no way to teach a man to read the Bible . . . which did not also enable him to read the radical press.' Keith Thomas observes that 'the uneven social distribution of literacy skills greatly widened the gulf between the classes'; but he illustrates also the fear that 'if the poor learned to read and write they would become seditious,

---

[46] Foucault, *History of Sexuality*, p. 101. See Jonathan Dollimore and Alan Sinfield, 'Culture and Textuality: Debating Cultural Materialism', *Textual Practice* 4:1 (1990), p. 95; and Jonathan Dollimore, 'Sexuality, Subjectivity and Transgression: The Jacobean Connection', *Renaissance Drama* 17 (1986), pp. 53–82.

[47] Jonathan Goldberg, 'Speculations: *Macbeth* and Source', in Howard and O'Connor, *Shakespeare Reproduced*, pp. 244, 247. See also Jonathan Goldberg, *Writing Matter: From the Hands of the English Renaissance* (Stanford, Calif.: Stanford University Press, 1990), esp. pp. 41–55.

atheistical, and discontented with their humble position.'[48] Both may occur, in varying degrees; it was, and is, all to play for.

It is to circumvent the entrapment model that I have generally used the term *dissident* rather than *subversive*, since the latter may seem to imply achievement – that something *was subverted* – and hence (since mostly the government did not fall, patriarchy did not crumble) that containment must have occurred. 'Dissidence' I take to imply refusal of an aspect of the dominant, without prejudging an outcome. This may sound like a weaker claim, but I believe it is actually stronger insofar as it posits a field necessarily open to continuing contest, in which at some conjunctures the dominant will lose ground while at others the subordinate will scarcely maintain its position. As Jonathan Dollimore has said, dissidence may provoke brutal repression, and that shows not that it was all a ruse of power to consolidate itself, but that 'the challenge really *was* unsettling'.[49]

The implications of these arguments for literary criticism are substantial, for it follows that formal textual analysis cannot determine whether a text is subversive or contained. The historical conditions in which it is being deployed are decisive. 'Nothing can be intrinsically or essentially subversive in the sense that prior to the event subversiveness can be more than potential; in other words it cannot be guaranteed a priori, independent of articulation, context and reception', Dollimore observes.[50] Nor, independently of context, can anything be said to be safely contained. This prospect scandalizes literary criticism, because it means that meaning is not adequately deducible from the text-on-the-page. The text is always a site of cultural contest, but it is never a self-sufficient site.

It is a key proposition of cultural materialism that the specific historical conditions in which institutions and formations organize and are organized by textualities must be addressed. That is what Raymond Williams was showing us for thirty years. The entrapment model is suspiciously convenient for literary criticism, because it means that little would be gained by investigating the specific historical effectivity of texts. And, indeed, Don Wayne very shrewdly suggests that the success of prominent new historicists may derive in large part from their skills in close reading – admittedly of a far wider range of texts – which satisfy entirely traditional criteria of performativity in academic criticism.[51] Cultural materialism calls for modes of knowledge that literary criticism scarcely possesses, or even knows how to discover – modes, indeed, that hitherto have been cultivated distinctively within that alien other of essentialist humanism, Marxism. These knowledges are in part the provinces of history and other social sciences – and, of course, they bring in their train

---

[48] Williams, *Culture*, pp. 94, 110; Keith Thomas, 'The Meaning of Literacy in Early Modern England', in Gerd Baumann, ed., *The Written Word: Literacy in Transition* (Oxford: Clarendon Press, 1986), pp. 116, 118.

[49] Dollimore, 'Shakespeare, Cultural Materialism, Feminism and Marxist Humanism', p. 482. See also Holstun, 'Ranting at the New Historicism'.

[50] Dollimore and Sinfield, *Political Shakespeare*, p. 13; discussed in Dollimore and Sinfield, 'Culture and Textuality'. See also Alan Liu's argument that we need to consider not only subjects and representation, but action: Liu, 'Power of Formalism', pp. 734–5.

[51] Wayne, 'New Historicism', pp. 801–2. See also Culler, *Framing the Sign*, p. 37; Porter, 'History and Literature', pp. 253–6.

questions of historiography and epistemology that require theory more complex than the tidy poststructuralist formula that everything, after all, is a text (or that everything is theatre). This prospect is valuable in direct proportion to its difficulty for, as Foucault maintains, the boundaries of disciplines effect a policing of discourses, and their erosion may, in itself, help to 'detach the power of truth from the forms of hegemony (social, economic and cultural) within which it operates at the present time' in order to constitute 'a new politics of truth'.[52]

Shakespearean plays are themselves powerful stories. They contribute to the perpetual contest of stories that constitutes culture: its representations, and our critical accounts of them, reinforce or challenge prevailing notions of what the world is like, of how it might be. 'The detailed and substantial *performance of a known model* of "people like this, relations like this", is in fact the real achievement of most serious novels and plays', Raymond Williams observes;[53] by appealing to the reader's sense of how the world is, the text affirms the validity of the model it invokes. Among other things, *Othello* invites *recognition* that this is how people are, how the world goes. That is why the criteria of plausibility are political. This effect is not countered, as essentialist humanists have long supposed, by literary quality; the more persuasive the writing, the greater its potential for political intervention.

The quintessential traditional critical activity was always interpretive, getting the text to make sense. Hence the speculation about character motivation, image patterns, thematic integration, structure: the task always was *to help the text into coherence.* And the discovery of coherence was taken as the demonstration of quality. However, such practice may feed into a reactionary politics. The easiest way to make *Othello* plausible in Britain is to rely on the lurking racism, sexism, and superstition in British culture. Why does Othello, who has considerable experience of people, fall so conveniently for Iago's stories? We can make his gullibility plausible by suggesting that black people are generally of a rather simple disposition. To explain why Desdemona elopes with Othello and then becomes so submissive, we might appeal to a supposedly fundamental silliness and passivity of women. Baffled in the attempt to find motive for Iago's malignancy, we can resort to the devil, or the consequence of skepticism towards conventional morality, or homosexuality. Such interpretations might be plausible; might 'work', as theatre people say; but only because they activate regressive aspects of our cultural formation.

Actually, coherence is a chimera, as my earlier arguments should suggest. No story can contain all the possibilities it brings into play; coherence is always selection. And the range of feasible readings depends not only on the text but on the conceptual framework within which we address it. Literary criticism tells its own stories. It is, in effect, a subculture, asserting its own distinctive criteria of plausibility. Education has taken as its brief the

[52] 'The Political Function of the Intellectual', trans. Colin Gordon, *Radical Philosophy* 17 (1977), p. 14; see Eve Tavor Bannet, *Structuralism and the Logic of Dissent* (London: Macmillan, 1989), pp. 170–83.

[53] Williams, *Marxism and Literature*, p. 209.

socialization of students into these criteria, while masking this project as the achievement by talented individuals (for it is in the program that most should fail) of a just and true reading of texts that are just and true. A cultural materialist practice will review the institutions that retell the Shakespeare stories, and will attempt also a self-consciousness about its own situation within those institutions. We need not just to produce different readings but to shift the criteria of plausibility.

---

10 Catherine Belsey

From *Towards Cultural History – in Theory and Practice*

Textual Practice, volume 3, number 2, 1989, pp. 159–68.

I

Is there a place for English in a postmodern world? Does an academy where twentieth-century textual practice breaks down the nineteenth-century boundaries between disciplines offer English departments any worthwhile job to do? Can we still seriously set out to teach our students literature?

I start from the assumption that English as it has traditionally been understood, as the study of great literary works by great authors, has no useful part to play in a pedagogy committed to a politics of change. In the course of the 1980s the institution of English has been firmly stripped of its mask of polite neutrality by Peter Widdowson, Chris Baldick, Terry Eagleton and Terence Hawkes, among others.[1] As their analyses reveal, the conservatism of traditional English lies primarily in two main areas: first, its promotion of the author-subject as the individual origin of meaning, insight, and truth; and second, its claim that this truth is universal, transcultural and ahistorical. In this way, English affirms as natural and inevitable both the individualism and the world picture of a specific western culture, and within that culture the perspective of a specific class and a specific sex. In other words, a discipline that purports to be outside politics in practice reproduces a very specific political position.

But I start equally from the assumption that there is no special political or pedagogical merit in severing all ties with the texts the institution of English has done its best to make its own. It would be ironic if a theory of difference left us unable to differentiate between Bradley's *Othello* and Leavis's, and between these *Othello*s and all the others we might produce for quite other

---

[1] Peter Widdowson, ed., *Re-Reading English* (London: Methuen, 1982); Chris Baldick, *The Social Mission of English Criticism, 1848–1932* (Oxford: Oxford University Press, 1983); Terry Eagleton, *Literary Theory: An Introduction* (Oxford: Basil Blackwell, 1983); Terence Hawkes, *That Shakespeherian Rag* (London: Methuen, 1986).

purposes. It would be still more ironic if by a kind of political ultra-leftism we abandoned *Othello* and the entire institution with all its (precisely institutional) power – and handed it back without a struggle to those for whom a politics of change is more of a threat than a promise. The works that the institution of English has done everything to appropriate are there to be reclaimed and reappropriated, and there is no reason why this should not be done from within the institution. The texts are available to be reread as the material for a history of meanings and values and practices in their radical discontinuity. In this way new work might be expected to come from the English department itself, and not just from somewhere else called, say, Cultural Studies. My project for English, therefore, is not to abandon it but to *move* it – towards cultural history.

Much of the work of the institution has been, of course, a process of exclusion. The canon of great books by great authors has been important not only for what it affirms – the value and the coherence of admissible readings of those works it recognizes. As every feminist, for example, knows, its importance also lies in what it refuses. Dale Spender has recently unearthed nearly 600 novels from the century before Jane Austen, by a hundred women novelists who were taken seriously in their own period. As she points out, Ian Watt's extremely influential book, *The Rise of the Novel*, takes no account of their existence. As far as the institution is concerned, the novel was invented by men. *The Rise of the Novel* is subtitled *Studies in Defoe, Richardson and Fielding*.[2]

The relegation of certain authors, of particular texts and, above all, of specific textual practices helps to police the boundaries of truth. Texts which are most obviously difficult to recuperate, which most obviously challenge conservative assumptions about race, class, or gender, have been systematically marginalized as 'flawed', or banished from view (and in consequence from print) as inadequate, not *literature*. They are, of course, flawed and inadequate according to literary standards invoked precisely to marginalize them – standards which have denied their own relativity, and indeed the cultural and historical specificity of imposing 'literary standards' at all.

The cultural history I should like to see us produce would refuse nothing. While of course any specific investigation would find a specific focus, both chronologically and textually, no moment, no epoch, no genre and no form of signifying practice would be excluded a priori from the field of enquiry. Cultural history would have no place for a canon, and no interest in ranking works in order of merit. Stephen Greenblatt's discussion of the reformer Tyndale, for instance, in his book *Renaissance Self-Fashioning,* shows some of the advantages of linking literature with a manual of religious politics in the analysis of sixteenth-century subjectivity. Greenblatt treats *The Obedience of a Christian Man* not as background in the conventional way, but as text.[3] Indeed, Louis Adrian Montrose, like Greenblatt an American New Historicist, identifies his own position in terms which closely resemble the project I am trying to define here. New Historicism is new, Montrose points out, 'in its

---

[2] See Dale Spender, *Mothers of the Novel* (London: Pandora, 1986), pp. 115–37.
[3] Stephen Greenblatt, *Renaissance Self-Fashioning: From More to Shakespeare* (Chicago: University of Chicago Press, 1980).

refusal of traditional distinctions between literature and history, between text and context; new in resisting a traditional opposition of the privileged individual – whether an author or a work – to a world "outside" '.[4] In a rather different way, Jacqueline Rose's book on *Peter Pan* also rejects traditional distinctions and oppositions. Rose brings together children's fiction, the notion of the child and the history of sexuality in ways that throw into relief the limitations on our knowledge imposed by conventional value-judgments and conventional reading practices.[5] Without wanting to deny the specificity of fiction, of genre and, indeed, of the individual text, cultural history would necessarily take all signifying practice as its domain.

And that means that the remaining demarcation lines between disciplines would not survive the move. Signifying practice is not exclusively nor even primarily verbal. We need, for example, to align ourselves with art historians. I have invoked portraits in the analysis of changing meanings of gender relations.[6] John Barrell and Norman Bryson have both in different ways demonstrated much more extensively the kind of work that becomes possible when writing and painting are brought into conjunction, without treating one as the background which explains the other.[7] And perhaps more eccentrically, but only marginally so, the allocation of domestic space is replete with meanings for the cultural historian. The medieval move of the feast from the hall to the great chamber, which was also for sleeping in (or rather, to the great chambers, since the lady, if she was involved in the feast at all, was likely to dine in her own chamber),[8] and the subsequent isolation of the family dining-room from the servants' quarters, is as significant in charting the history of the meaning of the family as is the current vogue for open-plan living. What is at stake in each of these changes is the definition of the family unit. And meanwhile, Girouard's account of the development of the privy in his book on the English country house constitutes a mine of information indispensable to any truly thorough analysis of the bourgeois disavowal of the body.[9]

II

As this rudimentary reading list reveals, I don't imagine that cultural history is my own invention. It is necessary only to point to the work of Christopher Hill and E.P. Thompson, or of Philippe Ariès and Marina Warner, to give authority

---

[4] Louis Adrian Montrose, 'The Elizabethan Subject and the Spenserian Text', in Patricia Parker and David Quint, eds, *Literary Theory/Renaissance Texts* (Baltimore, Md.: Johns Hopkins University Press, 1986), pp. 303–40, 304.

[5] Jacqueline Rose, *Peter Pan, or the Impossibility of Children's Fiction* (London: Macmillan, 1984).

[6] Catherine Belsey, 'Disrupting Sexual Difference: Meaning and Gender in the Comedies', in John Drakakis, ed., *Alternative Shakespeares* (London: Methuen, 1985), pp. 166-90; *The Subject of Tragedy: Identity and Difference in Renaissance Drama* (London: Methuen, 1985).

[7] John Barrell, *The Dark Side of the Landscape: The Rural Poor in English Painting, 1730–1840* (Cambridge: Cambridge University Press, 1980); Norman Bryson, *Word and Image: French Painting of the Ancien Régime* (Cambridge: Cambridge University Press, 1981).

[8] Mark Girouard, *Life in the English Country House* (Harmondsworth: Penguin Books, 1980).

[9] Girouard, *Life in the English Country House*, pp. 245–66.

to such a project. Here fiction is one source, and not necessarily a privileged one, of knowledge about the past. Meanwhile, the recent phase of feminist criticism received a considerable impetus from three books published in 1970 by Kate Millett, Germaine Greer, and Eva Figes. All three discussed literature, and all three refused to isolate it from the culture of which it formed a part. The writings of Freud and Barbara Cartland, for example, were invoked by these feminists, and were treated neither as explanatory metalanguage in the first case, nor as cultural context in the second, but in both instances as texts alongside Shakespeare, D.H. Lawrence, and Norman Mailer. And, of course, the transformation of English into cultural history would be unthinkable without the example of Raymond Williams, who above all established a tradition of radical critical work from within the institution of English itself.

But in listing this methodologically and politically disparate group of writers, I become conscious of the need at this stage to clarify precisely what it is that cultural history enables us to know, and to reflect on why it is that we might want to know it. Without intending at all to diminish the radical importance of their work, or my own debts to all of them, I am not now sure that every form of knowledge that each of these authors has pursued is either available to us on the one hand or politically productive on the other.

Early in *Of Grammatology*, Derrida, whose admirers have so often presented him as contemptuous of history, suggests that there remains to be written a history of writing itself, or rather, a history of what he calls 'the system of signified truth'.[10] What Derrida is proposing here is the story of God, of the transcendental signified which holds all other meanings in place, and he offers a series of quotations from different historical moments which identify the truth as alternatively God or his surrogates, nature, reason, the self. (Derrida is explicitly discussing a continuity here, but he of all people would hardly be likely to rule out some very significant differences between these terms.) And early in volume 2 of *The History of Sexuality* Foucault, whose admirers are so often anxious to see his work in opposition to Derrida's, gives a general account of his own project: 'what I have held to, what I have tried to maintain for many years, is the effort to isolate some of the elements that might be useful for a history of truth.'[11] For all their important differences, Derrida and Foucault both identify a mode of history which is profoundly political. To possess the truth is to have the right to act in its name. Truth stands outside culture as a guarantee of legitimacy. Despite the familiar romance of truth, secretly so dear to academics, in which the special and solitary hero sets out to go beyond the bounds of convention on a lonely quest for transcendental presence, in historical practice the metaphysics of truth has licensed torture, exploitation, and mass murder. Poststructuralism now displays truth as a linguistic tyranny which arrests the proliferation of meanings, assigns values and specifies norms. Truth recruits subjects. The history of truth is the history of our subjection. Its content is the knowledges that constitute us as subjects, and that define and delimit what it is possible for us to say, to be and to do.

[10] Jacques Derrida, *Of Grammatology*, trans. Gayatri Chakravorty Spivak (Baltimore, Md.: Johns Hopkins University Press, 1976), p. 15.
[11] Michel Foucault, *The History of Sexuality, Volume 2: The Use of Pleasure*, trans. Robert Hurley (London: Viking Press, 1986), p. 6.

It might be worth a digression here to stress the argument that to abandon truth is not necessarily to embrace the free-for-all of radical subjectivism. And it is not inevitably to endorse a politics of relativism or, worse, expediency. The proposition is that we cannot *know* that any existing language maps the world adequately, that there can be no certainty of a fit between the symbolic and the real. This is not the same as encouraging people to subscribe to whatever conviction happens to come into their heads, or inciting them to make things up. Nor is it to settle for believing them when they do. It is perfectly possible to recognize lies without entailing the possibility of telling the truth, least of all the whole truth. It would be very naive indeed to claim that people do not from time to time set out to deceive each other, or that institutions and states do not practise cover-ups on a deplorable scale. But what they conceal is what they know, and since there can be no guarantee that any system of differences maps the world accurately, knowledge is necessarily culturally and discursively relative. This does not exonerate the liars. They are culpable. But neither does it support the belief that in order to be able to denounce lies, we have to cling to a metaphysics of truth. Language is a system of differences, not of binary oppositions. As Foucault argues in another but related context, alternatives which only offer either the old constraints or no constraints at all are 'simplistic and authoritarian', and we should refuse to be coerced by them.[12] You can tell it like you know it, in accordance with the rules of the discourse, without having to claim that you're telling it like it (absolutely, metaphysically, incontrovertibly) *is*.

It is my empirical observation, offered here for debate, that whereas men in general have the greatest difficulty in surrendering the concept of truth, women in general do so without much trouble. The explanation is almost certainly not biological. The cultural construction of women – as of other marginal groups – tends to include rather less emphasis on the possession of truth. Marginal subjects commonly have an oblique relationship to the world map which guarantees the imaginary knowing, mastering autonomy of those who speak from the centre of a culture. The map always represents a knowledge of which those at the margins are at least partly the objects rather than the subjects, and from which they are at least from time to time excluded. Their identity as subjects is thus less evidently dependent on the reaffirmation of the map itself. Conversely, however, marginality of this kind protects women from the fear that if the world is not exactly as we have mapped it, perhaps it is not there at all, or the conviction that the alternative to truth is chaos or absence. As women, we know that, whatever form it may take, the real is there and is independent of our will: we are, after all, consistently assaulted, constrained, defined and reconstructed by it. Cartesian doubt, Catharine MacKinnon points out, 'comes from the luxury of a position of power that entails the possibility of making the world as one thinks it to be'.[13] Most women, however

[12] Michel Foucault, 'What is Enlightenment?', in Paul Rabinow, ed., *The Foucault Reader* (Harmondsworth: Penguin Books, 1986), pp. 32–50, 43.

[13] Catharine A. MacKinnon, 'Desire and Power: A Feminist Perspective', in Cary Nelson and Lawrence Grossberg, eds, *Marxism and the Interpretation of Culture* (London: Macmillan, 1988), pp. 105–21, 113.

individually powerful, have only a sporadic or oblique hold on that luxury; they can therefore relinquish the totalizing narratives of their culture with relative equanimity.

III

If the ultimate objective of a politically radical cultural history is the history of truth, its location is the history of meanings. Not exactly concerned with images and representations, in so far as those terms indicate an exteriority, gesture towards a presence which is always elsewhere, cultural history is nevertheless not quite a history of behaviour or conduct either. The project is to identify the meanings in circulation in earlier periods, to specify the discourses, conventions and signifying practices by which meanings are fixed, norms 'agreed' and truth defined. Cultural history is thus a history of 'experience' only, as Foucault puts it, 'where experience is understood as the correlation between fields of knowledge, types of normativity, and forms of subjectivity in a particular culture'.[14] The constraints on knowledge, normativity, and subjectivity are the ranges of meaning culturally and discursively available. What it is possible to 'experience' at any specific moment is an effect of what it is possible to say. (Not, of course, what I am personally capable of formulating, but *what can be said* and thus known.) And in case this proposition should be interpreted as a piece of unregenerate structuralism, it is perhaps useful to reaffirm that meanings are always plural, subject to excess, in process, contradictory, sites of struggle.

It is important to bear in mind, too, that wherever there is a history of subjection to norms and truths, there is also a history of resistances. Power produces resistance not only as its legitimation, as the basis for an extension of control, but as its defining difference, the other which endows it with meaning, visibility, effectivity. The work of Foucault is an important influence here. His position is often represented, by Foucault's admirers and his detractors alike, as negative, nihilistic, an account of power as a new transcendental signified, irreducible and irresistible in its omnipresence. Some of the New Historicists have borrowed from Foucault in order to produce an account of history, especially Renaissance history, which is so close in many ways to the kind of cultural history I am proposing here that it seems important to attempt to distinguish between the two. Of course, New Historicism is by no means a unified phenomenon, and any generalization is likely to obliterate important differences of emphasis. But if it is possible to point to general tendencies, this is a form of cultural history in which power is commonly seen as centred, usually in the monarchy, and is held to produce opposition only in order to legitimate its own extension. In practice, this analysis owes more to functionalism than it does to Foucault, who locates power not in a centre, but in knowledges, discourses, micro-exchanges, and who everywhere proclaims its precariousness, its instability. On the assumption that political usefulness, not the author's opinion, is our concern, Foucault's work can be read,

---

[14] Foucault, *The Use of Pleasure*, p. 4.

selectively, I admit, but no less productively for that, as a history of resistances – of ballad-mongers, fools, criminals, deviants and suicides who heroically repudiate the positions that power produces for them.

If there is a general distinction to be made between the project of the New Historicists and what I am proposing here, it lies in the inscription of struggle. Too often in the work of Stephen Greenblatt and Jonathan Goldberg, for all its elegance, scholarship, and subtlety, power is represented as seamless and all-pervasive, while resistance, where it exists at all, is seen as ultimately self-deceived. Texts are understood as homogeneous, monologic, in the last instance non-contradictory, because the uncertainties they formulate are finally contained by the power they might seem to subvert.[15] The cultural history I propose is a story of conflicting interests, of heroic refusals, of textual uncertainties. It tells of power, but of power which always entails the possibility of resistance, in so far as it inevitably requires a differentiating other.

To this extent, then, I share the position of the British Cultural Materialists, who tend to stress subversion rather than containment. But in this case too it seems to me important to draw distinctions between an existing practice and the project I am outlining.[16] It is even less clear here than in the case of New Historicism that there is a single, homogeneous body of work to which the term Cultural Materialism refers. The phrase was originally invoked by Raymond Williams, and was subsequently adopted by Jonathan Dollimore and Alan Sinfield as the subtitle of their important and challenging collection of essays on *Political Shakespeare*.[17] It seems to imply an allusion to the Althusserian concept of ideology as a material practice, and to propose that culture, like Althusser's ideology, is relatively autonomous and is in consequence itself a site of contradiction and struggle. The structuralist analysis of the materiality of language had made it possible for Althusser to break with a vulgarized Marxist treatment of ideology as the *expression* of a struggle which was *really* taking place elsewhere, in the economy. Now the economic, the political, and the ideological could be thought as distinct instances, relatively independent, developing unevenly, but linked together to the extent that each might also constitute a condition of the possibility of developments in the others. Althusser's term 'ideology', however, though indispensable in enabling theory to break with the empiricist recuperation of Marx, has come in time to seem rather a blunt instrument, if only because of the uneasy distinction in Althusser's own writing between *ideologies* and *ideology in general*. (It was at this point that Foucault's work on the power relations inscribed in knowledges-as-discourses offered the possibility of a more focused analysis of cultural practice.) In the usage of Dollimore and

---

[15] See Greenblatt, *Renaissance Self-Fashioning*; Jonathan Goldberg, *James I and the Politics of Literature* (Baltimore, Md.: Johns Hopkins University Press, 1983). But for exceptions to these generalizations, see Louis Adrian Montrose, '"Shaping Fantasies": Figurations of Gender and Power in Elizabethan Culture', *Representations* 2 (1983), pp. 61–94, and 'The Elizabethan Subject and the Spenserian Text'.

[16] On a visit to the United States in 1988 I was surprised to discover that I was a Cultural Materialist.

[17] Jonathan Dollimore and Alan Sinfield, eds, *Political Shakespeare: New Essays in Cultural Materialism* (Manchester: Manchester University Press, 1985).

Sinfield the looser term, 'culture', in conjunction with the silent allusion to Marxism in the word 'materialism', appears to promise a form of analysis which takes into account post-Althusserian work on the textual inscription of struggle.

It is disappointing, therefore, to find that in Dollimore's introduction to *Political Shakespeare* the emphasis is on cultural subversion as a unitary phenomenon, as an 'idea', which is 'represented' (re-presented) in texts, and that the real struggle is once again elsewhere:

> the mere thinking of a radical idea is not what makes it subversive . . . one might go further and suggest that not only does the idea have to be conveyed, it has also actually to be used to refuse authority *or* be seen by authority as capable and likely of being so used.

'Ideas' apparently have materiality only if they are in some not very clearly specified way *put into* practice, or *perceived as* able to be so. Later in the same paragraph an idea is subversive because it is 'taken up' and helps to precipitate 'historical change'.[18] There is no space in Dollimore's account of Cultural Materialism for the theoretical developments of recent years, for the analysis of textuality as inherently unstable, or for the identification of culture as itself the place where norms are specified and contested, knowledges affirmed and challenged, and subjectivity produced and disrupted.

If meanings are not fixed and guaranteed, but as Derrida has consistently argued, indeterminate, differed and deferred, invaded by the trace of otherness which defines and constitutes the self-same, texts necessarily exceed their own unitary projects, whether these are subversion or containment, in a movement of instability which releases new possibilities in the very process of attempting to close them off. And if power generates the possibility of resistance as its defining difference, the signified truth necessarily produces alternative knowledges, not only for political motives, as functionalism proposes, in order to master them, but also as a structural necessity, because without them it lacks definition. Only an eternal verity (universal truth) can hold the network of meanings in place. But it does so in a perpetual conflict with its others, both internal and external, which is the condition of its existence as knowledge. If we succeed in relativizing the truth, then we release as material for analysis the play of signification, Foucault's 'games of truth',[19] which necessarily have more than one player, or more than one side, and which are not a reflection of the struggle for power, but its location. To give a historical account of what constitutes us as subjects is to specify the possibilities of transgressing the existing limits on what we are able to say, to be and to do.[20]

IV

What has this to do with the institution of English? Everything, I believe. More than any other discipline, English has been concerned with the study of

---

[18] Dollimore and Sinfield, eds, *Political Shakespeare*, p. 13.
[19] Foucault, *The Use of Pleasure*, pp. 6–7.
[20] Foucault, 'What is Enlightenment?', p. 46.

signifying practice. Traditionally we have not only analysed meanings (philosophy does that too), and we have not only been concerned with social relations (history and sociology are too). Supremely, English departments have attended to the formal properties of texts, their modes of address to readers and the conditions in which they are intelligible. Cultural history needs to appropriate and develop those strategies, putting them to work not in order to demonstrate the value of the text, or its coherence as the expression of the authorial subjectivity which is its origin, but to lay bare the contradictions and conflicts, the instabilities and indeterminacies, which inevitably reside in any bid for truth. We need only extend the range of texts we are willing to discuss, to put on the syllabus . . .

That 'only' is there to cheer us up, to make it all sound easy. I'm not sure how easy it is. But if we can interpret Shakespeare, we can surely learn to interpret fashion, and music – and privies. Fredric Jameson has succeeded with an ease which may be deceptive (or which at least may be hard to emulate) in bringing together fiction, painting, music, film, and architecture in his polemical and controversial account of the postmodern condition.

Jameson's essay, 'Postmodernism, or the Cultural Logic of Late Capitalism', is a discussion of changes in signifying practice itself: not simply changes in meaning in the conventional sense, but changes in form.[21] It is impossible to consider postmodernism without paying attention to its mode of address, its disruption of the subject-object couple produced and reproduced by the signifying practices of classic realism. What Jameson fears – and others celebrate – is the dispersal of the knowing subject of humanism, in possession of the objects of its knowledge, and able to map the world. In my book *The Subject of Tragedy* I suggested that the subject of humanism was installed as a consequence of a parallel shift in signifying practice in the sixteenth and seventeenth centuries. My aim there was not to declare a nostalgia for the world we have lost, but to chart a revolution in the system of signification, which had radical implications for the subjectivity that is its effect. There is a great deal more work to be done on the specificity of modes of address and the history of the subject. And if this particular task seems to me especially urgent, that is perhaps because our culture places the subject at the centre of the system of signified truths, identifies it as the absolute, extra-linguistic presence which is the origin and guarantee of the fixity of meaning, and targets nuclear weapons on the Soviet Union in defence of its (imaginary) freedom. If in the twentieth century truth has at last become plural, it is still inclined to be subjective, the unique and inalienable property of each unique individual subject.

Or it was. Because the tyranny of truth (including the subjective truth) becomes visible to us now only in consequence of the postmodern condition. It is no accident, but a precise effect of cultural history, that postmodern practice and poststructuralist theory coincide in their assault on truth to the extent that they do.

This is not to say that our own position as individuals – for or against truth,

---

[21] Fredric Jameson, 'Postmodernism, or the Cultural Logic of Late Capitalism', *New Left Review* 146 (1984), pp. 53–92.

theory, change – is determined for us in advance: that too is a site of struggle, of subjections and resistances. There are choices constantly to be made, but they are political choices, choices of subject-position, not recognitions of the truth. It is, however, to emphasize our location within a continuing history, and the relativity of our own meanings, knowledges and practices. And perhaps this above all is the pedagogic and political importance of cultural history. It addresses and constitutes students, readers, practitioners who are themselves an effect of the history they make.

It goes without saying (I hope) after all this that I am not proposing that we should set out in quest of a new truth, simply reconstituting our dispersed, postmodern subjectivities round new objects of knowledge. Still less that we reconstruct the institution of English in support of a more comprehensive metanarrative, a more thorough mapping of the world, a new system centred on a new transcendental signified. Nor on the other hand is cultural relativity the ground of a simple libertarianism, making the texts do whatever we like. This part of my argument is difficult to formulate, since the discourse of a non-empiricist knowledge barely exists as yet, but I am persuaded that we should not abandon the notion of rigour, the project of substantiating our readings, or a commitment to historical specificity. We shall need principles of selection, since without them no individual project would be thinkable. But at the same time, the cultural history I visualize is predicated on the relativity of knowledges, on history as a process of production, and on that process as political intervention.

If, however, it takes for granted the relativity of our certainties, it also assumes the relativity of our subjection. The transcendental subject, outside and above the objects of its knowledge, is also the most deeply subjected being, at the mercy of the system of signified truth of which it is an effect. Conversely, the subjectivity which is imbricated in the knowledges it participates in and helps to produce has more options at its disposal. Modes of resistance – or, to use Pêcheux's terms, counter-identification, the rejection of what is dominant, and disidentification, the production of alternative knowledges, alternative subject positions – are no longer seen as eccentric or psychotic, as a threat to the very being of the subject itself. A subjectivity explicitly constituted in and by its own knowledges does not 'disintegrate' in consequence of contradiction and conflict. And equally, it escapes to some degree the reaffirmation of the lack which stems from the exteriority of a knowledge whose objects are always finally elsewhere, beyond the grasp of the subject. The readings we should make would not be a quest for lost presence, but a contribution to a continuing process of production.

The project, then, is a history of meanings, and struggles for meaning, in every place where meanings can be found – or made. Its focus is on change, cultural difference and the relativity of truth. And its purpose is to change the subject, involving ourselves as practitioners in the political and pedagogic process of making history, in both senses of that phrase.

11 Lee Patterson

From *Historical Criticism and the Claims of Humanism*

Negotiating the Past: The Historical Understanding of Medieval Literature, University of Wisconsin Press: Madison, Wisconsin, 1987, pp. 62–74.

By treating cultural history as a text, New Historicism is able to bring to bear the formidable techniques of interpretation that literary criticism has been developing for the past fifty years or so. The result is a series of readings of great subtlety and power, readings that anatomize the shifting imperatives and ambitions of Renaissance culture without subjecting them to easy – or indeed any – resolution: history is finally as undecidable as poetry, as of course it must be when read as a poem. Absorbing the historical into the textual, New Historicism endows it with the irresolution that, for deconstruction, characterizes textuality per se. But there is a price to pay for this absorption. To adopt an interpretive method that assumes that history is not merely known through but constituted by language is to act as if there are no acts other than speech acts. But while we can all agree that language cannot be prised off the world, that whatever nonverbal, nonsymbolic reality exists can be known only by means of linguistic mediation, this does not allow us to abandon the category of the historically real entirely. History is impelled by consequential and determinative acts of material production: building cities, making wars, collecting wealth, imposing discipline, seizing and denying freedom – these are material processes that, while enacted in terms of and made known by symbolic forms, possess a palpable force and an intentional purposiveness, however we may finally come to understand them, that stand against the irresolutions and undecidabilities valued by contemporary techniques of interpretation. It is true that the literary historian must perforce operate within the closed world of textuality, and that he must not hypostasize a part of his evidence as the historically real. But our experience also teaches us that the historically real – as economic, political, social, and material reality – does indeed exist, and that action in the world has a presence and consequentiality that cannot be evaded. To apply the conditions of our scholarship to life is an almost inevitable transaction, but it in fact denatures, because it dematerializes, our historical existence. Indeed, the lines of influence ought really to run the other way, from our lives to our scholarship: in dealing with the textuality by which the historical makes itself known, we must not merely acknowledge but seek to accommodate, in however inevitably partial a fashion, something of the palpability and unavoidability of historical action.

My concern that the skeptical self-cancellations of contemporary textuality should not subvert the category of the historically real is derived not from some notion of philosophical correctness: indeed, since the historically real cannot exist apart from the textuality by which it is made known, deconstruction is surely right to insist that the priority of neither element can ever finally be demonstrated. Rather, it is the political consequences entailed by such a subversion that seem to me particularly persuasive. For in foregrounding the self-contradictions that haunt historical action, New Historicism discloses a world strangely drained of dynamism, in which every effort to enact change issues in a reaffirmation of the status quo, and where the continually renegotiated antagonisms of Renaissance culture are always already inscribed within a space of stasis. It arrives, in fact, at a paradox: on the one hand Renaissance culture is an arena of social contradictions engaged in ceaseless strife, and yet on the other hand, nothing happens. On the one hand, New Historicism sets itself against the monologic idealism of traditional *Geistesgeschichte*, with its insistence upon cultural homogeneity, and yet on the other ends up presenting a Renaissance as synchronically isolated and politically uniform as anything we find in Tillyard's *Elizabethan World Picture*.[1] The terms with which Greenblatt designates this condition are containment and subversion: Renaissance discourses *contain* subversion, in the double sense that they simultaneously elicit and control it, grant it a space for its enactment but finally encompass and disarm it.[2] Cultural oppositions may require continual renegotiation, but the results are always the same.

An illuminating instance of this process is offered by Greenblatt in 'Loudun and London', where he describes how the attempt 'to exorcise the theatricality of exorcism' through execution simply reinstated the theatrical. But the authorities did not stop there in their attempt to gain control. Rather, they instituted a public act of confessional guidance, in which the priestly exorcist would whisper in the ear of the possessed: 'In effect, the theatre of possession and exorcism is made to cede place to a mute public spectacle and an inaudible, private discourse of spiritual interiority.'[3] What Greenblatt traces here is an early stage in the 'negotiation of cultural power' by which public display gives way to private manipulation. The end of this story is not only easy to imagine but has in fact already been written, in Foucault's *Discipline and Punish*. There Foucault argues that in the late eighteenth century the dangers of execution as a display of power were fully recognized, so that the public enactment of authority was replaced with the secret, inward manipulation of the subject – a process that has now reached its fulfilment in the monolithic carceral society of the modern world, with its inescapable reproduction of itself within each individual.

---

[1] The term 'monologic' is used by Greenblatt to characterize the old historicism over against which the New Historicism is to be defined; see his Introduction to *The Power of Forms in the English Renaissance* (Norman, Okla.: Pilgrim Books, 1982) pp. 3–6.

[2] Stephen Greenblatt, 'Invisible Bullets: Renaissance Authority and Its Subversion', *Glyph* 8 (1981), pp. 40–61; in 'The Politics of Renaissance Literature: A Review Essay', *English Literary History* 49 (1982), pp. 514–42, Jonathan Goldberg has shrewdly noted that 'there is in Greenblatt's work too great a need not to express the possibility that what he calls containment may not in fact have been absolute, a need related to the desire of his project to contain all in a controlling frame' (p. 533). And Goldberg adds, in commenting on Montrose's work, 'Change needs to be accounted for; the possibility that change can occur must be read into texts that appear to confirm power, and into the institutions – court, theatre – that appear to preserve power' (p. 528). It is sometimes difficult to remember, in reading New Historicist accounts, that the English Renaissance reached its culmination in 1642 with a revolution.

[3] Stephen Greenblatt, 'Loudon and London', *Critical Inquiry* 12 (1986), p. 332.

The underwriting presence of Foucault in Greenblatt's account is symptomatic of his pervasive influence throughout New Historicism generally. For one thing, Foucault's argument that culture can be best understood through the analysis of the discursive practices that constitute its reality is another, and less depoliticized, way to bridge the gap between history and textuality than the solution offered by deconstruction. And for another, the central, almost obsessive focus of New Historicist attention is upon Foucault's own topic – power – and power understood in a specifically Foucauldian rather than Marxist way. That is, for Foucault power is not a capacity possessed by one group in society that advantageously deploys it against another, as the Marxist account of class struggle would have it, but rather a capacity that inhabits the very sinews and nerves of the body politic. To imagine that power is possessed or controlled by someone would be to imagine a space outside power, a wholly free and autonomous place from which power issues but which is itself uncontrolled. But to imagine such a place is to fall prey to the central cunning by which power enforces itself, that is, to imagine that one is somehow autonomous, a pure subjectivity from which unconditioned actions can issue, an individual. As Frank Lentricchia has cogently argued, for Foucault power is virtually a metaphysical principle:

> In his social theory power tends to occupy the 'anonymous' place which classical treatises in metaphysics reserved for substance: without location, identity, or boundaries, it is everywhere and nowhere at the same time. . . . To put it as Foucault puts it is to suggest that power has no predominant direction, no predominant point of departure, no predominant point of terminus. Like the God of theism, it is ubiquitous; unlike God it has no intention.[4]

And unlike God, its effects are malevolent. Foucault provides the ultimate fulfilment of a nightmare vision of a world so perfectly administered (Adorno), so thoroughly bureaucratized (Weber), that reality itself is constituted through the insidious, invisible workings of power. 'The exercise of power', says Foucault, 'is a total structure of actions brought to bear upon possible actions; it incites, it induces, it seduces, it makes easier or more difficult; in the extreme it constrains or forbids absolutely; it is nevertheless always a way of acting upon an acting subject or acting subjects *by virtue of their acting or being capable of action.*'[5] The very entrance upon a field of action implicates the agent in a web of power relations that predetermines the scope and direction of his action. Power may presuppose freedom, but it remains itself the primary term: freedom is simply that which power requires for its actions, and is thus brought into being in order to provide the necessary conditions for power's enactment.

This totalizing vision of an entrapping world organized not primarily but exclusively by structures of domination and submission, implicit in much New Historicist work, becomes an explicit source of concern in Greenblatt's *Renaissance Self-Fashioning*. Greenblatt rather ruefully acknowledges that

---

[4] Frank Lentricchia, 'Reading Foucault (Punishment, Labour, Resistance): Part Two', *Raritan* 2:1 (1982), pp. 50–1.
[5] Michel Foucault, 'The Subject and Power', in Herbert L. Dreyfus and Paul Rabinow, *Michel Foucault: Beyond Structuralism and Hermeneutics* (Chicago: University of Chicago Press, 1982), p. 220 (my italics).

although the topic of his book is the creation of the Renaissance self, in the course of its writing 'the human subject itself began to seem remarkably unfree, the ideological product of the relations of power in a particular society.'[6] Similarly, in the struggle between containment and subversion, containment remains the dominant mode, as in all logic it must since it has itself summoned up subversion in order to reconfirm, over and over, its dominance. Given this prescribed dynamic, individual and contingent political action is revealed as an illusion: whatever acts may be undertaken, they are instantly inscribed within already established structures. Hence the New Historicist refusal to specify authorial intention: the most that Greenblatt will say about Jacobean theatrical representations of exorcism is that 'they do the state some service', as of course they inevitably must, since all cultural activity can serve only to confirm the authority always already in place; at one point in his essay on *A Midsummer Night's Dream* Montrose describes the play as attempting to assert royalist values that it then unwittingly undoes, but he later reverses the lines of force by presenting it as an attempt at subversion that is inevitably inscribed within an authoritative ideology.[7] More tendentiously, for Montrose Spenser's *Shepheardes Calender,* and indeed all Elizabethan pastoral, serves to legitimize hierarchical power structures by representing them as benign, a reading that ignores the fact that Spenser clearly intended his poem as an attack upon specific political practices supported by Elizabeth.[8] It is quite true that specific and explicit intention can never fully govern the meaning of a text, that literature serves to constitute cultural reality in ways it can never fully know and that may run counter to its own most insistent purposes. But simply to set aside these intentions and purposes as unworthy of discussion is effectively to silence dissent; and by raising analysis to a level at which individual actions and motives become submerged into a totalized

---

[6] Stephen Greenblatt, *Renaissance Self-Fashioning: From More to Shakespeare* (Chicago: University of Chicago Press, 1980), p. 256. Greenblatt continues: 'Whenever I focused sharply upon a moment of apparently autonomous self-fashioning, I found not an epiphany of identity freely chosen but a cultural artifact. If there remained traces of free choice, the choice was among possibilities whose range was strictly delineated by the social and ideological systems in force.' This is a concern also voiced by the book's otherwise enthusiastic reviewers. See, for example, Louis Adrian Montrose, 'A Poetics of Renaissance Culture', *Criticism* 23 (1981), pp. 349–59; and Thomas M. Greene, *Comparative Literature* 34 (1982), pp. 184–6. In 'The Politics of Renaissance Literature' Goldberg describes the book as offering a 'frighteningly totalistic and implicitly totalitarian vision' (p. 529).

[7] Greenblatt, 'Loudun and London', p. 341; Montrose, ' "Shaping Fantasies": Figurations of Gender and Power in Elizabethan Culture', *Representations* 2 (1983), pp. 74, 84–5.

[8] Louis Montrose, ' "Eliza, Queene of Shepheardes," and the Pastoral of Power', *English Literary Renaissance* 10 (1980), pp. 153–82; see also 'Gifts and Reasons: The Context of Peele's *Araygnement of Paris*', *English Literary History* 47 (1980), pp. 433–61, and ' "The perfecte paterne of a Poete": The Poetics of Courtship in *The Shepheardes Calender*', *Texas Studies in Language and Literature* 21 (1979), pp. 34–67. For the anti-Elizabethan politics of *The Shepheardes Calender*, see David Norbrook, *Poetry and Politics in the English Renaissance* (London: Routledge & Kegan Paul, 1984), pp. 59–90. Norbrook concludes: 'In *The Shepheardes Calender* Spenser established a political rhetoric that was to remain popular until the Civil War. The figure of the shepherd poet became associated with the kind of policies adopted by Leicester and his political heir, the Earl of Essex: a militant foreign policy and at home a religious policy that was reasonably sympathetic to the more radical brethren, while not necessarily favouring all radical demands' (p. 89).

vision of a monolithic culture is to beg the question by adopting a method that can prove only the hypothesis at issue.[9] The Foucauldian vision of a carceral society is dangerously self-confirming: the individual disappears because the historian stops looking for him, just as the nonpolitical yields wholly to a decoding that reveals it to have been political all along.[10] There is no space outside power because power is the only term in the analyst's arsenal.

While thus setting itself up as providing a dialogic alternative to the mono-logic idealism of traditional historicism, New Historicism finds itself in danger of falling into an analogous narrowness. The valence has been reversed but the condition remains the same: where old historicism saw Renaissance culture as conforming to the norm of Tillyard's benign *Elizabethan World Picture*, the New Historicists now see it as organized according to the malign principle of power. Quite against its explicit intentions, New Historicism effects a mono-lithic totalization, suppressing the individual in favour of the general and the disparate in favour of the homogenous. Similarly, while New Historicism seeks to promote the power of discourse – 'The Power of Forms', to use Greenblatt's title – it ends up representing discourse as in fact impotent: language may consti-tute reality but is itself constrained by rules and procedures so intricately inter-woven into its fabric as to be impervious to investigation and change.

Finally, New Historicist investigation is as relentlessly synchronic as any *Geistesgeschichte*. Sharing the current distrust of diachronic historicism, a distrust impelled by the discrediting of the concept of the origin, the collapse of the classic model of cause-and-effect causality, and the unpersuasiveness of evolutionary and teleological claims, New Historicism seeks instead to achieve what Geertz calls 'thick description', an analysis of the conditions of cultural production. No longer believing that cultural phenomena can be usefully explained as effects of anterior causes, New Historicism is released from the narrow criterion of relevance that constrained older literary historians. The result is both an enlightening extension of the range of materials to be brought to bear upon a text – New Historicist essays typically begin with an apparently out of the way anecdote or event in order eventually to show how it too bespeaks the central problematic of the culture as a whole – and yet a weakening of explanatory force. For if the New Historicists rightly refuse to reduce the text to an effect of either a straightforward authorial intention or a determinant social context, they also decline to specify the ground of comparison – the historically real – that supports their analyses. Neither the period consciousness of *Geistesgeschichte* nor the class struggle of Marxism provides them with adequate explanatory categories for cultural production, with the result that the critic withdraws from the task of explanation entirely and settles for the less definitive act of interpretation. At issue here is the same question raised by Adorno in his debate with Benjamin

---

[9] As Norbrook trenchantly points out, 'If, as so often in the Renaissance period, authorial intention has a substantial and under-acknowledged political element, to ignore the intention is effectively to depoliticize' (*Poetry and Politics in the English Renaissance*, p. 8).

[10] For two instances of this decoding in contemporary Renaissance studies, see Arthur Marotti, ' "Love is not love": Elizabethan Sonnet Sequences and the Social Order', *English Literary History* 49 (1982), pp. 396–428; and Frank Whigham, *Ambition and Privilege: The Social Tropes of Elizabethan Courtesy Theory* (Berkeley, Calif.: University of California Press, 1984).

over Benjamin's *Passagenarbeit*. For Adorno, Benjamin's juxtapositioning of disparate cultural elements could yield results only if grounded in a critical perspective secured by its political commitments. Otherwise his instances of nineteenth-century culture became images that simply instantiated contradictions and could not serve as materials for a historical understanding to be developed through critical analysis.[11] At heart, in other words, the question was – and remains – whether cultural analysis is possible without an explicit commitment to a specific philosophy of history, a specific definition of the real. Can history be written without causality? And if not, is causal explanation possible without a foundational commitment to some narrative of historical action, be it the fulfilment of the Spirit, the rise of a heroic bourgeoisie, or the class struggle entailed by social inequality?

This question presents itself with some urgency for the medievalist because New Historicism, despite its laudable self-consciousness, in fact operates largely according to a traditional historiographical scheme that not only sets the Renaissance over against the Middle Ages but understands the opposition in terms originally established by nineteenth-century liberal philology. That is, the crucial heuristic category for New Historicism remains the individual versus society, although with the valence of the opposition now reversed. For Burckhardt, the Renaissance was the time in which man asserted his individuality, as opposed to the corporatist, collectivist Middle Ages in which 'man was conscious of himself only as a member of a race, people, party, family, or corporation – only through some general category.'[12] For the New Historicists, on the other hand, the Renaissance is the time when man discovers that the individuality he is seeking to assert does not in fact exist, that selfhood is not atemporally given but socially constituted.[13] From this

[11] A brief account of the debate is offered by Susan Buck-Morss, *The Origin of Negative Dialectics* (New York: Free Press, 1977), pp. 143–6.

[12] Jacob Burckhardt, *The Civilization of the Renaissance in Italy* (London: Phaidon Books, 1965), p. 81.

[13] In *Renaissance Self-Fashioning* Greenblatt argues that 'there are always selves – a sense of personal order, a characteristic mode of address to the world, a structure of bounded desires – and always some sense of deliberate shaping in the formation and expression of identity. . . . Moreover, there is considerable empirical evidence that there may well have been less *autonomy* in self-fashioning in the sixteenth century than before, that family, state, and religious institutions impose a more rigid and far-reaching discipline upon their middle-class and aristocratic subjects. . . . What is essential is the perception – as old in academic writing as Burckhardt and Michelet – that there is in the early modern period a change in the intellectual, social, psychological, and aesthetic structures that govern the generation of identities. This change is difficult to characterize in our usual ways because it is not only complex but resolutely dialectical. If we say that there is a new stress on the executive power of the will, we must say that there is the most sustained and relentless assault upon the will; if we say that there is a new social mobility, we must say that there is a new assertion of power by both family and state to determine all movement within the society; if we say that there is a heightened awareness of the existence of alternative modes of social, theological, and psychological organization, we must say that there is a new dedication to the imposition of control upon those modes and ultimately to the destruction of alternatives' (pp. 1–2). In *Radical Tragedy: Religion, Ideology, and Power in the Drama of Shakespeare and His Contemporaries* (Chicago: University of Chicago Press, 1984), Jonathan Dollimore argues that the Jacobean period saw the emergence of 'a conception of subjectivity legitimately identified in terms of materialist perspective rather than one of essentialist humanism' (p. 249) – i.e., subjectivity as a function of the reification of the self entailed by capitalist modes of production. See also Don E. Wayne, *Penshurst: The Semiotics of Place and the Poetics of History* (Madison, Wisc.: University of Wisconsin Press, 1984).

perspective, then, it is the Middle Ages that is the time of heroic individuality while the Renaissance emerges from feudalism into the reification and alienation entailed by capitalism.[14] Indeed, one might almost be back with Ruskin, for whom Gothic freedom of expression was destroyed by 'the poison-tree of the Renaissance', initiating a decline that culminated in the monolithic regimentation and pervasive alienation of the nineteenth-century factory – the Foucauldian locus of the carceral society.

My point is not simply that New Historicism is perhaps not so new after all; indeed, since our entire cultural situation has not moved much beyond the nineteenth-century opposition of left and right wing, however these may be variously defined, we can hardly expect our literary criticism to do so either. The issue is not how to get beyond the opposition – which, if we grant the inescapability of the political, in practice means how to evade it – but rather how to locate one's scholarly work within it in a way consistent with what one takes one's political values to be. Hence my point here is that New Historicism (and probably this is an effect of its insistence on its novelty) has in ways perhaps unbeknownst to itself found itself in a conservative political posture. At the most basic level, the Foucauldian account of cultural formation that the New Historicists have adopted, by depoliticizing power, calls into question the efficacy of local and contingent political action: since all of life is always already inscribed within and predetermined by structures of dominance and subordination, the powers-that-be will always be the powers-that-be. At a more local level, New Historicism typically focuses its attention not on the subversive and suppressed elements of society but on the dominating structures – and largely without criticism: the court, the aristocracy, the upwardly mobile. Indeed, in its attentive recreation of the ways in which Elizabethan and Jacobean monarchs used cultural productions in order to sustain their dominance it too often displays an uncritical celebration of what Fernand Braudel once called 'that *Adelswelt* to which [the historian] is secretly drawn'.[15]

Given both its explicit polemic against a reactionarily 'idealist' old historicism, and its own commitment not only to thc priority of the social but to conceptualizing it in terms of instability and contradiction, the conservative drift of New Historicism is best understood as an unintended embarrassment. Indeed, this unintentionality shows in vivid terms how a prevailing ideology can come to dominate even antithetical theoretical formations, regardless of their sophistication. The late 1970s and 1980s are self-evidently a time of hegemonic conservatism, in which the privatization of value has reached new extremes and in which the cult of success has become an explicit and unashamed justification for the crudest forms of economic and social injustice. To think that the academy is somehow exempt from this process would be naive, and yet academic discourse still maintains an objectivist style that implicitly denies the relevance of the writer's own social situation to his work of investigation. My point is not that the New Historicists are grasping and

---

[14] For a lucid description of the Marxist theory of the generation of the sense of autonomous individuality by capitalism, see István Mészáros, *Marx's Theory of Alienation* (London: Merlin Press, 1970), pp. 255–8.

[15] Fernand Braudel, *On History,* trans. Sarah Matthews (Chicago: University of Chicago Press, 1980), p. 125. For instances of this attraction, see the works of Orgel, Goldberg, and Whigham cited above.

materialist seekers after fame and fortune who are betraying the noble values of their humanist discipline; not only can I not exempt myself from exactly the same charge, since the writing of this book is undertaken within a system of punishments and rewards that has an unmistakably prescriptive force, but phrasing the issue in these terms both invokes a set of indefensible assumptions and obscures a more central if difficult point. For while we may agree that it is necessary to stand against the dominant ideology of our times, it is the immense difficulty of doing so that must be acknowledged. Indeed, perhaps the lesson that the unintended conservatism of New Historicism teaches is that if you do not have an explicit politics – an ideology – then one will certainly have you.

To assume that the social totality prescribes not only the terms of every local and contingent opposition but the course of their contestation – that the progressive and the reactionary are two sides of the same repressive coin, subversion a function of containment – is not only to foreclose the possibility of political progress but in effect to annul the local and the contingent entirely. This is a recipe for despair: human beings have no other arena for action than the here and now, make no decisions that are not local, assert no values that are not contingent. Our daily lives are the only lives we have: there is no escaping from the historically specific, and it is in terms of this specificity that we must decide what work to do and how to do it. Our scholarly activity, in other words, can never be guided by some impossible norm of correctness but only by the relation we want to establish to the social and political formations governing our own historical moment.

These formations are at the moment deeply antipathetic to just the kind of small-scale, tactical activity that is our most available way of interacting with the world and participating in its development. It is not just the academic who has his historical irrelevance forced upon him; it is everybody. The homogenization of value and the annulment of the individual have reached extraordinary lengths in contemporary America; the culture industry has achieved a virtually undisputed dominance over American consciousness; corporate, military, and institutional interests pursue their goals with little restraint; and the most vigorous political formation at work in the United States is a fundamentalist conservatism dedicated to the growth of state power and the further eradication of difference. But if indeed Foucault's dystopic vision of the carceral society is on the way to fulfilment, then surely our scholarly task should be to stand against it. There is, for instance, something scandalous in the fact that the current, virulent attacks on humanism issue from two diametrical points on the political compass, the religious right and the theoretical left. How is it that the academic intellectual has come to conspire in his own demise? Almost twenty years ago Adorno understood this process with prescient clarity: 'The more individuals are really degraded to functions of the social totality, as it becomes more systematized, the more will man pure and simple, man as a principle with the attributes of creativity and absolute domination, be consoled by exaltation of his mind.'[16] The contemporary

---

[16] Theodor Adorno, 'Subject and Object', (1969) in Andrew Arato and Eike Gebhardt, eds, *The Essential Frankfurt School Reader* (New York: Urizen Books, 1978), p. 500.

theoretical effort to subvert the false stability of the ideology of the subject is best understood not as a simple emancipation from reified bourgeois categories but rather as a totalizing intellectualism correlative to the hegemonic homogenization that characterizes our time. Of course, to propose the recuperation of humanism will inevitably be seen by many as simply the reaction of an offended liberalism. But if we cannot return to the transhistorical bourgeois individual with his dominating ego and self-identical subjectivity, neither can we afford to dispense with the category of individualism altogether. To deprive the human agent of any purchase upon the social whole is to signal the end of a politics we desperately need.

But even if the force of these political considerations be granted, what is their relevance to the problems and procedures of literary historicism? To begin with, they entail a criticism that insists not only upon the dialectical nature of its relation to its own time but upon the negativity of that dialectic, upon adopting an antagonistic stance to the depersonalized, depoliticized, and tranquillized homogenization accomplished by modern American culture. Specifically, then, we must be alert at the level of critical method to the dangers of what the Frankfurt School thinkers called 'identity theory', the underwriting assumption of those forms of historicism that would reduce difference and opposition to sameness by collapsing together subject and object, either through an idealist appropriation of the object world (as in *Geistesgeschichte*) or through a materialist economism (as in Marxism). On the contrary, our work should seek to preserve and understand threatened categories of difference, the imperative that Adorno called 'the morality of thought':

> The morality of thought lies in a procedure that is neither entrenched nor detached, neither blind nor empty, neither atomistic nor consequential. . . . Nothing less is asked of the thinker today than that he should be at every moment both within things and outside them – Munchhausen pulling himself out of the bog by his pig-tail becomes the pattern of knowledge which wishes to be more than either verification or speculation.[17]

Not the least of these categories of difference, and one with which medievalists are almost obsessively concerned, is that between the present-as-subject and the past-as-object. This is not, it must be insisted, a difference that can be theorized: the otherness of the past, and the demands of recognition and self-restraint it places upon us, can become the subject of homiletic urgings but not – as the failure of objectivism and the largely negative character of hermeneutics show – of theoretical prescriptions.[18] In attempting to understand the past, we inevitably enter into elaborate and endless negotiations, struggles between desire and knowledge that can never be granted closure. But negotiations can take place only between two equal and independent parties, and this fiction – a fiction because the past can never exist independently of our

[17] Theodor Adorno, *Minima Moralia: Reflections from Damaged Life*, trans. E.F.N. Jephcott (London: New Left Books, 1974), p. 74.

[18] For comments on Hans Robert Jauss's most recent effort to theorize it in terms of Medieval Studies, see Lee Patterson, *Negotiating the Past: The Historical Understanding of Medieval Literature* (Madison, Wisc.: University of Wisconsin Press, 1987), Ch. 1, n. 9.

memory of it – must be consciously and painfully maintained. The paradox involved is again well illuminated by Adorno:

> The preponderant exertion of knowledge is destruction of its usual exertion, that of using violence against the object. Approaching knowledge of the object is the act in which the subject rends the veil it is weaving around the object. It can do this only where, fearlessly passive, it entrusts itself to its own experience. In places where subjective reason scents subjective contingency, the primacy of the object is shimmering through – whatever in the object is not a subjective admixture.[19]

The contradictions in this passage pile up because historical understanding is by definition a vacillation between contradictions that must not yield to closure.

Another antinomy whose irresolution must be respected is, as we have seen, that between the individual and the totality. In literary-historical terms this respect presents itself in the form of intention, an interpretive category that contemporary criticism has largely written off as a vestige of positivism. To be sure, there are constraints upon intention, and serious ones: writing comes into being within a socially determined context and by means of a socially constituted discourse, and it always makes meanings beyond and often other than those the author intended. Clearly the present is endowed with a capacity to understand the past in ways that it cannot understand itself: history takes place behind man's back as well as in front of his face. But a text is also a function of specific human intentions, in the sense both of self-consciously maintained purposes and of impulses that may be incapable of articulation but nonetheless issue from a historical intentionality, and it is a large part of our task to understand how these intentions went into its making. Much of what we come to know about texts was also available to their makers, albeit in a variety of unfamiliar cognitive forms, and to empower our critical abilities by devaluing theirs is to initiate an exchange that will ultimately rebound upon ourselves. To grant the social totality unfettered sway over the individual, who is then reduced to a helpless mediator of historical forces that can be fully understood only by the modern historian, is to invoke an 'absolute historicism', in Gramsci's phrase, that entraps us all. Adorno's famous critique of Benjamin is relevant here:

> Before his Medusan glance, man turns into a stage on which an objective process unfolds. For this reason Benjamin's philosophy is no less a source of terror than a promise of happiness.[20]

---

[19] Adorno, 'Subject and Object', p. 506. On this passage, see also Martin Jay, *Adorno* (Cambridge, Mass.: Harvard University Press, 1984), pp. 73–4. In *Minima Moralia* Adorno offers a similar account of the difficult reliability of aesthetic experience: 'Anyone who, drawing on the strength of his precise reaction to a work of art, has ever subjected himself in earnest to its discipline, to its immanent formal law, the compulsion of its structure, will find that the objections to the merely subjective quality of his experience vanish like a pitiful illusion: and every step that he takes, by virtue of his highly subjective innervation, towards the heart of the matter, has incomparably greater force than the comprehensive and fully backed-up analyses of such things as "style", whose claims to scientific status are made at the expense of such experience. This is doubly true in the era of positivism and the culture industry, where objectivity is calculated by the subjects managing it' (p. 70).

[20] Theodor Adorno, *Prisms*, trans. Samuel Weber and Shierry Weber (Cambridge, Mass.: MIT Press, 1981), p. 235.

Whatever individualism we seek to sustain must, to be sure, insist upon its historicity: the idea of the individual arises at certain historical moments and becomes submerged at others. But it is clearly not an idea dependent simply upon capitalism (how then can we explain its twelfth-century presence?), and neither can it be read as simply a function of subjection. The self may be made, but it is also self-made.

Finally, a correlative historical category that literary scholars cannot really do without is that of literature itself. That this is a *historical* category is beyond dispute, and that its boundaries, definitions, and purposes change over time is also true. Contemporary criticism characteristically understands it as an agency for authoritarian and conservative forces: the canon of literary works is devised in order to enforce hegemonic interests. But this is not always true: in the Middle Ages many of the texts we now call literary carved out for themselves, without the benefit of a theory of the literary, a space of ideological opposition. It is, moreover, precisely their negative relationship to the dominant formations of their time that make such texts as, for example, the Chartrian poems, the *Roman de la rose, Piers Plowman,* and the *Canterbury Tales* such accurate indices of the historical world from which they arise and upon which they reflect. This is not to say that they are not themselves conditioned by social forces that remain outside their own articulation, forces that the historian can recuperate; but it is to argue that they bear a privileged relation to their historical moment, and that we must respect and rely upon this privilege. These texts can hardly tell us everything we want or need to know about the past, but when securely located at the centre of our investigations (as not objects but subjects) they can help us to negotiate an otherwise enigmatic terrain.

---

12 Marjorie Levinson

From *The New Historicism: Back to the Future*

Marjorie Levinson, Marilyn Butler, Jerome McGann and Paul Hamilton, *Rethinking Historicism: Critical Readings in Romantic History*, Blackwell: Oxford, 1989, pp. 18–23, 50–55.

We have seen within Romantic studies over the past five years a new zeal to position literary works within a historical domain. More dramatically, many of us use that domain to identify and interrogate the work's representational choices. The enthusiasm attending this 'new historicist' investigation marks our sense of emancipation. We trust to our contextual and retextualizing procedures to put us beyond the interpretative norms imposed by the poetry and sanctified by the most influential of this century's criticism of that poetry.

In light of these interests and attitudes, the name we have given our critical practice executes a Freudian slip of the first order. By the word 'historicism' – a repetition of a nineteenth-century coinage – we confess our share in the very fictions we claim to de-mystify. Let me add another twist to this irony by suggesting that it is precisely our interest in the Romantic ideology – I shall say, its interest in us – that puts us in position to elucidate and transvalue the poetry of the early nineteenth century. We are, in short, situated to read that literature dialectically.

This business of interest is a question of historical conjunctures, not enthusiasm. Or, 'enthusiasm' will do so long as we construe it as a dynamic response to objective relations. The immediate distinction between today's interest and the relatively sustained study of the Romantics conducted throughout most of this century is the widespread, spontaneous and, by its account, non-strategic revaluation now under way in the academy. Eliot's devaluation, an isolated campaign, was largely a tactical manoeuvre determined by his revaluation on behalf of another literature, that of the sixteenth and early seventeenth centuries. Moreover, the entire literary discussion was plainly advanced as an exercise in contemporary social instruction. Yale's influential seriousness aligned itself early on with a theoretical project. This, we might say, was the effective interest of its philosophic and formal operation upon the Romantic canon. Certainly, Eliot's depreciation and Yale's appreciation can and should be read as dynamic reflections of social change and as part of the field which includes the poetry in question. Today's criticism differs in its untheorized and unselfconsciously political situation. This gives it a special place – a place privileged, ironically, by the kind and extent of its possession by the object it studies. The special intelligence of this criticism will come from its opportunity to investigate its object within the terrain of subjective knowledge and practice.[1]

There are the meanings you choose, and then there are the meanings that choose you. In the case of our new historicism, one can discern at least four orders of determination, only two of which will I elaborate in this essay.[2] Before I begin that account, let me characterize the project to which it contributes as a reading of a body of work produced over the past five years, a corpus that includes my own studies.[3] Since I hope to discover what is entailed by our practice, mine will be a highly generalizing representation of a wide range of critical work. I think many of us are curious about the meaning of our interest and anxious to see how we can best pursue it now, in light of our recent experience. I hope this curiosity will allow for the necessarily reductive way I shall conduct this inquiry. Let me also observe that my topic is that new historicism which has emerged within Romantic studies. I say 'our' historicism to distinguish this critical endeavour from that movement in

---

[1] This model of knowledge derives from Georg Lukács's postulate of the proletariat as capitalism's working self-consciousness and thus as the internal surpassing of the special epistemological bind required by that economic order. See 'Reification and the Consciousness of the Proletariat', in *History and Class Consciousness,* trans. Rodney Livingstone (Cambridge, Mass.: MIT Press, 1971), pp. 83–222.

[2] These four orders are our resistance to Yale, our revisionary interest in historical scholarship, the historiographic forms of the nineteenth century, and the Marxian methodology.

[3] (1) Alan Bewell, David Bromwich, Jim Chandler, Jerome Christensen, Kurt Heinzelman, Kenneth Johnston, Anne Mellor, Cliff Siskin, Olivia Smith; (2) John Barrell, Marilyn Butler, Laurence Goldstein, Paul Hamilton, Alan Liu, Jerry McGann, Marjorie Levinson, David Simpson. The two groupings represent a discrimination along methodological and political lines.

Renaissance studies associated with Stephen Greenblatt, Louis Montrose, Frank Whigham, and others.

The new historicism – a direct assault upon Yale's present-mindedness and an attempt to surpass the extrinsic and binary contextualism of twentieth-century scholarship – has emerged as a kind of systems analysis, an approach that, by its very form, indicates yet a third critical target.[4] By our functionalist exercises in closed-field intertextuality, we tacitly reject that teleological formalism associated with the old historicism, the dominant form of nineteenth-century historiography. Ours is an empirically responsible investigation of the contemporary meanings informing literary works (their parts, their production, their reception), as well as other social texts.[5] We regard these meanings as systematically interrelated within the period in question, but since we do not organize the system by a dynamic concept of ideology on the one hand, and of structural determination on the other, our

---

[4] We inscribe our reaction to the historical studies of the past fifty years in our multiply pregnant self-designation. By the locution 'new historicism' – with its resonance to the 'new criticism' and its grammatical rejection of the subordinate adjectival form 'historical' – we pronounce the critical invasiveness of our scholarly procedures. We dissolve the intrinsic – extrinsic distinctions felt to govern the old, historical scholarship so as to move beyond the peripheral, illustrative character of that exercise.

Our rejection of Yale's present-mindedness is a more complicated matter. One might even glimpse in the reactive empiricism which regularly surfaces in today's criticism an idealism not all that different from Yale's more manifestly tendentious abstractness. I refer to the way in which 'politics' or 'history' gets *practically* identified with that otherwise abandoned domain: the absolute, irreducible, matter-of-fact. To install a Real in this binary fashion is of course to construct another ghost town, and one a good deal more dangerous than New Haven, as its ghosts are so much more lifelike. Moreover, our tendency to homogenize text and context by collapsing them all into the category 'social text' – a consequence of our semiotic sophistication – consorts very strangely with our postulate of a Real which is some kind of final intransigence. In short, we seem oddly reluctant to think dialectically. Either we reduce text and context to 'social text' – mediations both, their authority intertextual, not extrinsic – or we elevate literature and life to the status of self-authorizing immediacies.

[5] Today's historicism is a historically informed investigation of the representational acts that made and make both literary objects and their receptions. The idea is to situate politics within the work and, typically, at the level of its allusive structure. Literary mode of production (roughly, form), and ideology as it operates to realize this given productive mode in particular ways for particular writers (roughly, style), do not have an important place in this criticism. Historicists tend to focus on representational objects as these figure by displacement, absence or distortion in the work. When they *do* reflect on the verbal surface as such, they generally treat it as a mimetic dimension as well: a reference to some extraliterary occurrence of a particular linguistic item. Or, style is read as an authorial selection of a particular political code, its partisanship clearly established within the domain of contemporary culture.

By 'politics', historicists seem to intend actual circumstances and their apparent interrelations, as well as the covert logic obtaining among these data in the contemporary mind. Rarely are these configurations set within a larger, and in some way compelling objective field. In note 4, I observe a tendency in our criticism to synonymize 'politics' with the Real of the poet's time and place. The manner in which the work figures (disfigures, deconstructs or dismisses), this referential order indicates both the work's ideological position and the conflicts pertaining to that place. 'Position' tends to be treated as a static phenomenon rather than a dynamic, problem-solving function. Historicists do not, that is, generally assume the ongoing proliferation of positions by a contradiction-engendering base of any kind. As for 'ideology', this appears to mean something like involuntary insertion in a cultural force field. This insertion carries with it or is constituted by a set of attitudes and beliefs not easily accessible to consciousness but theoretically available to the ideological subject.

inquiries do not give rise to a meaningful historical sequence. In the absence of some such model of epochal relatedness, questions concerning our own critical interest cannot materialize. By suppressing such questions, we do not, as we think, *surpass* the old historicism with its providential coherences and one-way dialectics, we install it at the heart of our practice. It is precisely our failure to articulate a critical field that sights *us* even as we compose *it*, that brings back the positivism, subjectivism and relativism of the rejected historicist methodology.

Where our historicism genuinely surpasses its nineteenth-century namesake is in its adoption of some specifically Marxian critical methods and values. Our interest in motivating *objectively* the special differences of Romantic works and responses – like our sensitivity to their contradictions and discontinuities – is a Marxian emphasis and a real departure from both the empiric formalism and the gradualism of Romantic historiography. Where we fall back into the received Romantic field is in our failure, first, to objectify our own subjectivity (that is, our way of *producing* that value), and second, to articulate the subject-object, present-past, criticism-poetry polarities as a mode of relation. As it is, we seem determined *not* to make anything of the historical differentials precipitated by our criticism.

One important corollary of this restraint is our failure to *represent* the critical practice which, by its cross-referencing, relates phenomena that were, in the past's immanent and differentiated experience of itself, either not related, differently related or unselfconsciously related. *We* are the ones who, by putting the past to a certain use, put it in a certain order. While most of us know this, we seem not to consider that this interest of ours in a certain use might also be an *effect* of the past which we study, and that our mode of critical production could be related to that past as to the absent cause which our practice instantiates. What I'm describing is a specifically *transhistorical* dialectic, one that invents the critic as Schlegel's prophet looking backwards.

By thinking along these lines, we learn to manage some basic hermeneutic binds. Here is Tony Bennett (who, for today's historicists, is the likelier influence than Stanley Fish, the larger and more stationary target of this critique), on the task which faces Marxist criticism. This task is not, Bennett says,

---

Those who produce the new historicism are trying to respond to the so-called failure of empiricism less antithetically than the scholarship of this century reacted to the hegemony of the new criticism. Now that the poststructuralisms have demonstrated the absolutely mediated form in which history is lived and remembered – the narrativity of historical knowledge and experience – we fold text and context into a variegated but homogeneous batter. Rather than tell stories, in the sense of genetic narrations or accounts of developing projects, historicists favour a cross-referencing mode of analysis, wherein the mechanical relations of social to literary text are traced in both directions. This preference for marble cakes over layer cakes would seem to betray a wish to live that 'molarity' we image. In lieu of this Imaginary solution, a collapse of the text – context distinction as this got formulated in particular works and periods, we might *develop* that difference and then *relate* it to the contradiction between our own everyday life and our professional consciousness. We might use our *own* longing in order to illuminate the continuity dreams of the works we study; by that practice, we begin to refocus, maybe even to alter the form of our wishes.

that of reflecting or of bringing to light the politics which is already there, as a latent presence within the text which has but to be made manifest. It is that of *actively politicizing* the text, of *making its politics for it*, by producing a new position for it within the field of cultural relations and, thereby, new forms of use and effectivity within the broader social process.[6]

This kind of thinking (in the text [essentialism]/outside the text [pragmatism]: passive reflecting, elucidating/active politicizing, use) is predialectical and therefore not the task of a Marxist or any other criticism today. Bennett's either/or formulation puts us in fact in a single box: namely, a privileging of the text's original or its most belated position. If we choose not to rehearse the politics produced for the work by the way it got written and, initially, read, then we must crisply depose the authority of first things, which is to say, we transfer that authority to last or latest things. This use-value pragmatism, which cordons off from criticism the present, or its special modes of cultural consumption, describes as well a commodity concept of literature. It imagines a work capable of dissolving the traces of its production and its history of receptions. The proposition that we can in any simple sense 'make a poem's politics for it' is also a definition of a text which descends – or rather, ascends – to us as a pure form. If essentialism is the danger of the first option, relativism and formalism are the perils of the second. Interestingly, historicism proper (the nineteenth-century variety) resolves in practice into this particular, and illusory, Scylla and Charybdis.

We want to articulate the literatures of the past in such a way as to accommodate the contingency of the present – the wilfulness of our textual politics – and at the same time, to configurate that freedom with the particular past that is retextualized. We want a framework that will explain the objective value of a belated criticism, one which reads into the work anticipations that were *not* present in the text's contemporary life, only in its posthumous existence, an existence that turns around and *plants itself* in the past. Within such a framework, today's criticism can assume its properly active, interested, 'subject' role and simultaneously figure as part of the objective field which includes the work: its original political position and its reception history.

Of course, to articulate this framework means giving up our notion of time as something different from histories (of matter, we might say, as something different from energy). It means conceiving the epochal distinctiveness of Romantic poetry not, chiefly, as a function of natural and therefore monolithic temporality, but as a result of determinate differences obtaining between the productive formations of the early nineteenth century and the late twentieth century, of the different ideological tasks defined by those formations, and finally, of the diverse kinds or levels of relatedness which those basic differences establish.

Our embrace of the Marxian methodology is a delicately selective affair and it is also a rejection of the Marxian content, or of the synoptic imperative which is the law of that content. Our reluctance to relate ourselves by difference to the objects we study is an attempt to save the present and its subjectivity from objectification by a critically transformed past. With a

---

[6] Tony Bennett, *Formalism and Marxism* (London: Methuen, 1979), pp. 167–8.

predictable irony, our conscientiously heterodox empiricism – our refusal to *repeat* the Romantic form of knowledge: literally, a refusal of the narrative principle that governs romance – locates our freedom within the mythic, untransformed past we have taken such pains to dismantle. Indeed, our discreetly truncated dialectics construct that particular myth all over again. We have, in short, and very much against our will, reified the Romantic science.

Let me put a happier accent on this irony and at the same time establish the character of my own interest in the subject. I have suggested that in some respects, our new and scandalous criticism is a reprise of our critical object: the Romantic ideology. I have also implied, however, that a world – or worlds – of difference separates the original from its reproduction. (More specifically, 'the alienation of the objectified result is not the same as the alienation at the point of departure. It is the passage from one to the other that defines [the subject].'[7]) We may characterize our new historicism as that 'thought which is lost and alienated in the course of [the] action so that it may be rediscovered by and in the action itself'.[8] To say this – to quote Sartre in this context – is a way of suggesting that our consciousness of Romantic poetry is the consciousness *of* that practice ('of' in the genitive sense) produced as a moment in the course of its accomplishment. We use the fact of our interest, then, to plot our position within the objective field radiating from or including both the object we study and the existence we create for ourselves (the future we project for ourselves) by that study. Since our critical practice has already figured 1798 and 1988 – or certain sectors of those formations – as part of a developing, leap-frogging totalization, we have no choice but to study this phenomenon. By 'totalization' – which is here Sartre's word – I mean to describe a structure that comes into being only through the dialectical practice of the present, which is read as the delayed effect of that structure. We define the structure of the past as an absent cause promoting a range of effects that, at a certain historical moment, configurate with an origin to which they are related by difference and distance. At that moment – which we regard as a unique opportunity for critical translation – the origin coalesces as a structure, one which is really, suddenly, there in the past, but only by the retroactive practice of the present. Our totalizing act thus becomes part of the movement by which history continually reorganizes itself. Even as we wait upon the real development of that history as the sufficient condition for our critical acts, these acts also hasten that development. This is to say that we really *are* part of the object we study, subject to the changes that our study effects.[9]

---

[7] Jean-Paul Sartre, *Search for a Method*, trans. Hazel Barnes (New York: Random House, 1968), p. 99, note 4.

[8] Sartre, *Search for a Method*, p. 33, note 9.

[9] This construct represents a crossing of Althusser's concept, structural causality, and Sartre's discussion of totalization. See Louis Althusser and Etienne Balibar, *Reading Capital*, trans. Ben Brewster (London: New Left Books, 1970), pp. 184–93; Sartre, *Search for a Method*, pp. 133–66; and *Critique of Dialectical Reason*, ed. Jonathan Ree, trans. Alan Sheridan-Smith (London: New Left Books, 1982), pp. 53–252. I am indebted to Fredric Jameson's own implicit alignment of these positions, *The Political Unconscious* (Ithaca, NY: Cornell University Press, 1981), pp. 33–58, 74–102.

How then *should* we position ourselves towards the literatures of the past? How to avoid historicism's Hobson's choice of contemplation or empathy, a discourse of knowledge or of power? One might propose that in a real and practical way, *we are the effects* of particular pasts, to which we are related by distance and difference. Those pasts could be bound to us as the absent cause is linked to the effects which embody it. To say this is to identify that second and difficult Real of which Althusser writes – not the binary opposite to the age's Imaginary but that which resists symbolization absolutely – with the future, some *particular* future. By our ideological practice, we produce Wordsworth's absolute Real and in so doing, we catapult *our* Real to some unimaginable point in the future. We do this with a certain panache; we *send* the content of our criticism beyond its phrase. We *invite* the generations that succeed us to tread us down: totalize our phrases and violate our knowledge. If this violence presses out our Real in symbolic form, then we will have anticipated the future and there *will have been* a meaning to that which we suffer in our lives because we cannot conceive it. This is an ironic view of history as lived and a comic view of history as reproduced by the future. It is, following Benjamin, the gift of the destructive character.

How do we know which past we are in position to realize; which past is ready to begin its posthumous life now? This is a question that can only be answered in a practical and circular way. One asks oneself which periods are generating the most interest and producing the most interesting criticism. Which group of critics seems most passionate, most defensive and extreme? Which is the most awkward in its rhetoric and difficult in its forms of argumentation? Which discourse sounds the most theological? Exciting work is always being done across the board; one needs to find out which group of historians feels most vividly a sense of mission and of solidarity.

We know there are moments when two ages call to each other in powerful ways. Naturally, there are strong local reasons – institutional reasons – for these conjunctions. But we must also wonder if there aren't other orders of explanation. Might we not be part of a developing, leap-frogging logic? Are we, or could we *make* ourselves the consciousness of the Romantic movement produced as a moment in the accomplishment of that action? To ask this is to wonder who we are that we produce the Romantics in just this way. It is also to inquire who *they* are, to have produced us in just this way. Once again, we go *back* to the future.

To ask these questions is to insist that we rewrite the past with the full complement of contemporary knowledges. It is also to name ourselves as producers of the past *as past* and thus of history's meaning, even as we bring out the historical overdetermination of our productive acts and even as we renounce a fully dialectical knowledge of ourselves. We define ourselves as a potential structure to be actualized by whatever generation it is that turns around and seeks us out as its way of living its present. This model is, among other things, a way to establish the absolute difference between past and present but also to see that this difference is a form of complicity.

For the old historicism, the alleged project was to restore to the dead their own, living language, that they might bespeak themselves. Historicism defined, as we know, a sort of ventriloquism – a virtuoso variety. The dummy really seems to speak; the ventriloquist does not move his lips.

By contrast, the critical work I've been describing should be called translation. One of the phrases that recurs throughout today's criticism is 'rewriting the past'. We refresh the cliché by way of Benjamin's great essay, 'The Task of the Translator'. The formal analogy gains a certain force from Benjamin's own sense of its relevance to our Romantic concerns.

> It is no mere coincidence that the word 'ironic' here [apropos the relation of translation to original] brings the Romanticists to mind. They, more than any others, were gifted with an insight into the life of literary works which has its highest testimony in translation. To be sure, they hardly recognized translation in this sense, but devoted their entire attention to criticism, another, if a lesser, factor in the continued life of literary works.[10]

Benjamin asks a shocking question: 'Is a translation meant for readers who do not understand the original?' He goes on, 'For what does a literary work "say"? . . . It "tells" very little to those who understand it.' There is, naturally, a conventional – indeed, a Romantic – way of reading the remark. I paraphrase: 'Great literature, as all good readers know, has no content. It has transmuted all that raw facticity into soul and form.' There is also, however, the strong reading: literature tells very little to those whose ideology reproduces it, who can represent it to themselves, conceive it – in short, understand it. Such readers can be 'edified' by the work (and we recall Benjamin's scorn for edification). They can, that is, be 'built up, improved' (the root meaning of 'edify'). They cannot, however, be taken apart, and this is what art, for most of us, seems to be about. The translation, then, is meant for those who come at some *particular* 'later', one that compels them to produce their lives in a way not just different from but antagonistic to the way of the original. Because of this, they cannot read the original properly. Therefore they can put it to work.

To put this practically, we could say that all works become avant-garde at a particular point in time which is the beginning of their posthumous existence. The job of the translator-critic – our job – is to produce this point of departure. We can only do this by producing a bad, a literal, translation, one that, by misunderstanding the spirit of the original, *represents* the work's resistance to those who 'do not speak its tongue', who do not share, that is, its ideology. Translation of this kind pronounces the original's ineffability yet preserves its silence. It demonstrates the original's strong difference from the present age, and, at the same time, shows that only this age, these barbarians, can change the work and be changed by it. This parodic translation is, then, the exemplary act of literary appreciation since it is the only repetition that leaves the original intact. It is also the most invasive kind of criticism imaginable. Or, to rewrite Benjamin's question, and as an answer, *originals* are meant for those who do not understand them; they are meant for the criticism of the future.

This is the real power of art-works – not just to survive (the classic 'classic' definition) but to flare up at a certain moment, thereby introducing their

---

[10] Walter Benjamin, 'The Task of the Translator', in *Illuminations*, ed. Hannah Arendt, trans. Harry Zohn (New York: Harcourt, Brace and World, 1968), pp. 69–82.

distinct order of production into the alien formations of another age. One is reminded of that trusty translation metaphor, 'old wine in new bottles'. The phrase is a good one so long as it is taken to signify the *contradiction* between old and new. It is this friction that realizes the old, and that gives the new – the critique or translation – *its* power to flare up later. Only by the differential of another intention can the intention of those first words crystallize. This sort of dialogism is exactly the aim of that critical ravishing, that literalism, I have described.[11]

In order to use what is thrust upon us – Romantic poetry or its academic form, historicism – our criticism must first be abstract: a repetition detoured through the concepts of the present. It must change: meaning, it must change the past, and let itself *be changed* by its own invention. Finally, it must give pleasure. Thus do we prescribe that 'libidinal investment' Jameson has discussed. We ask of our criticism a susceptibility to reduction, such that the present can use it for its own exercises in the imaginary. We do all this because the literatures of the past, if left to themselves, confront us as despotic structures: what Sartre calls totalities as opposed to totalizations. The more resonant phrase is 'practico-inert'. It's not a question, as historicism thought, of calling up the past and making it speak. The past is with us all the time and it never stops speaking. Without an aggressive re-enactment of the past, it reenacts us. One thinks of that nightmare of familiarity – that terrible, because imperial, family romance, 'The Shining'. One thinks of those importunate ghosts and feels the hideousness of the past when it gets *passively* re-enacted.

Benjamin tells us 'it is not the highest praise of a translation . . . to say that it reads as if it had originally been written in that language.' This business of re-totalizing is a corrosive affair. Benjamin advises a 'literal rendering of the syntax which proves words rather than sentences to be the primary element of the translator'. We have seen in our reading of Wordsworth's sonnet how material a rewriting of the past this protocol entails.[12] Benjamin finds at the end

---

[11] Here's what comes of all this shuttling. Or, here's what results from the ravishing of our textual brides. Our appreciation of the thoroughly Romantic character of Wordsworth's poem ['The world is too much with us' (ed.)] – its critical production of the past – thoroughly modernizes it. By our work, we are positioned to recognize in Wordsworth's strategies of inwardness (his opposition of the private, revelatory moment to the sordid social realities of contemporary culture), the technique of Eliot and Pound. In Wordsworth as in the high modernists, the utopian move is accomplished by and is identical with the reactionary, regressive move. The evocation of the noble past – the transparency and wholeness of the classical (i.e. pre-capitalist) cultures – is at once escape from, critique and 'ideological duplication' of the age's mean materialism. Moreover, we feel in Wordsworth, and precisely within his most humanistic longings, the same fascist edge we brush up against in Eliot and Pound: the same longing for a government that is oneself but other and that inhabits the individual as a god might do. The wish is for a creed made by human beings an art – but one that somehow breaks free of its makers and their inevitably corrupt interests, returning to liberate them from their meanness, their guilt. This terrible dream of what Stevens calls the 'major man' is also a radical, monistic solution to the problem Sartre has defined as *the* problem of historical investigation: that of *relating* inside to outside, individual to collective life. There is, of course, a modernist *comic* solution – Joyce's, for instance – and this is a genuine critical action. This difficult response is the dialectical rewriting of the inside – outside dualism, a response that we recognize as the desideratum of both the Marxian and Freudian hermeneutics.

[12] For Levinson's reading of Wordsworth's sonnet 'The world is too much with us' (composed 1802–4, published 1807) see the original version of this essay, pp. 35–49. [ed.]

of this process a 'pure language – which no longer means or expresses anything but is, as expressionless and creative Word, that which is meant in all languages'. To take the mystical edge off this and to coordinate it with some earlier remarks, we may identify this Word with the Real which resists symbolization absolutely and which is therefore experienced as necessity. By our criticism, we configurate our own, unimaginable Real with the Real of 1802, and while we cannot *remember* that Real – cannot, therefore, teach it – we can, by our bad repetition, represent it. The effect one hopes to produce by one's criticism is that of shock: deep familiarity and profound difference. It took 150 years to hear 'The world is too much with us, late and soon' with a certain ring. This is definitely *not* the ring heard by Wordsworth's contemporaries. One hopes it is a ring different enough from all those sounds and some of our own, and in the right ways, for it to make Wordsworth's phrase re-sound, to make it 'tell', in Benjamin's sense, which is the opposite of 'teach'.

Up until now, Romantic poetry was not categorically different from the literary output of any other age. Because it lacked a distinctive kind of pastness, it had no distinctive presentness either. To read Romantic poetry tendentiously – for ourselves – we effectively read it by its own latest dream. In the selfsame motion and by feeling the lateness of our dream, we alter our own language. 'The basic error of the translator is that he preserves the state in which his own language happens to be instead of allowing his language to be powerfully affected by the foreign tongue.' The translator-critic does not redeem the past, he – or she – conceives it, by an action that might remind us of Yeats's 'Leda and the Swan', an action that produced Helen, Troy, Homer and history. We do *to* the past what it could not do *for* itself. We see it clearly in the idea of it.

SECTION THREE

Soundings

The final part of the Reader illustrates the application of the theoretical perspectives surveyed in the first two parts to the practice of interpretation. Its aim is to demonstrate how profoundly and diversely cultural materialism and cultural poetics have transformed our perception of the classics of the literary canon.

This section embraces novels, plays and poetry, and it ranges in time from the *Oresteia* to the *Cantos*; but it starts off, appropriately, with a brace of contrasting essays on the Bard, on whose drama new historicism and cultural materialism cut their teeth. Both *Measure for Measure* and *The Tempest* revolve around omnipotent rulers who behave just like dramatists, and who thus provide perfect opportunities to examine the complicities of art with power. 'Although neither the dramatist nor the king is onstage,' Jonathan Goldberg observes, 'the Duke in *Measure for Measure* represents them both, the clearest emblem for the relationship of literature and politics in the Jacobean period.' It is the act of representation itself that forges the link between the theatre and the throne, and *Measure for Measure* can be read very profitably, as Goldberg's account confirms, as Shakespeare's meditation on the role of representation in sustaining absolute power, and the part played by the stage in enhancing the mystique of the sovereign, the playwright's own dark double. Shakespeare's claustrophobic Vienna, epitomized by the prisonhouse through which most of the cast pass, and policed by the Duke himself, the incarnation of surveillance, offers an irresistible image of the carceral culture depicted by Foucault in *Discipline and Punish*. The island Prospero patrols like some invisible voyeur plainly fits the bill as well, making it tempting to read *The Tempest* as a theatrical preview of the panopticon. But, as Francis Barker and Peter Hulme contend, in this play power proves far more vulnerable to anxiety about its implication in oppression. Barker and Hulme are led to this recognition by their admirably dialogic approach, which treats *The Tempest* as both historically constrained by its origins and ripe for progressive appropriation today. As a result their analysis of the play is more persuasive than cultural materialist accounts that rely solely on the imperatives of the present and reading against the grain. In the bizarre opening scene of Act IV, when Prospero's sudden recollection of Caliban's plot disrupts his celebratory masque, the play betrays, for Barker and Hulme, a 'fundamental disquiet concerning its own functions within the projects of colonialist discourse', and the massive investment of energy required to repress its political unconscious.

In the next essay, however, there seems to be no way to rescue Defoe's tale of another man marooned on an island from unqualified collusion in the history of subjection. In fact, in John Bender's compelling interpretation, not only does *Robinson Crusoe* lose whatever shreds of political innocence and heroic humanism may have clung to it, but its seminal status in the history of English fiction ensures that the novel itself, and ultimately writing as such, take the rap along with it. The grim thesis of this excerpt from *Imagining the Penitentiary* owes a huge debt, needless to say, to Foucault, its *spiritus rector*, and to *Discipline and Punish* in particular. But it is Bender's distinction to have made the connection between narrative and the nascent society of the spectacle, and to invite us to discern in the early masterpieces of the English novel a sinister schooling in techniques of restraint. Not even the notorious polyphony of the form, acclaimed by Mikhail Bakhtin as the secret of its subversiveness, can redeem it in Bender's eyes. For in the end, 'while it remains permissive in many respects, the novel oscillates between points of view that imply surveillance and enclosure. On the one hand stand novels in which readers enter the mental world of a single character and thereby fictionally view reality as a network of contingencies dependent upon observation; on the other lie novels in which readers ally themselves with the controlling power of an omniscient narrator.'

The paranoid suspicion that all imaginative writing, and especially the literature of the eighteenth century, might turn out to be a blueprint for Bentham's panopticon is rapidly dispelled by Heather Glen's reading of Blake's poem 'London'. It is instructive to juxtapose this essay with Bender's because 'London' mirrors much the same predicament as Defoe describes, obliging us likewise to 'enter the mental world of a single character and thereby fictionally view reality as a network of contingencies dependent upon observation'. Without recourse to the ubiquitous Foucault, to whom her book *Vision and Disenchantment* owes nothing, Glen discovers in Blake's song of experience a bleak, constricted universe governed by the Medusan gaze of power; but she also discerns in the language of 'London' resources which demystify the logic of surveillance and expose it to critique. The ostensible detachment of the speaker/spectator is confounded by the poem's disclosure that 'what he observes is the objectification of his own activity', and that he is 'dominated by what he hears, trapped within the world on which he is trying to comment'. The apocalyptic urban spectacle of violence, disease and desolation incriminates the eye that beholds it and, indeed, the pen that puts it into words. Blake implicitly arraigns himself and the reader for their share in replicating a plight whose depiction imparts 'a haunting poetic sense of that which is missing'. Through this 'negative articulation of alternative possibility', however,

> Blake makes it very clear that the disaster portrayed here is not inevitable. It has not been imposed by an unchangeable social order, nor is it the product of 'the ancient curse', the inborn evil of mankind. In 'London' it is shown to be the inevitable result of particular, chosen modes of relating to others, here manifested throughout a whole society. And this realization in one sense does imply its opposite: what has been humanly chosen and created can be humanly reversed.

It strikes me as no accident, moreover, that Glen reaches these conclusions as the result of a scrupulous analysis of specific words, whose complex historical connotations she excavates, and after considering Blake's revisions in his notebooks and the impact of his engraving technique on the poem's plot. New historicists and cultural materialists regularly treat texts as pretexts to explore other sorts of discourse, as local expressions of a larger cultural law, or as confirmations of the theoretical preconceptions they have brought to bear on them. But, as Lee Patterson suggests in Section Two and Heather Glen demonstrates here, a healthy regard for the creative individuality and deliberate intent of the author at work with the language can deliver less predictable revelations.

The long shadow of Foucault falls across Nancy Armstrong's inquiry into the politics of domestic fiction in 1848, returning us to a more diagnostic style of critical discourse. This time, however, *The History of Sexuality* takes the lead in a trenchant feminist analysis of the function of the novel in the symbolic economy of Victorian culture. The idea of internalized surveillance from *Discipline and Punish* and the concept of the grotesque body developed by Bakhtin in *Rabelais and His World* play the supporting roles, as Armstrong unmasks the ploys devised by narrative to occlude the political reality of nineteenth-century Britain. The discipline of sociology, pioneered in this period by Shuttleworth and Mayhew, and the groundbreaking fiction of Gaskell, Dickens, Thackeray and the Brontës serve the same oblique purpose: to disguise a social problem as a sexual problem by deflecting attention on to transgressive female figures, and especially the demonized figure of the prostitute. In this critical scenario the madwoman in Rochester's attic, the insatiable ghost of Heathcliff's Cathy and the mutilated corpse of Nancy, the tender-hearted whore in *Oliver Twist*, are unavailable for conscription as insurgent outsiders. They might *seem* obvious recruits for the resistance, glaring faultlines in the fabric of coercion, but that only makes them more effective as double-agents of the patriarchal state from the start. 'It is no accident', remarks Armstrong, 'that all the monstrous women in question have other than middle-class origins. Resembling Bakhtin's figure of the grotesque body in several ways, this kind of female body is open, permeable, and ambiguously gendered. In her, other sexual behaviours linger on as archaic forms that are both powerless and terrible. And as these cultural materials are contained within the body of a deranged woman, all threats of social disruption suddenly lose their political meaning and are just as suddenly quelled.'

The contrast between the critical vision of Nancy Armstrong and that of Jerome McGann could hardly be starker. Given the centrality to his argument of Benjamin's 'Theses on the Philosophy of History', with their stern admonition that 'There is no document of civilization which is not at the same time a document of barbarism', McGann needs no reminding of how deeply the cultural treasures of the canon are contaminated by the history of violence and injustice that produced them. But he refuses to believe that this is the whole story, and he puts forward instead, in theory and in practice, a way of reading the great texts of the literary tradition that could release them from fossilization by old and new historicists alike. Contextualizing is crucial, but not of the kind that imprisons the work in its orthodox perception of itself, erasing all trace of divided loyalties and involuntary premonitions:

When we think of poems 'in their historical contexts', our historicist biases – even in their 'New Historicist' modes – take those 'contexts' to be located primarily in the past, or – if we have read our Nietzsche and Foucault with care – in the present and the past. And when we think even more deeply about such matters we also understand that these historical contexts are multiple and conflicting: heteroglossial, as Bakhtin would say. But if it is true that all futures are functions of the past (and the present), then we must expect to find those futures being carried out in the works that seem to be speaking and acting only from the past.

Poems imagine more than they know. The *Oresteia* is a far greater work, in those future contexts of reality it had not discussed and did not desire, than it is when we read it merely in the context of its own grandiose – and mistaken – self-conceptions.

To reread Aeschylus, Blake and Pound from this perspective is to reveal three mighty prophets against empire. It is also, perhaps, one more step, as McGann's eloquent essay suggests, towards a critical practice consistent with the Third World imagination of which Frantz Fanon dreamed: a criticism committed to eroding our imperialist culture by unshackling the proleptic potential of its finest literature.

13 Jonathan Goldberg

Measure for Measure as Social Text[1]

James I and the Politics of Literature: Jonson, Shakespeare, Donne, and their Contemporaries, Johns Hopkins University Press: Baltimore and London, 1983, pp. 230–9.

With Shakespeare, instrumentality, or, as Stephen Greenblatt calls it, improvisation, is everything.[2] Shakespeare's relation to his culture remains difficult to summarize, not because he is apart from it, but because he assumes no fixed relationship to it. This has often made it possible to act as if Shakespeare was some timeless figure, a man for all times and yet of none. This is, palpably, erroneous. Yet, opposing attempts, for instance E.M.W. Tillyard's,[3] to moor his political and historical attitudes in a morass of Elizabethan commonplaces, have foundered. As Greenblatt says, it seems untrue to characterize Shakespeare as a Tudor propagandist, but equally unconvincing to speak of him as a Marlovian rebel; it is false, too, to locate him (with Jonson) on some *via media*. The space of Shakespearean representation is, Greenblatt concludes, radically unstable, a place of improvisation where all the beliefs of the culture are trotted out, tried on, but where none is ultimately adopted. This is not Keatsian negative capability exactly; rather, Shakespeare occupies a thoroughly theatrical space. But, we must add, his theatrical space is inscribed in a cultural theatre. James, we need hardly recall, viewed himself as an exemplary performer onstage. Shakespearean improvisation partakes of the royal mode; it achieves the show of transparency, the heart of inscrutability, to which the king's double language aspired.

Unlike Jonson or Donne, Shakespeare appears to have had no firsthand dealings with the king. Yet their paths crossed significantly. When James came to the throne, his first act in the literary realm was to take the theatres under his patronage. Shakespeare's company, as we all know, became the King's Men. As part of his entertainment, James demanded court performances of plays; the King's Men were favoured, and many plays by their leading playwright were performed at court. This is about as far as one can faithfully state the relationship between Shakespeare and the king. Many critics have gone further and have supposed that royal patronage circumscribed the subject matter and

---

[1] Title provided by the editor of the present volume with the permission of the author and Johns Hopkins University Press. [ed.]

[2] *Renaissance Self-Fashioning: From More to Shakespeare* (Chicago: University of Chicago Press, 1980), pp. 222 ff., esp. pp. 227–8, 252–4.

[3] In, for example, *Shakespeare's History Plays* (1944; reprint, New York: Collier Books, 1962). Perhaps the most useful account of Shakespeare's relation to the political and social beliefs of his time is W. Gordon Zeeveld's *The Temper of Shakespeare's Thought* (New Haven, Conn.: Yale University Press, 1974).

attitudes expressed in plays, or involved commissioning plays for court performance. This does not seem to have been the case. Plays performed by the King's Men, like *Sejanus*, could be suspected of sedition and atheism. Plays performed at court were always drawn from the public repertory, and there is no example of a play written for court. Even the plays chosen for court performance need not have been overtly adulatory or even topically suitable, *Othello*, for instance, being one play chosen for the marriage celebrations of Princess Elizabeth, nor were the companies performing always in good standing with the court. To take one example, Marston's *The Dutch Courtesan*, performed several times before the king, derives some of its humour from dialects, and the Scots – and thus James and his favourites – are not immune.[4] Cocledemoy, the witty knave and parodist, determining that he 'must dissemble, must disguise' takes first the identity of 'a Northerne Barbar' (2.1. 205–7) named Andrew Sharke (2.2.3). The name combines the patron saint of Scotland with Scottish rapacity. Yet, presumably, the play pleased the king for much the same reasons that Jonson's antimasques succeeded. James countenanced what he would not have tolerated behind his back.

In the canon of Shakespeare's works, one play that has induced frequent speculation about the relationship of playwright and king is *Measure for Measure*.[5] We have been assured that it was written for court performance in 1604 (it seems clear that it was performed before the king on Christmas that year), or, at the very least, that the text we have is one revised for that performance.[6] And we have been told that the Duke mouths James's opinions and apes his actions. These claims are as easily answered: no plays were written for court performance; we know too little about the status of Shakespeare's texts to be able to determine that the one we have is a court revision; the opinions that the Duke and James share can be found readily in many political treatises of the time; much as some of the Duke's acts may recall James's, more do not – for instance, his crucial disguise as a monk has no literal counterpart in James's career. Yet criticism is no doubt correct in feeling that *Measure for Measure* has some special relationship to the king. In

---

[4] Citations from Marston's *The Dutch Courtesan*, ed. Peter Davison (Berkeley and Los Angeles: University of California Press, 1968).

[5] Citations from the Penguin edition, ed. R.C. Bald (Baltimore, Md.: 1956). The topicality of *Measure for Measure* is the burden of Josephine Waters Bennett's *Measure for Measure as Royal Entertainment* (New York: Columbia University Press, 1966) and an appendix to David Lloyd Stevenson, *The Achievement of Shakespeare's Measure for Measure* (Ithaca, NY: Cornell University Press, 1966). Occasional arguments are the subject of Richard Levin's attack, 'The King James Version of *Measure for Measure*', *Clio* 3 (1974), pp. 129–96 (reprinted in his *New Readings vs. Old Plays* [Chicago: University of Chicago Press, 1979]) and his debate over Roy Battenhouse's '*Measure for Measure* and King James', *Clio* 7 (1977), pp. 193–215, in *Clio* 7 (1977), pp. 217–6. Levin characteristically attacks straw men; Battenhouse's predictably theological reading (in which James is lectured by Shakespeare for not being a Catholic) is easily answered, as are the literalisms of much topical criticism. Still, as Battenhouse says ('*Measure for Measure* and King James', p. 221), Levin is merely a skeptic, and he sidesteps any real confrontation with the play. It is surely incontrovertible that Shakespeare is of his time; the question is how to describe that relation accurately, not to dismiss it out of hand.

[6] This point is made by J. Dover Wilson in the New Cambridge edition, and by John Wasson in '*Measure for Measure*: A Text for Court Performance?', *Shakespeare Quarterly* 21 (1970), pp. 17–24. J.W. Lever in the Arden edition points to many of the limits in this argument about the text.

the pages that follow, that relationship, and with it, Shakespeare's relationship to his culture, are explored through the crucial notion that links theatre and culture in James's time: representation. Perhaps one hardly need say more than this, that *Measure for Measure* is a play about substitution, replacement – and thus, re-presentation.[7] In it, the power of theatre bears a royal stamp. Hence, it is not surprising to find Josephine Waters Bennett spinning out this fantasy about the play:

> If the author himself acted the part of the Duke, then there could be no suggestion that the Duke was, or represented, King James. He *is* Shakespeare, acting a play which exemplifies what King James had written about kingcraft (that is, he is the King's puppet), and, in the last act, producing a play he has created (as the Duke) to resolve all difficulties and make everything come out right in the end. Shakespeare as actor and playwright is the 'God on earth' of his play, manipulating the other characters like puppets, and creating Lucio, the puppet who talks back to his creator. He is the God-Ruler in his world of make-believe, as King James thought himself to be in the real world.[8]

Se non è vero (and there is not a shred of evidence for any of the suppositions here) *è ben trovato.*

Not even the vagaries of stage tradition support Bennett's supposition that Shakespeare took the Duke's part. Yet her literalistic fantasy is based on an inchoate insight. The Duke plays two roles that overlap: as a monarch he has powers so extensive that Angelo can say that 'your grace, like power divine, / Hath looked upon my passes' (5.1. 365–6) – like James he rules by Divine Right. Hence, he is also responsible for Angelo's 'passes' as well as those of other characters in the play. He authorizes and authors their actions, and Angelo's career, in the seat of government and in bed with Mariana, is entirely scripted by the Duke. In the Duke, Shakespeare has written a role that represents his powers as playwright as coincident with the powers of the sovereign. This is more than the analogical statement that dramatist and king rule their realms, for the Duke reigns in both; dramatist and monarch represent each other, a doubleness housed in his single person. In her study of *Measure for Measure*, Bennett wavers in identifying the Duke with James; without realizing why, she is nonetheless correct; the play of representation does not invite exact identification. The Duke plays his part in two costumes, as ruler and as friar.[9] He is split, and he casts the

---

[7] The most cogent treatment of this point is Nancy S. Leonard's, 'Substitution in Shakespeare's Problem Comedies', *English Literary Renaissance* 9 (1979), pp. 281–301.

[8] Bennett, *Measure for Measure as Royal Entertainment*, p. 137.

[9] The Duke's double form leads to a particularly breathtaking display of power when he consigns Mariana to Angelo: 'I have confessed her and I know her virtue' (5.1.522). This seems to be an ultimate violation of privacy, and a demonstration of the confluence of sovereign power with the confessional. It is comprehended in the argument of Michel Foucault's *The History of Sexuality, Volume 1: An Introduction*, trans. Robert Hurley (New York: Pantheon Books, 1978). Foucault argues that the law that maintains sovereignty is entangled with the law that constitutes desire (see, e.g., pp. 81, 113); the confession is the form of discourse in which sex is made to speak, and the history of sexuality is the history of its being put into discourse. Sexuality is not, for Foucault, a natural phenomenon but 'a historical construct' (p. 105, cf. pp. 155–7), and in sexuality one has a 'dense transfer point for relations of power' (p. 103). In *Measure for Measure*, the Duke's two forms – as Angelo and as friar – are forms of the virtues upon which government rests, justice and religion. Both meet in sexuality in the play, the underlying privacy dragged into public.

characters into doubling, substitutive roles as well. In these re-presentational procedures, the play offers an image of its relation to sovereign power.

The play opens in a manner that characterizes its proceedings throughout. The Duke starts a disquisition on the nature of rule, 'Of government the properties to unfold' (1.1.3), but gets no further than this opening clause. Instead of words, the Duke points to Escalus, to whom he speaks, as the embodiment of the words about government he would have spoken. Although the dramatic procedure is not absolutely clear, its representational force is: as exemplar, Escalus doubles and embodies the Duke's learning and knowledge of government, and the Duke has 'unfolded' himself in Escalus. Since Escalus embodies the words, an audience might presume that the Duke is resigning his powers to him, since his 'commission' (1.1.13) embraces 'our city's institutions, and the terms / For common justice' (1.1.10–11). This supposition proves false immediately. Instead, the reins of power are handed to Angelo. The Duke thus puts two commissioners in his place as his representatives. Escalus seconds the Duke's choice of Angelo, but Angelo does not. The doubling thus produces division, too. 'Let there be some more test made of my mettle / Before so noble and so great a figure / Be stamped upon it' (1.1.48–50), Angelo asks. 'No more evasion' is the Duke's evasive reply.

The Duke has 'unfolded' himself in Angelo, who wishes, like the Duke, to refuse to play his part. Yet we cannot know how far Angelo represents the Duke, for we do not know why the Duke has chosen Angelo, or even if he knows why. When, later, it seems that Angelo's refusal to play his part stems from an incipient awareness of his unworthiness to administer a law he himself would violate, we do not know whether this is the Duke's case as well, although Lucio suggests that it is. Lucio exists to suggest that such analogies are identities and that the 'Duke of dark corners' (4.3.154–5) 'had some feeling of the sport' (3.2.112). 'The Duke yet would have dark deeds darkly answered' (3.2.165–6). Yet there is no reason to believe Lucio. What we can know is that the exercise of sovereign power and dramatic power as the play opens depends upon the enactment of substitutions whose analogical force remains mysterious. 'Do you call, sir, your occupation a mystery?' (4.2.30), Pompey the bawd turned executioner asks the hangman Abhorson, whose name at least suggests that he is an alter ego. His avowal of the mystery of his occupation echoes in a play where 'though you change your place, you need not change your trade' (1.2.104–5), as Pompey counsels Mistress Overdone, Madam Mitigation as he also calls her. The same places are forever reoccupied. Hence the whorehouse becomes a prison, a bawd an executioner, men's heads pay for maidenheads. Substitution is the law of the play and inherent in justice, the law of society as well. The 'mystery' in these multiple replacements and substitutions centres on the Duke, sovereign in both realms.

'What figure of us think you he will bear?' (1.1.16), the Duke asks Escalus about Angelo, a central question throughout the play. How does Angelo represent the Duke and how far does such representation go? Angelo's pun on *mettle* in the first scene suggests that he is a coin stamped with the Duke's figure. Sovereign power, real and stamped, sustains the exchange system of society, the endless refiguration of the king in representative acts of substitution. At the end of *Measure for Measure*, the Duke replays the opening scene anew, departing and reinvesting himself in Angelo and Escalus. 'The

Duke's in us' (5.1.293), Escalus says. Interior inhabitation there matches Angelo's condition; the Duke has 'lent him our terror, dressed him with our love' (1.1.19). Similarly, the absent Duke dons a friar's habit and is dressed with love. Thus, the Duke's language of figuration, supplementation ('Elected him our absence to supply' [1.1.18]), and investiture for his deputy predicts his own form in the play that follows. Angelo may well be called the Duke's 'motion generative' (3.2.104), his puppet. The substitute occupies the seat of power. But if 'the body politic be / A horse whereon the governor doth ride' (1.2.154–5), then public rule has private – and sexual – implications. The law of Vienna connects these two spheres, enforcing the fact that the private sphere is realized in public. The properties of government unfolded from the opening line of the play onward continually catch individual desire within the web of the body politic. This is 'the state, whereon [Angelo] . . . studied' (2.4.7).[10]

Thus the substitutions within the play are not exactly duplicative, but a series of analogies in which differences are crucial though unfathomable. Hence, at the end of the play, Angelo is in Claudio's position, having repeated his crime (so, too, have Lucio and Elbow, both virgin violators), and the Duke appears to be in Angelo's place, offering redemption to Isabella in exchange for sexual favours. Yet Angelo's crime seems monstrous whereas Claudio's seemed no crime at all, and the Duke's wooing of Isabella, even though he offers marriage, seems at least as much an assault upon her integrity as Angelo's proposition.

The final unsettling refigurations of *Measure for Measure* return the play to its initial premise, the unfolding of individual and communal government, and provide a mirror for the cultural situation of the play. No exact replay of James at all, the play yet manages to catch at central concerns: in the disguised Duke, the king's divided self; in the relations between privacy and the public, the play between internal and external theatres of conscience; in the Duke's actions, the combination of absence and presence through which James claimed authority. More specifically, commentators have felt that the Duke's initial decision to sneak away from Vienna reflects upon James and his aversion to crowds.

> I'll privily away; I love the people,
> But do not like to stage me to their eyes;
> Though it do well, I do not relish well
> Their loud applause and aves vehement,
> Nor do I think the man of safe discretion
> That does affect it.
>
> (1.1.67–72)

What genuinely seems to reflect James's government in this decision is the function of the Duke's retirement. Although, like James, the Duke could be accused (and is, by Lucio) of having little interest in running the government,

---

[10] In *Shakespeare and Society* (New York: Schocken Books, 1967), Terence Eagleton sees the crime of Claudio and Julietta as their attempt to keep sexual union private: 'Personal action, to be real, must be available for social verification' (p. 67).

delegating all responsibility to others, he does not retire to country pleasures; rather, he rules in absence, through others and in disguise. His presence-in-absence figures a mode of power. James claimed it; Tiberius exemplifies it. Power-in-absence is the central stance of absolutism necessary to maintain prerogatives and the secrets of state. The complexity of the relationship of *Measure for Measure* to this absolutist mode, and to its cultural situation, lies in the fact that the Duke, who professes complete power and control, is not in fact all-powerful. Lucio's accusations have force; the Duke's plots cause us discomfort and strain our credulity, too. Yet the Duke even asserts control over what he cannot control. His withdrawal figures his inability and his disinclination to enact his powers; yet his power lies in withdrawing.

The two Dukes – absolute and absent – meet in Act 5 when the two Dukes of the play – Vincentio and Friar Lodowick – confront each other. The Duke, having returned, disappears once again to return disguised anew. He faces his delegates, Escalus and Angelo, dispensing the Duke's Justice ('The Duke's in us' [5.1.293]). They unfold him. Responding to their attempt to send him to prison – the place where virtually everyone in the play arrives so that it reconstitutes the world and erases the margin between the world outside the prison walls and that within – he protests that the Duke has no power over him:

> The Duke
> Dare no more stretch this finger of mine than he
> Dare rack his own: his subject am I not,
> Nor here provincial. My business in this state
> Made me a looker-on here in Vienna.

(5.1.311–15)

The Duke's *double entendres* stem from a doubleness that runs throughout the play (notably present in Angelo's second scene with Isabella where his *sense* fails to meet hers).[11] Self-referentiality is self-divisive: 'His subject am I not.' More crucially, these *double entendres* point to the nature of the absolutist ruler – 'nor here provincial' – his separateness from the state he rules. Only he is not subject in such a state, and it is his special status - his aloneness, the fact that he is *sui generis* – that makes him no 'provincial' even at home, and always a 'looker-on', observing, a divine status. The Duke assumes this stance repeatedly, as did James, modelling himself on God in his lieutenancy, standing in place of God. The Duke represents James's Divine Right claims; as a divine – a friar – he claims the right not to be subject to the Duke.

From this stance, the Duke enacts his power, dispensing grace. The return of 'royal grace' (5.1.3) in the final act recasts the Duke's divine actions throughout; but the point about grace is made best by Lucio: 'Grace is grace, despite of all controversy: as, for example, thou thyself art a wicked villain, despite of all grace' (1.2.24–6). As he explains, grace is and is not grace. The wit of Lucio's statement lies in the way a tautology and identification ('grace

---

[11] On the meanings of *sense* and for a reading of the play that emphasizes much that is unsettling in it, see William Empson's 'Sense in *Measure for Measure*' in *The Structure of Complex Words* (Ann Arbor, Mich.: University of Michigan Press, 1967). For a reading of the play in which theatricality casts doubt upon the Duke's powers and virtues, see Ann Righter [Barton], *Shakespeare and the Idea of the Play* (London: Chatto and Windus, 1962; Harmondsworth: Penguin, 1967), pp. 158–62.

is grace') becomes exclusionary and self-divisive. That which refers to itself cannot be contained. This explains the Duke's inexplicable behaviour. Grace is grace despite the law; it lies beyond the boundaries. Just as Pompey can rename Mistress Overdone and call her Madame Mitigation, so bawdry – the Duke's bed trick, for instance – becomes grace in this play. In the exchanges that lead up to Lucio's definition of grace, this situation is epitomized by the pirate who stole the commandment 'thou shalt not steal' and thus remained pious, breaking no commandment, yet remained a pirate, too. These equivocations are suspended in the figure of the Duke and in his various deputies in the play – in Angelo, of course, and even in Elbow, the elbow of the law if not its right hand.

ELBOW.   Bless you, good father friar.
DUKE.   And you, good brother father. What offence hath this man made you, sir?
ELBOW.   Marry, sir, he hath offended the law; and sir, we take him to be a thief too, sir.
(3.2.10–14)

The Duke's parodic greeting scores a reflective point, as does Elbow's bumbling doubling of Pompey's offences – for in the play one could offend the law and yet be innocent. The Duke does – and his extension of grace makes it true for Angelo as well as Claudio. They are measured by his own measure. The pirate's loophole is extended to them, in the form of Ragozin the pirate's head. Even Barnardine, who resists the Duke's attempts to manipulate the plot through representative, substitutive acts, is also reprieved at the end. Nothing and nobody escapes the Duke's grasp. He makes the strongest opposing themes of the play, restraint and liberty, one. By a principle like the allophanic extension of Donne's poem on the Somerset wedding, all the characters reflect the Duke and become engaged in his schemes. 'The doubleness of the benefit defends the deceit from reproof' (3.1.250–1), the Duke-as-friar tells Isabella, recommending her lying to Angelo and Mariana's lying in her place. The benefit may be double, yet it also leads Isabella to experience the reported death of Claudio, her accusation of unchastity, and imprisonment. All this, the Duke affirms, is for her good, as is, presumably, his final grace – wooing her, and presenting – re-presenting – Claudio as a double of himself, 'as like almost to Claudio as himself' (5.1.485). In the play, tautology is the Duke's truth, and with it all's good, all's one, reflecting him, serving his ends.

We know that we will never know his ends, that the Duke's motives, unrepresented, can never be known. We see a play of representation in which the rule of doubleness is, from the Duke's perspective, endlessly to his credit, representing multiple mirrors of his powers. Yet representation maintains, from the start, its opacity precisely because the principle of substitution opens up unfathomable differences, making it unclear whether we should read grace-as-grace or grace-despite-grace. We see this when Isabella cannot hear what Angelo says to her, and he assumes that she either is ignorant or pretending to be (2.4.74–5). And we see it uproariously when Escalus attempts to determine what was done to Elbow's wife (2.1). This, of course, will be a vital question later in the play, when it turns out that Angelo has done nothing more than sleep with his betrothed. 'Do you hear how he misplaces?' (2.1.84), Escalus's question about Elbow's speech – the speech of a constable of the Duke's, an administrator of his justice – applies to all who are replaced in the play – from the Duke in his habit, to Angelo in his. 'O place, O form, / How often dost thou with thy case, thy habit, / Wrench awe from fools, and tie the wiser souls / To thy false seeming' (2.4.12–15).

The enactment of justice is always a scene of representation, putting into language what has occurred, doubling an event in words. In *Measure for Measure*, both events and words share a doubleness, and language when it is most accurate unspeaks itself. Thus, Angelo speaks 'empty words' (2.4.2) and would have 'good Angel' inscribed on the devil's horn (2.4.16), a duplicitous autonomy that follows from a tautology – 'Blood, thou art blood' (2.4.15). Such is the language of things and the nature of events. Claudio's deed 'with character too gross is writ on Juliet' (1.2.150), and Angelo tells Isabella, 'I do arrest your words' (2.4.134), demanding that she put her body where her mouth was. Instead, she repeats herself. The play operates within language, Claudio apprehended 'for a name . . . 'tis surely for a name' (1.2.164, 166). He knows the double nature of 'the demigod Authority': 'on whom it will, it will; / On whom it will not, so: yet still 'tis just' (1.2.116, 118–19). Authority speaks a language – the Duke's – in which what is and what is not remain the same, always just. The power of authority takes root in language itself, endlessly reduplicative, endlessly re-presenting. 'I hope here be truths', Pompey affirms in his first dealing with the law (2.1.120); and this character, who has more names than any other character in the play – Thomas Tapster, bawd, caitiff, varlet, Hannibal, Pompey Bum – and whose change in 'mysteries' mirrors the Duke's transformation, tells a central truth no matter how much he lies.

> ESCALUS.   How would you live, Pompey? By being a bawd? What do you think of the trade, Pompey? Is it a lawful trade?
> POMPEY.   If the law would allow it, sir.
>
> (2:1.211–14)

The law to which Pompey refers is the law of Vienna: the law of representation. Representation includes acts of restatement and of interpretation as well as the dramatic act of renaming.

Shakespeare's Vienna is a curious locale, a landscape of Italianate vice (and with a cast of characters whose names are largely Italian) with its leader, the Duke, bearing an Italian title. It is a dramatic domain as another mirror for princes suggests: 'This play is the image of a murder done in Vienna. Gonzago is the duke's name; his wife, Baptista' (*Hamlet*, 3.2.30–1).[12] The dominant trope of *Measure for Measure* is the unfolding of government, the revelation of the politicization of the body, of the single cloth that links public and private spheres. No one is free from another's construction, everyone does himself wrong 'whether thou art tainted or free' (1.2.40–1), for 'every true man's apparel fits your thief' (4.2.42). All men are clothed similarly, free or restrained, innocent or criminal. All are subject to the Duke and his endless scheming and mysterious plotting. All: even the Duke; he, too, is caught within the web, part of the vice he wishes to separate himself from, and, in the last act, caught in his own dramatic manipulations. It is not merely that Lucio 'makes' the Duke (5.1.352, 511); his act of revelation and unmasking suggests the contained subversion that deconstructs what the Duke constructs. Lucio's

---

12 *Hamlet*, ed. Willard Farnham (Baltimore, Md: Penguin, 1957).

claims that he 'spoke ... according to the trick' (5.1.499–500) deny autonomy in his act; his lie tells a truth. For, although he pretends that his words were given him by the Duke and form part of his play, they do form part of the play, one in which he and the Duke have parts, actuating each other, operating as bound antagonists, linked as firmly as main masque and antimasque in a courtly entertainment. These are the measures of *Measure for Measure*, the principle of representation that prescribes a single law for the state and the theatre. In this elusive relationship, the king, the author, and the text of the play all have a part.

Measure for Measure suggests that the essential question that links politics and literature in the Jacobean period is representation. By representing representation, Shakespeare contributes to the discourse of his society and to its most pressing questions about prerogative, power, and authority. These questions also affect him, and his meditation on the nature of rule is inevitably self-scrutinizing as well. Although neither the dramatist nor the king is onstage, the Duke in *Measure for Measure* represents them both, the clearest emblem for the relationship of literature and politics in the Jacobean period. As the careers of Jonson and Donne, and their more explicit confrontation with royal power, suggest, the dilemma of representation that Shakespeare takes as his subject is at the heart of the relationship of literature to royal power, of the words of the poet to the king's language. For Donne, words came from the king directly; for Jonson, double language provided a reflecting glass; for Shakespeare, re-presenting assured autonomy. It was his law, and the king's.

---

14 Francis Barker and Peter Hulme

'Nymphs and Reapers Heavily Vanish': The Discursive Con-texts of The Tempest

Alternative Shakespeares, ed. John Drakakis, Methuen: London and New York, 1985, pp. 191–205.

I

No one who has witnessed the phenomenon of midsummer tourism at Stratford-upon-Avon can fail to be aware of the way in which 'Shakespeare' functions today in the construction of an English past: a past which is picturesque, familiar and untroubled. Modern scholarly editions of Shakespeare, amongst which the Arden is probably the most influential, have seemed to take their distance from such mythologizing by carefully locating the plays against their historical background. Unfortunately such a move always serves, paradoxically, only to highlight in the foregrounded text preoccupations and values which turn out to be not historical at all, but eternal. History is thus recognized and abolished at one and the same time. One of the aims of this essay is to give a closer account of this mystificatory negotiation of 'history', along with an examination of the ways in which the relationship between text and historical context can be more adequately formulated. Particular reference will be made to the way in which, in recent years, traditional notions of the historical sources of the text have been challenged by newer analyses which employ such terms as 'intertextuality' and 'discourse'. To illustrate these, a brief exemplary reading will be offered of *The Tempest*. But to begin with, the new analyses themselves need setting in context.

II

The dominant approach within literary study has conceived of the text as autotelic, 'an entity which always remains the same from one moment to the next';[1] in other words a text that is fixed in history and, at the same time, curiously free of historical limitation. The text is acknowledged as having been produced at a certain moment in history; but that history itself is reduced to being no more than a background from which the single and irreducible meaning of the text is isolated. The text is designated as the legitimate object of literary criticism, *over against* its contexts, whether they be arrived at through the literary-historical account of the development of particular traditions and genres or, as more frequently happens with Shakespeare's plays, the study of 'sources'. In either case the text has been separated from a surrounding ambit of other texts over which it is given a special pre-eminence.

In recent years, however, an alternative criticism, often referred to as 'structuralist' and 'poststructuralist', has sought to displace radically the primacy of the autotelic text by arguing that a text indeed 'cannot be limited by or to . . . the originating moment of its production, anchored in the intentionality of its author'.[2] For these kinds of criticism exclusive study of the moment of production is defined as narrowly 'historicist' and replaced by attention to successive *inscriptions* of a text during the course of its history.[3] And the contextual background – which previously had served merely to highlight the profile of the individual text – gives way to the notion of *intertextuality* according to which, in keeping with the Saussurean model of

---

[1] E.D. Hirsch, *Validity in Interpretation* (New Haven, Conn.: Yale University Press, 1967), p. 46.
[2] Tony Bennett, 'Text and History', in Peter Widdowson, ed., *Re-Reading English* (London: Methuen, 1982), p. 227; drawing on the argument of Jacques Derrida, 'Signature Event Context', *Glyph* 1 (1977), pp. 172–98.
[3] For the theory behind the concept of inscription see Renée Balibar, *Les Français fictifs: le rapport des styles littéraires au français national* (Paris: Hachette, 1974) and 'National Language, Education, Literature', in Francis Barker *et al.*, eds, *The Politics of Theory* (Colchester: University of Essex, 1983); Pierre Macherey and Etienne Balibar, 'On Literature as an Ideological Form: Some Marxist Propositions', *Oxford Literary Review* 3 (1978), pp. 4–12; and Tony Davies, 'Education, Ideology and Literature', *Red Letters* 7 (1978), pp. 4–15. For an accessible collection of essays which put this theory to work on the corpus of English literature, see Widdowson, ed., *Re-Reading English*.

language, no text is intelligible except in its differential relations with other texts.[4]

The break with the moment of textual production can easily be presented as liberatory; certainly much work of importance has stemmed from the study of inscription. It has shown for example that texts can never simply be *encountered* but are, on the contrary, repeatedly constructed under definite conditions: *The Tempest* read by Sir Walter Raleigh in 1914 as the work of England's national poet is very different from *The Tempest* constructed with full textual apparatus by an editor/critic such as Frank Kermode, and from the 'same' text inscribed institutionally in that major formation of 'English Literature' which is the school or university syllabus and its supporting practices of teaching and examination.[5]

If the study of the inscription and reinscription of texts has led to important work of historical description, it has also led to the formulation of a political strategy in respect of literary texts, expressed here by Tony Bennett when he calls for texts to be 'articulated with new texts, socially and politically mobilized in different ways within different class practices'.[6] This strategy also depends, therefore, on a form of intertextuality which identifies in all texts a potential for new linkages to be made and thus for new political meanings to be constructed. Rather than attempting to derive the text's significance from the moment of its production, this politicized intertextuality emphasizes the present *use* to which texts can now be put. This approach undercuts itself, however, when, in the passage from historical description to contemporary rearticulation, it claims for itself a radicalism which it cannot then deliver. Despite speaking of texts as always being 'installed in a field of struggle',[7] it denies to itself the very possibility of combating the dominant orthodoxies. For if, as the logic of Bennett's argument implies, 'the text' were wholly dissolved into an indeterminate miscellany of inscriptions, then how could any confrontation between different but contemporaneous inscriptions take place: what would be the ground of such a contestation?[8] While a genuine difficulty in theorizing 'the text' does exist, this should not lead inescapably to the point where the only option becomes the voluntaristic ascription to the text of meanings and articulations derived simply from one's own ideological preferences. This is a procedure only too vulnerable

---

[4] Intertextuality is a term coined by Julia Kristeva in *Le Texte du roman* (The Hague: Mouton, 1970) from her reading of the seminal work of Mikhail Bakhtin: *Rabelais and his World*, trans. Hélène Iswolsky (Cambridge, Mass.: MIT Press, 1968); *Problems of Dostoevsky's Poetics* (Ann Arbor, Mich.: Ardis, 1973); *The Dialogic Imagination: Four Essays*, ed. Michael Holquist, trans. Caryl Emerson and Michael Holquist (Austin, Texas: University of Texas Press, 1981).

[5] For Raleigh's *Tempest* see Terence Hawkes, 'Swisser-Swatter: Making a Man of English Letters', in John Drakakis, ed., *Alternative Shakespeares* (London: Methuen, 1985) pp. 26–46; Kermode is editor of the Arden edition of *The Tempest* (London: Methuen, 1954); on the formation of 'English' see Davies, 'Education, Ideology and Literature'.

[6] Bennett, 'Text and History', p. 224.

[7] Bennett, 'Text and History', p. 229.

[8] Stanley Fish, *Is There a Text in this Class?: The Authority of Interpretive Communities* (Cambridge, Mass.: Harvard University Press, 1980), p. 165. Fish, whose general argument is similar to Bennett's, admits that in the last analysis he is unable to answer the question: what are his interpretative acts interpretations *of*?

to pluralistic incorporation, a recipe for peaceful co-existence with the dominant readings, not for a contestation of those readings themselves. Struggle can only occur if two positions attempt to occupy the same space, to appropriate the 'same' text; 'alternative' readings condemn themselves to mere irrelevance.

Our criticism of this politicized intertextuality does not however seek to reinstate the autotelic text with its single fixed meaning. Texts are certainly not available for innocent, unhistorical readings. Any reading must be made from a particular position, but is not *reducible* to that position (not least because texts are not infinitely malleable or interpretable, but offer certain constraints and resistances to readings made of them). Rather, different readings struggle with each other on the site of the text, and all that can count, however provisionally, as knowledge of a text, is achieved through this discursive conflict. In other words, the onus on new readings, especially radical readings aware of their own theoretical and political positioning, should be to proceed by means of a *critique* of the dominant readings of a text.

We say critique rather than simply criticism, in reference to a powerful radical tradition which aims not merely to disagree with its rivals but to *read their readings*: that is, to identify their inadequacies and to explain why such readings come about and what ideological role they play.[9] Critique operates in a number of ways, adopting various strategies and lines of attack as it engages with the current ideological formations, but one aspect of its campaign is likely to have to remain constant. Capitalist societies have always presupposed the naturalness and universality of their own structures and modes of perception, so, at least for the foreseeable future, critiques will need to include an *historical* moment, countering capitalism's self-universalization by reasserting the rootedness of texts in the contingency of history. It is this particular ground that what we have been referring to as alternative criticism runs the risk of surrendering unnecessarily. As we emphasized earlier, the study of successive textual inscriptions continues to be genuinely important, but it must be recognized that attention to such inscriptions is not logically dependent on the frequent presupposition that *all* accounts of the moment of production are either crudely historicist or have recourse to claims concerning authorial intentionality. A *properly* political intertextuality would attend to successive inscriptions without abandoning that no longer privileged but still crucially important *first* inscription of the text. After all, only by maintaining our right to make statements that we can call 'historical' can we avoid handing over the very notion of history to those people who are only too willing to tell us 'what really happened'.

---

[9] Marx's work was developed out of his critique of the concepts of classical political economy that had dominated economic thought in the middle of the nineteenth century. We choose here to offer a critique of Kermode's introduction to the Arden *Tempest* because of the *strengths* of his highly regarded and influential work.

III

In order to speak of the Shakespearean text as an historical utterance, it is necessary to read it with and within series of *con-texts*.[10] These con-texts are the precondition of the plays' historical and political signification, although literary criticism has operated systematically to close down that signification by a continual process of occlusion. This may seem a strange thing to say about the most notoriously bloated of all critical enterprises, but in fact 'Shakespeare' has been force-fed behind a high wall called Literature, built out of the dismantled pieces of other seventeenth-century discourses. Two particular examples of the occlusive process might be noted here. First, the process of occlusion is accomplished in the production of critical meaning, as is well illustrated by the case of Caliban. The occlusion of his political claims – one of the subjects of the present essay – is achieved by installing him at the very centre of the play, but only as the ground of a nature/art confrontation, itself of undoubted importance for the Renaissance, but here, in Kermode's account, totally without the historical contextualization that would locate it among the early universalizing forms of incipient bourgeois hegemony.[11] Secondly, source criticism, which might *seem* to militate against autotelic unity by relating the text in question to other texts, in fact only obscures such relationships. Kermode's paragraphs on 'The New World' embody the hesitancy with which Shakespearean scholarship has approached the problem. Resemblances between the *language* of the Bermuda pamphlets and that of *The Tempest* are brought forward as evidence that Shakespeare 'has these documents in mind' but, since this must remain 'inference' rather than 'fact', it can only have subsidiary importance, 'of the greatest interest and usefulness', while clearly not 'fundamental to [the play's] structure of ideas'. Such 'sources' are then reprinted in an appendix so 'the reader may judge of the verbal parallels for himself', and the matter closed.[12]

And yet such closure proves premature since, strangely, source criticism comes to play an interestingly crucial role in Kermode's production of a site for *The Tempest*'s meaning. In general, the fullness of the play's unity needs protecting from con-textual contamination, so 'sources' are kept at bay except for the odd verbal parallel. But occasionally, and on a strictly *singular* basis, that unity can only be protected by recourse to a notion of source as explanatory of a feature otherwise aberrant to that posited unity. One example of this would be Prospero's well-known irascibility, peculiarly at odds with Kermode's picture of a self-disciplined, reconciliatory white magician, and therefore to be 'in the last analysis, explained by the fact that [he] descend[s] from a bad-tempered giant-magician'.[13] Another would be Prospero's strange perturbation which brings the celebratory masque of Act 4 to such an abrupt conclusion, in one reading (as we will demonstrate shortly) the most important

---

[10] Con-texts with a hyphen, to signify a break from the inequality of the usual text/context relationship. Con-texts are themselves *texts* and must be *read with*: they do not simply make up a background.

[11] Kermode, ed., *The Tempest*, pp. xxxiv–lxiii.

[12] Kermode, ed., *The Tempest*, pp. xxvii–xxviii.

[13] Kermode, ed., *The Tempest*, p. lxiii.

scene in the play, but here explained as 'a point at which an oddly pedantic concern for classical structure causes it to force its way through the surface of the play'.[14] In other words the play's unity is constructed only by shearing off some of its 'surface' complexities and explaining them away as irrelevant survivals or unfortunate academicisms.

Intertextuality, or con-textualization, differs most importantly from source criticism when it establishes the necessity of reading *The Tempest* alongside congruent texts, irrespective of Shakespeare's putative knowledge of them, and when it holds that such congruency will become apparent from the constitution of discursive networks to be traced independently of authorial 'intentionality'.

IV

Essential to the historico-political critique which we are proposing here are the analytic strategies made possible by the concept of *discourse*. Intertextuality has usefully directed attention to the relationship *between* texts: discourse moves us towards a clarification of just what kinds of relationship are involved.[15]

Traditionally *The Tempest* has been related to other texts by reference to a variety of notions: *source*, as we have seen, holds that Shakespeare was influenced by his reading of the Bermuda pamphlets. But the play is also described as belonging to the *genre* of pastoral romance and is seen as occupying a particular place in the *canon* of Shakespeare's works. Intertextuality has sought to displace work done within this earlier paradigm, but has itself been unable to break out of the practice of connecting text with text, of assuming that single texts are the ultimate objects of study and the principal units of meaning.[16] Discourse, on the other hand, refers to *the field* in and

---

[14]   Kermode, ed., *The Tempest*, p. lxxv.

[15]   Colin MacCabe, 'On Discourse', *Economy and Society* 8:4 (1979), pp. 279-307, offers a helpful guide through some of discourse's many usages. The concept of discourse at work in the present essay draws on Michel Foucault's investigation of the discursive realm. A useful introduction to his theorization of discourse is provided by Foucault's essays, 'Politics and the Study of Discourse', *Ideology and Consciousness* 3 (1978), pp. 7–26 and 'The Order of Discourse', in Robert Young, ed., *Untying the Text: A Post-structuralist Reader* (London: Routledge & Kegan Paul, 1981). Foucault's most extended theoretical text is *The Archaeology of Knowledge*, trans. Alan Sheridan (London: Tavistock, 1972). However, a less formal and in many ways more suggestive treatment of discourse is practised and, to a certain extent theorized, in his early work on 'madness' and in more recent studies of the prison and of sexuality, where discourse is linked with both the institutional locations in which it circulates and the power functions it performs: see *Madness and Civilization: A History of Insanity in the Age of Reason*, trans. Richard Howard (London: Tavistock, 1967); *Discipline and Punish: The Birth of the Prison*, trans. Alan Sheridan (London: Allen Lane, 1977); *The History of Sexuality, Volume 1: An Introduction*, trans. Robert Hurley (London: Allen Lane, 1979). For a cognate approach to discourse see the theory of 'utterance' developed by Valentin Voloshinov, *Marxism and the Philosophy of Language*, trans. Ladislaw Matejka and I.R. Titunik (New York: Seminar Press, 1973).

[16]   On the weakness of Kristeva's own work in this respect see Jonathan Culler, *The Pursuit of Signs* (London: Routledge & Kegan Paul, 1981), pp. 105–7.

through which texts are produced. As a concept wider than 'text' but narrower than language itself (Saussure's *langue*), it operates at the level of the enablement of texts. It is thus not an easy concept to grasp because discourses are never simply observable but only approachable through their effects just as, in a similar way, grammar can be said to be *at work* in particular sentences (even those that are ungrammatical), governing their construction but never fully present 'in' them. The operation of discourse is implicit in the regulation of what statements can and cannot be made and the forms that they can legitimately take. Attention to discourse therefore moves the focus from the interpretative problem of meaning to questions of instrumentality and function. Instead of *having* meaning, statements should be seen as *performative of* meaning; not as possessing some portable and 'universal' content but, rather, as instrumental in the organization and legitimation of power-relations – which of course involves, as one of its components, control over the constitution of meaning. As the author of one of the first modern grammars said, appropriately enough in 1492, 'language is the perfect instrument of empire.'[17] Yet, unlike grammar, discourse functions effectively precisely because the question of codifying its rules and protocols can never arise: the utterances it silently governs speak what appears to be the 'natural language of the age'. Therefore, from within a given discursive formation no general rules for its operation will be drawn up except against the ideological grain; so the constitution of the discursive fields of the past will, to some degree, need comprehending through the excavatory work of historical study.

To initiate such excavation is of course to confront massive problems. According to what we have said above, each individual text, rather than a meaningful unit in itself, lies at the intersection of different discourses which are related to each other in a complex but ultimately hierarchical way. Strictly speaking, then, it would be meaningless to talk about the unity of any given text – supposedly the intrinsic quality of all 'works of art'. And yet, because literary texts *are* presented to us as characterized precisely by their unity, the text must still be taken as a point of purchase on the discursive field – but in order to demonstrate that, athwart its alleged unity, the text is in fact marked and fissured by the interplay of the discourses that constitute it.

V

The ensemble of fictional and lived practices, which for convenience we will simply refer to here as 'English colonialism', provides *The Tempest*'s

---

[17] Antonio de Nebrija, quoted in Lewis Hanke, *Aristotle and the American Indians* (Bloomington, Ind.: Indiana University Press, 1959), p. 8.

dominant discursive con-texts.[18] We have chosen here to concentrate specifically on the figure of usurpation as the nodal point of the play's imbrication into this discourse of colonialism. We shall look at the variety of forms under which usurpation appears in the text, and indicate briefly how it is active in organizing the text's actual diversity.[19]

Of course conventional criticism has no difficulty in recognizing the importance of the themes of legitimacy and usurpation for *The Tempest*. Indeed, during the storm-scene with which the play opens, the issue of legitimate authority is brought immediately to the fore. The boatswain's peremptory dismissal of the nobles to their cabins, while not, according to the custom of the sea, strictly a mutinous act, none the less represents a disturbance in the normal hierarchy of power relations. The play then proceeds to recount or display a series of actual or attempted usurpations of authority: from Antonio's successful palace revolution against his brother, Prospero, and Caliban's attempted violation of the honour of Prospero's daughter – accounts of which we hear retrospectively; to the conspiracy of Antonio and Sebastian against the life of Alonso and, finally, Caliban's insurrection, with Stephano and Trinculo, against Prospero's domination of the island. In fact it could be argued that this series *is* the play, in so far as *The Tempest* is a dramatic action at all. However, these rebellions, treacheries, mutinies and conspiracies, referred to here collectively as usurpation, are not *simply* present in the text as extractable 'Themes of the Play'.[20] Rather, they are differentially embedded there, figural traces of the text's anxiety concerning the very matters of domination and resistance.

Take for example the play's famous *protasis*, Prospero's long exposition to Miranda of the significant events that predate the play. For Prospero, the real beginning of the story is his usurpation twelve years previously by Antonio, the opening scene of a drama which Prospero intends to play out during *The Tempest* as a comedy of restoration. Prospero's exposition seems unproblematically to take its place as the indispensable prologue to an

---

[18]   In other words we would shift the emphasis from the futile search for the texts Shakespeare 'had in mind' to the establishment of significant patterns within the larger discursive networks of the period. The notion of 'English colonialism' can itself be focused in different ways. The widest focus would include present con-texts, the narrowest would concentrate on the con-texts associated with the initial period of English colonization of Virginia, say 1585 to 1622. In the first instance many of the relevant texts would be found in the contemporary collections of Richard Hakluyt, *The Principal Navigations, Voyages, Traffiques and Discoveries of the English Nation* [1589], 12 vols (Glasgow: James MacLehose, 1903–5) and Samuel Purchas, *Purchas His Pilgrimes* [1625], 20 vols (Glasgow: James MacLehose, 1905–7). For congruent approaches see James Smith, '*The Tempest*', in *Shakespearian and Other Essays* (Cambridge: Cambridge University Press, 1974), pp. 159–261; Charles Frey, '*The Tempest* and the New World', *Shakespeare Quarterly* 30 (1979), pp. 29–41; Stephen Greenblatt, *Renaissance Self-Fashioning: From More to Shakespeare* (Chicago: University of Chicago Press, 1980), Ch. 4; and Peter Hulme, 'Hurricanes in the Caribbees: The Constitution of the Discourse of English Colonialism', in Francis Baker *et al.*, eds, *1642: Literature and Power in the Seventeenth Century* (Colchester: University of Essex, 1981), pp. 55–83.

[19]   See Pierre Macherey, *A Theory of Literary Production*, trans. Geoffrey Wall (London: Routledge & Kegan Paul, 1978). Macherey characterizes the literary text not as unified but as plural and diverse. Usurpation should then be regarded not as the centre of a unity but as the principle of a diversity.

[20]   Kermode's second heading (Kermode, ed., *The Tempest*, p. xxiv).

understanding of the present moment of Act 1, no more than a device for conveying essential information. But to see it simply as a neutral account of the play's prehistory would be to occlude the contestation that follows insistently throughout the rest of the first act, of Prospero's version of true beginnings. In this narration the crucial early days of the relationship between the Europeans and the island's inhabitants are covered by Prospero's laconic 'Here in this island we arriv'd' (1.2.171). And this is all we would have were it not for Ariel and Caliban. First Prospero is goaded by Ariel's demands for freedom into recounting at some length how his servitude began, when, at their first contact, Prospero freed him from the cloven pine in which he had earlier been confined by Sycorax. Caliban then offers his compelling and defiant counter to Prospero's single sentence when, in a powerful speech, he recalls the initial mutual trust which was broken by Prospero's assumption of the political control made possible by the power of his magic. Caliban, 'Which first was mine own King', now protests that 'here you sty me / In this hard rock, whiles you do keep from me / The rest o'th'island' (1.2.344–6).

It is remarkable that these contestations of 'true beginnings' have been so commonly occluded by an uncritical willingness to identify Prospero's voice as direct and reliable authorial statement, and therefore to ignore the lengths to which the play goes to dramatize its problems with the proper beginning of its own story. Such identification hears, as it were, only Prospero's play, follows only his stage directions, not noticing that Prospero's play and *The Tempest* are not necessarily the same thing.[21]

But although different beginnings are offered by different voices in the play, Prospero has the effective power to impose his construction of events on the others. While Ariel gets a threatening but nevertheless expansive answer, Caliban provokes an entirely different reaction. Prospero's words refuse engagement with Caliban's claim to original sovereignty ('This island's mine, by Sycorax my mother, / Which thou tak'st from me' [1.2.333–4]). Yet Prospero is clearly disconcerted. His sole – somewhat hysterical – response consists of an indirect denial ('Thou most lying slave' [1.2.346]) and a counter accusation of attempted rape ('thou didst seek to violate / The honour of my child' [1.2.349–50]), which together foreclose the exchange and serve in practice as Prospero's only justification for the arbitrary rule he exercises over the island and its inhabitants. At a stroke he erases from what we have called Prospero's play all trace of the moment of his reduction of Caliban to slavery and appropriation of his island. For, indeed, it could be argued that the series of usurpations listed earlier as constituting the dramatic action all belong to that play alone, which is systematically silent about Prospero's own act of usurpation: a silence which is curious, given his otherwise voluble preoccupation with the theme of legitimacy. But, despite his evasiveness, this moment ought to be of decisive *narrative* importance since it marks Prospero's self-installation as ruler, and his acquisition, through Caliban's enslavement, of the means of supplying the food and labour on which he and

---

[21] This is a weak form of the critical fallacy that, more chronically, reads Prospero as an autobiographical surrogate for Shakespeare himself. On some of the theoretical issues involved here see Foucault, 'What is an Author?' in J.V. Harari, ed., *Textual Strategies: Perspectives in Post-structuralist Criticism* (London: Methuen, 1979), pp. 141–60.

Miranda are completely dependent: 'We cannot miss him: he does make our fire, / Fetch in our wood, and serves in offices / That profit us' (1.2.313–15). Through its very occlusion of Caliban's version of proper beginnings, Prospero's disavowal is itself performative of the discourse of colonialism, since this particular reticulation of denial of dispossession with retrospective justification for it, is the characteristic trope by which European colonial regimes articulated their authority over land to which they could have no conceivable legitimate claim.[22]

The success of this trope is, as so often in these cases, proved by its subsequent invisibility. Caliban's 'I'll show thee every fertile inch o' th' island' (2.2.148) is for example glossed by Kermode with 'The colonists were frequently received with this kindness, though treachery might follow', as if this were simply a 'fact' whose relevance to *The Tempest* we might want to consider, without seeing that to speak of 'treachery' is already to interpret, from the position of colonizing power, through a purported 'description'. A discursive analysis would indeed be alive to the use of the word 'treachery' in a colonial context in the early seventeenth century, but would be aware of how it functioned for the English to explain to themselves the *change* in native behaviour (from friendliness to hostility) that was in fact a *reaction* to their increasingly disruptive presence. That this was an explanatory trope rather than a description of behaviour is nicely caught in Gabriel Archer's slightly bemused comment: 'They are naturally given to trechery, howbeit we could not finde it in our travell up the river, but rather a most kind and loving people.'[23] Kermode's use of the word is of course by no means obviously contentious: its power to shape readings of the play stems from its continuity with the grain of unspoken colonialist assumptions.

So it is not just a matter of the occlusion of the play's initial colonial moment. Colonialist legitimation has always had then to go on to tell its own story, inevitably one of native violence: Prospero's play performs this task within *The Tempest*. The burden of Prospero's play is already deeply concerned with producing legitimacy. The purpose of Prospero's main plot is to secure recognition of his claim to the usurped duchy of Milan, a recognition sealed in the blessing given by Alonso to the prospective marriage of his own son to Prospero's daughter. As part of this, Prospero reduces Caliban to a role in the supporting subplot, as instigator of a mutiny that is programmed to fail, thereby forging an equivalence between Antonio's initial *putsch* and Caliban's revolt. This allows Prospero to annul the memory of his failure to prevent his expulsion from the dukedom, by repeating it as a mutiny that he will, this time, forestall. But, in addition, the playing out of the colonialist narrative is thereby completed: Caliban's attempt – tarred with the brush of Antonio's supposedly self-evident viciousness – is produced as final and irrevocable confirmation of the natural treachery of savages.

---

[22] This trope is studied in more detail in Peter Hulme, *Colonial Encounters: Europe and the Native Caribbean, 1492–1797* (London: Methuen, 1986), chs 3 and 4. See also Francis Jennings, *The Invasion of America: Indians, Colonialism and the Cant of Conquest* (New York: Norton, 1976).

[23] Gabriel Archer, 'The Description of the Now Discovered River and County of Virginia . . .' [1607], in D. Quinn *et al.*, eds, *New American World* (London: Macmillan, 1979), V.

Prospero can plausibly be seen as a playwright only because of the control over the other characters given him by his magic. He can freeze Ferdinand in mid-thrust, immobilize the court party at will, and conjure a pack of hounds to chase the conspirators. Through this physical control he seeks with considerable success to manipulate the mind of Alonso. Curiously though, while the main part of Prospero's play runs according to plan, the subplot provides the only real moment of drama when Prospero calls a sudden halt to the celebratory masque, explaining, aside:

> I had forgot that foul conspiracy
> Of the beast Caliban and his confederates
> Against my life: the minute of their plot
> Is almost come.

                                                                  (4.1.139–42)

So while, on the face of it, Prospero has no difficulty in dealing with the various threats to his domination, Caliban's revolt proves uniquely disturbing to the smooth unfolding of Prospero's plot. The text is strangely emphatic about this moment of disturbance, insisting not only on Prospero's sudden vexation, but also on the 'strange hollow, and confused noise' with which the Nymphs and Reapers – two lines earlier gracefully dancing – now 'heavily vanish'; and the apprehension voiced by Ferdinand and Miranda:

FERDINAND.   This is strange: your father's in some passion
                        That works him strongly.
MIRANDA.   Never till this day
                        Saw I him touch'd with anger, so distemper'd.

                                                                  (4.1.143–5)

For the first and last time Ferdinand and Miranda speak at a distance from Prospero and from his play. Although this disturbance is immediately glossed over, the hesitation, occasioned by the sudden remembering of Caliban's conspiracy, remains available as a site of potential fracture.

The interrupted masque has certainly troubled scholarship, introducing a jarring note into the harmony of this supposedly most highly structured of Shakespeare's late plays. Kermode speaks of the 'apparently inadequate motivation' for Prospero's perturbation,[24] since there is no obvious reason why he should so excite himself over an easily controllable insurrection.

What then is the meaning of this textual excess, this disproportion between apparent cause and effect? There are several possible answers, located at different levels of analysis. The excess obviously marks the recurrent difficulty that Caliban causes Prospero – a difficulty we have been concerned to trace in some detail. So, at the level of character, a psychoanalytic reading would want to suggest that Prospero's excessive reaction represents his disquiet at the irruption into consciousness of an unconscious anxiety concerning the grounding of his legitimacy, both as producer of his play and, *a fortiori*, as governor of the island. The by now urgent need for action forces upon Prospero the hitherto repressed contradiction between his dual roles as

---

[24] Kermode, ed., *The Tempest*, p. lxxv.

usurped and usurper. Of course the emergency is soon contained and the colonialist narrative quickly completed. But, none the less, if only for a moment, the effort invested in holding Prospero's play together as a unity is laid bare.

So, at the formal level, Prospero's difficulties in staging his play are themselves 'staged' by the play that we are watching, this moment presenting for the first time the possibility of distinguishing between Prospero's play and *The Tempest* itself.

Perhaps it could be said that what is staged here in *The Tempest* is Prospero's anxious determination to keep the subplot of his play in its place. One way of distinguishing Prospero's play from *The Tempest* might be to claim that Prospero's carefully established relationship between main and subplot is reversed in *The Tempest*, whose *main* plot concerns Prospero's anxiety over his *sub*plot. A formal analysis would seem to bear this out. The climax of Prospero's play is his revelation to Alonso of Miranda and Ferdinand playing chess. This is certainly a true *anagnorisis* for Alonso, but for us a merely theatrical rather than truly dramatic moment. *The Tempest*'s dramatic climax, in a way its only dramatic moment at all, is, after all, this sudden and strange disturbance of Prospero.

But to speak of Prospero's anxiety being staged by *The Tempest* would be, on its own, a recuperative move, preserving the text's unity by the familiar strategy of introducing an ironic distance between author and protagonist. After all, although Prospero's anxiety over his subplot may point up the *crucial* nature of that 'sub' plot, a generic analysis would have no difficulty in showing that *The Tempest* is ultimately complicit with Prospero's play in treating Caliban's conspiracy in the fully comic mode. Even before it begins, Caliban's attempt to put his political claims into practice is arrested by its implication in the convention of clownish vulgarity represented by the 'low-life' characters of Stephano and Trinculo, his conspiracy framed in a grotesquerie that ends with the dubiously amusing sight of the conspirators being hunted by dogs, a fate, incidentally, not unknown to natives of the New World. The shakiness of Prospero's position is indeed staged, but in the end his version of history remains *authoritative*, the larger play acceding as it were to the containment of the conspirators in the safely comic mode, Caliban allowed only his poignant and ultimately vain protests against the venality of his co-conspirators.

That this comic closure is necessary to enable the European 'reconciliation' which follows hard on its heels – the patching up of a minor dynastic dispute within the Italian nobility – is, however, itself symptomatic of the text's own anxiety about the threat posed to its decorum by its New World materials. The lengths to which the play has to go to achieve a legitimate ending may then be read as the quelling of a fundamental disquiet concerning its own functions within the projects of colonialist discourse.

No adequate reading of the play could afford not to comprehend *both* the anxiety and the drive to closure it necessitates. Yet these aspects of the play's 'rich complexity' have been signally ignored by European and North American critics, who have tended to listen exclusively to Prospero's voice: after all, he speaks their language. It has been left to those who have suffered colonial usurpation to discover and map the traces of that complexity by reading in full measure Caliban's refractory place in both Prospero's play and *The Tempest*.[25]

VI

We have tried to show, within the limits of a brief textual analysis, how an approach via a theory of discourse can recognize *The Tempest* as, in a significant sense, a play imbricated within the discourse of colonialism; and can, at the same time, offer an explanation of features of the play either ignored or occluded by critical practices that have often been complicit, whether consciously or not, with a colonialist ideology.

Three points remain to be clarified. To identify dominant discursive networks and their mode of operation within particular texts should by no means be seen as the end of the story. A more exhaustive analysis would go on to establish the precise articulation of discourses within texts: we have argued for the discourse of colonialism as the articulatory *principle* of *The Tempest*'s diversity but have touched only briefly on what other discourses are articulated and where such linkages can be seen at work in the play.

Then again, each text is more than simply an *instance* of the operation of a discursive network. We have tried to show how much of *The Tempest*'s complexity comes from its *staging* of the distinctive moves and figures of colonialist discourse. Discourse is always performative, active rather than ever merely contemplative; and, of course, the mode of the theatre will also inflect it in particular ways, tending, for example, through the inevitable (because structural) absence of any direct authorial comment, to create an effect of distantiation, which exists in a complex relationship with the countervailing (and equally structural) tendency for audiences to identify with characters presented – through the language and conventions of theatre – as heroes and heroines. Much work remains to be done on the articulation between discursive performance and mode of presentation.

Finally, we have been concerned to show how *The Tempest* has been severed from its discursive con-texts through being produced by criticism as an autotelic unity, and we have tried therefore to exemplify an approach that would engage with the fully dialectical relationship between the detail of the text and the larger discursive formations. But nor can theory and criticism be exempt from such relationships. Our essay too must engage in the discursive struggle that determines the history within which the Shakespearean texts will be located and read: it matters what kind of history that is.

[25] See for example George Lamming, *The Pleasures of Exile* (London: Michael Joseph, 1960) and Roberto Fernández Retamar, *Caliban: Apuntes sobre la Cultura de Nuestra América* (Buenos Aires: Editorial la Pleyade, 1973). Aimé Césaire's rewriting of the play, *Une Tempête*, 1969, has Caliban as explicit hero. For an account of how Caliban remains refractory for contemporary productions of *The Tempest* see Trevor R. Griffiths, '"This island's mine": Caliban and Colonialism', *Yearbook of English Studies* 13 (1983), pp. 159–80.

15 John Bender

Robinson Crusoe *and the Rise of the Penitentiary* [1]

Imagining the Penitentiary: Fiction and the Architecture of Mind in Eighteenth-Century England, University of Chicago Press: Chicago and London, 1987, pp. 52–61.

Experiences of transformation in marginal places of confinement figure centrally in *Robinson Crusoe* (1719), which presents a materially realistic delineation of consciousness shaped through the narration of confinement.

Here is Crusoe's situation liminally considered. Prior to the wreck, Crusoe lays stress on the unceremonious break with his parents and on the immaturity of obeying 'blindly the Dictates of my Fancy rather than my Reason'.[2] After the wreck, invoking the metaphor of condemnation and reprieve, he hovers at the boundary between life and death:

> I believe it is impossible to express to the Life what the Extasies and Transports of the Soul are, when it is so sav'd, as I may say, out of the very Grave; and I do not wonder now at that Custom, *viz*. That when a Malefactor who has the Halter about his Neck, is tyed up, and just going to be turn'd off, and has a Reprieve brought to him: I say, I do not wonder that they bring a Surgeon with it, to let him Blood that very Moment they tell him of it, that the Surprise may not drive the Animal Spirits from the Heart, and overwhelm him. (p. 46)

Crusoe's thinking here catches the primitive doubleness of marginal symbolism in the notion of bloodletting at the moment of reprieve: the wound that heals. His overarching metaphor assumes the liminal prison because Newgate launched the condemned onto the infamous road terminating at Tyburn gallows and held the fortunate few who returned with reprieves until their transportation abroad. Indeed, we later discover that Crusoe has been simultaneously alive and dead throughout most of the book, for legally he has undergone '*Civil Death*' (pp. 283–4).

During the island confinement he subjects his entire previous standard of life to criticism; his initiative rises to the re-creation, often in parodic forms, of virtually every craft or social comfort known in England. Time becomes conjectural after he loses track during a delirious, nearly fatal, illness, and its value becomes immeasurably small during his ceaseless labours to shape the island into a microcosm of European life. Having undergone his own rite of passage, Crusoe undertakes Friday's instruction and eventually institutes a facsimile of civil society on the basis of truths he has discovered about human nature. Finally, Crusoe himself, as the Governor, reprieves certain mutineers

---

[1] Title provided by the editor of the present volume with the permission of the author and the University of Chicago Press. The opening paragraph of this excerpt and subsequent footnotes have been abridged by the author. [ed.]

[2] Daniel Defoe, *Robinson Crusoe*, ed. J. Donald Crowley (London: Oxford University Press, 1972), p. 40. Further references are to this edition.

and commutes their sentences to a form of transportation: the colonization of
the island. He thus closes the liminal cycle with full acceptance of axiomatic
social values, including the use of reprieves as tokens in the system of
patrician patronage through which the gentry exercised authority.[3] Although
Crusoe never settles down to realize them, the social prospects implied by his
entry into the class of substantial landholders have been enacted prospectively
on the island through his journeys from sea coast fort to inland country seat, as
well as by his exercises in governance. In the end, however much greater his
fortunes might have been had he remained in Brazil instead of undertaking the
fateful voyage, Crusoe does achieve a new economic status well above his
father's 'middle state'.

Yet the liminal account, like Crusoe's metaphor of reprieve, seems artificial
– not false, but insufficient or old-fashioned – because Defoe centres the work
on Crusoe's obsession with finding an account of his mental life that coheres
sequentially, causally, and spiritually. Solitude is the occasion, narrative the
medium, and prison the overarching figure:

> Now I began to construe the Words mentioned above, *Call on me, and I will deliver
> you*, in a different Sense from what I had ever done before; for then I had no Notion
> of any thing being call'd Deliverance, but my being deliver'd from the Captivity I
> was in; for tho' I was indeed at large in the Place, yet the Island was certainly a
> Prison to me, and that in the worst Sense in the World; but now I learn'd to take it in
> another Sense: Now I look'd back upon my past Life with such Horrour, and my
> Sins appear'd so dreadful, that my Soul sought nothing of God, but Deliverance
> from the Load of Guilt that bore down all my Comfort: As for my solitary Life it was
> nothing; I did not so much as pray to be deliver'd from it, or think of it. (pp. 96–7)

Here, as in the wreck, Crusoe's terms are directly religious. But in context the
theological referents are subordinate to the machinations of Defoe's narrative
as it struggles – repeatedly retelling the early phases of the story – to trace the
reformation of Crusoe's conscience. We move from 'just history of fact', to
straight journal, to journal interrupted and dissolved by reflection. Defoe uses
the 'real' words of Crusoe's chronicle to certify the truth of reflections that at
first break into the texture of the vital pages surrounding the delirium and
eventually overtake them entirely. Narrative in its relation to consciousness is
the actual subject here: accounts of the self *are* the self, and fuller, more
circumstantial accounts placed in a reflective context are more true than mere
chronicles or journals. This section of *Robinson Crusoe* stands at a decisive
juncture in the history of the novel because of its literal quest through generic
types for some material equivalent to the formation of thought. This quest
structures Defoe's 'realism' as a mode of representation that incorporates and
subordinates the others into what Bakhtin calls polyglossia.[4] Before our very

[3] See Douglas Hay, 'Property, Authority, and the Criminal Law', in Douglas Hay *et al.*, eds,
Albion's Fatal Tree: Crime and Society in Eighteenth-Century England (New York: Pantheon,
1975), pp. 17–63.
[4] On 'polyglossia' as a form of contradiction and as the essence of the novel – that is, its
ability to contain contradictory voices – see Mikhail Bakhtin, 'From the Prehistory of Novelistic
Discourse' and 'Discourse in the Novel', in *The Dialogic Imagination*, ed. Michael Holquist,
trans. Caryl Emerson and Michael Holquist (Austin, Texas: University of Texas Press, 1981),
especially pp. 50–60 and 277–84.

eyes, the new, reflective, consciousness-centred form displaces the genres it has subsumed, a state of affairs traced in Defoe's text by Crusoe's progressive dilution of his ink until the journal fades into illegibility a few pages following the passage quoted above.

During Crusoe's 'solemn' observance of the second anniversary of his shipwreck, the prison metaphor recurs, again yoked with solitude. Here the two terms fall into clear opposition, signifying states of mind before and after Crusoe's correct understanding of deliverance some two months earlier. To be imprisoned is to be subject to random misery:

> I was a Prisoner lock'd up with the Eternal Bars and Bolts of the Ocean, in an uninhabited Wilderness, without Redemption: In the midst of the greatest Composures of my Mind, this would break out upon me like a Storm, and make me wring my Hands, and weep like a Child: Sometimes it would take me in the middle of my Work, and I would immediately sit down and sigh, and look upon the Ground for an Hour or two together; and this was still worse to me; for if I could burst out into Tears, or vent my self by Words, it would go off, and the Grief having exhausted it self would abate.   (p. 113)

But to comprehend solitude is to be spiritually and mentally whole, as well as to function materially:

> I spent the whole Day in humble and thankful Acknowledgments of the many wonderful Mercies which my Solitary Condition was attended with . . . I gave humble and hearty Thanks that God had been pleas'd to discover to me, even that it was possible I might be more happy in this Solitary Condition, than I should have been in a Liberty of Society, and in all the Pleasures of the World. That he could fully make up to me, the Deficiencies of my Solitary State, and the want of Humane Society by his Presence . . . supporting, comforting, and encouraging me to depend upon his Providence here, and hope for his Eternal Presence hereafter.   (p. 112)

Meanings outnumber terms here as the notion of prison slides from the liminal, arbitrary, openly public realm into the private realm of reflective thought.

Several things are happening. First, the liminal experience, while present, is losing its tangibility, and its habitual, external forms are assuming a negative tinge. Second, the outcome of punishment is now being represented as mental reformation. Third, errant personality is reconstituted as self-consciousness by solitary reflection. Finally, the ability to function materially is specifically attributed to the proper inner comprehension of life as a story, each circumstance of which is meaningful. We see the mythology of reform taking shape here. Prison, now equated with solitary reflection, is first viewed as negative, random, punitive, vengeful; but it slides into another thing entirely – something salubrious, beneficent, reformative, and productive of wealth and social integration. Crusoe's illness can be read, in this light, as a prospective allegory of the move from the old, fever-ridden jails to the clean, healthy, contemplative solitude of the penitentiaries.

Crusoe equates having a self with being able to account for his crime, and his story literally enacts a quest for some narrative equivalent to personality. Just as his construction of material surrogates of European civilization is indistinguishable from the narration of his story, so is novelization inseparable from the reformation of his consciousness. Friday's advent enables Crusoe to test the power of narrative to constitute the self. Crusoe must teach him the causes and raise him up into the crafts before Friday is recognizable as human and Crusoe's self-construction is socially validated.

When Crusoe ends his confinement by subjugating the mutineers with the purely fictional personage of the Governor, both the self and the authority it projects are shown as narrative constructs that effect material ends.

> When I shew'd my self to the two Hostages, it was with the Captain, who told them, I was the Person the Governour had order'd to look after them, and that it was the Governour's Pleasure they should not stir any where, but by my Direction; that if they did, they should be fetch'd into the Castle, and be lay'd in Irons; so that as we never suffered them to see me as Governour, so I now appear'd as another Person, and spoke of the Governour, the Garrison, the Castle, and the like, upon all Occasions. (p. 271)

The fiction of the Governor becomes real through its own enactment: the mutineers are divided, manoeuvred into submission, and, where of sound character, reconverted to the service of established order. The five incorrigibles, imprisoned in the island's fortified cave during the recapture of the English captain's ship, benefit ultimately from clemency at Crusoe's hand in his role as the Governor; they are left to colonize the island under threat of execution should they return to England. Viewed one way, they, like Moll Flanders, are reprieved and transported; but from another perspective they have become convicts in Crusoe's penitentiary, condemned to reformation according to a narrative of his making. His story will be their regime:

> I then told them, I would let them into the Story of my living there, and put them into the Way of making it easy to them: Accordingly I gave them the whole History of the Place, and of my coming to it; shew'd them my Fortifications, the Way I made my Bread, planted my Corn, cured my Grapes; and in a Word, all that was necessary to make them easy: I told them the Story also of the sixteen *Spaniards* that were to be expected; for whom I left a Letter, and made them promise to treat them in common with themselves. (p. 277)

Crusoe has altered from a lord of nature, alone with the savage Friday, to a lord of men who appears at last, ceremoniously clothed, in *propria persona* as the Governor. Having defined a consciousness located at the juncture of the mental and the material, having mapped it first on the terrain of his island and then on Friday's malleable mentality, Crusoe now rehearses his authority and renders it tangible through fiction. Once he has construed himself and discovered the enabling force of narrative, Crusoe uses the explanatory power of story-telling to exert control over the mutineers and to police the future civic order he envisions upon the arrival of the sixteen Spaniards. Upon Crusoe's departure, the island and its furniture exchange their metaphorical standing as prison for that of an actual penal colony with his fortress at its civic centre and his story as its master narrative.

Although Defoe's hero is castaway on a deserted island, the formulation of imprisonment that lies at *Robinson Crusoe*'s figurative core assumes and incorporates the experience of the city as the seat of power. Defoe's tale is an archaeology of urban geographical, social, psychological, and legal forms. Crusoe maps the island according to the polarity between city and country even before he is able to populate it, and the architectural traces of his ingenuity, so minutely fabricated in the telling, become instruments of power once the mutineers arrive. This is especially clear in the case of Crusoe's fortified cave, the evolution of which is synonymous with the narration of his story, because it serves at once as a prison in which he holds the mutineers and the seat of authority personified in the Governor. Built first to shield its resident from harm and then elaborated to provide a base for his farming and hunting, the fortress becomes a walled city that can contain and subjugate as well as defend. Crusoe's building programme retraces the ancient etymology of the English word 'town' and the French word 'ville', earlier forms of which referred first to enclosed places or camps, then to farms or manors, and finally to governed urban habitations.

Crusoe tests and revalidates forms of hegemony characteristic of urban culture, the ordering principles of the governed city. With the convergence of Friday, the Spanish captain, the mutineers, the English captain, and the prospective arrival of sixteen Spanish castaways from the mainland (signifying, like so many tribes, the varying modes of social order), Defoe retrieves that moment in human history described by Lewis Mumford as 'the first time the city proper becomes visible': 'The first beginning of urban life . . . was marked by a sudden increase in power in every department and by a magnification of the role of power itself in the affairs of men.'[5] Of course Defoe's narrative cannot re-create the original city but instead must represent it from the vantage point of modern civilization – thus Crusoe's salvage operations, and his construction of what amounts to a deserted city waiting for its test of viability. The architectural fabric by which Crusoe laboriously masters the island, like the articles reclaimed from the shipwreck, store up power as surely as gunpowder stores propulsive force. They form a stockpile of the urban estate that, no less than Crusoe's hoard of gold, must wait to be expended.

It has become a commonplace of literary history to trace the emergence of the realist novel to the concentration of literate audiences in early modern cities.[6] Collaterally, from the broad perspective of social theory, the origin of written history within the purview of the city situates narrative in 'a special form of "container", a crucible for the generation of power on a scale unthinkable in non-urban communities'.[7] Critics of the novel risk more by making too little of these congruent analyses than by making too much.

Traditionally the two most distinctive spatial traits of the city were, at its centre, the compound containing governmental and religious buildings and, at its periphery, the surrounding walls. These also were the two habitual sites of

[5] Lewis Mumford, 'University City', in Carl H. Kraeling and Robert M. Adams, eds, *City Invincible* (Chicago: University of Chicago Press, 1960), p. 7.

[6] See especially Ian Watt, *The Rise of the Novel: Studies in Defoe, Richardson and Fielding* (Berkeley, Calif.: University of California Press, 1959), pp. 45–6 and 177–82. My treatment of the relationship between narrative and cities, in general, and between the realist novel and the urban metropolis, in particular, is at once more literal, more encompassing, and less dependent upon the concept of class than Watt's.

[7] Anthony Giddens, *A Contemporary Critique of Historical Materialism* (Berkeley, Calif.: University of California Press, 1981), p. 96. In the following section I employ various terms from Giddens.

prisons, which thus lay deep in the syntactic structure articulating the space of the city. Viewed on the large canvas of world time, written narrative rests with prison at the generative axis of the city as the enclosed seat of authority and the site of surveillance. In ancient Sumer, for example, the origins first of written language and then of inscribed narrative have been traced to the requirements of civic administration:

> The keeping of written 'accounts' – regularised information about persons, objects and events – generates power that is unavailable in oral cultures. The list is . . . not just an aid to the memory, but a definite means of encoding information. Lists do not represent speech in any sort of direct way, and . . . the early development of writing thus signals a sharper break with speech than might be imagined if we suppose that writing originated as a visual depiction of the spoken word. In Sumer, listing led eventually to the further development of writing as a mode of chronicling events of a 'historical' nature. . . . These 'event lists' form the first known 'written histories', and eventually built up to span a large number of generations.[8]

Considered on this scale, the claim that novels often lay to the narration of historical truth becomes an assertion of the authority latent in written representation.

As Mikhail Bakhtin says, all of the traditional literary genres, 'or in any case their defining features, are considerably older than written language and the book, and to the present day they retain their ancient oral and auditory characteristics. Of all the major genres only the novel is younger than writing and the book: it alone is organically receptive to new forms of mute perception, that is, to reading.'[9] The novel, the genre of writing par excellence, formally embodies the fabric of urban culture: the very self-consciousness concerning the narration of minute particulars that defines it implies not merely an awareness of being watched but the technical ability to keep track by writing and to retrieve by reading. Compilation, investigation, justification, adjudication, letters, lists, receipts, journals, records, evidentiary detail, testimony – the written traces of merchandise and manners – here is the stuff both of cities and of novels.

Defoe's pervasive listings – his accountings, inventories, census reports, bills of lading, logs, and diaries – fictionally reinscribe the origins of writing as the medium of power. Among the first products of Crusoe's confinement are the lists contained in his journal, at once prototypes of his ultimate published narrative and integral parts of it. But early in the story we see writing, the means of civic commerce, go faint as Crusoe dilutes and finally exhausts his ink in a trail of scarcely legible script. Defoe underscores the social structure implicit in records when, because of his delirium, Crusoe's marking of the calendar also becomes indefinite. On the island Crusoe's solitary, gestural use of writing calls attention to its usual function as a medium of exchange. For written language, which represents its objects abstractly and renders them transferable across time and space, is to talk and oral fable as money, which

[8] Giddens, *A Contemporary Critique of Historical Materialism*, p. 95.

[9] Bakhtin, *The Dialogic Imagination*, p. 3. I am concerned with the extent to which narrative order itself modifies the diversity and antiauthoritarianism ('heteroglossia') that, for Bakhtin, define the novel. Chapter 7 of *Imagining the Penitentiary* suggests that transparent representation in the realist novel encompasses, contains, and reshapes apparent heterodoxy.

gains value only as a medium of exchange, is to labour and its tangible products. Defoe probes and reoriginates the link between money and writing, which, in recent times, has been traced archaeologically to exceedingly ancient trade tokens, impressions of which appear to have formed the earliest inscriptions, a primitive, protocuneiform script. Crusoe is forced back into an existence based only on use value rather than exchange. He must put aside his hoards of money and stash his manuscripts.

In *Robinson Crusoe*, Defoe stages an explanatory myth showing how Crusoe's isolation and enclosure enable him to constitute power through the storage and allocation of resources. Only gradually does Crusoe master the physical potential of the island and store up enough provisions to consider allocating some to another person. At first his sense of control seems childish or illusory, and he suffers horrible fears that his authoritative resources might not be sufficient to protect him from visiting savages. However, his power becomes instrumental when luck and skillful deployment enable him to subdue the two cannibals who separate from their clan to pursue Friday, the object of their feast. His rescue of Friday provides a subject on whom to exercise authority.

As Friday becomes Crusoe's loyal subject (a human resource), he participates in an elementary linguistic, educational, and social structure in which Crusoe accumulates enough power to mount a direct assault, destroying all but four of the twenty-one cannibals who visit the island intent upon making a banquet of Friday's father and the Spanish captain. Defoe's representation of the signal stages of civilization is lucid. Crusoe represses the primitive, devouring power latent, as Elias Canetti suggests, in the sharp, smooth, orderly array of teeth.[10] His island government sublimates cannibalistic dominance into a mimicry of toleration as state policy:

> My Island was now peopled, and I thought my self very rich in Subjects; and it was a merry Reflection which I frequently made, How like a King I look'd. First of all, the whole Country was my own meer Property; so that I had an undoubted Right of Dominion. *2dly*, My People were perfectly subjected: I was absolute Lord and Law-giver; they all owed their Lives to me, and were ready to lay down their Lives, *if there had been Occasion of it*, for me. It was remarkable too, we had but three Subjects, and they were of three different Religions. My Man *Friday* was a Protestant, his Father was a *Pagan* and a *Cannibal*, and the *Spaniard* was a Papist: However, I allow'd Liberty of Conscience throughout my Dominions: But this is by the Way. (p. 241)

When Defoe has the Spanish captain interpose an objection to immediate colonization of the island by shipmates abandoned among savages on the mainland, he goes out of his way to elucidate the relationship between physical resources and power in social formations:

> He told me, he thought it would be more advisable, to let him and the two other [*sic*], dig and cultivate some more Land, as much as I could spare Seed to sow; and that we should wait another Harvest, that we might have a Supply of Corn for his Country-men when they should come; for Want might be a Temptation to them to

---

[10] Elias Canetti, *Crowds and Power*, trans. Carol Stewart (New York: Viking Press, 1962), pp. 207–11.

disagree, or not to think themselves delivered, otherwise than out of one Difficulty into another. You know, says he, the Children of *Israel*, though they rejoyc'd at first for their being deliver'd out of *Egypt*, yet rebell'd even against God himself that deliver'd them, when they came to want Bread in the Wilderness. (p. 246)

In this same context, though implements are lacking, writing becomes an issue for the first time since the ink was exhausted more than twenty years before. The authoritative language that Crusoe intends to have the force of a written charge assumes the marked stiffness of legislative prose:

And now having a full Supply of Food for all the Guests I expected, I gave the *Spaniard* Leave to go over to the *Main*, to see what he could do with those he had left behind him there. I gave him a strict Charge in Writing, Not to bring any Man with him, who would not first swear in the Presence of himself and of the old *Savage*, That he would no way injure, fight with, or attack the Person he should find in the Island, who was so kind to send for them in order to their Deliverance; but that they would stand by and defend him against all such Attempts, and where-ever they went, would be entirely under and subjected to his Commands; and that this should be put in Writing, and signed with their Hands: How we were to have this done, when I knew they had neither Pen or Ink; that indeed was a Question which we never asked. (p. 248)

Only eight days later Crusoe sights the mutinous vessel, the mastery of which will prove his salvation.

Except for the one invocation of writing in Crusoe's charge to the Spanish captain, his ambassador to the mainland castaways, his demonstrations of power remain oral and physical until after he has staged the appearance of a settled government so as to overcome and imprison the mutineers. But at the moment of departure, when he tells the technical secrets of life on the island to the prison colony he leaves behind, Crusoe's letter to the expected Spaniards reintroduces writing in order to explain the constitution of his city-state and to govern its future behaviour. His letter attempts to store up authority across time just as his treasure has stored up value. And indeed, as if to acknowledge the ancient covalence of writing and money, within a page of text Defoe refurbishes the disused currency:

When I took leave of this Island, I carry'd on board for Reliques, the great Goat's-Skin-Cap I had made, my Umbrella, and my Parrot; also I forgot not to take the Money I formerly mention'd, which had lain by me so long useless, that it was grown rusty, or tarnish'd, and could hardly pass for Silver, till it had been a little rubb'd, and handled; as also the Money I found in the Wreck of the *Spanish* Ship. (p. 278)

Money, writing, listing, urban enclosure, social authority, forced confinement – all are obsessions of Defoe's, and these elements remain central to our sense of the novel in general.

Reference to large-scale social theory merely works to confirm motive forces embedded in the novel. The novel acts out, it represents iconically, the interplay between the unbounded heterogeneity of population in cities (their polyglot assembly of voices) and the bounded unity of their walls, fortified compounds, governmental structures, and systems of communication (their inscription of 'facts', their insistence on point of view, and their assimilation of authority from approved genres through parody, burlesque, irony). 'From the beginning', as Lewis Mumford says, 'the city exhibited an ambivalent character it has never wholly lost: it combined the maximum amount of protection with the greatest incentives to aggression: it offered the widest possible freedom and diversity, yet imposed a drastic system of compulsion and regimentation.'[11] My stance necessarily stresses the subordination of diversity to civic rule and, in the case of the novel, to narrative order. But the novel's generic instability persists because the diversity it encompasses and the authority it projects are reciprocal opposites, each defined by the representation of its antithesis, each always containing the other. Still, while it remains permissive in many respects, the novel oscillates between points of view that imply surveillance and enclosure. On the one hand stand novels in which readers enter the mental world of a single character and thereby fictionally view reality as a network of contingencies dependent upon observation; on the other lie novels in which readers ally themselves with the controlling power of an omniscient narrator. In this light, it is of more than incidental significance that Defoe served as a spy and a government agent – the very human medium of surveillance – and that he repeatedly suffered imprisonment.

---

16 Heather Glen

Blake's 'London': The Language of Experience[1]

Vision and Disenchantment: Blake's 'Songs' and Wordsworth's 'Lyrical Ballads', Cambridge University Press: Cambridge, 1983, pp. 208–19.

Unlike 'The human Image' or 'The Human Abstract', 'London' identifies its speaker as a lonely wanderer, who passes through the streets of a particular city, and sees it from a lamenting distance:

> I wander thro' each charter'd street,
> Near where the charter'd Thames does flow
> And mark in every face I meet
> Marks of weakness, marks of woe.
>
> In every cry of every Man,
> In every Infants cry of fear,
> In every voice; in every ban,
> The mind-forg'd manacles I hear.

---

[11] Lewis Mumford, *The City in History* (New York: Harcourt, Brace & World, 1961), p. 46.
[1] Title provided by the editor of the present volume with the permission of the author and Cambridge University Press. [ed.]

In choosing to present his vision of social disaster thus, Blake was engaging with a familiar literary mode. The assumption of a stance of 'observation', freely passing judgment on that which is before it, is common to much eighteenth-century literature: 'There mark what ills the scholar's life assail'.[2] But nowhere is it more prominent than in that which attempts to describe London, a place of bewildering diversity, changing and growing rapidly, in which a new kind of anonymity and alienation was becoming a remarked-upon fact of life.[3] Indeed, it seems that in the literature of London the implications of this state were beginning to become an explicit preoccupation. Thus, Ben Sedgly in 1751:

> No man can take survey of this opulent city, without meeting in his way, many melancholy instances resulting from this consumption of spirituous liquors: poverty, diseases, misery and wickedness, are the daily observations to be made in every part of this great metropolis: whoever passes along the streets, may find numbers of abandoned wretches stretched upon the cold pavement, motionless and insensible, removed only by the charity of passengers from the danger of being crushed by carriages, trampled by horses, or strangled with filth in the common sewers.[4]

'Take survey of', 'meeting in his way', 'observations to be made', 'whoever passes along the streets may find' – the sense throughout is of an anonymous and freely observing stranger, rather than of a member of a society who sees himself as shaped by it and interacting with others within it. Perhaps such a perspective is natural in a documentary work such as Sedgly's. But this sense of the self in the city is central, too, to much of the most powerful imaginative literature of the century, literature which is after all not merely a description of or meditation upon the world, but the recreation of a certain mode of being within it. It is a sense that informs the novels of Defoe: the figures of Roxana and Colonel Jack and Moll Flanders move through the streets from adventure to adventure with a freedom from social constraint which is only possible because of the nature of London life.[5] It is to be found in Gay's *Trivia* and *The Beggar's Opera*; in Boswell's *Journal*; in Johnson's *London*, and even in those of his essays which seem to have nothing to do with London at all:

> He that considers how little he dwells upon the condition of others, will learn how little the attention of others is attracted by himself. While we see multitudes passing before us, of whom perhaps not one appears to deserve our notice, or excites our sympathy, we should remember, that we likewise are lost in the same throng, that

---

[2] Johnson, 'The Vanity of Human Wishes', l. 159. The opening lines of this poem are perhaps the dramatization *par excellence* of this stance:
'Let observation with extensive view, / Survey mankind, from China to Peru; / Remark each anxious toil, each eager strife, / And watch the busy scenes of crouded life.'

[3] See George Rudé, *Hanoverian London, 1714–1808* (London: Secker and Warburg, 1971), Ch. 1; Raymond Williams, *The Country and the City* (London: Chatto and Windus, 1973), pp. 142–52; Max Byrd, *London Transformed: Images of the City in the Eighteenth Century* (New Haven, Conn., and London: Yale University Press, 1978).

[4] Ben Sedgly, *Observations on Mr. Fielding's Enquiry* (London, 1751), pp. 22–3, quoted in Byrd, *London Transformed*, p. 23.

[5] See Byrd, *London Transformed*, esp. pp. 26–8, for an excellent discussion of this. Cf. also Richard Sennett, *The Fall of Public Man* (Cambridge: Cambridge University Press, 1977), pp. 28–122, on the more general issue of 'role-playing' within the eighteenth-century city.

eye which happens to glance upon us is turned in a moment on him that follows us, and that the utmost which we can reasonably hope or fear is to fill a vacant hour with prattle, and be forgotten.[6]

Here, the tone is one of judicious moralizing. But the imagery is that of the confusing eighteenth-century London street, in which relations with one's fellow beings involve attracting attention, deserving notice, glancing and turning, even *exciting* sympathy: in which the other is the object of observation rather than one with whom one interacts. And the supposedly free individual who sees those who pass before him as a mighty spectacle is himself 'lost in the same throng'.

The eighteenth-century London street was not, then, merely a place where suffering and distress could be seen on a hitherto unprecedented scale: it was also a place where that sense of the other as object – often as feeble and wretched object – which Blake exposes in 'The Human Abstract' ('we . . . make somebody Poor') was the dominant mode of relationship. And it is a sense which is an ironic point of reference in 'London'. For this poem begins with a speaker who seems to be a detached observer, who wanders 'thro'' the streets of the city and 'marks' the sights before him. Yet his is not the lively and distinctive London of Defoe or Gay or Johnson: what he records is not variety, but sameness. To him, both streets and river are simply 'charter'd': the different faces which pass all bear the same message, 'Marks of weakness, marks of woe'. And the tight quatrain with its present indicative tense conveys not flexible responsiveness to constantly changing possibilities, but entrapment. What this speaker sees is fatally linked to the way in which he sees it. In the notebook draft, the second word of the third line was 'see': Blake's alteration limits any incipient sense of freedom. The triple beat of 'mark' – an active verb materializing into two plural nouns – registers a new consciousness of this 'I''s implication in the world 'thro'' which he wanders. What he observes is the objectification of his own activity.

'Mark' is not the only change which Blake made in this stanza. In the notebook draft, the first two lines read:

I wander thro' each dirty street,
Near where the dirty Thames does flow.[7]

The substitution, in the engraved version, of 'charter'd', signals a complex process of poetic thought. For 'charter'd' in 1793 was a word at the centre of political debate: a word whose accepted meaning of 'granted privileges or rights' had been challenged by Paine a year earlier, in a book whose sales had by now reached 200,000:

It is a perversion of terms to say, that a charter gives rights. It operates by a contrary effect, that of taking rights away. Rights are inherently in all the inhabitants; but charters, by annulling those rights in the majority, leave the right by exclusion in the hands of a few . . . all charters have no other than an indirect negative operation.

[6] Samuel Johnson, *The Rambler*, 159.
[7] Geoffrey Keynes, ed., *The Complete Writings of William Blake* (Oxford: Oxford University Press, 1972), p. 170. Subsequent page references are to this edition.

They do not give rights to A, but they make a difference in favour of A by taking away the right of B, and consequently are instruments of injustice.[8]

No contemporary of Blake's could have read the two altered opening lines of his poem as an objective description of the trading organization of the city. Their repetition of 'charter'd' forces into prominence the newly, ironically recognized sense that the very language of 'objective' description may be riddled with ideological significance: that beneath the assurance of polite usage may lurk another, 'cheating' meaning.[9] And this sense informs the stanza in a peculiar way. It is as though beneath the polite surface – the observer in London wandering the streets of a city whose 'charter'd' organization he notes, as the guidebooks noted its commercial organization, and whose manifestations of distress and depravity he, like hundreds of other eighteenth-century writers, remarks – there is another set of meanings, which are the *reverse* of those such description could customarily bear. They are not meanings private to Blake: and they are meanings which focus in those sound-linked and repeated words, 'mark' and 'charter'd'.

The ambiguities of 'charter'd' had been explicitly debated: those of 'mark' are perhaps less obvious. Yet Blake, altering the poem in his notebook, has done an extraordinary thing. He has chosen a term commonly found in polite descriptions of London, to indicate the expected attitude of detached interest, and used it in such a way as to evoke a whole cluster of powerful, far from detached and far from polite resonances – resonances which question the value and perhaps even the possibility of such detachment. For 'mark' was not simply used by polite gentlemen to indicate the different sights of London to one another: it was, in the late eighteenth century, a word used on the streets of

---

[8] Paine, *Rights of Man*, ed. Henry Collins (Harmondsworth: Penguin, 1969), pp. 242–3. On the sale of the volume, see Henry Collins's Introduction to this edition, p. 36, and Richard D. Altick, *The English Common Reader* (Chicago and London: University of Chicago Press, 1959), p. 70. For a fuller discussion of the debate over 'charters', see David Erdman, *Blake: Prophet against Empire*, rev. edn (Princeton, NJ: Princeton University Press, 1969), pp. 276–7 and E.P. Thompson, 'London', in *Interpreting Blake*, ed. Michael Phillips (Cambridge: Cambridge University Press), pp. 6–10. An interesting footnote is provided by Burke himself, who seems to have drawn attention to this ambiguity in the word as early as 1784: 'The charters, which we call by distinction *great*, are public instruments of this nature; I mean the charters of King John and King Henry the Third. The things secured by these instruments may, without any deceitful ambiguity, be very fitly called the *chartered rights of men*.

'These Charters have made the very name of a Charter dear to the heart of every Englishman. But, Sir, there may be, and there *are* Charters, not only different in nature, but formed on principles the *very reverse* of those of the great Charter. Of this kind is the Charter of the East-India Company. *Magna Charta* is a Charter to restrain power, and to destroy monopoly: the East India Charter is a Charter to establish monopoly, and to create power. Political power and commercial monopoly are *not* the rights of men; and the rights to them derived from Charters, it is fallacious and sophisticated to call "the Chartered Rights of men". These Chartered Rights ... do at least suspend the natural rights of mankind at large; and in their very frame and constitution are liable to fall into a direct violation of them.' (Taken from 'a short Abstract from Mr. Burke's celebrated speech upon the East India Bill, in which the line of distinction between the different sorts of Charters is drawn with great truth and great precision', *Chartered Rights* [1784]).

[9] Cf. Blake's notebook entry of these years: 'Why should I care for the men of thames, / Or the cheating waves of charter'd streams?' (p. 166).

London by those who were by no means gentlemen, those artisan classes whose newly articulate radical politics were still intertwined with, and sometimes framed in the language of, prophetic millenarianism. Such men did not casually wander through the city marking the sights: with desperate intensity they turned from the Bible to the world around them to read the signs of the coming millennium. The 'marks' which they saw were the 'marks' of God's promise, or – more often – those of damnation, the signs of a rotten society:

> And he causeth all, both small and great, rich and poor, free and bond, to receive a mark in their right hand, or in their foreheads:
> And that no man might buy or sell, save he that had the mark, or the name of the beast . . .
>
> (Revelation 13:16–17)

In this, their 'marking' was akin to that of the prophet or the judge:

> And the LORD said unto him, Go through the midst of the city, through the midst of Jerusalem, and set a mark upon the foreheads of the men that sigh and that cry for all the abominations that be done in the midst thereof.
>
> (Ezekiel 9:4)

(This latter 'marker' is a 'man clothed with linen, which *had* the writer's inkhorn by his side' [9:3].)[10] And a mark on the face (in part, surely, a reference to the very real marks on the faces of the London crowd)[11] would to them suggest Cain, the 'man of blood' (p. 176) marked by God, the builder of the first city (referred to in *Poetical Sketches* as 'Cain's city built with murder' [p. 41]). Cain's was a city built in 'the Land of Nod', which in the Hebrew was the land of wandering. These biblical allusions, abstruse though they may seem to the modern reader, would have been felt very immediately by anyone familiar with the language of London streets in the 1790s: felt not as pointing to a particular interpretation – the 'marker' as Ezekiel, or the 'marks' as marks of sin ('weakness') or pity ('woe') but as signalling a stance towards the city at once very different from that of conventional polite observation, and posing a radical challenge to it.[12]

---

[10] These 'marks' are marks of salvation. Harold Bloom, *Poetry and Repression* (New Haven, Conn.: Yale University Press, 1976) argues that this is 'the precursor-text' of the poem. This seems rather literal-minded, and at odds with the pervasive sense that the marks, like the marks of the Beast, might be marks of damnation. Michael Ferber, '"London" and its Politics', *English Literary History* 48 (1981), pp. 310–38, prefers (similarly rather literally) to trace them to Revelation, but argues that it is 'best to dwell little on either of them, lest you wander entirely out of the poem' (p. 320). I would point less to a specific allusion – a key to the message of the poem – than to a whole cluster of biblical resonances, whose importance consists in their evocation of a quite different – and much more engaged – contemporary usage of 'mark' than that of polite convention.

[11] Sennett, *The Fall of Public Man*, p. 70. The notion of reading character from the face would have been familiar to Blake from Lavater's *Essays on Physiognomy*, for the first volume of which (1789) he had engraved three plates.

[12] For further discussion of the suggestiveness of 'mark' see E.P. Thompson, 'London', pp. 10–14; Heather Glen, 'The Poet in Society: Blake and Wordsworth on London', *Literature and History* 3 (1976), pp. 2–28; Stan Smith, 'Some Responses to Heather Glen's "The Poet in Society"', *Literature and History* 4 (1976), pp. 94–8.

The feeling of this opening stanza is, then, most unlike that of other eighteenth-century accounts of London – a feeling not of detachment, but of involvement, not of emancipation, but of constriction. And it is a feeling which by the second stanza has become dominant:

In every cry of every Man,
In every Infants cry of fear,
In every voice; in every ban,
The mind-forg'd manacles I hear.

The illusory freedom of 'wandering' and 'marking', the visible 'marks of weakness, marks of woe', have given way to sounds, sounds which by their nature are less controllable than visual images.[13] The syntactic structure, with main verb and subject postponed until the last two words, is exact in its effect: this speaker is dominated by what he hears, trapped within the world on which he is trying to comment. And the repeated 'every', 'every', 'every', with the monotonously regular rhythm, conveys an impression of sameness even in difference. Almost overwhelmed by that which surrounds him, this thinly present 'I' reduces all to the same miserable message. The world of London debate and dissent, of real controversy and real suffering, of real passing people on the streets, which is in some sense there in the first stanza – at a remove, but felt, in those charged words 'marks' and 'charter'd', and in the images of streets and Thames and of faces meeting and moving on – has here been further abstracted, even, paradoxically, as it threatens to engulf him.

And this sense of entrapment within a world in which no possibility of change can be seen is taken up and confronted in the final line of the stanza. Like 'charter'd', the image of 'mind-forg'd manacles' evokes a contemporary political debate – a debate which concerns precisely this paradox. On the one hand, radical thinkers claimed that crime and suffering ('weakness' and 'woe') were the result of social oppression and official mystification. Godwin in 1793 was to affirm: 'In reality the chains fall off of themselves when the magic of opinion is dissolved.'[14] On the other, conservatives argued that 'human nature' made social control absolutely necessary:

Society cannot exist, unless a controlling power upon will and appetite be placed somewhere; and the less of it there is within, the more there must be without. It is ordained in the eternal constitution of things, that men of intemperate minds cannot be free. Their passions forge their fetters.[15]

On the one hand, the ills of society are traced to the 'objective' manacles of repression, on the other to the 'subjective' failings of human nature. And

---

[13] This point is well made by Thompson, 'London', pp. 18–19.

[14] Godwin, *Enquiry Concerning Political Justice*, ed. Isaac Kramnick (Harmondsworth and Baltimore, Md., 1976), p. 149. See Thompson, 'London', p. 15, and Ferber, '"London" and its Politics', pp. 321 ff., on Blake's change in the draft from 'german' (signifying, as Ferber notes, 'a kind of German yoke theory aimed at the House of Hanover') to 'mind-forg'd': a change which – like his use of 'charter'd' – does not simply place him on the radical side of a contemporary debate, but offers a rather more complex perspective on it.

[15] Edmund Burke, *Letter to a Member of the National Assembly* (1791), in Burke, *Writings and Speeches* (London: Beaconsfield edn, n.d.), IV, pp. 51–2.

Blake's use of the image seems an ironic commentary on both sides of the debate. The other-denying mechanisms of repression which are visible and audible all around his speaker are intimately present in the 'mind' which seeks to distance and to judge: the one cannot be said to cause the other, for both are interlocked. The facts which have been presented as alien and unalterable are the manifestations of an activity: that distancing of the other, that inability to realize transforming human *potentia* ('these flowers of London town') which has been implicit in his speaker's stance toward the world no less than in the abstracting (and constricting) legal process of chartering, and the 'bans' which seek licence and prohibit human freedoms. These 'manacles', binding the hands that might help one another, are 'forg'd' *both* for *and* by 'the mind', There is, significantly, no direction as to whose mind is meant, for this is a condition from which no member of the society, including he who judges it, is exempt. 'Mind-forg'd manacles' expresses both dismay at what the speaker 'hears' and a defeated self-reflexiveness: there can be no position of detachment in this world, and any compassion within it is impotent.

The recognition implicit in this image is analogous to that at the end of 'The Human Abstract': 'There grows one in the Human Brain.' Yet this poem does not, like that, end here. What follows is at once integrally related to and yet startlingly different from what has preceded it:

How the Chimney-sweepers cry,
Every blackning Church appalls,
And the hapless Soldiers sigh
Runs in blood down Palace walls

But most thro' midnight streets I hear
How the youthful Harlots curse
Blasts the new-born Infants tear
And blights with plagues the Marriage hearse.

Instead of a monotonous, stereotyped picture of passive misery there are vivid images of violent activity: instead of the abstracted 'marking' of a solitary 'I' there is a sharply realized, surrealistic vision of a whole network of social relationships. The syntactic structure in which the 'I' is nominally in control becomes confused: the rhythm changes from iambic regularity to heavy trochees. Blake is alluding to real sights here, as his readers would have recognized: to the smog which covered late eighteenth-century London like a pall, and whose blackening effect on the buildings was frequently noted;[16] to the anti-war slogans that were beginning to be daubed with paint on the walls of public buildings.[17] But these familiar sights here become signs of the inner logic of the society: they constitute a concrete realization of that which has been implicit in the poem from the beginning. The essential mode of

---

[16] E.g. Priscilla Wakefield, *Perambulations in London* (1809), p. 146. Ferber, '"London" and its Politics', p. 325, discusses the different possible meanings of 'appals' and concludes: 'I think it makes the line more coherent to entertain the paradox of the church paling at the chimney sweeper's cry while blackening on its own, than to imagine the cry doubling that blackening by casting a pall.'

[17] John Brewer, *Party Ideology and Popular Politics at the Accession of George III* (Cambridge: Cambridge University Press, 1976), p. 153.

relationship within this city – between its institutions and its people – is here portrayed as one of *marking* – blackening, daubing with blood, blighting with plague. The violence of these two stanzas – of the Sweep and Soldier, outside of and marking church and palace, of the harlot, excluded from the society yet infecting it – is the mirror-image of that detached observation, isolated and alienated yet imprinting all with its own damning stamp, dramatized in the opening stanza.

Yet if it is a mirror-image, it is one which is realized in a way in which the image of London in the first two stanzas is not – more definite, more active, more complex. It is not simply that where there were 'faces' there are now actual people, the Chimney Sweeper, the Soldier, the Harlot: the social interconnections which in the first two stanzas were obscured by abstraction have become manifest. The 'marking' of a series of passing impressions has given way to a much more immediate vision of London as a city composed of human beings, not passing and separate, but in relationship. It is a distorted relationship, and felt more directly as such: that reversal of norms which was obliquely registered in the ironic use of 'charter'd' focuses finally in the concrete image of the 'Marriage hearse'. And the previously almost undifferentiated cries are not simply clearer and more distinctive: they have a force of a kind unperceived before. No longer are they the passive signs of a generalized 'weakness' and 'woe': they have taken on a startling – and by the last stanza actively destructive – materiality. The cries have become marks.

The first two stanzas of 'London', then, offer an alienated, observer's account of the city through which, oddly, reversed meanings seem to run: at the third stanza, with startling suddenness, those meanings leap into life. The hidden exclusiveness of 'charter'd' ('charters . . . leave the right by exclusion in the hands of a few')[18] becomes objectified in the Palace walls deaf to the 'sigh' which marks them, and in the excluding wall which provides no answer to the Chimney Sweeper's cry. And in the final stanza observation turns to revelation, as the 'impolite' biblical meanings of mark become prominent, with the image of the Harlot and of a plague from which none is spared.[19] The effect is extraordinary. And it brings to mind a third, and not irrelevant, meaning of 'mark'.

'London' seems much closer to Blake's own voice than do many others of the *Songs of Experience*: most obviously, this is because of the way in which it pushes beyond exposure of its speaker's limitations (such as we find in 'Holy Thursday' or 'A Poison Tree') into a more apocalyptic mode. But there is another sense in which it seems to come from Blake, rather than from an anonymous speaker – from 'The Author & Printer W Blake.' For the poem is a relief engraving, made by a process of deliberate and corrosive 'marking'. And the materialization of the Chimney Sweeper's, Soldier's, Harlot's cries recalls, by analogy, this other process in which words become marks – the process of engraving and printing in which Blake was more intimately involved than any other English poet. 'London', like the other Songs, was

[18] Paine, *Rights of Man*, quoted above: see note 6.
[19] See Thompson, 'London', p. 23, for a discussion of the image of the Harlot in English radical Dissent in the eighteenth century.

produced in two stages. The first was the preparation of the stereotype plate. Blake traced his text and design in gum arabic – which is resistant to acid – upon paper: he then applied the paper to the surface of a copper plate. When the plate was exposed to acid, those surfaces not covered with gum arabic were eaten away, and the upraised lines of the design and the words appeared, as in mirror-writing, reversed.[20] This is the 'method' which he described in *The Marriage of Heaven and Hell*: 'printing in the infernal method, by corrosives, which in Hell are salutary and medicinal, melting apparent surfaces away, and displaying the infinite which was hid' (p. 154). Once this first stage was carried out, the page was then printed from the stereotype and coloured.

The production of protruding stereotype 'marks' within which a reversed meaning was contained and the printing of the real design of which these were but a mirror-image, was thus a familiar process to Blake – and one which he seems to have seen as intrinsically linked to the vision he sought to present.[21] And it is a process which has a curious parallel in the progression of this poem. For the marks which Blake made would appear in relief when corroded by acid, when that which surrounded them was eaten away – just as the 'marking' of the speaker in the first two stanzas traces a single message which becomes more and more prominent as the surrounding world becomes less and less realized. The 'marks' on the plate were the reverse of what was ultimately to appear as the design. And the startling reversal in 'London', from a 'marking' speaker to the visible, actual, violent 'marks' of the two final stanzas – 'marks' which mirror back his own 'marking', not as a reflection but as a realization of the hidden interconnections of a society in which any position of control is illusory – bears an extraordinary resemblance to that moment of reversal with which Blake would have been most familiar: the moment when the relief outline suddenly takes on an existence seemingly independent of the engraver, as the printed result appears. There is even an analogue to the colouring of the page in the colours which appear for the first time in the third stanza, the 'blackning Church' and the blood of the Soldier, the submerged pun of 'appalls'. And the fire which is portrayed halfway down the page recalls the Devil's activity in *The Marriage of Heaven and Hell*: 'with corroding fires he wrote the following sentence now perceived by the minds of men, & read by them on earth' (p. 150).

To read the poem with this in mind is, I think, to come closer to its essential feeling than it is to see it as a statement either of moral outrage or despair. It is more like the voice of a 'marking' prophet – 'If you go on So, the result is So' (p. 392); a prophet whose 'marking' is also that of the artist, disclosing the hidden logic of a whole society in a way which transcends rational analysis, creating something which becomes independent of – and capable of questioning – his own activity, as the work of art achieves a revelatory life, beyond anything its creator may consciously have intended. The first half of

---

[20] David Bindman, *Blake as an Artist* (Oxford: Oxford University Press, 1977), p. 43, offers a clear account of this process.

[21] See Robert N. Essick, 'Blake and the Traditions of Reproductive Engraving', *Blake Studies* 5:1 (1972), pp. 59–103.

the poem, with its alienated, abstracting speaker, both dramatizes that mode of relationship which 'makes somebody Poor', and exposes the nature of a society in which it is dominant. In the London depicted here, there is no sense of human potentiality, and no creative change: this world simply is. Reciprocal human relationships in which otherness is acknowledged and the needs of all harmonized do not exist: the only relationships – as the recurrent imagery of licensing and prohibition, of buying and selling, of human passivity and misery suggests – are instrumental ones. People have become objects. And the intrinsic import of this is made strikingly manifest in the two final stanzas. 'If you go on So' – in the mode presented in *Songs of Experience* – the linear mode of control and domination, in which there is no realization of the uniqueness of others, no respect for difference or attempt to meet human needs – 'the result is So': a destructive 'blighting' of the whole society. And it is a 'result' which is not projected into the future, but which, the relentless present tense insists, is implicit in what is.

Yet the effect is not one of defeat: these two final stanzas have none of the flattened immobility of 'There souls of men are bought and sold.' Partly, this is because of their 'revolutionary' suggestiveness: those who in the other fragment are passive victims here have a terrible force. There are certainly seditious resonances here, in the familiar subversive figure of the Chimney Sweeper, the possible allusion to anti-war protest in 'Runs in blood down palace walls', even in the dramatic rendering of the voices of the oppressed (in 1795 *Pigott's Political Dictionary* was to define *Groan* simply as 'Sedition'). But Blake's vision is far from simply revolutionary, as a comparison with a modern, anti-colonialist vindication of violence reveals:

> when it is their turn to be broken in, when they are taught what shame and hunger and pain are, all that is stirred up in them is a volcanic fury whose force is equal to that of the pressure put upon them . . . first, the only violence is the settler's; but soon they will make it their own; that is to say, the same violence is thrown back upon us as when our own reflection comes forward to meet us when we go towards a mirror.[22]

The violence which erupts in the closing stanzas of 'London' *is* the mirror-image of that denied and suppressed violence implicit in 'charter'd' and 'mark'. Yet if Blake shows this, he also shows that such mirror-imaging provides no escape: for his poem remains locked within the present indicative tense. His images of violence are also images of impotence: the Soldier's sigh 'runs down' the outside of the palace; the Chimney Sweeper and the church remain paralysingly locked together ('to appall' is to dismay into inactivity, rather than to stir into action); the Harlot's curse, effective though it may be, offers no release. The 'revolutionary' import of these images does not, it seems, point toward potential change: and it is not centrally from this that the feeling of excitement in these stanzas comes. Rather, it comes from that surrealistic sharpness of realization, in which meanings hidden from conventional vision are suddenly made manifest: the vividness with which that

---

[22] Jean-Paul Sartre, Preface to Frantz Fanon, *The Wretched of the Earth* (Harmondsworth: Penguin, 1967), p. 15.

which in the first two stanzas was distanced and abstracted leaps into life before us, as the work of art leaps into life before the artist.

It is not, however, a realization which is also a transformation, like the growing vision of the children as angels in the Innocent 'Holy Thursday'. The satisfaction here is of a wholly different kind: one which has led one critic to say of the poem that it 'shuts like a box'.[23] If we begin with an isolated observer 'marking' the faces he passes we end with an isolated Harlot and the suggestion of faces blighted with plague: if we begin with a city licensed out to trade we end with love as a financial transaction. That which in the opening stanzas was abstracted by convention is here simply exposed in its human reality. And by the final stanza the speaker merely registers what is around him: the compassion perhaps implicit in his recognition of 'weakness' and 'woe', of the 'haplessness' of the Soldier, has been reduced to passivity by the force of the two doubly emphasized final verbs.[24]

Yet embedded within the stanza is a haunting poetic sense of that which is missing; a sense which Fredric Jameson has declared to be the only way in which 'the concept of freedom' can arise in 'a stagnant time':

> an ontological impatience in which the constraining situation itself is for the first time perceived in the very moment in which it is refused . . . a sudden perception of an intolerable present which is at the same time, but implicitly and however dimly articulated, the glimpse of another state in the name of which the first is judged.[25]

The closing lines of 'London' contain just such a negative articulation of alternative possibility. For through their images of the babe and of tears, and that forceful final verb 'Blasts', plays a disquietingly counterpointing allusion:

> And pity, like a naked new-born babe,
> Striding the blast, or heaven's cherubin, hors'd
> Upon the sightless couriers of the air,
> Shall blow the horrid deed in every eye,
> That tears shall drown the wind.
>
> (*Macbeth*, 1.7.21–5)

These lines seem to have fascinated Blake; one of his large colour prints of 1795 was an illustration of them. And that sense of the enormous power of the apparently helpless, of the radical nature of the claim that is made by trust, the transcendent force of 'Pity', which is at their centre, is also central in *Songs of Innocence*: 'Then like a mighty wind they raise to heaven the voice of song', 'Then cherish pity; lest you drive an angel from your door.' Here, at the end of 'London', their evocation underlines, even amidst the images of violence, the absence of any such potency. 'Blasts' has become a verb, cancelling out those drowning tears; this babe has none of the paradoxical 'striding' energy of Shakespeare's – he is 'reducd to misery'. And that 'pity' which in the earlier passage rides out and vanquishes the storm of evil is here nowhere to be found. Unlike the Innocent 'Holy Thursday', this poem does not urge towards action,

[23] Thompson, 'London', p. 23.
[24] Both words are strongly sound-linked: each stands at the beginning of a line.
[25] Fredric Jameson, *Marxism and Form: Twentieth-Century Dialectical Theories of Literature* (Princeton, NJ: Princeton University Press), pp. 84–5.

suggesting the disturbing possibility of a revalued 'Pity': rather, the allusions to *Macbeth* all point towards its paralysing obliteration:

But most thro' midnight streets I hear
How the youthful Harlots curse
Blasts the new-born Infants tear
And blights with plagues the Marriage hearse.

Blake makes it very clear that the disaster portrayed here is not inevitable. It has not been imposed by an unchangeable social order, nor is it the product of 'the ancient curse', the inborn evil of mankind. In 'London' it is shown to be the inevitable result of particular, chosen modes of relating to others, here manifested throughout a whole society. And this realization in one sense does imply its opposite: what has been humanly chosen and created can be humanly reversed. As the 'ancient Proverb' of the 1792 notebook affirms:

Remove away that black'ning church,
Remove away that marriage hearse,
Remove away that — of blood,
You'll quite remove the ancient curse.

(p. 176)

---

17 Nancy Armstrong

The Politics of Domestic Fiction: Dickens, Thackeray and the Brontës[1]

Desire and Domestic Fiction: A Political History of the Novel, Oxford University Press: New York and Oxford, 1987, pp. 177–86.

The novels of 1848 begin with violent scenes of punishment and exclusion: Hindley's brutal denigration of Heathcliff in *Wuthering Heights*; Jane Eyre's night of torment in the red-room; Joseph Sedley's abrupt rejection of Becky in *Vanity Fair*; the gratuitous suffering that workers endure at the hands of Bounderby and Carson in novels by Dickens and Elizabeth Gaskell. And each of these scenes of unjustified punishment generates tremendous outrage on behalf of the powerless. To begin with, the violence itself seems to have an external cause. In one form or another, history has intruded upon the household and disrupted its traditional order. The Napoleonic wars in *Vanity Fair* destroy Amelia's traditional hopes for happiness and foster Becky's reckless ambitions. History in the form of archaic inheritance laws and British colonialism similarly disrupts conventional romance in *Jane Eyre* when Rochester's house is found to contain an extra chamber hiding a wife he

---

[1] Title provided by the editor of the present volume with the permission of the author and Oxford University Press. [ed.]

married for her fortune and brought home from the East Indies years before. In contrast with the manor houses of Richardson and Austen, Brontë's Thornfield Hall cannot contain its historical materials, and she feels compelled to destroy the house before she allows Jane and Rochester to marry. The ruthless operations of capitalism enacted by Heathcliff dismantle the families that organize *Wuthering Heights*, as he supplants the legal heir to the Earnshaw estate and then proceeds to overturn every traditional relationship in the novel. The introduction of new historical material is yet more conspicuous in *Mary Barton*, where domestic relationships must somehow be rescued out of the stuff of the new sociology.

It is curious that when Mrs Gaskell represents the problem in explicitly political terms –

> Living in Manchester, but with a deep relish and fond admiration for the country, my first thought was to find a frame-work for my story in some rural scene; and I had already made a little progress in a tale, the period of which was more than a century ago, and the place on the borders of Yorkshire, when I bethought me how deep might be the romance in the lives of some of those who elbowed me daily in the busy streets of the town in which I resided. I had always felt a deep sympathy with the careworn men, who looked as if doomed to struggle through their lives in strange alternations between work and want; tossed to and fro by circumstances, apparently even in greater degree than other men.[2]

– the disruption of violence appears to have no political cause. Although *Mary Barton* begins by lamenting the ever-widening gap between classes, Gaskell soon devotes all her rhetorical ingenuity to outlawing the practice of combination. In contrast with Shuttleworth[3] and the many others who wrote about conditions in the city, she writes as a novelist and thus as a woman. As such, she can claim to 'know nothing of Political Economy, or of the theories of trade' (p. 38). For a historical study, however, the strategies that Gaskell's fiction actually shares with the writing of Shuttleworth and others are more important than the ways in which her fiction differs from their empirical data.

The conventions of sociology are just as important as sentimental convention in determining how the problem of the workers' condition came to be understood. The two modes of writing work hand in hand to confine political disruption within an apolitical framework. Although Mrs Gaskell includes political material in its most topical form, history virtually disappears from her novel as class conflict comes to be represented as a matter of sexual misconduct and a family scandal.[4] The other novels I am considering similarly uncover a sexual scandal as the source of disturbances that tear a family apart. The bond linking Catherine to Heathcliff – across time and space and in

---

[2] Elizabeth Gaskell, *Mary Barton: A Tale of Manchester Life*, ed. Stephen Gill (Harmondsworth: Penguin, 1970), p. 37. Citations of the text are to this edition.
[3] James Phillips Kay Shuttleworth, *The Moral and Physical Condition of the Working Classes Employed in the Cotton Manufacture in Manchester* [1832] (London: Frank Cass, 1970). [ed.]
[4] For a discussion of the relationship between courtship and politics in mid-Victorian novels, see Ruth Yeazell, 'Why Political Novels Have Heroines: *Sybil, Mary Barton*, and *Felix Holt*', *Novel* 18 (1985), pp. 126–44.

violation of marriage laws – causes her ghost to disrupt Lockwood's slumber. This compels him in turn to solicit the history of sexual relations that identifies the bond between Catherine and Heathcliff as the secret cause of all the disruptive events in the novel. Such illicit desire is also the ultimate truth we discover in *Jane Eyre*. Beneath all the sexual adventures comprising Rochester's history, Jane uncovers the far greater scandal of a marriage based solely on money and lust that preclude a companionate relationship. And what else creates change in *Vanity Fair* if not Becky's subversive sexual behaviour? It is she who deprives Amelia of a loving husband well before Thackeray has him killed off on the battlefield at Waterloo.

Which returns us, then, to the question of the monstrous women for whom this fiction is remembered: what role did they play in the historical process I have been sketching? As I have explained in earlier chapters, the eighteenth century was concerned with representing the legitimate alliance of the sexes. But by the high Victorian period, that alliance had to displace and resolve a very different political conflict. As Foucault notes in *The History of Sexuality*, there came a point during the nineteenth century when 'the legitimate couple, with its regular sexuality, had a right to more discretion. It tended to function as a norm, one that was stricter' than an earlier notion of sexuality, but one that was less subject to representation as well.[5] *Pamela* fails to be a good novel in present-day terms largely because Richardson goes on, after Mr B acknowledges Pamela's desirability as a wife, to describe their state of perfect matrimony. But even at that he stops short of describing the perfect wedding night he claims is theirs at last to enjoy. Foucault reminds us, however, that during the nineteenth century,

> what came under scrutiny was the sexuality of children, mad men and women, and criminals; the sensuality of those who did not like the opposite sex; reveries, obsessions, petty manias, or great transports of rage. It was time for all these figures, scarcely noticed in the past, to step forward and speak, to make the difficult confession of what they were. (pp. 38–9)

Such figures overshadow the normal characters in the novels of the late 1840s, but perhaps nowhere so obviously as in work of the Brontës.

No reader forgets Rochester's 'bad, mad, and embruted' wife as she is represented here:

> In the deep shade, at the further end of the room, a figure ran backwards and forwards. What it was, whether beast or human being, one could not, at first sight tell: it grovelled, seemingly, on all fours; it snatched and growled like some strange wild animal; but it was covered with clothing; and a quantity of dark, grizzled hair, wild as a man, hid its head and face.[6]

Or consider the last view we receive of the woman who drives Heathcliff to commit crimes against the family in *Wuthering Heights*. As he recounts it, ' "I

---

[5] Michel Foucault, *The History of Sexuality, Volume 1: An Introduction*, trans. Robert Hurley (New York: Pantheon, 1978), p. 38. Citations of the text are to this edition.

[6] Charlotte Brontë, *Jane Eyre*, ed. Richard J. Dunn (New York: Norton, 1971), pp. 257–8. Citations of the text are to this edition.

got the sexton to remove the earth off her coffin lid, and opened it. I thought once, I would have stayed there, when I saw her face again – it is hers yet – he had hard work to stir me; but he said it would change, if the air blew on it." [7] Representing the last of the earlier generation of Earnshaws and embodying their pre-individualistic notion of identity, the same woman lives on into the present as a ghostly child. In this form, she enters the sleep of the utterly modern individual who has invaded her bedroom and peered into the books that bear traces of her personal history. In a scene where Brontë deliberately neglects to draw distinctions between subjective and objective experience, this ghostly woman grasps Lockwood, the intrusive narrator, with 'a little ice-cold hand'. Such encroachment by a female upon the male consciousness turns the room into something resembling the scene of rape, only here the features of aggressor and victim are grotesquely confused along with the features of gender. As the narrator describes, 'I pulled its wrist on to the broken pane, and rubbed it to and fro till the blood ran down and soaked the bedclothes; still it wailed, "let me in!" and maintained its tenacious grip, almost maddening me with fear' (p. 30). Unlike the desire that threatened to take forms of rape or adultery in earlier fiction, this material cannot be domesticated by marriage. It is definitely outside of culture.

Thackeray uses a similar figure of boundary dissolution to represent certain human desires that cannot be included within the novel, at least not in any literal way or realistic mode of description. On discovering Becky's infidelity, her husband tears up their household, reducing it to 'a *heap* of tumbled vanities lying in a wreck', and sends her back to the streets from which she came (italics mine). [8] It is significant that once outside the bounds of polite society, Becky loses her sharp socioeconomic delineation. To represent what a woman in this state becomes, Thackeray resorts to a literary figure, the sirens of classical mythology. Apparently they 'look pretty enough when they sit upon a rock and beckon you to come', but, the narrator warns, when they sink into their own element – in this case, the city – 'those mermaids are about no good, and we had best not examine the fiendish marine cannibals, feasting on their pickled victims' (p. 617). As the classical figure for misdirected desire is rewritten for a Victorian audience, we should note, it loses its aesthetic features and takes on those of a savage. No matter how closely Becky may resemble the people of polite society, that resemblance is at best superficial. Her sexual behaviour reveals her origins in another class.

Henry Mayhew's famous classification system for criminal behaviour in *London Labour and London Poor* (1862) can be viewed as a blatant attempt by a middle-class intellectual to transform the problem of an impoverished working class by translating this social dilemma into sexual terms. [9] In constructing his system of all the criminal types populating London, Mayhew

---

[7] Emily Brontë, *Wuthering Heights*, ed. William M. Sale, Jr (New York: Norton, 1972), p. 228. Citations of the text are to this edition.

[8] William Makepeace Thackeray, *Vanity Fair*, ed. Geoffrey and Kathleen Tillotson (Boston: Houghton Mifflin, 1963), p. 516. Citations of the text are to this edition.

[9] Henry Mayhew, *London Labour and London Poor* [1862] (New York: Dover, 1968), IV, p. 35. Citations of the text are to this edition.

cut through the political categories – distinctions based on one's source of income and place within a competitive economy – that had been isolated and refined in the earlier writing on political economy. For Mayhew, the first and most basic social distinction among men was the profound gulf between those who worked and those who did not. Among those who *would* not work were all criminal types, according to Mayhew. Such a view toward the vast number of unemployed that characterized Victorian England may help to explain how capitalism became relatively stable by the mid-nineteenth century despite continuing fluctuations in the economy. As Thomas Laqueur reminds us:

> The great divisions in early nineteenth century society were not between the middle and the working classes but between the idle and the non-idle classes, between the rough and the respectable, between the religious and the non-religious. All of these divisions ran across class lines. The puritan ethic was therefore not the monopoly of the owners of capital; it was the ideology of those who worked against those who did not.[10]

While this binary opposition was forged in the sociological descriptions of the 1830s and 1840s, the second half of the nineteenth century would make such categories impervious to interrogation. In *London Labour and London Poor*, Mayhew begins straightforwardly enough to map out the various kinds of crime that comprise London lowlife, but his description abruptly swerves away from crimes against property. It departs from the world of male deviance and singles out prostitution as the figure for virtually all other forms of criminal behaviour:

> Literally construed, prostitution is the putting of anything to vile use; in this sense perjury is a species of prostitution, being an unworthy use of the faculty of speech; so again, bribery is a prostitution of the right of voting; while prostitution, specially so called, is the using of her charms by a woman for immoral purposes. . . . Be the cause, however, what it may, the act remains the same, and consists in the base perversion of a woman's charms – the surrendering of her virtue to criminal indulgence. (p. 35)

We should note the reflex that makes the woman into the agent of her own prostitution ('the using of her charms by a woman', 'the surrendering of her virtue'). It is worth pausing over this curious tendency to view prostitution as the only crime that seems to be its own cause. The role that prostitution plays in Mayhew's classification system as a whole is also worth noting. In his description, prostitution is at first only one category among the many kinds of crime committed by people who will not work. But eventually the category balloons into an elaboration comprising half the entire volume and becomes both the figure for crime in general and the implicit source of all crime. Not only does sexual conduct provide the basis for Mayhew's entire catalogue of urban criminal types, but the theme of prostitution provides him with a means of comparing all modern cultures and those of earlier periods as well. In short, Mayhew's description of London advances a notion of deviance that aims at the labouring poor but that can be extended to other cultures. His urban

---

[10] Thomas Walter Laqueur, *Religion and Respectability: Sunday Schools and Working Class Culture, 1780–1850* (New Haven, Conn.: Yale University Press, 1976), p. 239.

sociology therefore provides the general basis for anthropological procedures.

After his exhaustive study of prostitution throughout time and geographical location, Mayhew begins the section entitled 'Thieves and Swindlers' by offering an analogy for the curious structure of his project: 'In tracing the geography of a river it is interesting to go to its source. . . . We proceed in a similar manner to treat of the thieves and swindlers of the metropolis' (p. 273). At the source of urban criminal culture, he discovers a female who is precisely what the domestic woman is not, and he describes her in the same terms as he described the prostitute:

> Thousands of our felons are trained from their infancy in the bosom of crime. . . .
> Many of them are often carried to the beershop or gin palace on the breast of
> worthless drunken mothers, while others, clothed in rags, run at their heels or hang
> by the skirts of their petticoats. (p. 273)

By way of this reference to Mayhew, I want to call attention to the importance of the prostitute in nineteenth-century political thought, which uses this figure to evaluate people in terms that have nothing to do with their economic circumstances or political position.[11] Yet sexual conduct is clearly a political language. It places both individuals and cultures on a moral continuum that declares any sexual behaviour other than legitimate monogamy as perverse and criminal. Mayhew not only specifies an elaborate system of normal desires and a standard for the conduct of private life. He also uses that historically specific model of sexuality as a universal and timeless one.

In turning now to the fictional use of the prostitute, we find that she is also the figure underlying all the monstrous women under consideration. An early Victorian novel and not yet Dickens's full-blown treatment of the relationship between money and love, the two halves of the Victorian world, *Oliver Twist* (1837) provides one of the clearest illustrations of the rhetorical purpose of the prostitute's almost obligatory appearance in fiction. Dickens's characterization of Nancy, the good-hearted prostitute, demonstrates how a uniquely Victorian logic was formulated out of the materials of an earlier moment in history. In her, the dangerous elements that must be abolished in the prostitute are clearly present as such rather than, as in later novels, dispersed among the features of her less obvious avatars. Nancy is the figure of illicit sexuality; her behaviour confuses money with sex. But if Nancy commits the crime of prostitution and – worse yet – delivers Oliver over to Fagin, her devotion to her man Sikes surpasses any other affiliation in the novel, and she ultimately is the one who returns Oliver to polite society by divulging the secret of his pedigree. Paradoxically, then, Nancy is the antithesis of the absent mother and an alternative source of nurturance as well as a surrogate for that mother. It has to be the mixing of illicit sexual features with the attributes of the good mother that makes her body the site of sexual violence. More than any other scene in the Dickens repertoire, including even the death of little Nell, the scene in which Sikes bludgeons his prostitute-lover to death both fascinated and appalled the audiences who flocked to hear

---

[11] For a discussion of the prostitute in Victorian England, see Judith R. Walkowitz, *Prostitution and Victorian Society: Women, Class, and the State* (Cambridge: Cambridge University Press, 1980).

Dickens's reading performances.[12] The power of the scene has everything to do with the fact that Nancy is the representation of another class sexuality as well as a positive figure. Her mutilated body expresses intense hostility toward the working classes, even though Dickens represents them as victims who need to be rescued. One could say this body provided a field where two notions of the family confronted one another and the old gave way to the new.

Having noted the habit of Victorian culture to sexualize all combination, that is, to render all collective forms of social organization as sexual violations, one still must ask what the novel did differently. The dramatic reappearance of domestic fiction during the late 1840s suggests that these novels had their own role to play. They not only contained disorder within the household, but they also gave it female form. In other words, coming between Shuttleworth in the 1830s and Mayhew in the 1860s, novels further displaced the conflict between competing social formations as they turned combination into a female who lacked femininity. It is no accident that all the monstrous women in question have other than middle-class origins. Resembling Bakhtin's figure of the grotesque body in several ways, this kind of female body is open, permeable, and ambiguously gendered. In her, other sexual behaviours linger on as archaic forms that are both powerless and terrible. And as these cultural materials are contained within the body of a deranged woman, all threats of social disruption suddenly lose their political meaning and are just as suddenly quelled.

With the murder of Nancy, the collective ethos of the urban underworld in *Oliver Twist* is demoralized and the characters scattered. The transformation of the prostitute's body into a battered corpse instantly criminalizes the merry gang of thieves who rescue Oliver from certain starvation. But the murder of Nancy also provides a way of containing this alternative form of social organization within a figure of combination and a way of transforming that figure into one that can be subjected to middle-class authority. Nancy appears in several forms throughout the novel, but the one that most closely resembles the monstrous women of the Brontës' fiction is not the woman who has been reduced to a pool of gore, though indeed, in the narrator's words, 'it was a ghastly figure to look upon' (p. 323). Instead, she assumes truly Gothic proportions only after her murder and as she lives on in the mind of her

---

[12] Dickens began to write *Oliver Twist* when *Pickwick Papers* was first appearing in serial form. Throughout his career, he included excerpts entitled 'Sikes and Nancy' in his public reading performances. The death of Nancy remained a set piece in his repertoire despite the fact his doctors had warned him that reading this particular episode severely overexcited him and endangered his life. The same strategies for dealing with the culture of poverty that appear in this novel shape John Forster's *The Life of Charles Dickens* (London: Chapman and Hall, 1872) as well as every novel Dickens subsequently wrote. On this point, see J.S. Schwarzbach, *Dickens and the City* (London: Athlone, 1979), p. 12. But the novel's wide reception, however mixed it was at first, suggests that in bringing the city back into fiction, *Oliver Twist* offered a form of narrative thinking in which the political fantasies of a new generation of readers, as well as the scars of Dickens's traumatic childhood, were inscribed. In the winter of 1838, to cite a notable instance from Kathleen Tillotson's commentary in the Clarendon edition of *Oliver Twist*, the young Queen Victoria was finding the novel 'excessively interesting' reading, even while an earlier generation of readers, represented by her mother and Lord Melbourne, admonished Victoria for 'reading light books' and expressed their distaste for this one's 'low, debasing style'. See *Oliver Twist*, ed. Kathleen Tillotson (Oxford: Clarendon Press, 1966), p. 600. Citations of the text are to this edition.

killer.[13] It is not as a material body at all that she exercises her power, then, but as a psychological one:

> For now, a vision came before him, as constant and more terrible than that from which he had escaped. Those widely staring eyes, so lustreless and so glassy, that he had better borne to see them than to think upon them, appeared in the midst of darkness: light in themselves, but giving light to nothing. There were but two, but they were everywhere. If he shut out the sight, there came the room with every well-known object – some, indeed, that he would have forgotten, if he had gone over its contents from memory – each in its accustomed place.   (pp. 327–8)

As she comes back to haunt the criminal, we should note, the figure of the prostitute works on the side of legitimate authority. She exercises a panoptical power that sees deep into the hearts of men and from whose gaze they cannot hope to escape, it is so all-encompassing. This power is a form of social control in its own right and is in fact required to bring the novel to a successful conclusion. As her figure is contained within the framework of Sikes's subjectivity, it turns his body against him, makes him visible wherever he goes, and drives him finally to serve as his own executioner:

> 'The eyes again!' he cried, in an unearthly screech.
> Staggering as if struck by lightning, he lost his balance and tumbled over the parapet. The noose was at his neck. It ran up with his weight, tight as a bow-string, and swift as the arrow it speeds.   (p. 347)

It is certainly a significant event when a novel represents an execution that is not performed by the state but by the criminal himself. And it is even more significant when the power of the state is enhanced simply by knowledge of the crime, as if such knowledge were in itself a remedy. Coming after the murder of Nancy and performed by Sikes's own conscience, his execution is staged in a manner that makes no demands on liberal sympathies. In contrast with the state execution of Fagin, the execution of Sikes is arranged so that readers can simply enjoy the extinction of a professed class enemy. His death is not only a public execution, but also a scene on the scaffold that he stages for himself.

Like sociology, the novel represents the disruption of domestic order in terms of combination; the destruction of boundaries between nature and culture reveals itself in a mixture of genders and generations and associates the scene of such dissolution with filth and disease. These qualities would be exaggerated in the cities of slightly later novels such as *Bleak House* and *Our Mutual Friend*, but the novels of the 1840s already observe the figurative logic of sociological description. They use scenes of discipline to restore the household disrupted by aberrant forms of desire. By way of a remedy, each novel offers up a static tableau that represents the family in a highly idealized and decidedly modern form. One glimpses such a scene through the window of Wuthering Heights as the Earnshaw family history ends. Here the household encloses a new generation of lovers within a radically exclusive space that is divided according to sex and to function. Thus we see the young Catherine deliberately departing from earlier sentimental heroines as she educates Hareton for a gentleman's role:

[13] On the notion of the 'new Gothic', see Robert B. Heilman, 'Charlotte Brontë's "New" Gothic', in Ian Watt, ed., *The Victorian Novel: Modern Essays in Criticism* (New York: Oxford University Press, 1971), pp. 166–7.

He was a young man respectably dressed, and seated at a table, having a book before him. His handsome features glowed with pleasure, and his eyes kept impatiently wandering from the page to a small white hand over his shoulder, which recalled him by a smart slap on the cheek whenever its owner detected such signs of inattention.   (p. 243)

A similar scene of rehabilitation also concludes the courtship of Jane Eyre and Rochester. Tucked away from the world with an invalid husband, Jane describes their relationship in terms that endow her with all the panoptical powers we observed both in Dickens's Nancy and in the second Catherine of *Wuthering Heights*:

Literally, I was (what he often called me) the apple of his eye. He saw nature – he saw books through me; and never did I weary of gazing for his behalf, and of putting into words the effect of field, tree, town, river, cloud, sunbeam – of the landscape before us; of the weather around us – and impressing by sound on his ear what light could no longer stamp on his eye.   (p. 397)

It is in the use of disciplinary strategies that *Vanity Fair* resembles the other great novels of its day, as Thackeray leaves us in a world he imagines as a joyless bazaar partitioned off into booths. Such women as Becky Sharp pose no threat to us in this highly individuated world. And because they each have revealed some slightly twisted desire, these characters suddenly become more alike than different, and marriage among them resembles nothing so much as a prison.

I would like to suggest that these novels were making history as they turned scenes of punishment into those that represented order in terms resembling representations of the factory, prison, and schoolroom. Novels incorporated new political material and sexualized it in such a manner that only one resolution would do: a partitioned and hierarchical space under a woman's surveillance. Because it is the earliest and least psychological of the novels I have been considering in this chapter, *Oliver Twist* again offers the most revealing display of social redemption through the domestication of desire. After scattering the underworld characters and purging them from his novel, Dickens encloses Oliver himself within a household and places him with a cousin who is neither mother, nor sister, nor lover, but who has displaced all of these roles. In this way, the reconstituted family recalls the death of the original family that the novel had originally sought to restore. The novel ends with a scene that also marks the death of an earlier mode of fiction. No matter how much the present resembles the past homologically, an abyss opens between them when Oliver's true mother reappears as a name for which there can never be a referent. Even more so than Nancy, the prostitute, Agnes, the true mother, becomes a disembodied woman:

Within the altar of the old village church, there stands a white marble tablet, which bears as yet but one word, – 'Agnes!' There is no coffin in that tomb; and may it be many, many years, before another name is placed above it! But, if the spirits of the Dead ever come back to earth, to visit spots hallowed by the love – the love beyond the grave – of those whom they knew in life, I believe that the shade of Agnes sometimes hovers round that solemn nook. I believe it none the less because that nook is in a Church, and she was weak and erring.   (p. 368)

Like Emily Brontë, Dickens leaves us with the ghosts of fiction past, figures of desire that have no place to occupy within the social order but, for that very reason, all the more important a role to play in constituting the household.[14]

---

[14] I have discussed this point in 'Emily Brontë In and Out of Her Time', *Genre* 15 (1982), pp. 243–64.

18 Jerome McGann

The Third World of Criticism: From Aeschylus to Ezra Pound[1]

Marjorie Levinson, Marilyn Butler, Jerome McGann and Paul Hamilton, *Rethinking Historicism: Critical Readings in Romantic History*, Blackwell: Oxford, 1989, pp. 85–107.

There is no freedom, even for masters, in the midst of slaves.

Byron

At the conclusion of his great essay 'Concerning Violence' Frantz Fanon argues that 'The fate of the world depends upon' whether the first two worlds, and especially the first world, are able to operate from a non-colonialist imagination.[2] To Fanon this means that the first world must be forced to realize its obligation not merely to allow the Third World its independent development, but also to assist actively in that development, and with no strings attached.

The full argument is by this time a familiar one, though certainly no less important for that reason. What still surprises a Western reader of this essay is its exclusive rhetoric. Fanon's essay addresses the people of the Third World; indeed, not until the conclusion does he allow himself to think at all about the effect his words might have on the first two worlds. But at the end, for the first time in the essay, the people from those other two worlds are allowed in the room with Fanon and his audience, are allowed to listen, from the margin of Fanon's centre, to the urgency of his message.

What we hear, from our corner of that room, is 'what [the Third World] expects from those who for centuries have kept it in slavery'. The message is 'to rehabilitate mankind, and make man victorious, once and for all':

> This huge task which consists of reintroducing mankind into the world, the whole of mankind, will be carried out with the indispensable help of the European peoples, who themselves must realize that in the past they have often joined the ranks of our common masters where colonial questions were concerned. To achieve this the European peoples must first decide to wake up and shake themselves, use their brains, and stop playing the stupid game of Sleeping Beauty.[3]

From the vantage of the eavesdropping 'European peoples' – ourselves – this involves awakening from certain luxurious and heroic dreams. We are to stop projecting those grand illusions that proceed from small imaginations. If we are hearing Fanon at all we are hearing from his point of view – that is to say,

---

[1] Original title ('The Third World of Criticism') adapted by the editor of the present volume with the permission of the author and Basil Blackwell. [ed.]

[2] Frantz Fanon, *The Wretched of the Earth*, Preface by Jean-Paul Sartre, trans. Constance Farrington (New York: Grove Press, 1968), p. 105.

[3] Fanon, *The Wretched of the Earth*, p. 106.

from the point of view of a Third World, where the dialectic of the first two worlds is completely reimagined.

The problem here is not at all that we occupy a *different* world, but that in investing it with privilege we have generated the inertias of violence and domination that Fanon has spoken of. Nor is the problem simply that our heritage of violence has borne away an actual Third World. The problem is more acute, simple and closer to home: that in our violent histories we have acquired a certain kind of imagination, and that this imagination is written out in the treasuries of our kings and the gardens of our queens. Benjamin, who had a Third Imagination, could not 'contemplate without horror' the cultural treasures which descended into his hands: 'There is no document of civilization which is not at the same time a document of barbarism. And just as such a document is not free of barbarism, barbarism taints also the manner in which it was transmitted from one owner to another.'[4] This is the voice of a European person speaking to European peoples out of a Third Imagination. Benjamin's 'Theses on the Philosophy of History' deploy the rhetoric of the second world frequently, but in fact he lived an uneasy existence, at the margins of both of the first two worlds. For when he says that the task of the 'historical materialist' is 'to brush history against the grain'[5] he could not exclude the atrocious histories of the second world as well, where the violence of the first world has met its match.

What would it mean, then, to acquire a Third Imagination? On this question Fanon is clearer than Benjamin – even for European persons like ourselves. He sketches an answer (it is not written for us, but we can read it with profit) in his essay 'On National Culture'. According to Fanon, in the context of imperialism a national culture develops in three phases. (Fanon, of course, writes of these matters from the perspective of an actual citizen of the actual Third World; his analysis reflects on circumstances in the first two worlds as well, however, since the latter live through, by carrying out, the imagination of violence visited upon the Third World.) In the first phase of its development a cultural mode of violation is established and assimilated. In the second phase, when the violation is discovered, an effort is made to find a world elsewhere, an inviolate world: 'Past happenings of the byegone days of . . . childhood will be brought up out of the depths of . . . memory; old legends will be reinterpreted in the light of a borrowed estheticism and of a conception of the world which was discovered under other skies.'[6] This is a phase of enlightenment where the past is used to clarify conditions in the present. It prepares for the third phase, 'the fighting phase', when one 'turns himself into an awakener of the people', to 'shake' them from their lethargy.[7] The imagery echoes Fanon's call to a similar awakening of the 'European peoples' at the end of the essay 'Concerning Violence'.

In the third phase, past and present are conceived from the vantage of the future. In terms of an actual literary practice, the third phase means, for

[4] Walter Benjamin, *Illuminations*, ed. Hannah Arendt, trans. Harry Zohn (New York: Schocken Books, 1969), p. 256.

[5] Benjamin, *Illuminations*, p. 257.

[6] Fanon, *The Wretched of the Earth*, p. 222.

[7] Fanon, *The Wretched of the Earth*, pp. 222–3.

example, that 'The storytellers who used to relate inert episodes now bring them alive and introduce into them modifications which are increasingly fundamental.' 'Conflicts' are brought 'up to date and . . . modernize[d]', and 'The method of allusion is more and more widely used': 'The formula "This all happened long ago" is substituted with that of "What we are going to speak of happened somewhere else, but it might well have happened here today, and it might happen tomorrow."'[8] What Fanon means is that an imagination of the future, of what the future should be, determines both the writing and the reading of the texts we inherit and create. This third phase, which is one with the Third World, is the Third World's gift to 'the whole of mankind' – an objective and precisely an *alienated* perspective on the dialectic of violence of the first two worlds and all the 'inert episodes' which we fondly call our literary and cultural inheritance.

For the nations of the first and second worlds, with their imperialist histories, the awakening Fanon speaks of would expose new ranges of historical possibility – new configurations of the past, different imaginations of the present and the future. Our cultural productions generally represent those histories in forms of beauty and sublimity, though in fact they are histories which, as often as not, are founded in shameful and barbarous deeds. A critical awakening would strip away such modes of deception (and self-deception); it would entail a refusal to read our cultural deposits on their own ideological terms, and a refusal as well to develop new readings (or writings) that merely modernize and update those ideologies.

Initially this requires that our cultural works be alienated from the tradition that represents them as the best that has been known and thought in the world. This alienation does not mean, however, that the works should be debunked. Neither an antithetical nor a third reading can afford to deliver any part of cultural history into the hands of an imperial imagination. Rather, the works must be raised up from their narrowly imagined totalities, must be seen as part of that larger context that emerges when they are *specifically* situated, when they are delivered over to their historical and social localities. That critical event – the islanding of history and its works[9] – establishes the possibility of a proper sphere of totalization – one that is horizontally international, and vertically transcultural and transhistorical.

This islanding of the works of culture is especially crucial for readers in a Western tradition, where the intertexture of our cultural works, in particular of our poetry, has woven a net that is strangling human imagination. The burden of the past that weighs like a nightmare on the brain of the West is an imperial burden, the anxiety that it might not all be of one piece, that secret histories, forgotten facts, other imaginations operate in all that we do and make, and that our massive ignorance of these Othernesses is working to undermine what we do. Like Napoleon moving inexorably towards the capture of Moscow, Great Traditions follow their difficult and equivocal victories of imagination to an ultimate destruction.

[8] Fanon, *The Wretched of the Earth*, p. 240.
[9] I mean to recall here Marshall Sahlins's *Islands of History* (Chicago: University of Chicago Press, 1985), and in general the book's important demonstration of how an imperial culture encounters, and mistakes, the histories in which it is involved.

That destruction does not overtake the works of the past, it merely makes them inaccessible to people in the present who are unable to imagine them anew, objectively. Writers like Benjamin and Fanon call us towards that objectivity, to an imagining of poetical work in ways that will be trying to overcome the illusions those works themselves have helped to perpetuate. Every poem is an island that imagines itself a world; and it *is* a world – but not *the* world – because it is a world within and among other worlds. Its illusion of totality is a dream of a truth that can only come to be in the exposure of the meaning of the dream.

A work like the *Oresteia*, for example, dreams of a society to be founded for ever in an imagination of justice and civil harmony. This utopian dream is then realized in Aeschylus's work, which we have since continued to interpret in terms that accommodate its own self-conception. Yet such interpretations visit a serious injustice upon the *Oresteia* and its utopian dream of a just and harmonious society. Justice here depends upon the exposition of the objective and alienated truths of Aeschylus's dramatic work. Such an exposition can never be completed, of course, but it will not even advance beyond a mirror-stage unless the work is seen objectively.

As we know, the *Oresteia* deals with the impasse which a retributive system of justice develops for itself. Or rather, it *imagines* such a system at an impasse – for in fact one could have imagined it otherwise, could have told a different story in which retribution falls upon the guilty by hands that are other than familial hands.

But Aeschylus wants to imagine retributive justice at an impasse because he wants to celebrate not simply a 'universal' idea of justice, but the Athenian version of a universal idea of justice. The play is presented in Athens at a crucial and specific time, 458 BC, shortly after the passage of the revolutionary Ephialtic reforms.[10] Scholars have long recognized this topical dimension to the *Oresteia*, and in more recent years have reached a certain broad agreement that Aeschylus, though generally conservative, must have supported a number of these new legal reforms. The trilogy makes a significant ideological intervention in the immediate aftermath of the struggle between the reformers (like Ephialtes and Pericles) and the traditional authorities (like Kimon).

The Ephialtic reforms were an attempt to replace the traditional oligarchic legal structure with democratic structures. As such, they were equally bound up with certain international issues, and most specifically with the uneasy relations (and alliance) between Sparta and Athens following the Persian Wars. Sparta, of course, was an oligarchy, and Athens's alliance with her was maintained and supported, at the crucial period of the reforms, largely through the authority of men like Kimon, who were sympathetic to oligarchic structures.

The context in which the reforms were passed is important if we are to understand the *Oresteia*.[11] Athens had been asked to send a supporting force to Laconia to aid the Spartans in putting down the revolt of their helots in 463.

---

[10] The best single presentation of the historical and political context of the *Oresteia* is in Anthony J. Podlecki's *The Political Background of Aeschylean Tragedy* (Ann Arbor, Mich.: University of Michigan Press, 1966), Ch. 5.

[11] See George Grote, *A History of Greece* (New York: Harper, 1881), II, Chs 45–6.

Kimon argued successfully, against strong democratic opposition, to send an Athenian contingent, but when the army arrived in Laconia – with Kimon at its head – it was ignominiously sent away by the suspicious Lacedaemonians. Kimon returned to Athens in disgrace, the reforms were passed in 462/1 and Kimon was ostracized. But the reforms were not instituted without vigorous and widespread opposition, and great civic unrest in Athens. Ephialtes himself was assassinated shortly after the passage of the initial series of reforms.

The *Oresteia* is clearly preoccupied with all these matters; indeed, one of its principal objects, as we see most clearly at the end of *The Eumenides*, is to promote an ideal of civic harmony, and (reciprocally) to warn of the dangers that beset a society torn by internal and civil discord. At the end of *The Libation Bearers*, with Clytemnestra and Aegisthus now dead at the hands of the avenging Orestes, and with Orestes pursued by the Fates, the Chorus – dismayed at the prospect of a ceaseless process of internecine death – prays for an end to the bloodletting:

> Where
> Is the end? Where shall the fury of fate
> Be stilled to sleep, be done with?

(1074–6)[12]

The prayer recalls the refrain of the Chorus at the beginning of the *Agamemnon* ('Sing sorrow, sorrow: but good win out in the end'), and anticipates the conclusion of the trilogy, when the judgement of Athena – at the trial and immediately afterwards – produces the trilogy's final vision of civil harmony.

That vision is itself crucial to the resolution of the dramatic conflicts. After the acquittal of Orestes the Fates are at first implacable in their resentment, but Athena persuades them out of their wrath with benevolent promises. These are all founded in a conviction that Athens is destined for greatness:

> If you go away into some land of foreigners,
> I warn you, you will come to love this country. Time
> in his forward flood shall ever grow more dignified
> for the people of this city. And you, in your place
> of eminence beside Erechtheus in his house
> shall win from female and from male processionals
> more than all lands of men beside could ever give.

(851–7)

This is a social and a political vision, and it celebrates what the final courtroom scene dramatizes: Aeschylus's conviction that the institutions of Athens are the glory of Greece – indeed, the glory of the world. Important to the meaning of the conclusion of *The Eumenides* is the fact that a stranger to Athens, a guest, should go there to seek justice. Athens took a justifiable pride in her legal institutions, and specifically in the two fundamental principles: that rule should be maintained by law and not by men, and that everyone – guest and citizen alike – should have equal protection under the law. The conclusion of *The Eumenides* is a celebration of those legal institutions.

---

[12] I use here Richmond Lattimore's translation (Chicago: University of Chicago Press, 1953).

But the play is also celebrating something else – a treaty of alliance with Argos made in 461 at the urging of the (now politically dominant) reform party. This second focus of celebration is closely allied to the first. It is a celebration not of Athens's political institutions, however, but of her economic and political power. The two celebrations are connected in the reality of Athens's circumstances in the period 463–458, when Athens arrived at a position of enormous economic, military and political power and influence. This position was achieved gradually during the period following the Persian Wars, but most dramatically between 477 and 463, that is, between the founding of the Delian League – with Athens at its head – and the subjugation by Athens of various members who tried to revolt from the League. The important island of Thasos was reduced in 463 after a two-year struggle. During the fifteen-year period between the foundation of the League and the Ephialtic reforms, Athens's empire came into being.

These matters bear upon the *Oresteia* because the treaty with Argos is the play's device for focusing our attention on Athens's position in the Greek world at the time. Aeschylus draws our attention to Argos immediately, at the opening of the *Agamemnon* (24), when we are told that the king is returning home from the Trojan War to Argos. According to Homer, however, Agamemnon was the king of Mykenai, not of Argos. Scholars agree now that this change was made as a compliment to Athens's new ally.[13] The change was not an awkward one in any case since the Argives had recently conquered the ancient city of Mykenai and incorporated her into their domains.[14]

The conquest of Mykenai was the latest in a series of adventures that placed Argos in a position to rival Sparta for control of the Peloponnese. Athens sought the treaty with Argos – a defensive alliance against Sparta – immediately after the failure of Kimon's expedition into Laconia to aid Sparta. The alliance with Argos, in other words, was an international part of the democratic reforms being carried through by Ephialtes and Pericles. The alliance was meant to strengthen the Athenian Empire against its chief rival for power in Greece, Sparta.

Aeschylus alludes to this treaty with Argos three times in *The Eumenides* and in each case the passage imagines an alliance 'for the rest of time' (291, 670). In the final passage Orestes, speaking as the mouthpiece of Argos, swears to fight with Athens against those who come against her, and to be the 'gracious spirit' of all those others, her tributaries and her allies, who 'align their spears to fight beside her' (773–4). Orestes's oath of alliance is immediately followed by the scene in which Athena finally persuades the Furies to take up their office of benevolence towards Athens. Before the play concludes in its vision of civic harmony, Athena addresses the as yet unpersuaded Furies. 'Do not', she warns them,

> engraft among my citizens that spirit of war
> that turns their battle fury inward on themselves.
> No, let our wars range outward . . .
>
> (862–4)

[13] See e.g. James C. Hogan, *A Commentary on The Complete Greek Tragedies: Aeschylus* (Chicago: University of Chicago Press, 1984), pp. 31, 159–60.
[14] See Grote, *A History of Greece*, p. 411.

The prayer expresses at once Aeschylus's dismay at the recent civil discords in Athens between the rival democratic and aristocratic parties, and his confidence in the martial strength of the empire in face of her enemies. The confidence here is part of the trilogy's compliment to Argos, whose alliance added so much to Athenian imperial power vis-à-vis the other Greek cities, and especially the Lacedaemonians.

Yet hidden in the splendour of the play's conclusion, with its grandiose imagination of social harmony, is a terrible truth which the ideology of Aeschylus's trilogy could not see, but which the dramas are none the less forced to confront. For the fact is that this very alliance with Argos, which seemed to promise so much good, was the triggering event behind the (so-called) 'First' Peloponnesian War, and the first act in a tragic curve that would eventually plunge all of Greece into war and bring about the destruction of the empire so vaunted in the *Oresteia*. Athena, goddess though she is, cannot understand the full, tragic weight of her prayer for outward-ranging war. In its imagination of an end to the cycles of bloodshed, the *Oresteia* is prophesying an even greater cataclysm, and no end to the cycles of destruction. For the *Oresteia*'s imagination of justice and harmony are illusions, founded in a set of contradictory social structures (democracy and imperialism) which would only grow more extreme with the passing of time.

We do not understand how poetry works if we think that, because the Peloponnesian Wars took place after Aeschylus wrote the *Oresteia*, therefore the trilogy and those wars are not implicated in each other. We may imagine, rather, that the 'meaning' of a poetical work is structured by the historical limit of the author's life; and this imagining is all the more insisted upon when the 'meanings' we seek after are social and historical ones. But we are wrong in this imagining, because every poetical work casts itself along what Shelley called 'futurity'. In writing what amounts to an imaginative history of the present, poems thereby construct a past and a set of possible futures. One of the futures constructed in the *Oresteia* is 'an upright course clear through to the end' (995) and 'peace forever' (1046). But another future, more dreadful, is also constructed through the play *in the very illusions and contradictions that are borne along with that first, benevolent imagination of the future*. The tragic meaning of the *Oresteia* is not a mere quirk or irony of history; it is what the trilogy signified from the beginning, and what was most dramatically foregrounded in the celebrations of the treaty with Argos.

Poems move out into many futures, which are their own real futures as well, unknown to themselves. The *Oresteia* today means both more and less than it meant in 458 because its meaning – which is always localized in the present – carries along the many histories of meanings that were only initiated in the trilogy's first appearance. These meanings are sometimes lost, often recovered and always refashioned. If we read the *Oresteia*'s conclusion as an unequivocal celebration we will be reading it in terms of its initial self-conception; and we will be reading *out* of the work that other dominant line of meaning which is so closely connected to the celebratory meaning, and which is so intimately involved with the work's history – with the work as meaning in and through the history its own celebration calls our attention to.

We will, moreover, be reading in a way that projects a certain meaning into our own immediate circumstances. More clearly than most works of the past, the *Oresteia* seems to impinge upon ourselves and our present. This work and its significant history 'all happened long ago', but Fanon's suggestion – that 'it might well have happened here today, and it might happen tomorrow' – points towards the 'formula' that all criticism, whether consciously or not, adheres to. The tales told in the *Oresteia* are certainly happening here today, and will happen again tomorrow. The question is: how will we choose to read those tales – objectively, or in terms of their own (and our own) celebrations and self-conceptions?

Shelley wrote the *Prometheus Unbound* as a response to the future bequeathed to him by Aeschylus's *Prometheus Bound* and the (subsequently lost) *Prometheus Unbound*, with its celebratory reconciliation of 'the Champion with the Oppressor of mankind'.[15] Shelley's play is a reading of the lost Aeschylean drama according to Fanon's 'method of allusion' and 'modernization': not an imitation, but a remaking in terms of a more objective imagining of Aeschylus than the Greek dramatist would have intended. Aeschylean drama, however, like all poetry, lays down a rich deposit of incommensurate detail even as it follows its specific ideological commitments. In this way poetry always tells more than it knows, always carries within itself many opportunities for greater objectivity and truth.

Genesis, more than most texts, has worked assiduously to project a monomorphic image of its world; but even in Genesis the relics of a larger story remain, a story that includes many other cultures and civilizations as great, and as barbaric, as Israel's. The Israel of Genesis is an island in a greater world, and the more it insists that it is the centre of that world, the more it gives us glimpses of the actual, the whole, the objective truth.

To relinquish an empire is no easy task, and it can be, as Pericles once argued, dangerous as well.[16] To maintain one, however, is not merely wrong – which Pericles observed – it is even more dangerous. The dangers are especially acute in the case of empires like the Athenian and the American – empires, that is to say, that were acquired in a brief period and only half-purposefully, empires that developed in volatile political circumstances both at home and abroad.

To relinquish an imperial imagination is also a difficult if no less urgent task. Empires are maintained by imperial intellects. Cultural studies, and literary work in particular, function either to build or to unbuild such minds. In this respect Blake's work is exactly a prophecy against empire, a model of how the poetic moves against the perpetuation of empires and towards the development of less exploitive societies, less alienated imaginations. Literary work is the art of multiplicities and minute particulars, the science of *Un*buildings: one law for the lion and the ox *is* oppression.

In this context Shelley's famous words bear remembering:

> We have more moral, political and historical wisdom, than we know how to reduce to practice; we have more scientific and economical knowledge than can be

[15] From Shelley's Preface to *Prometheus Unbound*, in Donald H. Reiman and Sharon B. Powers, eds, *Shelley's Poetry and Prose* (New York: Norton, 1977), p. 133.

[16] See Thucydides, *The Peloponnesian War*, Book II, sec. 63.

accommodated to the just distribution of the produce which it multiplies . . . our calculations have outrun conception; we have eaten more than we can digest. The cultivation of those sciences which have enlarged the limits of the empire of man over the external world, has, for want of the poetical faculty, proportionately circumscribed those of the internal world; and man, having enslaved the elements, remains himself a slave.[17]

These are stirring words, and worthy of honour – not least because they are fully conscious that poetical work is not an aesthetic resort but an activity with real social investments and obligations. They are as well, however, words spoken out of that fundamental Romantic ideology which is epitomized in the Kantian aesthetic, but which is equally operative in the anti-Kantian Romantic programme first deployed by Blake. That is to say, Shelley – like Blake before him – takes it for granted that the redemption of the social order is the function of the 'poetical faculty'. For them, poetry and Imagination are not involved with the false consciousness of ideology.

Yet it is plain that this ascription of transcendent status to art and the Imagination is mistaken – indeed, is contradicted by the actual practice of Romantic artists themselves. Milton earlier established the model that, in place of a failed social order, one might establish the order of an inward paradise. But neither Blake nor Shelley – nor even Wordsworth, for that matter – accepted Milton's consolatory move. Their departures from Milton's model all differ somewhat, of course, but Blake's departure is especially significant because his work enacts an artistic practice that is committed to the transformation of society: the installation of the city of God (which for Blake means a *human* city) in England's green and pleasant land.

Blake understands that this will be a city of art, that is to say, a city in which all the work will be artists' work – work designed to move against (though it will never entirely defeat) what Shelley called 'Fate, Time, Occasion, Chance, and Change'. It will be a social order with no 'corporeal war', an order entirely cleansed of 'the Wastes of moral law'. None of these imaginations are 'inward' imaginations; they are emphatically political, institutional, even economic – as Blake's prose works repeatedly emphasize.

Blake's work is important, in this context, because it consistently foregrounds the material, social and institutional bases of its productive modes. Unlike Shelley and the other Romantics, he took none of art's productive processes and institutions for granted. An imaginative and poetical transformation of the social order is carried out at all levels and in every form of that order. His illuminated poems are especially clear examples of his understanding that if art is to be an agent of change, its agencies will be operating at the earliest stages of conception and through all later productive, distributive and reproductive phases. None of this must be allowed to escape poetry's concrete transformative deliberations.

If Blake's judgements about these matters went far beyond the other artists of his time – and I think they did – the irony is that he became, none the less, the most ineffectual of that period's many angels. No one had less influence on his age than Blake, and it would be many decades after his death before he

[17] From Shelley's 'Defence of Poetry', in Reiman and Powers, eds, *Shelley's Poetry and Prose*, pp. 502–3.

would begin to gather a public arena. And now he is an academic subject, central to the curriculum.

It was not what he had in mind. In *The Marriage of Heaven and Hell* 'the cherub with his flaming sword' – that is to say, the angel of the social apocalypse – '*is* hereby commanded to leave his guard at tree of life' (plate 14; my italics). But the angel of history did not appear to obey that poetic command, which Blake gave in this early poem and which he repeated in all his works throughout his career. (In fact, the command was obeyed as it was issued, only its accomplishment came in forms of truth which Blake had not thought of.) As with Aeschylus in *The Eumenides*, the future of Blake's work would bear along with that work, and for that work, as much history as it had imagined, but far more than it knew.

Are they fortuitous, these discordant artistic futures, and irrelevant to the ways we should understand and use our poetic resources? I do not think so. When we think of poems 'in their historical contexts', our historicist biases – even in their 'New Historicist' modes – take those 'contexts' to be located primarily in the past, or – if we have read our Nietzsche and Foucault with care – in the present and the past. And when we think even more deeply about such matters we also understand that these historical contexts are multiple and conflicting: heteroglossial, as Bakhtin would say. But if it is true that all futures are functions of the past (and the present), then we must expect to find those futures being carried out in the works that seem to be speaking and acting only from the past.

Poems imagine more than they know. The *Oresteia* is a far greater work, in those future contexts of reality it had not discussed and did not desire, than it is when we read it merely in the context of its own grandiose – and mistaken – self-conceptions. Its greatness is intimately bound up with its own imaginative capacities, which solicit the total appearance of the human truth of things – that is to say, their social and historical truth, in all its contradictions and emergencies. And the same is true for Blake's work, which, like the *Oresteia*, looked forward to the advent of a New Jerusalem. But it did not come. The violent would bear it away, and Blake would play his part in the closet dramas of the academy and the struggles in the auction salesrooms.

Blake's distinctly non-radical reception history is an irony very like the one we saw in the future of the *Oresteia*; the irony is no more an aberration for Blake's work, however, than it was for Aeschylus's. There are more things in Blake's heavens and hells than he thought of in his philosophy. Though his mode of artistic production involved a conscious effort to avoid the machineries of mercantile capitalism, it also ensured that his work would be expensive, even in his own way. The provenance histories of the illuminated works show that they have, with few exceptions, been sought after and owned by rich people and art connoisseurs.[18] Thus, although Blake's ideas and goals looked to the material transformation of unjust and exploitive social conditions, the 'vehicular forms' of these projects had, from the outset, small purchase among those who would be most interested in carrying out such social transformations. Unlike Shelley and Byron, for example, Blake was

[18] For information on the provenance histories of Blake's works see Gerald Bentley, Jr, *Blake Books* (Oxford: Oxford University Press, 1977).

unknown to the Chartists. He was delivered into the aesthetic hands of the Pre-Raphaelites through quietist religious agencies: that is to say, through that pious circle of men who called themselves the 'Ancients' and Blake the 'Interpreter' – men like John Linnell, George Cumberland, Frederick Tatham, George Richmond and of course Alexander Gilchrist.[19] Similarly, though we can see that, in Blake's day, the New Jerusalem Church and other dissenting sects drew their strength from the underprivileged, the character of religious non-conformity had changed drastically between 1790 and 1830. The Evangelical Movement, in the first two decades of the nineteenth century, moved closer to the ideological mainstream of English society – so much so, in fact, that it had become an important reforming movement even within the Church of England by 1820.[20] We should not be surprised, therefore, that Blake would ask to have the Anglican service read at his funeral in 1827. It may seem an odd turn of events in the career of this great antinomian figure, but he was first and last a Christian, and his own work remained open – as it still remains open – to those clerical interpretations which survive in the valley of their saying, which make nothing happen beyond what has been established as possible or acceptable.

Once again, however, this is a historical eventuality that lies hidden within Blake's own work. That his ideas and goals were partly mystified in themselves seems quite clear, and not simply from his sexist theory of the emanations,[21] or his decision to write in such a way that the figure of a privileged 'Interpreter' would become so central to that correspondent breeze known as 'Blake Studies'. Even more crucial to the historical meaning of Blake's work was his conviction, which he shared with every major poet of his age, that art is a non-ideological agency. Of course Blake understood very well that imagination and poetry are human acts embedded in their times of conflicting vision and contested human interests. But he also – and contradictorily – believed that there could be – had to be – an originary Prophet of such Losses who would not be subject to those losses. A New Day would dawn with the Dawning of the Imagination, when the unfallen Zoa – Los, the Zoa of Poetic Creation – would assume an empire over the world. This idea – the Romantic Ideology of the Poet as Genius – is one of the last infirmities of those noble Romantic minds.

It was, in addition, a mental infirmity which they themselves recognized – in others. The Romantic 'interpretation' of Milton – vulgarly, that Satan is the hero of *Paradise Lost* – is not something which, in their view, had been laid upon Milton's work anachronistically. Blake's *Milton* argued the case against the great Puritan on the basis of English history, and especially the history of English imperial interests as they developed between Milton's day, on the one hand, and Blake's during the Napoleonic Wars, on the other. Blake's argument

[19] See Gerald Bentley, Jr, *Blake Records* (Oxford: Oxford University Press, 1969). My Blake texts here are quoted from David V. Erdman, ed., *The Poetry and Prose of William Blake* (Berkeley, Calif: University of California Press, 1982).

[20] See Kenneth Scott Latourette, *A History of Christianity in the 19th and 20th Centuries* (Grand Rapids, Mich.: Zondervan, 1969), II, Chs 16–19.

[21] See Anne K. Mellor, 'Blake's Portrayal of Women', *Blake: An Illustrated Quarterly* 16 (1982–3), pp. 148–65.

is that Milton's works contributed largely to the construction of that evil history; indeed, the famous 'paradise within', which Milton preached, is revealed in Blake's revisionary poem as the 'cold bosom' and corrupted heart of 'Albion', who sleeps in righteousness on his 'Rock of Ages'.

> The Nations still
> Follow after the detestable Gods of Priam; in pomp
> Of warlike selfhood, contradicting and blaspheming . . .
> I will go down to the sepulcher to see if morning breaks!
> I will go down to self-annihilation and eternal death,
> Lest the Last Judgement come & find me unannihilate
> And I be siez'd & giv'n into the hands of my own Selfhood.
>
> (14: 14–16, 20–4)

Milton's work constructs an image of the paradisal and the elect through a reciprocal definition of the hellish and the damned. It is an image founded, therefore, quite literally, in sin. Its consequence is an imperial history which, in political terms, reappeared in Blake's day as a dynamic of the Elect (England), the Reprobate (France) and the Redeemable (that which remains, the Third World). In such a scheme that Third World is to be appropriated to the missionary zeal of an Elected design. But to Blake such a design is not merely moral righteousness, it is actual political imperialism. To Blake it is a design founded in England, reinstituted in Milton and thence dispersed across the world in a process of real historical events.

> Lambeth's Vale
> Where Jerusalems foundations began: where they were laid in ruins
> Where they were laid in ruins from every Nation & Oak Groves rooted . . .
> When shall Jerusalem return & overspread all the Nations
> Return: return to Lambeths Vale O building of human souls
> Thence stony Druid Temples overspread the Island white
> And thence from Jerusalems ruins, from her walls of salvation
> And praise: thro the whole Earth were reard from Ireland
> To Mexico & Peru west, & east to China & Japan: till Babel
> The Spectre of Albion frownd over the Nations in glory and war
> All things begin & end in Albions ancient Druid rocky shore.
>
> (4: 14–16, 18–25)

England's spectrous presence is called Babel, in the context of these historical references, because she works to build an imperial city and to sacrifice all other cities to that monomorphic empire. From the ruins of Jerusalem – a plural reality, as we know from the conclusion of Blake's last major prophecy – emerges Babel, the great figure of all the Buildings of Loss. Its more common name is the British Empire.

Blake deployed a poetical scheme for imagining all the buildings of loss as the Buildings of Los: as the city of art, 'great Golgonooza', a place that opened out to the world of eternity. And eternity, Blake's ultimate object in several senses, stood apart from history and time and space because it incorporated, like a Hegelian dialectic, all of human history within itself. But *in truth* the Hegelian dialectic and Blake's 'Eternity' are, like Kant's aesthetic, historical formations; and their historicity is revealed most dramatically when they enter the fullness of time, that is, when Blake's 'Eternity' – or Hegel's dialectic, or

Kant's aesthetic – are viewed in the perspective of a total form of history, which means that they are viewed in the perspective of a more encompassing – a more objective – form of history. That is the perspective of the unknown and the possible, the perspective which alone reveals the multiple histories that lie hidden, and as often as not repressed, within the works where they have been imagined, but where they are not recognized. These futures, which may be either terrible or wonderful, are the instruments through which all of history, past, present and future alike, is opened to change. Such an opening is what Blake supplied for Milton and his other cultural forebears. But while in this respect Blake, like Jesus, saved those others, of himself we have to think – it is one of the few (terrible) insights left to an imperialist imagination – that 'himself he could not save'. He could not, quite simply, because he had held back – because he had 'saved' – a part of his work that was to be placed for ever beyond the possibility of either fall or redemption.

In fact, there is nothing that can be set apart in that way; and the idea that Eternity exists outside of its various human imaginations (of which Blake's is only one) is an immortalist illusion. In Romantic art it reappears as the idea of the aesthetic, and while Blake fought against that idea, his own work ultimately submitted to its domination. Its illusory character, so far as poetic work is concerned, would not be fully and consciously re-exposed until the twentieth century, in the unfolding of Ezra Pound's great poetical project the *Cantos*. (I say *(re-)exposed* because the transcendentalizing of poetry and imaginative agencies is by no means characteristic of the cultural periods of the West – even the Christian West – before the coming of Romanticism.)

Had Byron begun writing *Don Juan* when he began *Childe Harold's Pilgrimage* in 1809, and had he gone on with it all his life and lived until (let us say) 1870 or so, he might have produced something comparable to the *Cantos*. I sketch this literary fantasy because it calls attention to certain important similarities, and even more important differences, between *Don Juan* and Pound's epic. In the first place, both works are produced in a seriatim process. *Don Juan* is published in six separate parts over a five-year period, and the separate volumes reflect that passage of time and its circumstantialities. The work replicates, in this respect, the serial publication of *Childe Harold's Pilgrimage*, which was issued in three separate volumes between 1812 and 1818, and which was written over a ten-year period. Byron's work refuses to proceed upon 'system'; the horizon of *Don Juan's* expectations is close and short, and the poem cultivates, as we know, a series of immediacies. 'Note or text, / I never knew the word which will come next' *(Don Juan*, IX, st. 41). With this deliberate cultivation of inconsequence (the word should be taken in several senses) Byron defies the highest poetical canons of his age, most especially those of Kant, Coleridge and Hegel. As he got further along with *Don Juan* he began to imagine a conclusion – the death of Juan on the guillotine in the Reign of Terror – and he seems to have begun to prepare for that event.[22] But in the work that we have, the seriatim process persists to the end.

---

[22] For Byron's plans to have Juan executed in the Reign of Terror see Jerome J. McGann, ed., *Byron: The Poetical Works* (Oxford: Oxford University Press, 1986), V, p. xxiii.

Unlike Byron, Pound began the *Cantos* with definite plans and preconceptions, nor did he put into question the Romantic criterion of Total Form. On the contrary, in setting out to write a *Commedia* appropriate to his epoch, Pound's plan was fairly dominated by the idea of Total Form. The idea captured him because, even more than the writers and poets of 1780–1830, Pound confronted an epoch – particularly from 1914, the year before he began the *Cantos* – that surpassed even Byron's age in its cultural fragmentation and social barbarity. 'These fragments you have shelved (shored)' (VIII, 1): that theme directs the *Cantos* from the first. But Pound's initial articulation works some telling puns on the words 'shelved' and 'shored': in addition to their obvious primary meanings, both words suggest 'fragments' that have come or been washed ashore, like Odysseus at Phaiakia or his other stopping places.

Pound's method for negotiating that treacherous world was what he called the periplum, or what he understood as point-by-point navigation. That method of proceeding is the equivalent of Byron's seriatim manoeuvres, only in Pound's case it is initiated in concert with a quest for Total Form (social as well as aesthetic, it should be understood). As it turned out, the production history of the *Cantos* became a kind of periplum in time. Ten separate 'books' of the work are printed from 1925 to 1969, and individual Cantos or parts of Cantos – some later revised or rejected altogether – were published in various magazines and journals. The first pieces of the poem appear in print in 1915, and to this day – Pound died in 1972 – further unpublished fragments continue to appear.[23]

It has been wittily (and justly) said that 'The eleven Pisan Cantos were written at a time [1945] when the poem including history found itself included in history.'[24] In truth, however, the *Cantos* were *always* 'included in history', as the production history of the poem emphasizes. The Pisan Cantos are special only because they dramatize that inclusion beyond any possibility of mistake or unawareness. For more than fifty years – 1915 to 1969 – the *Cantos* moved through the twentieth century, appearing at intervals to reflect the European/American mind back to itself. The effort was to bring (or restore) coherence to that mind. In the end – in the great tragic texts of *Drafts and Fragments* of 1969, a malebolge year of this century's Western and imperialist wars – Pound echoed Byron's 'Epistle to Augusta':[25]

> Tho' my errors and wrecks lie about me.
> And I am not a demigod,
> I cannot make it cohere.

(CXVI)

'I lost my center / fighting the world,' he remarks in the 'Notes for CXVII et seq.'; for in this quest after a 'paradiso/terrestre', Pound discovers that what

---

[23] For the bibliographical history of the *Cantos* see Donald Gallup, *Ezra Pound: A Bibliography* (Charlottesville, Va.: University Press of Virginia, 1983). A good discussion of the bibliography can be found in Alan Durant, *Ezra Pound: Identity in Crisis* (Brighton: Harvester Press, 1981), Ch. 3.

[24] George Kearns, *Guide to Ezra Pound's Selected Cantos* (New Brunswick, NJ: Rutgers University Press, 1980), p. 149.

[25] For the Byron text Pound is recalling see McGann, ed., *Byron: The Poetical Works*, IV, pp. 33–5 ('Stanzas to [Augusta]').

initially appeared as fragmentation and contradiction was precisely that: 'The dreams clash / and are shattered.'

The greatness of the *Cantos* is in large part a function of its chronology, and its involvement in the real history that is schematized in that chronology. The poem begins with the goal of Total Form as it had been framed and imperially imagined in the West between 1780 and 1915. The poem then tests that imagination as it continues to reimagine itself, more brutally than it ever did in the nineteenth century, from the First World War to Vietnam. The great *artistic* benefit to a work that has been produced over such a long period is that time and circumstances – if the poem is honest with itself – will play havoc with its most cherished illusions. In the *Cantos* we finally see, fully displayed, the brutal truth of the Western dialectic as Benjamin had framed it: 'There is no document of civilization which is not at the same time a document of barbarism.'

Of course, when the academy reads such a poem it has ways of avoiding its imaginations. One way is to celebrate the *Cantos* for its 'beauties', for its local achievements and its grand aspirations. These things are accepted. Reciprocally, the poem will have its horrors denounced, deplored or set aside: its antisemitism and racism, for example, or its unrepentant adherence to fascist programmes. If one takes this way with the poem, all these matters are accepted at face value, as if the beauties were evidently beauties and the horrors, horrors, as if they were all understandable to persons of sympathy and taste.

Another way is more critical. It will argue that somehow the beauties and the horrors are functions of each other, that the former will only have been gained – in so far as they *are* gained – through a concert with the latter. In this view the poem is internally self-contradicted, and is to be read as a moral exemplum or cautionary tale.[26]

But in truth neither this poem, nor any other poem or cultural product, ought to be read from such a safe – such an imperial distance. Not in the West, at any rate. The distanced reader is what Baudelaire knew to be a hypocritical reader. Pound's exposure of European and American imperialism loses none of its *objective* truth because it comes from a source which is in so many ways repellent and blind. To Pound it was a complex centred in England, a complex from which Germany and Italy sought to free themselves. But increasingly we can see that that complex is a parodic god whose centre is everywhere and whose circumference is nowhere. The European wars of this century were mugs' games – like Russia, France and England struggling with the Ottoman Empire at the end of the eighteenth century for control of Greece and the east Mediterranean trade routes. If Pound excepted Mussolini's Italy from the twentieth century's Western ways – if he excepted himself, and if he sought to represent his exceptional condition in the *Cantos* – we may think or say that he failed. But the more important thought is that the *Cantos* finally imagined the failure they did not know – imagined it throughout, as a total form, though that

---

[26] The second is the way Michael Bernstein has proceeded in his excellent *The Tale of the Tribe: Ezra Pound and the Modern Verse Epic* (Princeton, NJ: Princeton University Press, 1980). His book is at the same time a conscious critique of all readings of the *Cantos* that operate as if the poem were transparent to itself.

imaginative form only began to raise the failure into a form of consciousness in the last twenty-five years of the work's production.

During those years – 1945 to 1969 – the academy began its quest to 'understand' the *Cantos*, and to this day it has produced those two ways of reading the poem I have mentioned. Yet they will not do. The poem does not permit a distanced reading, and in this respect it carries out a definitive break with the Romantic ideology of immanent form (the Kantian 'aesthetic'). Immanent, 'readerly' criticism, the last serious bastion of this Kantian norm, reestablished aesthetic space in the reader after Modernism in art began the labour to disestablish it from the work.

The *Cantos* is important, therefore, because – as a poem evidently included in history – it has explained once again, more clearly than at any time since the eighteenth century, that all poems and cultural products are included in history – *including* the producers and the reproducers of such works, the poets and their readers and interpreters. But the *Cantos* is even more significant for its revelation of the meaning of history. To the historicist imagination, history is the past, or perhaps the past as seen in and through the present; and the historical task is to attempt a reconstruction of the past, including, perhaps, the present of that past. But the *Cantos* reminds us that history includes the future, and that the historical task involves as well the construction of what shall be possible. Delivered through the world over such a long and momentous period of time, the *Cantos* managed to gather into itself, and then foreground, parts of its own futurity. History in this poem thereby revealed itself as the fullness of time – a fullness whose shape(s) and direction(s) will never be completely known, though they will always be anticipated.

Poetical work, Aristotle said, is more philosophical than history. If this is so then it is also more 'historical' than history, as Nietzsche argued, because the 'history' that poems touch and re-present encompasses a far greater scale of possible, and therefore real, human times and events than the most careful and scholarly historical text. Indeed, the greatest of such texts – Herodotus, the Bible, Thucydides – have set themselves apart by actively embracing different types of imaginative procedures. Poetical works are historically overdetermined – littered with incommensurate materials that grow only more multiple when they are delivered over to further readings and uses. What they do not know – which is a great deal, the abyss of their ignorance – they will have imagined. The *Oresteia* and the *Cantos* are unusual only because they have so graphically displayed this faultline – ultimately catastrophic – of their non-consciousness; in this respect they epitomize the resources of all poetical discourse, whose knowledge is heterological.

When we read we construct our histories, including our futures. In our day, this peculiar Western moment, poetry's special contribution to that process – poetry's special form of 'reading' – comes as a set of complicating and undermining procedures. Calling into question all that is privileged, understood and given, including itself, this poetry operates under the signs of Difference and, most especially, of Change. And this poetry has thereby set us our models for reading the works that descend to us from 'tradition'. What is astonishing here is the way our literary inheritance seems to have anticipated these contemporary uses – seems, as it were, to have intended them.

Bibliography

The bibliography is divided into the following sections:

I   Origins and Influences
II   On History and Historicism
III   On Culture and Cultural Studies
IV   New Historicism and Cultural Materialism: Aims and Issues
V   Studies of Medieval Literature and Culture
VI   Studies of Renaissance Literature and Culture
VII   Studies of Eighteenth-Century Literature and Culture
VIII Studies of the Literature and Culture of the Romantic Period
IX   Studies of Victorian Literature and Culture
X   Studies of Twentieth-Century Literature and Culture
XI   Studies of American Literature and Culture
XII   Publishers' Series
XIII Journals

I Origins and Influences

Althusser, Louis 1969: *For Marx*, tr. Ben Brewster. London: Penguin Books.
—— 1971: *Lenin and Philosophy and Other Essays*, tr. Ben Brewster. London: New Left Books.
—— 1972: *Politics and History*, tr. Ben Brewster. London: New Left Books.
—— 1984: *Essays on Ideology*. London: Verso.
—— 1994: *Althusser: A Critical Reader*, ed. Gregory Elliott. Oxford: Blackwell.
Auerbach, Erich 1953: *Mimesis: The Representation of Reality in Western Literature*, tr. Willard R. Trask. Princeton, NJ: Princeton University Press.
Bakhtin, Mikhail 1968: *Rabelais and his World*, tr. Hélène Iswolsky. Cambridge, Mass., and London: MIT Press.
—— 1973: *Marxism and the Philosophy of Language*, tr. L. Matejka and I.R. Titunik. New York: Seminar Press.
—— 1981: *The Dialogic Imagination: Four Essays*, ed. Michael Holquist, tr. Caryl Emerson and Michael Holquist. Austin, Texas: University of Texas Press.
—— 1994: *The Bakhtin Reader: Selected Writings of Bakhtin, Medvedev and Voloshinov*, ed. Pam Morris. London: Edward Arnold.
—— and P.N. Medvedev 1978: *The Formal Method in Literary Scholarship: A Critical Introduction to Sociological Poetics*, tr. Albert J. Wehrle. Baltimore, Md., and London: Johns Hopkins University Press.
Benjamin, Walter 1968: *Illuminations*, ed. Hannah Arendt, tr. Harry Zohn. New York: Harcourt, Brace & World.

—— 1973: *Charles Baudelaire: A Lyric Poet in the Era of High Capitalism*, tr. Harry Zohn. London: New Left Books.

—— 1978: *Reflections: Essays, Aphorisms, Autobiographical Writings*, tr. Edmund Jephcott, ed. Peter Demetz. New York: Harcourt Brace Jovanovich.

—— 1979: *One-Way Street and Other Writings*, tr. Edmund Jephcott and Kingsley Shorter. London: New Left Books.

Derrida, Jacques 1976: *Of Grammatology*, tr. Gayatri Chakravorty Spivak. Baltimore, Md.: Johns Hopkins University Press.

—— 1978: *Writing and Difference*, tr. Alan Bass. Chicago: University of Chicago Press.

—— 1981: *Dissemination*, tr. Barbara Johnson. Chicago: University of Chicago Press.

—— 1982a: *Margins of Philosophy*, tr. Alan Bass. Chicago: University of Chicago Press.

—— 1982b: *Positions*, tr. Alan Bass. Chicago: University of Chicago Press.

—— 1991: *A Derrida Reader: Between the Blinds*, ed. Peggy Kamuf. New York: Columbia University Press.

—— 1992: *Acts of Literature*, ed. Derek Attridge. New York and London: Routledge.

Elias, Norbert 1978: *The Civilising Process: Vol. 1: The History of Manners*, tr. Edmund Jephcott. Oxford: Blackwell.

—— 1982: *The Civilising Process: Vol. 2: Power and Civility*. New York: Pantheon Books.

Foucault, Michel 1970: *The Order of Things: An Archaeology of the Human Sciences*, tr. Alan Sheridan. London: Tavistock.

—— 1972: *The Archaeology of Knowledge*, tr. Alan Sheridan. London: Tavistock.

—— 1977a: *Discipline and Punish: The Birth of the Prison*, tr. Alan Sheridan. London: Allen Lane.

—— 1977b: *Language, Counter-Memory, Practice: Selected Essays and Interviews*, ed. Donald F. Bouchard, tr. Donald F. Bouchard and Sherry Simon. Oxford: Blackwell.

—— 1978: *The History of Sexuality, Volume 1: An Introduction*, tr. Robert Hurley. New York: Pantheon.

—— 1980: *Power/Knowledge: Selected Interviews and Other Writings, 1972–1977*, ed. and tr. Colin Gordon. Brighton: Harvester Press.

—— 1984: *The Foucault Reader*, ed. Paul Rabinow. New York: Pantheon.

Geertz, Clifford 1973: *The Interpretation of Cultures: Selected Essays*. New York: Basic Books.

—— 1976: *The Religion of Java*. Chicago: University of Chicago Press.

—— 1980: *Negara: The Theatre State in Nineteenth-Century Bali*. Princeton, NJ: Princeton University Press.

—— 1983: *Local Knowledge: Further Essays in Interpretive Anthropology*. New York: Basic Books.

—— 1988: *Works and Lives: The Anthropologist as Author*. Stanford, Calif.: Stanford University Press.

Gramsci, Antonio 1971: *Selections from the Prison Notebooks*, ed. and tr. Quintin Hoare and Geoffrey Nowell Smith. London: Lawrence & Wishart.

Marcuse, Herbert 1964: *One-Dimensional Man: Studies in the Ideology of Advanced Industrial Society*. Boston, Mass.: Beacon Press.

—— 1968: 'The Affirmative Character of Culture', in his *Negations: Essays in Critical Theory*, tr. Jeremy J. Shapiro. London: Allen Lane.

Said, Edward 1978: *Orientalism*. New York: Pantheon Books.

Thompson, E.P. 1968: *The Making of the English Working Class*, rev. edn. Harmondsworth: Penguin Books.

—— 1978: *The Poverty of Theory and Other Essays*. London: Merlin Press.

Williams, Raymond 1958: *Culture and Society, 1780–1950*. London: Chatto & Windus.
—— 1973: *The Country and the City*. London: Chatto & Windus.
—— 1977: *Marxism and Literature*. Oxford: Oxford University Press.
—— 1979: *Politics and Letters: Interviews with New Left Review*. London: New Left Books.
—— 1980: *Problems in Materialism and Culture*. London: Verso.
—— 1981: *Culture*. Glasgow: Fontana.

II On History and Historicism

Abelove, Henry, *et al.* (eds) 1983: *Visions of History*. New York: Pantheon Books.
Ankersmit, Frank and Hans Kellner (eds) 1995: *The New Philosophy of History*. Chicago: University of Chicago Press.
Attridge, Derek, Geoff Bennington and Robert Young (eds) 1987: *Post-structuralism and the Question of History*. Cambridge: Cambridge University Press.
Bambach, Charles R. 1995: *Heidegger, Dilthey, and the Crisis of Historicism*. Ithaca, NY: Cornell University Press.
Braudel, Fernand 1980: *On History*, tr. Sarah Matthews. Chicago: University of Chicago Press.
CCCS (Centre for Contemporary Cultural Studes) 1980: *Making Histories: Studies in History-Writing and Politics*. London: Hutchinson.
Chakrabarty, Dipesh 1992a: 'The Death of History? Historical Consciousness and the Culture of Late Capitalism', *Public Culture*, 4, pp. 47–65.
—— 1992b: 'Postcoloniality and the Artifice of History: Who Speaks for "Indian" Pasts?', *Representations*, 37, pp. 1–26.
Copjec, Joan 1994: *Read My Desire: Lacan Against the Historicists*. Cambridge, Mass.: MIT Press.
Davis, Natalie Zemon 1988: *Fiction in the Archives*. Berkeley, Calif: University of California Press.
de Certeau, Michel 1988: *The Writing of History*, tr. Tom Conley. New York: Columbia University Press.
Fukuyama, Francis 1992: *The End of History and the Last Man*. New York: Free Press.
Gearhart, Suzanne 1987: 'History as Criticism: The Dialogue of History and Literature', *Diacritics*, 17, pp. 56–65.
Hamilton, Paul 1995: *Historicism*. London: Routledge.
Harlan, David 1989: 'Intellectual History and the Return of Literature', *American Historical Review*, 94, pp. 581–609.
Hartog, François 1988: *The Mirror of Herodotus: The Representation of the Other in the Writing of History*, tr. Janet Lloyd. The New Historicism: Studies in Cultural Poetics 5. Berkeley, Calif.: University of California Press.
Himmelfarb, Gertrude 1987: *The New History and the Old: Critical Essays and Reappraisals*. Cambridge, Mass.: Harvard University Press.
Horwitz, Howard 1988: ' "I Can't Remember": Skepticism, Synthetic Histories, Critical Action', *South Atlantic Quarterly*, 87, pp. 787–820.
Howard, Jean 1991: 'Feminism and the Question of History: Resituating the Debate', *Women's Studies: An Interdisciplinary Journal*, 19, pp. 149–57.
Jameson, Fredric 1979: 'Marxism and Historicism', *New Literary History*, 11, pp. 41–72.
LaCapra, Dominick 1983: *Rethinking Intellectual History*. Ithaca, NY: Cornell University Press.

—— 1986: *History and Criticism*. Ithaca, NY: Cornell University Press.
—— 1989a: 'On the Line: Between History and Criticism', *Profession*, 89, pp. 4–9.
—— 1989b: *Soundings in Critical Theory*. Ithaca, NY: Cornell University Press.
Lowenthal, David 1985: *The Past is a Foreign Country*. Cambridge and New York: Cambridge University Press.
—— 1994: *The Politics of the Past*. London and New York: Routledge.
Morris, Wesley 1972: *Toward a New Historicism*. Princeton, NJ: Princeton University Press.
New Literary History 1990: special issue on 'History and . . .', 21:2.
Orr, Linda 1986: 'The Revenge of Literature: A History of History', *New Literary History*, 18, pp. 1–22.
Pearce, Roy Harvey 1969: *Historicism Once More: Problems and Occasions for the American Scholar*. Princeton, NJ: Princeton University Press.
Sahlins, Marshall 1985: *Islands of History*. Chicago: University of Chicago Press.
Scott, Joan W. 1988: *Gender and the Politics of History*. New York: Columbia University Press.
Trouillot, Michel-Rolph 1995: *Silencing the Past: Power and The Production of History*. Boston, Mass.: Beacon Press.
Veyne, Paul 1986: *Writing History*. Middletown, Conn.: Wesleyan University Press.
White, Hayden 1973: *Metahistory*. Baltimore, Md.: Johns Hopkins University Press.
—— 1987: *The Content of the Form: Narrative Discourse and Historical Representation*. Baltimore, Md.: Johns Hopkins University Press.
—— 1989: '"Figuring the Nature of the Times Deceased": Literary Theory and Historical Writing', in Ralph Cohen (ed.), *The Future of Literary Theory*, London and New York: Routledge, pp. 19–43.

III On Culture and Cultural Studies

Batsleer, Janet, Tony Davies, Rebecca O'Rourke and Chris Weedon 1985: *Rewriting English: Cultural Politics of Gender and Class*. London: Methuen.
Bennett, Tony, *et al.* (eds) 1981: *Culture, Ideology and Social Process*. London: Batsford and Open University Press.
Bhabha, Homi 1994: *The Location of Culture*. London and New York: Routledge.
Brantlinger, Patrick 1990: *Crusoe's Footprints: Cultural Studies in Britain and America*. New York and London: Routledge.
Brenkman, John 1987: *Culture and Domination*. Ithaca, NY: Cornell University Press.
Chartier, Roger 1988: *Cultural History*. Ithaca, NY: Cornell University Press.
Clifford, James 1988: *The Predicament of Culture: Twentieth-Century Ethnography, Literature, and Art*. Cambridge, Mass.: Harvard University Press.
—— and George E. Marcus (eds) 1986: *Writing Culture: The Poetics and Politics of Ethnography*. Berkeley and Los Angeles: University of California Press.
Collins, Jim 1989: *Uncommon Cultures: Popular Culture and Post-modernism*. New York: Routledge.
Easthope, Antony 1991: *Literary Into Cultural Studies*. London and New York: Routledge.
Giroux, Henry A. (ed.) 1991: *Postmodernism, Feminism, and Cultural Politics: Redrawing Educational Boundaries*. Albany, NY: State University of New York Press.
——, David Shumway, Paul Smith and James Sosnoski 1985: 'The Need for Cultural Studies: Resisting Intellectuals and Oppositional Public Spheres', *Dalhousie Review*, 64, pp. 472–86.
Graff, Gerald and Bruce Robbins 1992: 'Cultural Criticism', in Stephen Greenblatt and Giles Gunn (eds), *Redrawing the Boundaries: The Transformation of English and*

American Studies, New York: Modern Language Association of America, pp. 419–36.

Grossberg, Lawrence, Cary Nelson and Paula Treichler (eds) 1991: *Cultural Studies*. New York: Routledge.

Gunn, Giles 1987: *The Culture of Criticism and the Criticism of Culture*. Oxford and New York: Oxford University Press.

Hall, Stuart 1990: 'The Emergence of Cultural studies and the Crisis of the Humanities', *October*, 53, pp. 11–23.

——, Dorothy Hobson, Andrew Lowe and Paul Willis (eds) 1980: *Culture, Media, Language: Working Papers in Cultural Studies,* 197–79. London: Unwin.

Hunt, Lynn (ed.) 1989: *The New Cultural History*. Studies on the History of Society and Culture. Berkeley, Calif., and London: University of California Press.

Jameson, Fredric 1991: *Postmodernism; or, The Cultural Logic of Late Capitalism*. Durham, NC: Duke University Press.

Johnson, Richard 1987: 'What Is Cultural Studies Anyway?', *Social Text*, 6:1, pp. 38–80.

Lears, T.J. Jackson 1985: 'The Concept of Cultural Hegemony: Problems and Possibilities', *The American Historical Review*, 90:3, pp. 567–93.

—— 1988: 'Power, Culture, and Memory', *The Journal of American History*, 75:1, pp. 137–40.

McCabe, Colin (ed.) 1986: *High Theory/Low Culture*. Manchester: Manchester University Press.

Nelson, Cary and Lawrence Grossberg (eds) 1988: *Marxism and the Interpretation of Culture*. Urbana, Ill.: University of Illinois Press.

News from Nowhere: Journal of Cultural Materialism 1990: No. 8: 'Futures for Critical and Cultural Theory'.

Punter, David (ed.) 1986: *Introduction to Contemporary Cultural Studies*. London: Longman.

Reed, Adolph, Jr. (ed.): *Race, Politics, and Culture*. New York: Greenwood.

Ross, Andrew 1989: *No Respect: Intellectuals and Popular Culture*. London and New York: Routledge.

Sahlins, Marshall 1975: *Culture and Practical Reason*. Chicago: University of Chicago Press.

Wagner, Roy 1981: *The Invention of Culture*, rev. edn. Chicago: University of Chicago Press.

Watkins, Evan 1985: 'Cultural Criticism and Literary Intellectuals', *Works and Days*, 3:1, pp. 11–31.

IV New Historicism and Cultural Materialism: Aims and Issues

Armstrong, Nancy, 'Introduction: Literature as Women's History', *Genre*, 19, pp. 347–69.

Barrell, John 1988: 'Introduction', in his *Poetry, Language and Politics*. Cultural Politics. Manchester: Manchester University Press.

Belsey, Catherine 1983: 'Literature, History, Politics', *Literature and History*, 9, pp. 17–27.

—— 1989: 'Towards Cultural History – in Theory and Practice', *Textual Practice*, 3:2, pp. 159–72.

—— 1991: 'Afterword: A Future for Materialist Feminist Criticism?', in Valerie Wayne, (ed.), *The Matter of Difference: Materialist Feminist Criticism of Shakespeare*, Hemel Hempstead: Harvester Wheatsheaf, pp. 257–70.

Braden, Gordon 1993: 'Greenblatt's Trajectory', *Raritan*, 13:1, pp. 139–50.

Dimock, Wai-chee 1991: 'Feminism, New Historicism, and the Reader', *American*

Literature: A Journal of Literary History, Criticism and Bibliography, 63, pp. 601–22.

Dollimore, Jonathan and Alan Sinfield 1990: 'Culture and Textuality: Debating Cultural Materialism', *Textual Practice*, 4, pp. 91–100.

—— (eds) 1994: *Political Shakespeare: Essays in Cultural Materialism*, 2nd edn: 'Foreword to the First Edition: Cultural Materialism'. Manchester: Manchester University Press.

During, Simon 1991: 'New Historicism', *Text and Performance Quarterly*, 11, pp. 171–89.

Edmundson, Mark 1995: *Literature Against Philosophy, Plato to Derrida: A Defence of Poetry*, Ch. 4: 'Foucault Inc'. Cambridge: Cambridge University Press.

Grady, Hugh 1993: 'Containment, Subversion – and Postmodernism', *Textual Practice*, 7, pp. 31–49.

Greenblatt, Stephen 1987: 'Capitalist Culture and the Circulatory System', in Murray Krieger (ed.), *The Aims of Representation*. New York: Columbia University Press.

—— 1990a: *Learning to Curse: Essays in Early Modern Culture*, Ch. 8: 'Towards a Poetics of Culture'. New York and London: Routledge.

—— 1990b: 'Culture', in Frank Lentricchia and Thomas McLaughlin (eds), *Critical Terms for Literary Study*, Chicago and London: University of Chicago Press, pp. 225–32.

—— 1990c: 'Resonance and Wonder', in Peter Collier and Helga Geyer-Ryan (eds), *Literary Theory Today*, Cambridge: Polity Press, pp. 74–90.

—— 1994: ' "Intensifying the Surprise as well as the School": Stephen Greenblatt interviewed by Noel King', *Textual Practice*, 8:1, pp. 114–27.

Gunn, Giles 1987: 'The Kingdoms of Theory and the New Historicism in America', *Yale Review*, 76, pp. 207–36.

Harpham, Geoffrey Galt 1991: 'Foucault and the New Historicism', *American Literary History*, 3, pp. 360–75.

Hawthorn, Jeremy 1996: *Cunning Passages: New Historicism, Cultural Materialism and Marxism in the Contemporary Literary Debate*. London: Edward Arnold.

Jehlen, Myra 1990: 'The Story of History Told by the New Historicism', in Gunter H. Lentz, Hartmut Keil and Sabine Brock-Sallah (eds), *Reconstructing American Literary and Historical Studies*. Frankfurt: Campus Verlag.

Kerrigan, William 1989: 'Individualism, Historicism, and New Styles of Overreaching', *Philosophy and Literature*, 13:1, pp. 115–26.

Leinwand, Theodore B. 1990: 'Negotiation and New Historicism', *Publications of the Modern Language Association of America*, 105, pp. 477–90.

Lentricchia, Frank 1988: *Ariel and the Police: Michel Foucault, William James, Wallace Stevens*, Ch. 1: 'Michel Foucault's Fantasy for Humanists'. Madison, Wisc.: University of Wisconsin Press.

Lindenberger, Herbert 1984: 'Toward a New History in Literary Studies', *Profession*, 22, pp. 16–23.

—— 1990: *The History in Literature: On Value, Genre, Institutions*. New York: Columbia University Press.

Litvak, Joseph 1988: 'Back to the Future: A Review Article on the New Historicism, Deconstruction, and Nineteenth-Century Fiction', *Texas Studies in Literature and Language*, 30, pp. 120–49.

Liu, Alan 1989: 'The Power of Formalism: The New Historicism', *English Literary History*, 56, pp. 721–71.

—— 1990: 'Local Transcendence: Cultural Criticism, Postmodernism, and the Romanticism of Detail', *Representations*, 32, pp. 75–113.

McGann, Jerome J. (ed.) 1985a: *Historical Studies and Literary Criticism*. Madison, Wisc.: University of Wisconsin Press.

—— 1985b: *The Beauty of Inflections: Literary Investigations in Historical Method and Theory*. Oxford: Clarendon Press.

—— 1988: *Social Values and Poetic Acts: The Historical Judgement of Literary Work*. Cambridge, Mass.: Harvard University Press.

—— 1989: *Towards a Literature of Knowledge*. Oxford: Clarendon Press.

—— 1991: *The Textual Condition*. Princeton Studies in Culture/Power/History. Princeton, NJ: Princeton University Press.

Miller, J. Hillis 1987: 'Presidental Address 1986: The Triumph of Theory, the Resistance to Reading, and the Question of the Material Base', *PMLA*, 102, pp. 281–91.

Montrose, Louis 1992: 'New Historicisms', in Stephen Greenblatt and Giles Gunn (eds), *Redrawing the Boundaries: The Transformation of English and American Studies*, New York: Modern Language Association of America, pp. 392–418.

New Literary History 1990; special issue on 'New Historicisms, New Histories, and Others', 21:3.

Newton, Judith Lowder, 'History as Usual?: Feminism and the "New Historicism"', *Cultural Critique*, 9, pp. 87–121.

Newton, K.M. 1990: *Interpreting the Text*, Ch. 6: 'Marxist Criticism, Cultural Materialism, the New Historicism'. Hemel Hempstead: Harvester Wheatsheaf.

Nicholls, Peter 1989: 'State of the Art: Old Problems and the New Historicism', *Journal of American Studies*, 23, pp. 423–34.

Patterson, Lee 1990: 'Literary History', in Frank Lentricchia and Thomas McLaughlin (eds), *Critical Terms for Literary Study*, Chicago and London: University of Chicago Press, pp. 250–62.

Pease, Donald 1991: 'Toward a Sociology of Literary Knowledge: Greenblatt, Colonialism, and the New Historicism', in Jonathan Arac and Barbara Johnson (eds), *Consequences of Theory: Selected Papers from the English Institute, 1987–88*. Baltimore, Md.: Johns Hopkins University Press.

Pigman, G.W. 1989: 'Self, Subversion, and the New Historicism', *Huntington Library Quarterly: A Journal for the History and Interpretation of English and American Civilization*, 52, pp. 501–8.

Porter, Carolyn 1988: 'Are We Being Historical Yet?', *South Atlantic Quarterly*, 87, pp. 743–86.

—— 1990: 'History and Literature: "After the New Historicism"', *New Literary History*, 21, pp. 253–72.

Prendergast, Christopher (ed.) 1995: *Cultural Materialism: On Raymond Williams*. Cultural Politics 9. Minneapolis, Minn.: University of Minnesota Press.

Roberts, Hugh 1990: 'Usage and Abusage: The New Historicism and History', *Eidos*, 9, pp. 175–93.

Rosenberg, Brian 1989: 'Historicizing the New Historicism: Understanding the Past in Criticism and Fiction', *Modern Language Quarterly*, 50, pp. 375–92.

Ross, Marlon B. 1990: 'Contingent Predilections: The Newest Historicisms and the Question of Method', *The Centennial Review*, 34, pp. 485–538.

Simpson, David 1988: 'Literary Criticism and the Return to "History"', *Critical Inquiry*, 14, pp. 721–47.

—— (ed.) 1991: *Subject to History: Ideology, Class, Gender*. Ithaca, NY, and London: Cornell University Press.

Sinfield, Alan 1994: *Cultural Politics – Queer Reading*. London: Routledge.

Thomas, Brook 1991: *The New Historicism and Other Old-Fashioned Topics*. Princeton, NJ: Princeton University Press.

Veeser, H. Aram (ed.) 1989: *The New Historicism*. London: Routledge.

—— 1994: *The New Historicism Reader*. London: Routledge.

Waller, Marguerite 1987: 'Academic Tootsie: The Denial of Difference and the Difference It Makes', *Diacritics*, 17, pp. 2–20.

Wayne, Don E. 1990: 'New Historicism', in Martin Coyle, Peter Garside, Malcolm Kelsall and John Peck (eds), *Encyclopedia of Literature and Criticism*, London: Routledge, pp. 791–805.

Wilson, Richard 1992: 'Introduction: Historicising New Historicism', in Richard Wilson and Richard Dutton (eds), *New Historicism and Renaissance Drama*, London: Longman, pp. 1–18.
Wilson, Scott 1995: *Cultural Materialism: Theory and Practice*. Oxford: Blackwell.

V   Studies of Medieval Literature and Culture

Aers, David 1980: *Chaucer, Langland and the Creative Imagination*. London, Boston and Henley: Routledge & Kegan Paul.
—— (ed.) 1986: *Medieval Literature: Criticism, Ideology and History*. Brighton: Harvester Press.
—— 1988a: *Community, Gender, and Individual Identity: English Writing, 1360–1430*. London and New York: Routledge.
—— 1988b: 'Rewriting the Middle Ages: Some Suggestions', *Journal of Medieval and Renaissance Studies*, 18, pp. 221–40.
—— (ed.) 1992: *Culture and History, 1350–1600: Essays on English Communities, Identities and Writing*. Hemel Hempstead: Harvester Wheatsheaf.
—— 1993: 'The Self Mourning: Reflections on *Pearl*', *Speculum*, 68:1, pp. 54–73.
—— and Lynn Staley 1996: *The Powers of the Holy: Religion, Politics, and Gender in Late Medieval English Culture*. University Park, Pa.: Pennsylvania State University Press.
Beckwith, Sarah 1993: *Christ's Body: Identity, Culture and Society in Late Medieval Writings*. London: Routledge.
Brownlee, Marina S., Kevin Brownlee and Stephen G. Nichols (eds) 1991: *The New Medievalism*. Parallax: Revisions of Culture and Society. Baltimore, Md., and London: Johns Hopkins University Press.
Bynum, Caroline Walker 1987: *Holy Feast and Holy Fast: The Religious Significance of Food to Medieval Women*. The New Historicism: Studies in Cultural Poetics 1. Berkeley, Calif.: University of California Press.
Delany, Sheila 1990: *Medieval Literary Politics: Shapes of Ideology*. Cultural Politics. Manchester and New York: Manchester University Press.
—— 1994: *The Naked Text: Chaucer's Legend of Good Women*. Berkeley, Los Angeles and London: University of California Press.
Ganim, John M. 1990: *Chaucerian Theatricality*. Princeton, NJ: Princeton University Press.
Gravdal, Kathryn 1991: *Ravishing Maidens: Writing Rape in Medieval French Literature and Law*. New Cultural Studies. Philadelphia, Pa.: University of Pennsylvania Press.
Hahn, Thomas (ed.) 1990: *Reconceiving Chaucer: Literary Theory and Historical Interpretation*. Special issue of *Exemplaria*, 2.
Hanawalt, Barbara (ed.) 1992: *Literature in Historical Context: Chaucer's England*. Minneapolis, Minn.: University of Minnesota Press.
Justice, Steven 1994: *Writing and Rebellion: England in 1381*. The New Historicism: Studies in Cultural Poetics 27. Berkeley, Calif., and London: University of California Press.
Knapp, Peggy 1990: *Chaucer and the Social Contest*. New York and London: Routledge.
Lochrie, Karma 1991: *Margery Kempe and Translations of the Flesh*. New Cultural Studies. Philadelphia, Pa.: University of Pennsylvania Press.
Nichols, Stephen (ed.) 1990: *The New Philology*. Special issue of *Speculum*, 65:1.
Patterson, Lee 1987: *Negotiating the Past: The Historical Understanding of Medieval Literature*. Madison, Wisc.: University of Wisconsin Press.
—— 1990a: 'On the Margin: Postmodernism, Ironic History, and Medieval Studies', *Speculum*, 65:1, pp. 87–108.

—— (ed.) 1990b: *Literary Practice and Social Change in Britain, 1380–1530*. New Historicism: Studies in Cultural Poetics 8. Berkeley, Calif., and Oxford: University of California Press.

—— 1991: *Chaucer and the Subject of History*. London: Routledge.

Rose, Mary Beth (ed.) 1988: *Women in the Middle Ages and the Renaissance: Literary and Historical Perspectives*. Ithaca, NY: Cornell University Press.

Scanlon, Larry 1994: *Narrative, Authority and Power: The Medieval Exemplum and the Chaucerian Tradition*. Cambridge: Cambridge University Press.

Spiegel, Gabriele M. 1990: 'History, Historicism, and the Social Logic of the Text in the Middle Ages', *Speculum*, 65:1, pp. 59–86.

—— 1993: *Romancing the Past: The Rise of Vernacular Prose Historiography in Thirteenth-Century France*. New Historicism: Studies in Cultural Poetics 23. Berkeley, Calif.: University of California Press.

Stock, Brian 1990: *Listening for the Text: On the Uses of the Past*. Baltimore, Md.: Johns Hopkins University Press.

Strohm, Paul 1989: *Social Chaucer*. Cambridge, Mass., and London: Harvard University Press.

—— 1992: *Hochon's Arrow: The Social Imagination of Fourteenth-Century Texts*. Princeton, NJ: Princeton University Press.

VI   Studies of Renaissance Literature and Culture

Achinstein, Sharon 1994: *Milton and the Revolutionary Reader*. Literature in History. Princeton, NJ: Princeton University Press.

Armstrong, Nancy and Leonard Tennenhouse (eds) 1987: *The Ideology of Conduct: Essays in Literature and the History of Sexuality*. Essays in Literature and Society. New York and London: Methuen.

—— 1992: *The Imaginary Puritan: Literature, Intellectual Labor and the Origins of Personal Life*. New Historicism: Studies in Cultural Poetics 12. Berkeley, Calif., and Oxford: University of California Press.

Barker, Francis 1984: *The Tremulous Private Body: Essays on Subjection*. London and New York: Methuen.

—— 1993: *The Culture of Violence: Essays on Tragedy and History*. Manchester: Manchester University Press.

——, Peter Hulme and Margaret Iversen (eds) 1991: *Uses of History: Marxism, Postmodernism and the Renaissance*. Manchester: Manchester University Press.

Barrell, John 1988: *Poetry, Language and Politics*. Cultural Politics. Manchester and New York: Manchester University Press.

Belsey, Catherine 1985: *The Subject of Tragedy: Identity and Difference in Renaissance Drama*. London and New York: Methuen.

Bennett, Susan 1995: *Performing Nostalgia: Shifting Shakespeare and the Contemporary Past*. London: Routledge.

Bishop, T.G. 1996: *Shakespeare and the Theatre of Wonder*. Cambridge Studies in Renaissance Literature and Culture. Cambridge and New York: Cambridge University Press.

Boose, Lynda E. 1987: 'The Family in Shakespeare Studies; or – Studies in the Family of Shakespeareans; or – The Politics of Politics', *Renaissance Quarterly*, 40, pp. 707–42.

Breitenberg, Mark 1996: *Anxious Masculinity in Early Modern England*. Cambridge Studies in Renaissance Literature and Culture. Cambridge and New York: Cambridge University Press.

Bristol, Michael D. 1985:*Carnival and Theater: Plebeian Culture and the Structure of Authority in Renaissance England*. London and New York: Methuen.

—— 1990: *Shakespeare's America, America's Shakespeare*. London: Routledge.

Bruster, Douglas 1992: *Drama and the Market in the Age of Shakespeare*. Cambridge Studies in Renaissance Literature and Culture 1. Cambridge: Cambridge University Press.

Collick, John 1989: *Shakespeare, Cinema, and Society*. Cultural Politics. Manchester and New York: Manchester University Press.

Collins, Stephen L. 1989: 'Where's the History in the New Literary Historicism? The Case of the English Renaissance', *Annals of Scholarship*, 6, pp. 231–47.

Cox, Virginia 1992: *The Renaissance Dialogue: Literary Dialogue in Its Social and Political Contexts, Castiglione to Galileo*. Cambridge Studies in Renaissance Literature and Culture 2. Cambridge: Cambridge University Press.

Crewe, Jonathan 1990: *Trials of Authorship: Anterior Forms and Poetic Reconstruction from Wyatt to Shakespeare*. New Historicism: Studies in Cultural Poetics 9. Berkeley, Calif., and Oxford: University of California Press.

de Grazia, Margreta 1991: *Shakespeare Verbatim: The Reproduction of Authenticity and the 1790 Apparatus*. Oxford: Clarendon Press.

—— 1995: 'Soliloquies and Wages in the Age of Emergent Consciousness', *Textual Practice*, 9:1, pp. 67–92.

——, Maureen Quilligan and Peter Stallybrass (eds) 1996: *Reconstructing Renaissance Culture: Object and Subject*. Cambridge and New York: Cambridge University Press.

—— and Peter Stallybrass 1993: 'The Materiality of the Shakespearean Text', *Shakespeare Quarterly*, 44, pp. 255–83.

Dollimore, Jonathan 1989: *Radical Tragedy: Religion, Ideology and Power in the Drama of Shakespeare and His Contemporaries*, 2nd edn. Hemel Hempstead: Harvester Wheatsheaf.

—— 1990: 'Shakespeare, Cultural Materialism, Feminism and Marxist Humanism', *New Literary History*, 21, pp. 471–93.

—— and Alan Sinfield (eds) 1994: *Political Shakespeare: Essays in Cultural Materialism*, 2nd edn. Manchester: Manchester University Press.

Drakakis, John (ed.) 1985: *Alternative Shakespeares*. London: Methuen.

Dubrow, Heather and Richard Strier (eds) 1988: *The Historical Renaissance: New Essays on Tudor and Stuart Literature and Culture*. Chicago and London: University of Chicago Press.

Erickson, Peter 1987: 'Rewriting the Renaissance, Rewriting Ourselves', *Shakespeare Quarterly*, 38, pp. 327–37.

Felperin, Howard 1987: 'Making it "Neo": The New Historicism and Renaissance Literature', *Textual Practice*, 1, pp. 262–77.

—— 1990: *The Uses of the Canon: Elizabethan Literature and Contemporary Theory*, Ch. 8: '"Cultural Poetics" versus "Cultural Materialism": The Two New Historicisms in Renaissance Studies'. Oxford: Clarendon Press.

Fuller, Mary C. 1995: *Voyages in Print: English Travel to America, 1576–1624*. Cambridge Studies in Renaissance Literature and Culture 7. Cambridge and New York: Cambridge University Press.

Fumerton, Patricia 1991: *Cultural Aesthetics: Renaissance Literature and the Practice of Social Ornament*. Chicago: University of Chicago Press.

Gallagher, Catherine 1994: *Nobody's Story: The Vanishing Acts of Women Writers in the Marketplace, 1670–1820*. New Historicism: Studies in Cultural Poetics 31. Berkeley, Calif.: University of California Press.

Gillies, John 1994: *Shakespeare and the Geography of Difference*. Cambridge Studies in Renaissance Literature and Culture 4. Cambridge and New York: Cambridge University Press.

Goldberg, Jonathan 1982: 'The Politics of Renaissance Literature: A Review Essay', *English Literary History*, 49, pp. 514–42.

—— 1983: *James I and the Politics of Literature: Jonson, Shakespeare, Donne, and their Contemporaries*. Baltimore, Md., and London: Johns Hopkins University Press.

—— 1984: 'Recent Studies in the English Renaissance', *Studies in English Literature*, 24, pp. 157–99.

—— 1990: *Writing Matter: From the Hands of the English Renaissance*. Stanford, Calif.: Stanford University Press.

—— 1992: *Sodometries: Renaissance Texts, Modern Sexualities*. Stanford, Calif.: Stanford University Press.

—— (ed.) 1994: *Queering the Renaissance*. Series Q. Durham, NC, and London: Duke University Press.

Grady, Hugh 1991: *The Modernist Shakespeare: Critical Texts in a Material World*. Oxford: Clarendon Press.

Greenblatt, Stephen 1980: *Renaissance Self-Fashioning: From More to Shakespeare*. Chicago and London: University of Chicago Press.

—— (ed.) 1982: *The Power of Forms in the English Renaissance*. Norman, Okla.: Pilgrim Books.

—— (ed.) 1988a: *Representing the English Renaissance*. Berkeley, Los Angeles and London: University of California Press.

—— 1988b: *Shakespearean Negotiations*. Oxford: Clarendon Press.

—— 1990: *Learning to Curse: Essays in Early Modern Culture*. New York and London: Routledge.

—— 1991: *Marvelous Possessions: The Wonder of the New World*. Oxford: Clarendon Press.

Gregerson, Linda 1995: *The Reformation of the Subject: Spenser, Milton, and the English Protestant Epic*. Cambridge Studies in Renaissance Literature and Culture 6. Cambridge and New York: Cambridge University Press.

Halpern, Richard 1991: *The Poetics of Primitive Accumulation: English Renaissance Culture and the Genealogy of Capital*. Ithaca, NY: Cornell University Press.

—— 1994: 'Shakespeare in the Tropics: From High Modernism to New Historicism', *Representations*, 45, pp. 1–25.

Harmon, Barbara Leah 1984: 'Refashioning the Renaissance', *Diacritics*, 14:1, pp. 52–65.

Harvey, Elizabeth D. and Katharine Eisaman Maus (eds) 1990: *Soliciting Interpretation: Literary Theory and Seventeenth-Century English Poetry*. Chicago and London: University of Chicago Press.

Hawkes, Terence 1986: *That Shakespeherian Rag: Essays on a Critical Process*. London and New York: Routledge.

—— 1992: *Meaning By Shakespeare*. London and New York: Routledge.

—— 1995: *King Lear*. Writers and Their Work. Plymouth: Northcote House.

Healy, Thomas 1992: *New Latitudes: Theory and English Renaissance Literature*. London: Edward Arnold.

—— 1994: *Christopher Marlowe*. Writers and Their Work. Plymouth: Northcote House.

Helgerson, Richard 1983: *Self-Crowned Laureates: Spenser, Jonson, Milton and the Literary System*. Berkeley, Calif.: University of California Press.

—— 1992: *Forms of Nationhood: The Elizabethan Writing of England*. Chicago and London: University of Chicago Press.

Holderness, Graham (ed.) 1988: *The Shakespeare Myth*. Cultural Politics. Manchester and New York: Manchester University Press.

—— 1992: *Shakespeare Recycled: The Making of Historical Drama*. Hemel Hempstead: Harvester Wheatsheaf.

——, Bryan Loughrey and Andrew Murphy 1995: 'What's the Matter? Shakespeare and Textual Theory', *Textual Practice*, 9:1, pp. 93–119.

——, Nick Potter and John Turner 1988: *Shakespeare: The Play of History*. London: Macmillan.

—— 1990: *Shakespeare: Out of Court*. London: Macmillan.

Holstun, James 1989: 'Ranting at the New Historicism', *English Literary Renaissance*, 19, pp. 189–225.

Howard, Jean E. and Marion F. O'Connor (eds) 1987: *Shakespeare Reproduced: The Text in History and Ideology*. New York and London: Methuen.

Jardine, Lisa 1989: *Still Harping on Daughters: Women and Drama in the Age of Shakespeare*, 2nd edn. Hemel Hempstead: Harvester Wheatsheaf.

—— 1996: *Reading Shakespeare Historically*. London and New York: Routledge.

Kamps, Ivo (ed.) 1995: *Materialist Shakespeare: A History*. London: Verso.

Kinney, Arthur F. and Dan S. Collins (eds) 1987: *Renaissance Historicism: Selections from 'English Literary Renaissance'*. Amherst, Mass.: University of Massachusetts Press.

Kinser, Samuel 1990: *Rabelais's Carnival: Text, Context, Metatext*. New Historicism: Studies in Cultural Poetry 10. Berkeley, Calif.: University of California Press.

Knapp, Jeffrey 1992: *An Empire Nowhere: England, America, and Literature from 'Utopia' to 'The Tempest'*. New Historicism: Studies in Cultural Poetics 16. Berkeley, Calif.: University of California Press.

Lestringant, Frank 1994: *Mapping the Renaissance World: The Geographical Imagination in the Age of Discovery*, tr. David Fausett. New Historicism: Studies in Cultural Poetics 32. Berkeley, Calif.: University of California Press.

Levin, Richard 1990: 'Unthinkable Thoughts in the New Historicizing of English Renaissance Drama', *New Literary History*, 21, pp. 433–47.

Levine, Laura 1994: *Men in Women's Clothing: Anti-theatricality and Effeminization, 1579–1642*. Cambridge Studies in Renaissance Literature and Culture 5. Cambridge: Cambridge University Press.

Lewalski, Barbara Kiefer 1993: *Writing Women in Jacobean England*. Cambridge, Mass.: Harvard University Press.

Loomba, Ania 1989: *Gender, Race, Renaissance Drama*. Cultural Politics. Manchester and New York: Manchester University Press.

Mallin, Eric Scott 1995: *Inscribing the Time: Shakespeare and the End of Elizabethan England*. New Historicism: Studies in Cultural Poetics 33. Berkeley, Calif.: University of California Press.

Marcus, Leah 1986: *The Politics of Mirth: Jonson, Herrick, Milton, Marvell, and the Defense of Old Holiday Pastimes*. Chicago: University of Chicago Press.

—— 1988: *Puzzling Shakespeare: Local Reading and Its Discontents*. New Historicism: Studies in Cultural Poetics 6. Berkeley, Calif., and London: University of California Press.

Marsden, Jean I. (ed.) 1991: *The Appropriation of Shakespeare: Post-Renaissance Reconstructions of the Works and the Myth*. New York and Hemel Hempstead: Harvester Wheatsheaf.

McCoy, Richard C. 1989: *The Rites of Knighthood: The Literature and Politics of Elizabethan Chivalry*. New Historicism: Studies in Cultural Poetics 7. Berkeley, Calif., and London: University of California Press.

McLuskie, Kathleen 1989: *Renaissance Dramatists*. Hemel Hempstead: Harvester Wheatsheaf.

Montrose, Louis A. 1986: 'Renaissance Literary Studies and the Subject of History', *English Literary Renaissance*, 16, pp. 5–12.

Mullaney, Steven 1988: *The Place of the Stage: License, Play and Power in Renaissance England*. Chicago and London: University of Chicago Press.

Neely, Carol Thomas 1988: 'Constructing the Subject: Feminist Practice and the New Renaissance Discourses', *English Literary Renaissance*, 18, pp. 5–18.

Norbrook, David 1984: *Poetry and Politics in the English Renaissance*. London: Routledge & Kegan Paul.

Orgel, Stephen 1975: *The Illusion of Power: Political Theater in the English Renaissance*. Berkeley, Calif.: University of California Press.

Parry, Graham 1981: *The Golden Age Restor'd: The Culture of the Stuart Court, 1603–42*. New York: St Martin's Press.

Pask, Kevin 1996: *The Emergence of the English Author: Pre-scripting the Life of the Poet in Early Modern England*. Cambridge Studies in Renaissance Literature and Culture. Cambridge and New York: Cambridge University Press.

Patterson, Annabel M. 1984: *Censorship and Interpretation: The Conditions of Writing and Reading in Early Modern England*. Madison, Wisc.: University of Wisconsin Press.

—— 1989: *Shakespeare and the Popular Voice*. Oxford: Blackwell.

—— 1991: *Fables of Power: Aesopian Writing and Political History*. Durham, NC: Duke University Press.

—— (ed.) 1992: *John Milton*. London: Longman.

—— 1993: *Reading Between the Lines*. London: Routledge.

—— 1994a: *Andrew Marvell*. Writers and Their Work. Plymouth: Northcote House.

—— 1994b: *Reading Holinshed's Chronicles*. Chicago: University of Chicago Press.

Pechter, Edward 1987: 'The New Historicism and Its Discontents: Politicizing Renaissance Drama', *Publications of the Modern Language Association of America* , 102, pp. 292–303.

—— 1995: *What Was Shakespeare? Renaissance Plays and Changing Critical Practice*. Ithaca, NY, and London: Cornell University Press.

Porter, Carolyn 1990: 'History and Literature: "After the New Historicism"', *New Literary History*, 21, pp. 253–72.

Quint, David 1993: *Epic and Empire: Politics and Generic Form from Virgil to Milton*. Literature in History. Princeton, NJ: Princeton University Press.

Rackin, Phyllis 1990: *Stages of History: Shakespeare's English Chronicles*. Ithaca, NY: Cornell University Press.

Rambuss, Richard 1993: *Spenser's Secret Career*. Cambridge Studies in Renaissance Literature and Culture 3. Cambridge: Cambridge University Press.

Shuger, Debora Kuller 1990: *Habits of Thought in the English Renaissance: Religion, Politics and the Dominant Culture*. New Historicism: Studies in Cultural Poetics 13. Berkeley, Calif., and Oxford: University of California Press.

—— 1994: *The Renaissance Bible: Scholarship, Sacrifice, and Subjectivity*. New Historicism: Studies in Cultural Poetics 29. Berkeley, Calif.: University of California Press.

Sinfield, Alan 1983: *Literature in Protestant England, 1560–1660*. London: Croom Helm.

—— 1992a: *Faultlines: Cultural Materialism and the Politics of Dissident Reading*. Oxford: Clarendon Press.

—— (ed.) 1992b: *Macbeth: Contemporary Critical Essays*. London: Macmillan.

Stallybrass, Peter and Allon White 1986: *The Politics and Poetics of Transgression*, Ch. 1: 'The Fair, the Pig, Authorship'. London: Routledge.

Strier, Richard 1995: *Resistant Structures: Particularity, Radicalism, and Renaissance Texts*. New Historicism: Studies in Cultural Poetics 34. Berkeley, Calif.: University of California Press.

Tennenhouse, Leonard 1986: *Power on Display: The Politics of Shakespeare's Genres*. New York and London: Methuen.

Vickers, Brian 1993: *Appropriating Shakespeare: Contemporary Critical Quarrels*, Ch. 4: 'New Historicism: Disaffected Subjects'. New Haven and London: Yale University Press .

Waller, Gary (ed.) 1991: *Shakespeare's Comedies*. London: Longman.

Wayne, Don E. 1984: *Penshurst: The Semiotics of Place and the Poetics of History.* Madison, Wisc.: University of Wisconsin Press.

Whigham, Frank 1984: *Ambition and Privilege: The Social Tropes of Elizabethan Courtesy Theory.* Berkeley, Calif.: University of California Press.

—— 1996: *Seizures of the Will in Early Modern English Drama.* Cambridge Studies in Renaissance Literature and Culture. Cambridge and New York: Cambridge University Press.

Wilson, Richard 1993: *Will Power: Essays on Shakespearean Authority.* Hemel Hempstead: Harvester Wheatsheaf.

—— and Richard Dutton (eds) 1992: *New Historicism and Renaissance Drama.* London: Longman.

VII   Studies of Eighteenth-Century Literature and Culture

Armstrong, Nancy 1987: *Desire and Domestic Fiction: A Political History of the Novel.* New York and Oxford: Oxford University Press.

—— and Leonard Tennenhouse (eds) 1987: *The Ideology of Conduct: Essays in Literature and the History of Sexuality.* Essays in Literature and Society. New York and London: Methuen.

—— 1992: *The Imaginary Puritan: Literature, Intellectual Labor and the Origins of Personal Life.* New Historicism: Studies in Cultural Poetics 21. Berkeley, Calif., and Oxford: University of California Press.

Barker-Benfield, G.J. 1992: *The Culture of Sensibility.* Chicago: University of Chicago Press.

Barrell, John 1983: *English Literature in History 1730–1830: An Equal, Wide Survey.* London: Hutchinson.

—— 1988: *Poetry, Language and Politics.* Cultural Politics. Manchester and New York: Manchester University Press.

—— 1992: *The Birth of Pandora and the Division of Knowledge.* Language, Discourse, Society. Basingstoke: Macmillan

Bender, John 1987: *Imagining the Penitentiary: Fiction and the Architecture of Mind in Eighteenth-Century England.* Chicago and London: University of Chicago Press.

—— 1992: 'Eighteenth-Century Studies', in Stephen Greenblatt and Giles Gunn (eds), *Redrawing the Boundaries: The Transformation of English and American Studies*, New York: The Modern Language Association of America, pp. 79–99.

Castle, Terry 1986: *Masquerade and Civilisation: The Carnivalesque in Eighteenth-Century English Culture and Fiction.* Stanford, Calif.: Stanford University Press.

Christensen, Jerome 1987: *Practicing Enlightenment: Hume and the Formation of a Literary Career.* Madison, Wisc.: University of Wisconsin Press.

Davis, Lennard 1983: *Factual Fictions: The Origin of the English Novel.* New York: Columbia University Press.

de Bolla, Peter 1989: *The Discourse of the Sublime: Readings in History, Aesthetics and the Subject.* Oxford: Basil Blackwell.

Erickson, Robert A. 1987: *Mother Midnight: Birth, Sex, and Fate in the Eighteenth-Century Novel.* New York: AMS Press.

Gallagher, Catherine 1994: *Nobody's Story: The Vanishing Acts of Women Writers in the Marketplace, 1670–1820.* New Historicism: Studies in Cultural Poetics 31. Berkeley, Calif.: University of California Press.

Harth, Philip (ed.) 1974: *New Approaches to Eighteenth-Century Literature.* New York: Columbia University Press.

Kelly, Veronica and Dorothea von Mücke (eds) 1994: *Body and Text in the Eighteenth Century.* Cambridge: Cambridge University Press.

Klancher, Jon P. 1987: *The Making of English Reading Audiences, 1740–1832*. Madison, Wisc.: University of Wisconsin Press.

Landry, Donna 1990: *The Muses of Resistance: Laboring-Class Women's Poetry in Britain, 1739–1796*. Cambridge: Cambridge University Press.

Marshall, David 1986: *The Figure of the Theater: Shaftesbury, Defoe, Adam Smith, and George Eliot*. New York: Columbia University Press.

Mullan, John 1988: *Sentiment and Sociability: The Language of Feeling in the Eighteenth Century*. Oxford: Clarendon Press.

Nussbaum, Felicity 1989: *The Autobiographical Subject: Gender and Ideology in Eighteenth-Century England*. Baltimore, Md.: Johns Hopkins University Press.

—— 1995: *Torrid Zones: Maternity, Sexuality, and Empire in Eighteenth-Century English Narratives*. Parallax: Revisions of Culture and Society. Baltimore, Md., and London: Johns Hopkins University Press.

—— and Laura Brown (eds) 1987: *The New Eighteenth Century: Theory, Politics, English Literature*. New York and London: Methuen.

Pollak, Ellen 1985: *The Poetics of Sexual Myth: Gender and Ideology in the Verse of Swift and Pope*. Chicago: University of Chicago Press.

Stafford, Barbara Maria 1991: *Body Criticism: Imaging the Unseen in Enlightenment Art and Medicine*. Cambridge, Mass.: MIT Press.

Stallybrass, Peter and Allon White 1986: *The Politics and Poetics of Transgression*, Ch. 2: 'The Grotesque Body and the Smithfield Muse: Authorship in the Eighteenth Century'. London: Routledge.

Straub, Kristina 1992: *Sexual Suspects: Eighteenth-century Players and Sexual Ideology*. Princeton, NJ: Princeton University Press.

Trotter, David 1988: *Circulation: Defoe, Dickens and the Economies of the Novel*. London: Macmillan.

Vance, Norman 1990: *Irish Literature: A Social History*, Ch. 3. Oxford: Blackwell.

VIII   Studies of the Literature and Culture of the Romantic Period

Aers, David, Jonathan Cook and David Punter 1981: *Romanticism and Ideology: Studies in English Writing, 1765–1830*. London: Routledge.

Barker, Francis, Jay Bernstein, Peter Hulme, Margaret Iversen and Jennifer Stone (eds) 1982: *1789: Reading Writing Revolution: Proceedings of the Essex Conference on the Sociology of Literature, July 1981*. Colchester: University of Essex.

Barrell, John 1983: *English Literature in History, 1730–1830: An Equal, Wide Survey*. London: Hutchinson.

—— 1988: *Poetry, Language and Politics*. Cultural Politics. Manchester and New York: Manchester University Press.

—— 1991: *The Infection of Thomas de Quincey: A Psychopathology of Imperialism*. New Haven, Conn.: Yale University Press.

Butler, Marilyn 1979: *Peacock Displayed: A Satirist in his Context*. London: Routledge & Kegan Paul.

—— 1981: *Romantics, Rebels and Reactionaries: English Literature and its Background, 1776–1830*. Oxford: Oxford University Press.

Carlson, Julie 1994: *In the Theatre of Romanticism: Coleridge, Nationalism, Women*. Cambridge Studies in Romanticism 5. Cambridge: Cambridge University Press.

Chandler, James K. 1984: *Wordsworth's Second Nature: A Study of the Poetry and Politics*. Chicago and London: University of Chicago Press.

Copley, Stephen and John Whale (eds) 1992: *Beyond Romanticism: New Approaches to Texts and Contexts, 1780–1832*. London and New York: Routledge.

Darnton, Robert 1982: *The Literary Underground of the Old Regime*. Cambridge, Mass.: Harvard University Press.

Duff, David 1994: *Romance and Revolution: Shelley and the Politics of a Genre*. Cambridge Studies in Romanticism 7. Cambridge: Cambridge University Press.

Eaves, Morris and Michael Fischer (eds) 1986: *Romanticism and Contemporary Criticism*. Ithaca, NY: Cornell University Press.

Eilenberg, Susan 1988: 'Wordsworth's "Michael": The Poetry of Property', *Essays in Literature*, 15, pp. 13–25.

—— 1992: *Strange Power of Speech: Wordsworth, Coleridge and Literary Possession*. New York and Oxford: Oxford University Press.

Ellis, Kate Ferguson 1989: *The Contested Castle: Gothic Novels and the Subversion of Domestic Ideology*. Urbana, Ill.: University of Illinois Press.

Everest, Kelvin (ed.) 1991: *Revolution in Writing: British Literary Responses to the French Revolution*. Milton Keynes: Open University Press.

Gallagher, Catherine 1994: *Nobody's Story: The Vanishing Acts of Women Writers in the Marketplace, 1670–1820*. New Historicism: Studies in Cultural Poetics 31. Berkeley, Calif.: University of California Press.

Glen, Heather 1983: *Vision and Disenchantment: Blake's 'Songs' and Wordsworth's 'Lyrical Ballads'*. Cambridge: Cambridge University Press.

Heinzelman, Kurt 1980: *The Economics of the Imagination*. Amherst, Mass.: University of Massachusetts Press.

Jacobus, Mary 1983: ' "That Great Stage Where Senators Perform": *Macbeth* and the Politics of Romantic Theater', *Studies in Romanticism*, 22, pp. 353–87.

—— 1990: *Romanticism, Writing, and Sexual Difference: Essays on 'The Prelude'*. Oxford: Clarendon Press.

Johnston, Kenneth R., *et al.* 1990: *Romantic Revolutions: Criticism and Theory*. Bloomington, Ind.: Indiana University Press.

Klancher, Jon P. 1987: *The Making of English Reading Audiences, 1740–1832*. Madison, Wisc.: University of Wisconsin Press.

—— 1989a: 'English Romanticism and Cultural Production', in H. Aram Veeser (ed.), *The New Historicism*, London: Routledge, pp. 77–88.

—— 1989b: 'Romantic Criticism and the Meanings of the French Revolution', *Studies in Romanticism*, 28, pp. 463–91.

Leask, Nigel 1988: *The Politics of Imagination in Coleridge's Critical Thought*. Basingstoke: Macmillan.

—— 1992: *British Romantic Writers and the East: Anxieties of Empire*. Cambridge Studies in Romanticism. Cambridge: Cambridge University Press.

Levinson, Marjorie 1986a: *Wordsworth's Great Period Poems*. Cambridge: Cambridge University Press.

—— 1986b: *The Romantic Fragment Poem: A Critique of Form*. Chapel Hill, NC: University of North Carolina Press.

—— 1988: *Keats's Life of Allegory: The Origins of a Style*. Oxford: Blackwell.

——, Marilyn Butler, Jerome McGann and Paul Hamilton 1989: *Rethinking Historicism: Critical Readings in Romantic History*. Oxford: Blackwell.

Liu, Alan 1984: 'Wordsworth: The History in "Imagination"', *English Literary History*, 51, pp. 505–48.

—— 1989a: *Wordsworth: The Sense of History*. Stanford, Calif.: Stanford University Press.

—— 1989b: 'Wordsworth and Subversion, 1793–1804: Trying Cultural Criticism', *Yale Journal of Criticism*, 2, pp. 55–100.

—— 1990: 'Local Transcendence: Cultural Criticism, Postmodernism, and the Romanticism of Detail', *Representations*, 32, pp. 75–113.

Mack, Anne and J.J. Rome 1989: 'Marxism, Romanticism and Postmodernism: An American Case History', *South Atlantic Quarterly*, 88, pp. 605–32.

Manning, Peter J. 1990: *Reading Romantics: Texts and Contexts*. New York: Oxford University Press.

McGann, Jerome J. 1983: *The Romantic Ideology: A Critical Investigation*. Chicago and London: University of Chicago Press.

—— 1985: *The Beauty of Inflections: Literary Investigations in Historical Method and Theory*. Oxford: Clarendon Press.

—— 1989: *Towards a Literature of Knowledge*. Oxford: Clarendon Press.

Mee, Jon 1992: *Dangerous Enthusiasm: William Blake and the Culture of Radicalism in the 1790s*. Oxford and New York: Clarendon Press.

Mellor, Ann K. (ed.) 1987: *Romanticism and Feminism*. Bloomington, Ind.: University of Indiana Press.

Morton, Timothy 1995: *Shelley and the Revolution in Taste: The Body and the Natural World*. Cambridge Studies in Romanticism 10. Cambridge: Cambridge University Press.

Parker, Reeve: 1987: 'Reading Wordsworth's Power: Narrative and Usurpation in the *Borderers*', *English Literary History*, 54, pp. 299–331.

—— 1988: '"In Some Sort Seeing with my Proper Eyes": Wordsworth and the Spectacles of Paris', *Studies in Romanticism*, 27, pp. 369–90.

Poovey, Mary 1984: *The Proper Lady and the Woman Writer: Ideology as Style in the Works of Mary Wollstonecraft, Mary Shelley, and Jane Austen*. Chicago: Chicago University Press.

Porter, Roy and Mikulás Teich (eds) 1988: *Romanticism in National Context*. Cambridge: Cambridge University Press.

Roe, Nicholas 1988: *Wordsworth and Coleridge: The Radical Years*. Oxford: Clarendon Press.

Schor, Esther H. 1994: *Bearing the Dead: The British Culture of Mourning from the Enlightenment to Victoria*. Literature in History. Princeton, NJ: Princeton University Press.

Simpson, David 1987: *Wordsworth's Historical Imagination: The Poetry of Displacement*. London: Methuen.

Siskin, Clifford 1988: *The Historicity of Romantic Discourse*. New York: Oxford University Press.

Smith, Olivia 1984: *The Politics of Romantic Language, 1791–1819*. London and New York: Oxford University Press.

Welsh, Alexander 1992: *The Hero of the Waverley Novels: with New Essays on Scott*. Literature in History. Princeton, NJ: Princeton University Press.

IX Studies of Victorian Literature and Culture

Arac, Jonathan and Harriet Ritvo (eds) 1991: *Macropolitics and Nineteenth-Century Literature: Nationalism, Exoticism, Imperialism*. New Cultural Studies. Philadelphia, Pa.: University of Pennsylvania Press.

Armstrong, Isobel 1993: *Victorian Poetry: Poetry, Poetics, Politics*. London and New York: Routledge.

Bailin, Miriam 1994: *The Sickroom in Victorian Fiction: The Art of Being Ill*. Cambridge Studies in Nineteenth-Century Literature and Culture 1. Cambridge: Cambridge University Press.

Beer, Gillian 1983: *Darwin's Plots: Evolutionary Narrative in Darwin, George Eliot and Nineteenth-Century Fiction*. London: Routledge & Kegan Paul.

Bivona, Daniel 1990: *Desire and Contradiction: Imperial Visions and Domestic Debates in Victorian Literature*. Cultural Politics. Manchester and New York: Manchester University Press.

Craft, Christopher 1994: *Another Kind of Love: Male Homosexual Desire in English*

Discourse, 1850–1920. New Historicism: Studies in Cultural Poetics 30. Berkeley, Calif.: University of California Press.

Gagnier, Regenia 1986: *Idylls of the Market Place: Oscar Wilde and the Victorian Public*. Stanford, Calif.: Stanford University Press.

Gallagher, Catherine 1985: *The Industrial Reformation of English Fiction: Social Discourse and Narrative Form, 1832–1867*. Chicago and London: University of Chicago Press.

—— and Thomas Laqueur (eds) 1987: *The Making of the Modern Body: Sexuality and Society in the Nineteenth Century*. Berkeley, Calif., and London: University of California Press.

Hall, Donald E. 1994: *Muscular Christianity: Embodying the Victorian Age*. Cambridge Studies in Nineteenth-Century Literature and Culture 2. Cambridge: Cambridge University Press.

Hamon, Philippe 1992: *Expositions: Literature and Architecture in Nineteenth-Century France*, tr. Katia Sainson-Frank and Lisa Maguire. New Historicism: Studies in Cultural Poetics 20. Berkeley, Calif., and London: University of California Press.

Kucich, John 1985: 'Narrative Theory as History: A Review of Problems in Victorian Fiction Studies', *Victorian Studies*, 28, pp. 657–75.

Ledger, Sally and Scott McCracken (eds) 1995: *Cultural Politics at the Fin de Siècle*. Cambridge: Cambridge University Press.

Levine, George 1988: *Darwin and the Novelists: Patterns of Science in Victorian Fiction*. Cambridge, Mass.: Harvard University Press.

Litvak, Joseph 1988: 'Back to the Future: A Review Article on the New Historicism, Deconstruction, and Nineteenth-Century Fiction', *Texas Studies in Literature and Language*, 30, pp. 120–49.

Lloyd, David 1987: *Nationalism and Minor Literature: James Clarence Mangan and the Emergence of Irish Cultural Nationalism*. The New Historicism: Studies in Cultural Poetics 3. Berkeley, Calif., and London: University of California Press.

Matus, Jill L. 1995: *Unstable Bodies: Victorian Representations of Sexuality and Maternity*. Manchester and New York: Manchester University Press.

McCormack, W.J. 1985: *Ascendancy and Tradition in Anglo-Irish Literary History, 1789–1939*. Oxford: Oxford University Press.

McGann, Jerome J. 1985: *The Beauty of Inflections: Literary Investigations in Historical Method and Theory*. Oxford: Clarendon Press.

Miller, D.A. 1987: *The Novel and the Police*. Berkeley and Los Angeles: University of California Press.

Newton, Judith Lowder 1990: 'Historicisms New and Old: "Charles Dickens" Meets Marxism, Feminism, and West Coast Foucault', *Feminist Studies*, 16, pp. 449–90.

Owen, Alex 1990: *The Darkened Room: Women, Power and Spiritualism in Late Victorian England*. New Cultural Studies. Philadelphia, Pa.: University of Pennsylvania Press.

Pointon, Marcia (ed.) 1989: *Pre-Raphaelites Reviewed*. Cultural Politics. Manchester University Press.

Poovey, Mary 1988: *Uneven Developments: The Ideological Work of Gender in Mid-Victorian England*. Chicago: University of Chicago Press.

Richards, Thomas 1990: *The Commodity Culture of Victorian Britain: Advertising and Spectacle, 1851–1914*. London: Verso.

Rothfield, Lawrence 1992: *Vital Signs: Medical Realism in Nineteenth-Century Fiction*. Literature in History. Princeton, NJ: Princeton University Press.

Shuttleworth, Sally 1984: *George Eliot and Nineteenth-Century Science: The Make-Believe of a Beginning*. Cambridge: Cambridge University Press.

Sinfield, Alan 1986: *Alfred Tennyson*. Oxford: Basil Blackwell.

—— 1994: *The Wilde Century: Effeminacy, Oscar Wilde and the Queer Moment*. London: Cassell.

Sussman, Herbert 1995: *Victorian Masculinities: Manhood and Masculine Poetics in Early Victorian Literature and Art.* Cambridge Studies in Nineteenth-Century Literature and Culture 3. Cambridge: Cambridge University Press.

Trotter, David 1988: *Circulation: Defoe, Dickens and the Economies of the Novel.* London: Macmillan.

Vance, Norman 1990: *Irish Literature: A Social History,* Ch. 4. Oxford: Blackwell.

Welsh, Alexander 1985: *George Eliot and Blackmail.* Cambridge, Mass.: Harvard University Press.

Widdowson, Peter 1989: *Hardy in History: A Study in Literary Sociology.* London: Routledge.

Yeazell, Ruth Bernard (ed.) 1986: *Sex, Politics and Science in the Nineteenth-Century Novel.* Baltimore, Md.: Johns Hopkins University Press.

X Studies of Twentieth-Century Literature and Culture

Arac, Jonathan 1989: 'The Struggle for the Cultural Heritage: Christina Stead Refunctions Charles Dickens and Mark Twain', *Cultural Critique,* 2, pp. 178–89.

Barker, Francis, Peter Hulme and Margaret Iverson (eds) 1992: *Postmodernism and the Re-reading of Modernity.* The Essex Symposia: Literature, Politics, Theory. Manchester: Manchester University Press.

Beer, Gillian 1989: *Arguing with the Past: Essays in Narrative from Woolf to Sidney.* London: Routledge.

Caesar, Adrian 1991: *Dividing Lines: Poetry, Class, and Ideology in the 1930s.* Cultural Politics. Manchester and New York: Manchester University Press.

Cairns, David and Shaun Richards 1988: *Writing Ireland: Colonialism, Nationalism and Culture.* Cultural Politics. Manchester and New York: Manchester University Press.

Connor, Steven 1995: *The English Novel in History, 1950 to the Present.* The Novel in History. London: Routledge.

Craft, Christopher 1994: *Another Kind of Love: Male Homosexual Desire in English Discourse, 1850–1920.* New Historicism: Studies in Cultural Poetics 30. Berkeley, Calif.: University of California Press.

Davies, Philip John (ed.) 1990: *Science Fiction, Social Conflict, and War.* Cultural Politics. Manchester and New York: Manchester University Press.

Deane, Seamus 1985: *Celtic Revivals.* London: Faber.

Dollimore, Jonathan 1991: *Sexual Dissidence: Augustine to Wilde, Freud to Foucault.* Oxford: Clarendon.

Fairhall, James 1993: *James Joyce and the Question of History.* Cambridge: Cambridge University Press.

Frazier, Adrian 1990: *Behind the Scenes: Yeats, Horniman, and the Struggle for the Abbey Theatre.* New Historicism: Studies in Cultural Poetics 11. Berkeley, Calif., and London: University of California Press.

Holderness, Graham 1982: *D.H. Lawrence: History, Ideology and Fiction.* Dublin: Gill and Macmillan.

Humm, Maggie 1991: *Border Traffic: Strategies of Contemporary Women Writers.* Cultural Politics. Manchester and New York: Manchester University Press.

Jordan, Glenn and Chris Weedon 1995: *Cultural Politics: Class, Gender, Race, and the Postmodern World.* Oxford and Cambridge, Mass.: Blackwell.

Lowe-Evans, Mary 1989: *Crimes Against Fecundity: Joyce and Population Control.* Irish Studies. Syracuse, NY: Syracuse University Press.

McCormack, W.J. 1985: *Ascendancy and Tradition in Anglo-Irish Literary History, 1789–1939.* Oxford: Oxford University Press.

McGann, Jerome J. 1993: *Black Riders: The Visible Language of Modernism.* Princeton, NJ: Princeton University Press.

News from Nowhere: Journal of Cultural Materialism 1989: No. 7: 'The Politics of Modernism'.

Paget, Derek 1990: *True Stories?: Documentary Drama on Radio, Screen, and Stage*. Cultural Politics. Manchester and New York: Manchester University Press.

Pinkney, Tony 1990: *D.H. Lawrence*. Hemel Hempstead: Harvester Wheatsheaf.

—— 1991: *Raymond Williams*. Bridgend: Seren.

Roberts, John 1990: *Postmodernism, Politics and Art*. Cultural Politics. Manchester and New York: Manchester University Press.

Ross, Andrew (ed.) 1988: *Universal Abandon?: The Politics of Postmodernism*. Cultural Politics 1. Minneapolis, Minn.: University of Minnesota Press.

Sinfield, Alan 1983 (ed.): *Society and Literature, 1945–1970: The Context of English Literature*. London: Methuen.

—— 1989: *Literature, Politics, and Culture in Post-War Britain*. Oxford: Blackwell; also published as New Historicism: Studies in Cultural Poetics 12. Berkeley, Calif.: University of California Press.

Smith, Stan 1982: *Inviolable Voice: History and Twentieth-Century Poetry*. Dublin: Gill & Macmillan.

Trotter, David 1993: *The English Novel in History, 1895–1920*. The Novel in History. London: Routledge.

Vance, Norman 1990: *Irish Literature: A Social History*, Chs 5–6. Oxford: Blackwell.

Williams, Raymond 1989: *The Politics of Modernism: Against the New Conformists*, ed. Tony Pinkney. London: Verso.

XI   Studies of American Literature and Culture

Agnew, Jean Christophe 1983: 'The Consuming Vision of Henry James', in Richard Wightman Fox and T.J. Jackson Lears (eds), *The Culture of Consumption, 1880–1980*, New York: Pantheon, pp. 65–100.

Baym, Nina 1984: *Novels, Readers, and Reviewers: Responses to Fiction in Antebellum America*. Ithaca, NY: Cornell University Press.

—— 1989: 'Early Histories of American Literature: A Chapter in the Institution of New England', *American Literary History*, 1, pp. 459–88.

Bentley, Nancy 1995: *Manners, Ethnography, and the Novel: The Discourse of Culture in Hawthorne, James and Wharton*. Cambridge: Cambridge University Press.

Bercovitch, Sacvan (ed.) 1986a: *Reconstructing American Literary History*. Cambridge, Mass.: Harvard University Press.

—— 1986b: 'The Problem of Ideology in American Literary History', *Critical Inquiry*, 12, pp. 631–53.

—— 1991: *The Office of 'The Scarlet Letter'*. Baltimore, Md.: Johns Hopkins University Press.

—— 1993: *The Rites of Assent: Transformations in the Symbolic Construction of America*. London and New York: Routledge.

—— and Myra Jehlen (eds) 1986: *Ideology and Classic American Literature*. Cambridge: Cambridge University Press.

Breitweiser, Mitchell 1990: *American Puritanism and the Defence of Mourning: Religion, Grief, and Ethnology in Mary White Rowlandson's Captivity Narrative*. Madison, Wisc.: University of Wisconsin Press.

Brown, Gillian 1990: *Domestic Individualism: Imagining Self in Nineteenth-Century America*. The New Historicism: Studies in Cultural Poetics 14. Berkeley, Calif., and London: University of California Press.

Buell, Lawrence 1986: *New England Literary Culture: From Revolution through Renaissance*. Cambridge and New York: Cambridge University Press.

Burbick, Joan 1994: *Healing the Republic: The Language of Health and the Culture of Nationalism in Nineteenth-Century America*. Cambridge: Cambridge University Press.

Carby, Hazel V. 1987: *Reconstructing Womanhood: The Emergence of the Afro-American Woman Novelist*. New York: Oxford University Press.

Colatrella, Carol and Joseph Alkana (eds) 1994: *Cohesion and Dissent in America*. Albany, NY: State University of New York Press.

Davidson, Cathy N. 1986: *Revolution and the Word: The Rise of the Novel in America*. New York: Oxford University Press.

Dimock, Wai-chee 1989: *Empire for Liberty: Melville and the Poetics of Individualism*. Princeton, NJ: Princeton University Press.

—— 1990: 'Scarcity, Subjectivity, and Emerson', *boundary 2*, 17, pp. 83–99.

Ferguson, Robert A. 1984: *Law and Letters in American Culture*. Cambridge, Mass.: Harvard University Press.

Fisher, Philip 1987: *Hard Facts: Setting and Form in the American Novel*. New York: Oxford University Press.

—— (ed.) 1991: *The New American Studies: Essays from Representations*. Berkeley, Calif.: University of California Press.

Gilmore, Michael T. 1985: *American Romanticism and the Marketplace*. Chicago: University of Chicago Press.

Gura, Philip F. *The Crossroads of American History and Literature*. University Park, Pa.: Pennsylvania State University Press.

Herbert, T. Walter 1993: *Dearest Beloved: The Hawthornes and the Making of the Middle-Class Family*. New Historicism: Studies in Cultural Poetics 24. Berkeley, Calif., and Oxford: University of California Press.

Jay, Gregory S. 1990: 'American Literature and the New Historicism: The Example of Frederick Douglass', *boundary 2*, 17, pp. 211–42.

Jehlen, Myra 1986: *American Incarnation: The Individual, the Nation, and the Continent*. Cambridge, Mass.: Harvard University Press.

Jordan, Cynthia 1989: *Second Stories: The Politics of Language, Form, and Gender in Early American Fictions*. Chapel Hill, NC: University of North Carolina Press.

Lang, Amy Schrager 1987: *Prophetic Woman: Anne Hutchinson and the Problem of Dissent in the Literature of New England*. Berkeley, Calif.: University of California Press.

Lentz, Gunter H., Hartmut Keil and Sabine Brock-Sallah (eds) 1990: *Reconstructing American Literary and Historical Studies*. Frankfurt: Campus Verlag.

Limón, José E. 1992: *Mexican Ballads, Chicano Poems: History and Influence in Mexican-American Social Poetry*. The New Historicism: Studies in Cultural Poetics 17. Berkeley, Calif., and London: University of California Press.

Machor, James L. (ed.) 1993: *Readers in History: Nineteenth-Century American Literature and the Contexts of Response*. Baltimore, Md., and London: Johns Hopkins University Press.

McGann, Jerome J. 1991: *The Textual Condition*. Princeton Studies in Culture/Power/History. Princeton, NJ: Princeton University Press.

—— 1993: *Black Riders: The Visible Language of Modernism*. Princeton, NJ: Princeton University Press.

Michaels, Walter Benn 1987: *The Gold Standard and the Logic of Naturalism: American Literature at the Turn of the Century*. The New Historicism: Studies in Cultural Poetics 2. Berkeley, Calif., and London: University of California Press.

—— and Donald E. Pease (eds) 1985: *The American Renaissance Reconsidered: Selected Papers from the English Institute, 1982–83*. Baltimore, Md.: Johns Hopkins University Press.

Nelson, Cary 1989: *Repression and Recovery: Modern American Poetry and the Politics of Cultural Memory, 1910–1945*. Madison, Wisc.: University of Wisconsin Press.

Pease, Donald E. 1987: *Visionary Compacts: American Renaissance Writings in Cultural Context*. Madison, Wisc.: University of Wisconsin Press.
Reed, T.V. 1992: *Fifteen Jugglers, Five Believers: Literary Politics and the Poetics of American Social Movements*. New Historicism: Studies in Cultural Poetics 22. Berkeley, Calif., and Oxford: University of California Press.
Reynolds, David S. 1988: *Beneath the American Renaissance: The Subversive Imagination in the Age of Emerson and Melville*. New York: Knopf.
Rogin, Michael Paul 1979: *Subversive Genealogy: The Politics and Art of Herman Melville*. Berkeley, Calif.: University of California Press.
—— 1990: 'Recolonizing America', *American Literary History*, 2, pp. 144–9.
Seltzer, Mark 1984: *Henry James and the Art of Power*. Ithaca, NY: Cornell University Press.
Shulman, Robert 1987: *Social Criticism and Nineteenth-Century American Fictions*. Columbia, Mo.: University of Missouri Press.
Thomas, Brook 1987: *Cross-Examinations of Law and Literature: Cooper, Hawthorne, Stowe, and Melville*. Cambridge and New York: Cambridge University Press.
Tompkins, Jane 1985: *Sensational Designs: The Cultural Work of American Fiction, 1790–1860*. New York and Oxford: Oxford University Press.
—— 1986: '"Indians": Textualism, Morality, and the Problem of History', *Critical Inquiry*, 13, pp. 101–19.
Warner, Michael 1990: *The Letters of the Republic: Publication and the Public Sphere in Eighteenth-Century America*. Cambridge, Mass.: Harvard University Press.
Weber, Donald 1990: 'Historicizing the Errand', *American Literary History*, 2, pp. 101–18.
Weinstein, Cindy 1995: *The Literature of Labor and the Labors of Literature: Allegory in Nineteenth-Century Fiction*. Cambridge: Cambridge University Press.
Wilson, Christopher P. 1989: 'Containing Multitudes: Realism, Historicism, American Studies', *American Quarterly*, 41, pp. 466–95.

XII Publishers' Series

Cambridge Studies in Renaissance Literature and Culture. General Editor: Stephen Orgel. Cambridge University Press.
Cambridge Studies in Romanticism. General Editors: Marilyn Butler and James Chandler. Cambridge University Press.
Cambridge Studies in Nineteenth-Century Literature and Culture. General Editors: Gillian Beer and Catherine Gallagher. Cambridge University Press.
Cultural Politics. (Founding General Editors: Jonathan Dollimore and Alan Sinfield.) Manchester University Press.
Cultural Politics. General Editors: *Social Text* Collective. University of Minnesota Press.
Literature in History. General Editors: David Bromwich, James Chandler and Lionel Gossman. Princeton University Press.
New Cultural Studies. General Editors: Joan DeJean, Carroll Smith-Rosenberg and Peter Stallybrass. University of Pennsylvania Press.
New Historicism: Studies in Cultural Poetics. General Editor: Stephen Greenblatt. University of California Press.
Parallax: Revisions of Culture and Society. General Editors: Stephen G. Nichols, Gerald Prince and Wendy Steiner. Johns Hopkins University Press.
Princeton Studies in Culture/Power/History. General Editors: Sherry B. Ortner, Nicholas B. Dirks and Geoff Eley. Princeton University Press.
The Novel in History. General Editor: Gillian Beer. Routledge.

XIII Journals

American Literary History
Cultural Critique
English Literary History
English Literary Renaissance
Literature and History
New Formations: A Journal of Culture/Theory/Politics
News from Nowhere: Journal of Cultural Materialism
Representations
Social Text
Textual Practice
Victorian Studies

Index

absolutism 71, 72, 113, 122
Adler, Doris 63
Adorno, Theodor xvi, 54, 94, 96–7, 99–102
adultery 77–8
Aers, David xii
Aeschylus x, 116, 169–73, 175
    The Oresteia 113, 116, 169–73, 175, 181
    Prometheus Bound 173
    Prometheus Unbound 173
Africa 5
agency 55–6, 68–9, 100
alternative culture 3, 24, 25
Althusser, Louis xii, 2–3, 17–21, 41, 42, 43, 49, 50, 51, 54, 63, 66, 67, 71, 88–9, 107, 108
Altick, Richard 149
American studies xii, xiii
anecdotes xvi, xvii
Annales school 50
anthropology 1, 7, 8, 10, 162
anxiety 78, 136
Argos 171, 172
Ariès, Philippe 84
Aristotle 8, 19, 181
Archer, Gabriel 134
Armstrong, Nancy 2, 115, 157–65
Asia 77
Athens 169–70, 172
Austen, Jane 83, 157
    Persuasion xvi
Australopithecines 5–6
authority 124, 132, 139, 143, 145

Baker, Houston 48
Bakhtin, Mikhail xii, 59, 114, 115, 116, 127, 139, 143, 163, 175
Baldick, Chris 82
Balibar, Etienne 107, 126

Balibar, Renée 126
Bannet, Eve Tavor 81
barbarism 4, 35, 63, 66, 115, 167, 180
Barker, Francis 4, 113, 125–37
Barrell, John 84, 103
Barth, Karl 17
base and superstructure xiv, 3, 22, 24, 26, 70
Battenhouse, Roy 118
Baudelaire, Charles 180
Belsey, Catherine xii, 4, 43, 74, 82–91
Bender, John 2, 114, 138–46
Benjamin, Walter xii, xvi–xvii, 4, 32–40, 96–7, 101, 108, 109–110, 167, 169
    Passagenarbeit 97
    'The Task of the Translator' 44, 109–10
    'Theses on the Philosophy of History' 4, 32–40, 44, 115, 167, 180
Bennett, Josephine Waters 118–19
Bennett, Tony 105–6, 126, 127–8
Bentham, Jeremy 2, 14–16, 114
Bentley, Gerald 175, 176
Bernstein, Michael 180
Bewell, Alan 103
Bible, the 79, 150, 181
    Ezekiel 150
    Genesis 173
    Revelation 150
Bindman, David 154
Blake, William 114, 116, 173–8
    'Holy Thursday' 156
    'The Human Abstract' 146, 148, 152
    'The human Image' 146
    'London' 114, 146–57
    The Marriage of Heaven and Hell 154, 175
    Milton 176
    Poetical Sketches 150
    Songs of Experience 155
    Songs of Innocence 156

Blanqui, Louis Auguste 37
Bloch, Ernst xvi
Bloom, Harold 150
body, the 84, 115, 124, 163–4
Boose, Lynda 53, 67, 68
Boswell, James
    Journal 147
Bourdieu, Pierre 66
bourgeois society 22, 25
Bradley, A. C. 82
Braudel, Fernand 98
Brazil 139
Brecht, Bertolt 34, 47
Brewer, John 152
Britain 77, 81, 115, 138, 141, 161, 174,
    177, 180
Bromwich, David 103
Brontë, Charlotte 115, 163
    Jane Eyre 157, 158, 159, 165
Brontë, Emily 115, 163
    Wuthering Heights xviii, 115, 157,
        158–60, 164–5
Brooks, David 52
Bryson, Norman 84
Buck-Morss, Susan 97
Burckhardt, Jacob 97
Burke, Edmund 149, 151
Burton, Robert
    The Anatomy of Melancholy 74
Butler, Judith 69
Butler, Marilyn 103
Byrd, Max 147
Byron, Lord 166, 175, 178–9
    Childe Harold's Pilgrimage 178
    Don Juan 178
    'Epistle to Augusta' 179

Cadiz 71
Caesar, Julius 72
Callaghan, Dympna 74, 76
Canetti, Elias 144
canon, the literary xv, xviii, 42, 83, 102,
    113, 115, 130
capitalism xvi, 25, 90, 97, 98, 102, 103,
    128, 161, 175
Cartland, Barbara 85
Catholicism 74
Césaire, Aimé 137
Chandler, James 103
Charles I 72
Chartists, the 176
Chartres, cathedral of 8
Chartrian poems 102

Chaucer, Geoffrey
    Canterbury Tales x, 102
Christ 20, 75
Christensen, Jerome 103
Christian criticism xiii
Churchill, Sir Winston 8
Church of England 176
city, the 141–3, 146
Clarke, John 77–8
class 26–7, 55, 66, 69, 78, 83
close reading xviii
Cohen, Walter 46, 51, 52, 55, 60, 70
Coleridge, Samuel Taylor 178
Collinson, Patrick 76
colonialism 113, 131–2, 134, 136–7,
    139, *see also* imperialism
confinement, *see* prisons and
    imprisonment
containment 56, 80, 89, 93, 95, 99, *see
    also* subversion
Coulanges, Fustel de 34
Cowhig, Ruth 63
Crews, Frederick 52
Culler, Jonathan 78, 80, 130
cultural history 82–91
cultural materialism ix–xviii, 1–3, 41,
    42–3, 44, 57, 61–82, 88–9, 113,
    115
cultural poetics xiv–xv, xvi, 1, 42, 113,
    see also new historicism; radical
    historicist criticism
cultural studies 83
culture xii, xiv, xvi, 1, 3, 5–10, 47, 69,
    81, 87, 88, 90, 94, 104
Cumberland, George 176

Davies, Tony 126
deconstruction x, xiv, xviii, 3, 31, 49, 51,
    53, 92, 94, *see also* Derrida,
    Jacques
Defoe, Daniel 148
    Colonel Jack 147
    Moll Flanders 141, 147
    Robinson Crusoe 114, 138–46
    Roxana 147
Democratic Party, the 46
Derrida, Jacques xii, 3–4, 28–32, 41,
    43, 49, 85, 89, 126
Dickens, Charles 115, 157, 163
    Bleak House 164
    Oliver Twist 115, 162–4, 165
    Our Mutual Friend 164
    Pickwick Papers 163
Dietzgen, Josef 36–7

Dietzgen, Wilhelm 37
différance 3–4, 28–32, *see also*
  Derrida, Jacques
discipline 12–14, *see also* prisons and
  imprisonment; surveillance
discourse 126, 130–1, 137
dissidence 71, 72–3, 76, 78–82
Dollimore, Jonathan x, xii, xv, 43, 67,
  73, 79, 80, 88–9, 97
dominant culture 3, 23, 24, 26, 28, 47,
  73, 76–7, 80
domination 43, 94, 98, 99, 132
Donne, John 117, 123, 125
Durant, Alan 179
Dusinberre, Juliet 74

Eagleton, Terry 82, 121
Edmundson, Mark xviii
eighteenth-century studies xiii
Eliot, T. S. 103, 110
Elizabeth I ('Virgin Queen') 59, 72, 95
emergent culture 3, 24–5, 27
Empson, William 122
Engels, Friedrich 66
England, *see* Britain
English studies 82–3, 89–91, 127
Enlightenment, the 7, 8, 9
entrapment 42, 70–3, 79–80, 94
Ephialtes 169–70, 171
Erdman, David 149
essentialist humanism 68, 80, 81, 97
Essex, Earl of 71, 72, 79, 95
Essick, Robert N. 154
estrangement xvii, 59
Evangelical Movement, the 176

Fanon, Frantz 116, 166–9, 173
Fascism 35, 36, 110, 180
faultlines 70–3, 76, 77, 78, 115, 181
feminism ix, 50, 52, 54, 67–9, 76, 83,
  85
Ferber, Michael 150, 151
feudalism 22, 98
Feuerbach, Ludwig 17, 18
Figes, Eva 85
Fish, Stanley 105, 127
Flaubert, Gustave 34
formalism ix, 46, 47, 51, 52, 59
Forster, John 163
Foucault, Michel xii, xvi, 1–2, 3, 11–16,
  41, 42, 43, 50, 64, 67, 78–9, 81,
  85–9, 93–4, 96, 98, 99, 113, 114,
  115, 116, 119, 130, 133, 159, 175
Fourier, François 37

France 180
Frankfurt School 47, 100
French Revolution 38
Freud, Sigmund 85, 102, 110
Frey, Charles 132
Fry, Paul xviii
Fuss, Diana 69
future and futurity xvi, xviii, 4, 32, 44,
  107, 108–11, 116, 156, 167–8, 172,
  175, 178, 181, *see also* utopia and
  utopianism

Gallagher, Catherine x, xii, 41, 42, 43,
  45–55, 58
Gallup, Donald 179
Gaskell, Mrs Elizabeth 115, 157
  Mary Barton 158
Gay, John 148
  The Beggar's Opera 147
  Trivia 147
Geertz, Clifford xii, 1, 5–10, 96
Geistesgeschichte 93, 96, 100
gender xii, 50, 52, 55, 78, 83, 84, *see
  also* feminism
Germany 180
Giddens, Anthony 64, 78, 142–3
Gilchrist, Alexander 176
Girouard, Mark 84
Glen, Heather 114–5, 146–57
Godwin, William 151
Goldberg, Jonathan 2, 61, 65, 79, 88,
  93, 95, 98, 113, 117–25
Golding, William
  Lord of the Flies 7
Goldstein, Laurence 103
Gordon, Colin 78
Gotha Programme 36
Goya, Francisco 15
Gramsci, Antonio xii, 3, 22, 23, 26, 69,
  100
grands récits ('grand narratives') xv,
  xvii, 43
Greece 170
Greenblatt, Stephen x, xii, xiii, xiv, 1,
  41–2, 43, 45, 55–60, 61, 63, 70–1,
  83, 88, 93–5, 97, 104, 117, 132
Greene, Gayle 67–8
Greene, Thomas M. 95
Greer, Germaine 85
Griffiths, Trevor R. 137
Grote, George 169, 171

Hakluyt, Richard 132
Hall, Stuart 76–7

Hamilton, Paul 103
Hawkes, Terence xvi, 82, 127
Hawthorne, Nathaniel 1, 10
Hay, Douglas 139
Hegel, G. W. F. 33, 39, 51, 177, 178
hegemony xv, 2, 3, 22–4, 26, 100, 102
Herodotus 181
Heidegger, Martin 29
Heilman, Robert B. 164
Heinzelman, Kurt 103
hermeneutics 17, 50, 100, 110
Hill, Christopher 76, 84
Hirsch, E. D. 126
historical materialism xvi, 4, 32–5, 39
historicism xiii, xvii, 4, 34, 39, 40, 55,
    57, 59–60, 93, 100, 102, 103–5,
    106, 108–9, 110, 126, *see also* new
    historicism
history xi, xii, xiv, xvii, 3–4, 31, 32–40,
    43, 51, 54, 55, 57, 80, 85, 91, 92,
    97, 100, 111, 125–6, 128, 137, 175,
    177–8, 181
Hitler, Adolf 8
Hogan, James C. 171
Holstun, James 70, 80
Holy Roman Empire 55
Homer 111, 171
Homo sapiens 5–6, 39
homosexuality 79, 81
Howard, Jean E. 58
Howard, John 15
Hulme, Peter 4, 113, 125–37
humanism 90, 99–100, 114
humanist criticism xiii

Ice Age 6, 7
identity 69, 86, 100
ideology 2, 4, 17–21, 22, 42, 47, 51,
    63–6, 68, 70, 71, 72, 73, 74, 76, 78,
    88, 99, 104, 109, 161
imperialism xii, 52, 54, 173, 177, 180,
    181
improvisation 117
incorporation 24–5
individualism 70, 82, 100
inscription 127–8
instrumentality, *see* improvisation
Ireland 72
Israel 173
Italy 18

James I 117–20, 121–2
Jameson, Fredric 78, 90, 107, 110, 156
Jansenism 20

Jardine, Lisa 76
Jauss, Hans-Robert 100
Java 9–10
Jay, Martin 101
Jefferson, Tony 77–8
Jennings, Francis 134
Jews 40
Johnson, Samuel 147–8
    'London' 147
    'The Vanity of Human Wishes' 147
Johnston, Kenneth 103
Jones, Ann Rosalind 76
Jonson, Ben 117, 118, 125
    Sejanus 118
Joyce, James 110

Kant 174, 177–8, 181
Kearns, George 179
Keats, John 117
Keller, Gottfried 34
Kermode, Frank 127, 128, 129–30,
    132, 135
Kimon 169–70
King's Men, the 117–18
Kitzinger, Celia 69
Klee, Paul 4, 35
Korean War 71
Kraus, Karl 38
Kristeva, Julia 127, 130

Laconia 169–70
Lamming, George 137
Langland, William
    Piers Plowman 102
language 3, 30–1, 61, 64, 78, 85, 92,
    110, 115, 124, 125, 126–7, 131
Laqueur, Thomas 161
Lassalle, Ferdinand 36
Latourette, Kenneth Scott 176
Lattimore, Richmond 170
Lawrence, D. H. 85
Leavis, F. R. 82
Lehman, David 52
Leicester, Earl of 95
Lentricchia, Frank 94
Lenz, Carolyn 67–8
Leonard, Nancy S. 119
Lever, J. W. 118
Levin, Richard 118
Levinson, Marjorie xii, xvii, 4, 44,
    102–11
liberal humanism 53
Liebknecht, Karl 37
Liebknecht, Wilhelm 36

Linnell, John 176
literature xviii, 27, 53, 102
Liu, Alan 70, 80, 103
local knowledge xviii
London 147–53, 155
Loomba, Ania 63
Lotze, Hermann 33
Lowell, Robert 1, 10
Lukács, Georg 47, 54, 103
Luxembourg, Rosa 37

MacArthur, General Douglas 71
MacCabe, Colin 130
McCanles, Michael xiii
McCarthy, Mary 46
Macdonald, Dwight 46
McGann, Jerome xvii, 4, 103, 115–16,
    166–81
Macherey, Pierre 51, 126, 132
MacKinnon, Catharine 86
McLuskie, Kathleen 67–8, 74
Mailer, Norman 85
Mallarmé, Stéphane 31
Marcuse, Herbert xvi, 50
Marlowe, Christopher 117
    Dr Faustus xviii, 59
    The Jew of Malta 63
marginality 49, 86
Marotti, Arthur 96
marriage 9, 73–8, 79, 165
Marston, John
    The Dutch Courtesan 118
Marx, Karl 18, 19, 36, 38, 54, 66, 70, 128
    Critique of the Gotha Programme 36
    The German Ideology 66
    The Jewish Question 18
    1844 Manuscripts 18
Marxism, xvi, 2, 3, 4, 18, 21, 22, 25–6,
    41, 45–55, 70, 71, 80, 88, 89, 94,
    96, 98, 100
Marxist criticism ix, x, xiii, 41, 46, 47,
    50, 103, 105–6, 110
masculinity 76, 78
materialism xv, xvi, 19, 89
Mayhew, Henry 115, 160–3
medieval studies xii, xiii, 97–8
Melbourne, Lord 163
Mellor, Anne K. 103, 176
Messiah 40
Mészáros, István 98
Michaels, Walter Benn xii
Middle Ages 97–8, 102
Middleton, Thomas
    The Changeling 59

Milan 134
Miller, D. A. 53
Miller, J. Hillis 70
Millett, Kate 85
Milton, John 174, 176–7, 178
    Paradise Lost 176
Modernism 46, 181
modernity xv, xvi
money 143–4, 145, 162
Montrose, Louis Adrian 58, 70, 71, 76,
    83–4, 88, 93, 95, 104
Morris, Wesley xiii
Moscow 168
Mullaney, Steven 65
Mumford, Lewis 142, 146
Mussolini, Benito 180
Mykenai 171

Napoleon 168
Napoleonic Wars 176
Nazis 4
Nebrija, Antonio de 131
Neely, Carol Thomas 57, 67–8, 69,
    76
negativity 49, 53
new criticism xiii–xiv, 105
new historicism ix–xviii, 1–3, 41–4,
    45–6, 51–5, 55–60, 67, 70, 71,
    83–4, 87–8, 92–9, 102–7, 115, 116,
    175, *see also* cultural poetics;
    radical historicist criticism
New Jerusalem 175, 176
New Left 46, 48, 50, 51
Newton, Judith 68
New World 129, 136
Nicholls, Peter 70
Nietzsche, Friedrich 37, 55, 116, 175,
    181
Norbrook, David 95, 96
novel, the 114, 143, 146, 164

Odysseus 179
Ohmann, Richard 68
oppositional culture 3, 24, 25
Orgei, Stephen 65, 98
Orkin, Martin 66
Ottoman Empire 180

Paine, Thomas 148–9, 153
panopticons and panopticism 1–2,
    14–16, 113, 114, 164, *see also*
    prisons and imprisonment;
    surveillance
Paris 38

Pascal, Blaise 20
patriarchy 67, 74, 75, 76, 115, *see also* feminism; gender; marriage
Patterson, Annabel 52
Patterson, Lee xii, 43–4, 92–102, 115
Pearce, Roy Harvey xiii
Pêcheux, Michel 91
Pechter, Edward 45, 55
Peloponnesian Wars 172
penitentiary, *see* prisons and imprisonment
Pericles 169, 171, 173
Perkins, William 75
petits récits ('little narratives') xvii
pharmakon 31
Phillips, William 46
plague, the 11–14
Plato xviii, 8, 31
plausibility 62, 65, 67, 69, 76, 78, 81–2
Podlecki, Anthony J. 169
Porter, Carolyn 45, 46, 52, 53, 71, 73, 80
positivity 53
postmodernism 90
poststructuralism ix, xiv, xvi, 1, 49, 70, 80, 85, 90, 105, 126
Pound, Ezra x, 110, 116, 178–81
    Cantos x, 113, 178–81
    Drafts and Fragments 179
power xv, 1–2, 12–16, 43, 45, 49, 50, 55, 64, 66, 67, 71, 72, 73, 76, 78, 87–8, 93–4, 96, 113, 120, 122, 132
Pre–Raphaelites 176
primitivism 7, 9
prisons and imprisonment 14–16, 99, 113, 122, 138–46, *see also* panopticons and panopticism; surveillance
progress 35, 36, 37–8
prostitution 161–3
Protestantism 74–5
psychoanalytic criticism ix, x
Purchas, Samuel 132

race and racism xii, xvii, 55, 66, 69, 73, 78, 81, 83, 97, 180
radical historicist criticism xi, xii, xvi, xvii, xviii, 1, 2, 41, 43
Rahv, Philip 46
Raleigh, Sir Walter 127
Ranke, Leopold von 34
Reformation, the 74
Reign of Terror, the 178
Renaissance, the 42, 58, 87, 92, 93, 95, 96, 97–8, 104, 129

Renaissance studies ix, 45, 58, 60
representation xv, 3, 17–20, 31, 46, 47, 48, 49, 51, 81, 87, 104, 113, 119–20, 123, 124, 125, 143
residual culture 3, 24–6, 27–8
resistance 43, 56–7, 67, 69, 78, 87–8, 89, 91, 115, 132
Retamar, Roberto Fernández 137
Richardson, Samuel 158, 159
Richmond, George 176
Righter, Ann 122
Roberts, Brian 77
Robespierre, Maximilien 38
Rogin, Michael xii
Roman de la Rose 102
Romantics, the 103, 106, 107, 108, 110, 111, 174, 176, 178, 181
Romantic studies xiii, 102–7
Rome (ancient) 38
Rose, Jacqueline 84
Rosenberg, Harold 46, 48
Rousseau, Jean-Jacques 31
Rudé, George 147
Russia 180

Sahlins, Marshall 168
Sartre, Jean-Paul 107, 110, 155
Saussure, Ferdinand de 3, 29–31, 126–7, 131
Schlegel, Friedrich von 105
Scholem, Gerhard (Gershom) 35
Schwarzbach, J. S. 163
Sedgly, Ben 147
semiology and semiotics 1, 31, *see also* signs and signification
Sennett, Richard 147, 150
Shakespeare, William xvi, 52, 55, 56–7, 59, 61, 64–5, 68, 76, 81, 82, 85, 90, 113, 117–119, 124–5, 129, 133
    Comedies 65, 79
    Cymbeline 65
    Hamlet xviii, 124
    Henry V 42, 72
    Histories (second tetralogy) 56–7
    King Lear 67, 77
    Macbeth 42, 71–2, 157
    Measure for Measure 65, 67, 77, 113, 117–25
    The Merchant of Venice 77
    A Midsummer Night's Dream 77, 95
    Othello 42, 61–3, 65–6, 69, 73–4, 75–8, 81, 82–3, 118
    Romeo and Juliet 77
    The Taming of the Shrew 77

Shakespeare, William – *cont.*
   The Tempest 4, 65, 77, 113, 125–37
   Tragedies 77
   The Winter's Tale 77
Shelley, Percy 172–4, 175
   'Defence of Poetry' 173–4
   Prometheus Unbound 173
Shepherd, Simon 66, 74
Shining, The (film) 110
Shuttleworth, James 115, 158, 163
Siberia xviii
Sidney, Sir Philip
   Arcadia 74
signs and signification 28–30, 47, 51
Simpson, David 103
Sinfield, Alan x, xii, xv, 1, 42–3, 61–82,
   88–9
Siskin, Clifford 103
Smith, Henry 75
Smith, James 132
Smith, Olivia 103
Smith, Stan 150
Social Democracy 36, 37
sociology 158, 161, 164
Sollers, Philippe 31
Sommerville, Johann 73
source studies 126, 129, 130
Soviet Union 26, 90
Sparta 169
Sparticists 37
spectacle, society of the 2, 114
Spender, Dale 83
Spenser, Edmund
   The Shepheardes Calender 95
Sprinker, Michael 51
Stalinism 46
Stallybrass, Peter 63
Stevens, Wallace 110
Stevenson, David Lloyd 118
Stone, Lawrence 75–6
Stratford-upon-Avon 125
Strohm, Paul xii
structuralism xiv, 71, 87, 88, 126
subjection 2, 16, 43, 85, 87, 114
subjects and subjectivity, 21, 44, 46, 49,
   50, 51, 54, 57, 66, 67, 68, 75, 85, 86,
   87, 89, 90–1, 97, 100, 104, 106, 122
substitution 119–21, 123
subversion 56, 80, 89, 93, 95, 98, 99,
   see also containment
Sumner, Colin 64
surveillance 12–16, 113, 114, 115, 143,
   146, 165, *see also* panopticons and
   panopticism

Swift, Jonathan
   Gulliver's Travels xviii

Tatham, Frederick 176
Taylor, Gary xvi
Tennenhouse, Leonard 76
textuality and intertextuality xvi, 3–4,
   43, 52, 79, 80, 92, 104, 126–8
Thackeray, William Makepeace 115,
   160
   Vanity Fair 157, 159, 160, 165
Thasos 171
thick description xviii, 96
Third World 166–7, 177
Thomas, Keith 79, 80
Thompson, Ann 68
Thompson, E. P. 77, 84, 149, 151, 153,
   156
Thucydides 173, 181
Tiberius 122
Tillotson, Kathleen 163
Tillyard, E. M. W. 93, 96, 117
Tompkins, Jane xii
Torah, the 40
totality and totalization xvii, 107–8, 110,
   168, 169
tradition 23
Trojan War 171
Troy 111
Truman, President Harry S. 71
truth 81, 85–7, 89
Turks 62, 65–6
twentieth-century studies xiii
Tylor, Sir Edward 5
Tyndale, William 83

ultra-leftism 79, 83
unconscious, political xv, 113
utopia and utopianism xvii, 47, 169, *see*
   also future and futurity

Venice and Venetians 62, 63, 66
Victoria, Queen 163
Victorian studies xiii
Vienna 113, 121, 122, 124
Vietnam War 57, 180
violence 66, 115, 153, 155, 158, 166–8
Virginia (USA) 132
Voloshinov, V. N. 68, 130

Wakefield, Priscilla 152
Walkowitz, Judith 162
Waller, Marguerite 45, 52
Warner, Marina 84

Wasson, John 118
Waterloo, Battle of 159
Watt, Ian 83, 142, 164
Wayne, Don 58, 70, 80
Weber, Max 94
Webster, John
    The Duchess of Malfi xvi
Whigham, Frank 96, 98, 104
Widdowson, Peter 82
Williams, Raymond xii, xv, 2–3, 22–8,
    42, 43, 70, 72, 78, 79, 80, 81, 85,
    88, 147
Wilson, J. Dover 118
Winstanley, Gerrard 75

Wordsworth, William 108, 174
    Lyrical Ballads xviii
    'The World is Too Much with Us'
        110–11
World War I 180
Wyatt, Sir Thomas 70–1

Yale school 103–4
Yeats, W. B.
    'Leda and the Swan' 111
Yeazell, Ruth 158

Zeeveld, W. Gordon 117